Love Hina

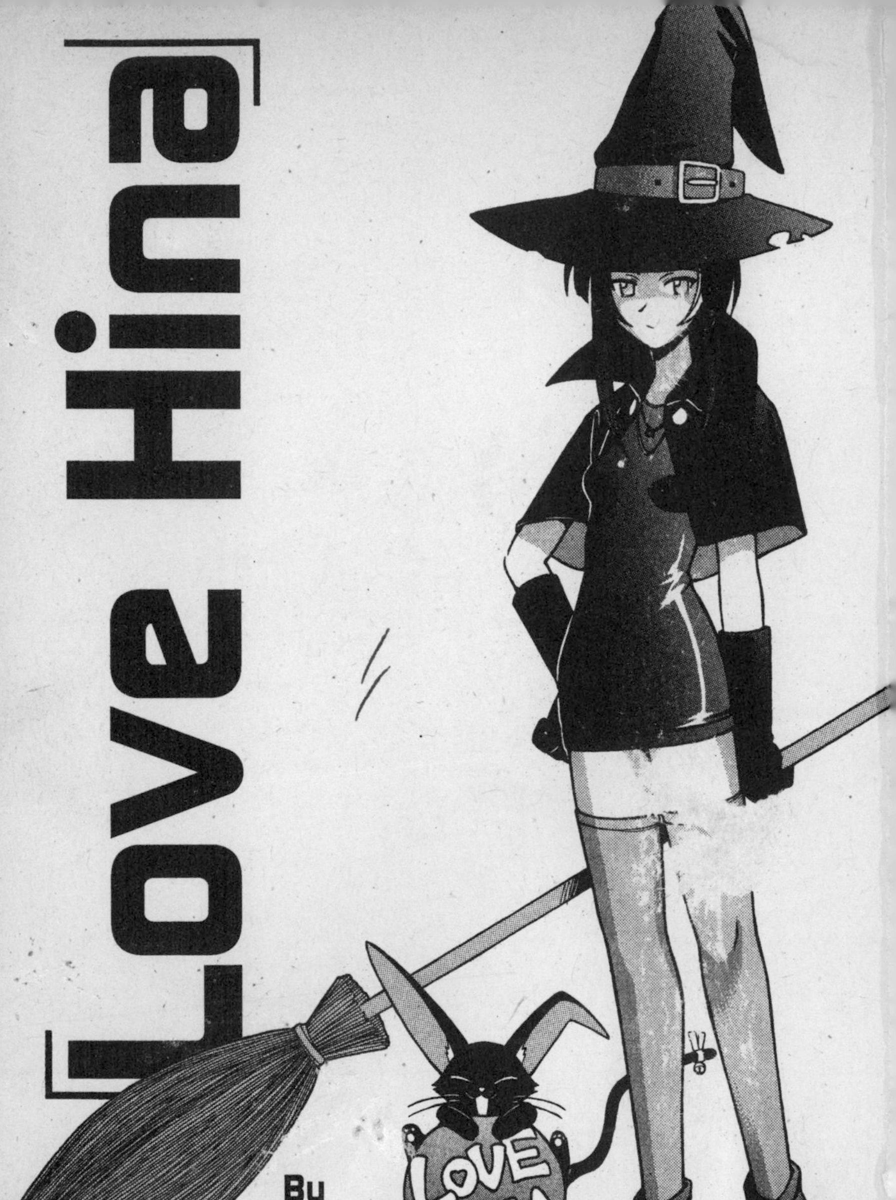
LOVE
HINA

By
Ken

Love Hina

By

Ken Akamatsu

Volume II

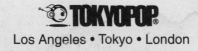
TOKYOPOP®
Los Angeles • Tokyo • London

Translator - Nan Rymer
English Adaptation - Adam Arnold
Associate Editors - Paul Morrissey & Tim Beedle
Retouch and Lettering - Marnie Echols
Cover Layout - Anna Kernbaum

Senior Editor - Mark Paniccia
Managing Editor - Jill Freshney
Production Coordinator - Antonio DePietro
Production Manager - Jennifer Miller
Art Director - Matt Alford
Editorial Director - Jeremy Ross
VP of Production - Ron Klamert
President & C.O.O. - John Parker
Publisher & C.E.O. - Stuart Levy

Email: editor@TOKYOPOP.com
Come visit us online at www.TOKYOPOP.com

A 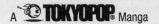 Manga

TOKYOPOP Inc.
5900 Wilshire Blvd. Suite 2000
Los Angeles, CA 90036

ISBN: 1-59182-117-7

First TOKYOPOP® printing: June 2003

10 9 8 7 6

Printed in the USA

Love Hina

The Story Thus Far...

Fifteen years ago, Keitaro Urashima made a promise to a girl that the two of them would go to Tokyo University together. For fifteen long years, Keitaro has slaved away at the books, stumbling through academia until the day he could take the university's entrance exam. Having failed three times already, having readied himself so thoroughly so as to fail again, and having discovered that the girl to whom he made that fateful promise is the girl that has recently studied with him, helping beat his fear of tests, at last the saga has ended, the impossible has become reality. Keitaro Urashima has finally managed to pass the entrance exam. This is one boy that won't live another year as a ronin. He is finally going to Tokyo U... or so he thought. For all the good twists of fate Keitaro had been given, sooner or later his bad luck would regain control. In a shocking turn of events, Keitaro breaks his leg just minutes before the opening ceremonies are about to commence. Hospitalized with no way of attending college, Keitaro goes for broke and confesses his love for Naru. As the two struggle to find an outlet to express their feelings, Keitaro makes a shocking revelation... that he wants to study abroad. But perhaps we are getting ahead of ourselves.

This chapter in Keitaro Urashima's life began well over a year ago when he inherited from his globe-trotting grandmother the Hinata House, an all-girls dormitory whose clientele is none too pleased that their new, live-in landlord is a man... or as close to a man as poor Keitaro can be. The lanky loser incessantly (and accidentally) crashes their sessions in the hot springs, walks in on them changing, and pokes his nose pretty much everywhere that it can get broken, if not by the hot-headed Naru - the mystery girl from fifteen years ago - then by one of the other Hinata inmates - Kitsune, a late-teen alcoholic with a diesel libido; Motoko, a swordsman who struggles with a feminine identity; Shinobu, a pre-teen princess with a colossal crush on Keitaro; Su, a foreign girl with a big appetite; Sarah, an orphaned ward resentful of being left there by her archeologist guardian; Mutsumi, an accident-prone lily also studying for her exams; and Haruka, Keitaro's aunt and de facto matriarch of Hinata House.

Now, Keitaro is stuck between a rock and a hard place as his passion for archeology has begun to outweigh his passion for Naru and to stay with the rest of the Hinata crew. Yet, should Keitaro manage to pass the course-screening test, whom will take over the responsibilities of taking care of Hinata House? And more importantly, what will the girls do for six months if they can't terrorize Keitaro?

CONTENTS

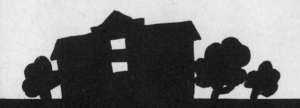

LOVE♡HINA

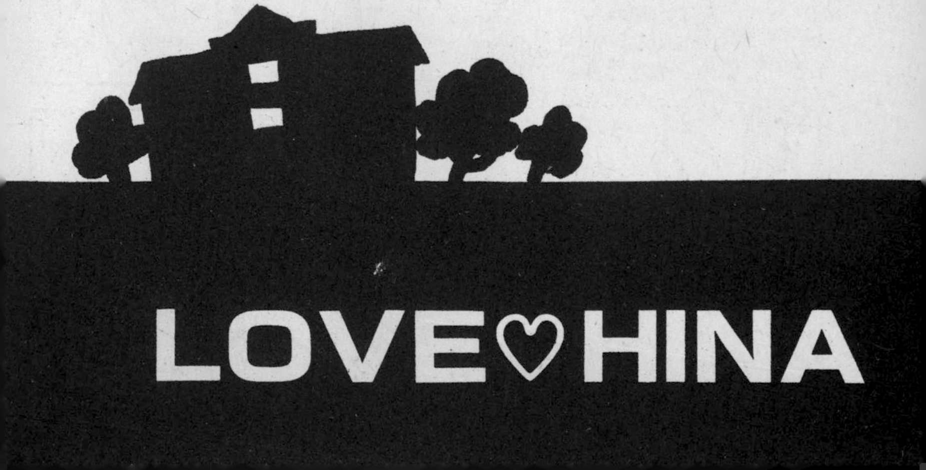

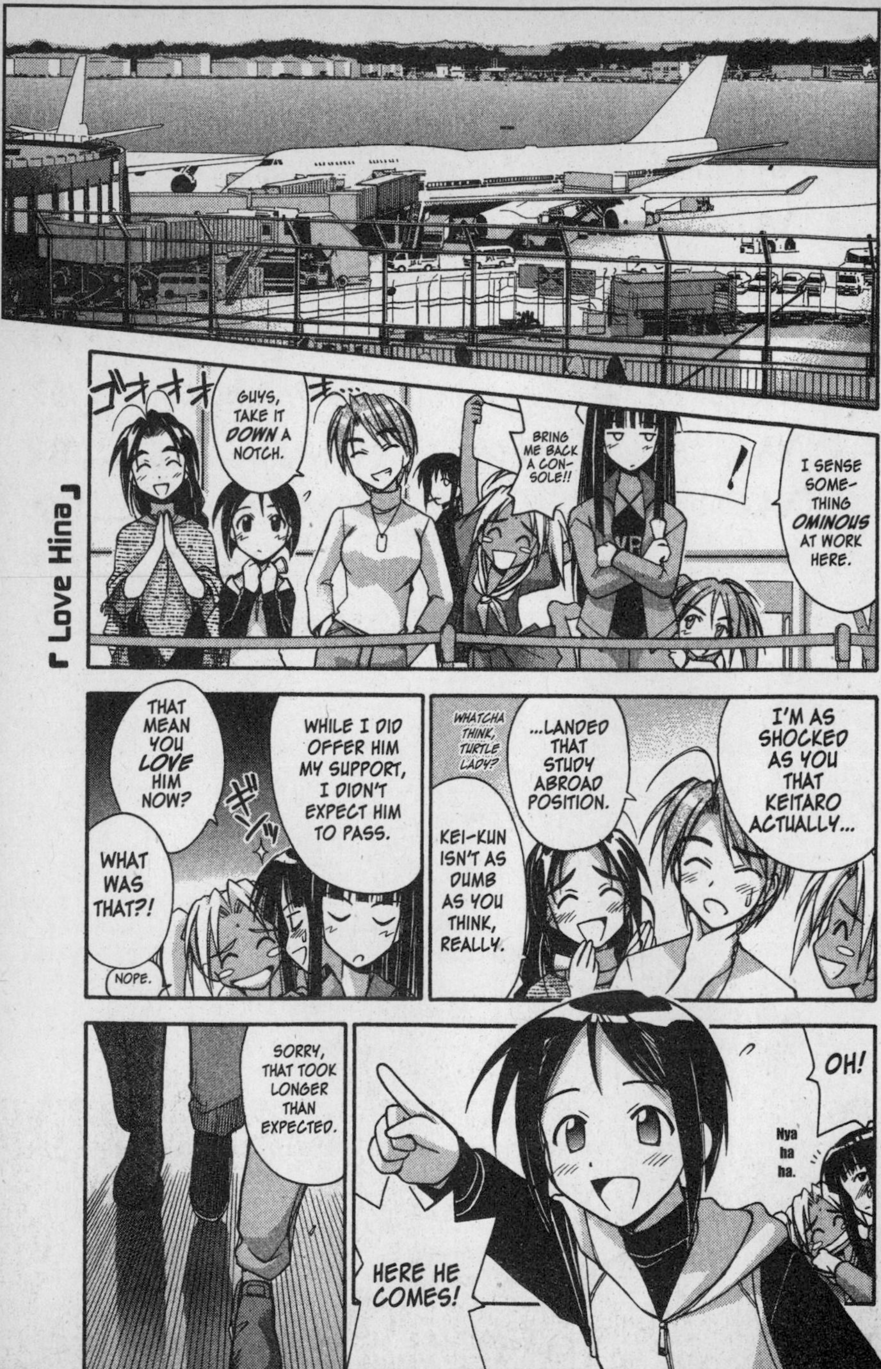
I SENSE SOMETHING OMINOUS AT WORK HERE.
!
BRING ME BACK A CONSOLE!!
GUYS, TAKE IT DOWN A NOTCH.
ゴオオオ
I'M AS SHOCKED AS YOU THAT KEITARO ACTUALLY...
...LANDED THAT STUDY ABROAD POSITION.
WHATCHA THINK, TURTLE LADY?
KEI-KUN ISN'T AS DUMB AS YOU THINK, REALLY.
WHILE I DID OFFER HIM MY SUPPORT, I DIDN'T EXPECT HIM TO PASS.
THAT MEAN YOU LOVE HIM NOW?
WHAT WAS THAT?!
NOPE.
OH!
Nya ha ha.
HERE HE COMES!
SORRY, THAT TOOK LONGER THAN EXPECTED.

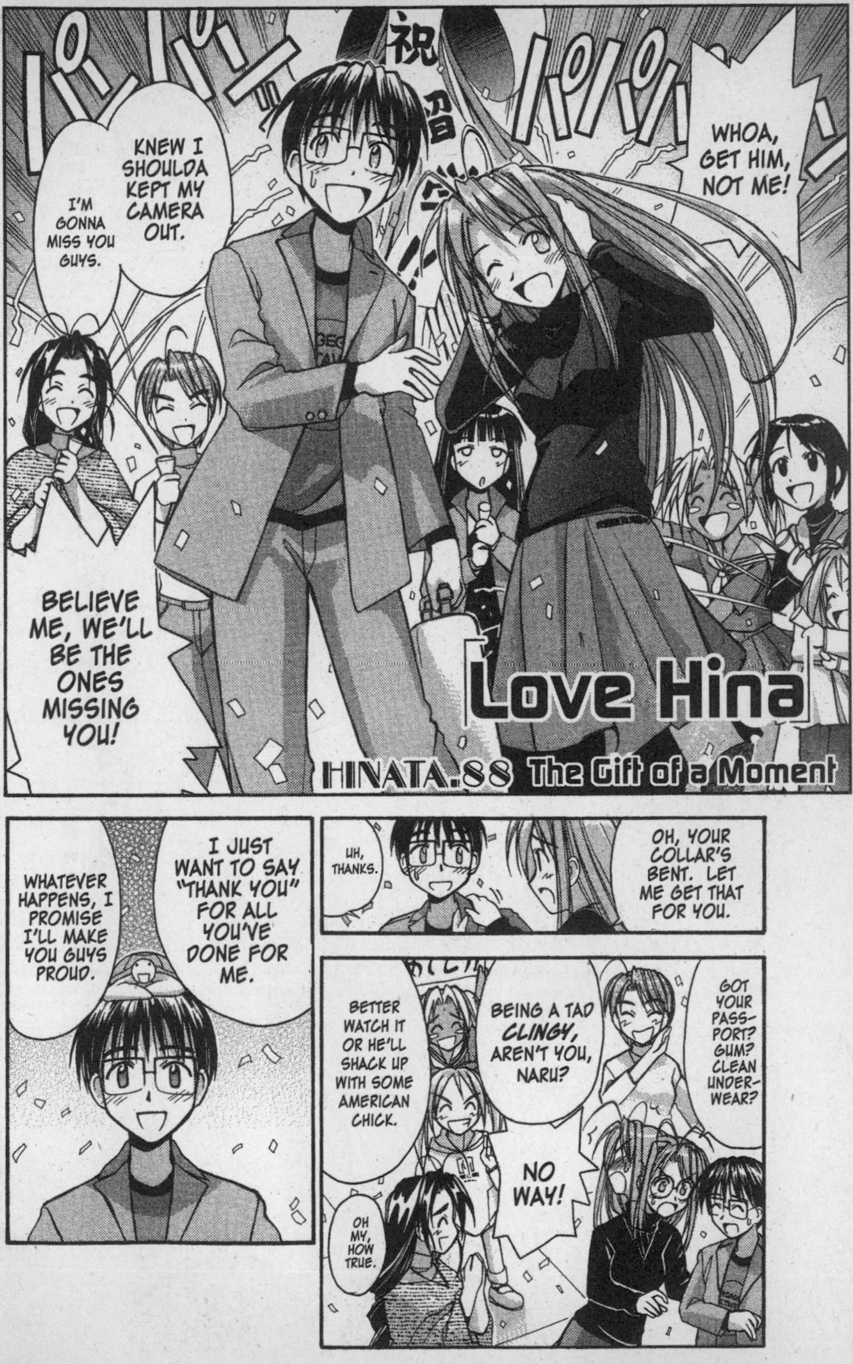

WHOA, GET HIM, NOT ME!
KNEW I SHOULDA KEPT MY CAMERA OUT.
I'M GONNA MISS YOU GUYS.
BELIEVE ME, WE'LL BE THE ONES MISSING YOU!
Love Hina
HINATA.88 The Gift of a Moment
OH, YOUR COLLAR'S BENT. LET ME GET THAT FOR YOU.
UH, THANKS.
GOT YOUR PASS-PORT? GUM? CLEAN UNDER-WEAR?
BEING A TAD CLINGY, AREN'T YOU, NARU?
BETTER WATCH IT OR HE'LL SHACK UP WITH SOME AMERICAN CHICK.
NO WAY!
OH MY, HOW TRUE.
I JUST WANT TO SAY "THANK YOU" FOR ALL YOU'VE DONE FOR ME.
WHATEVER HAPPENS, I PROMISE I'LL MAKE YOU GUYS PROUD.

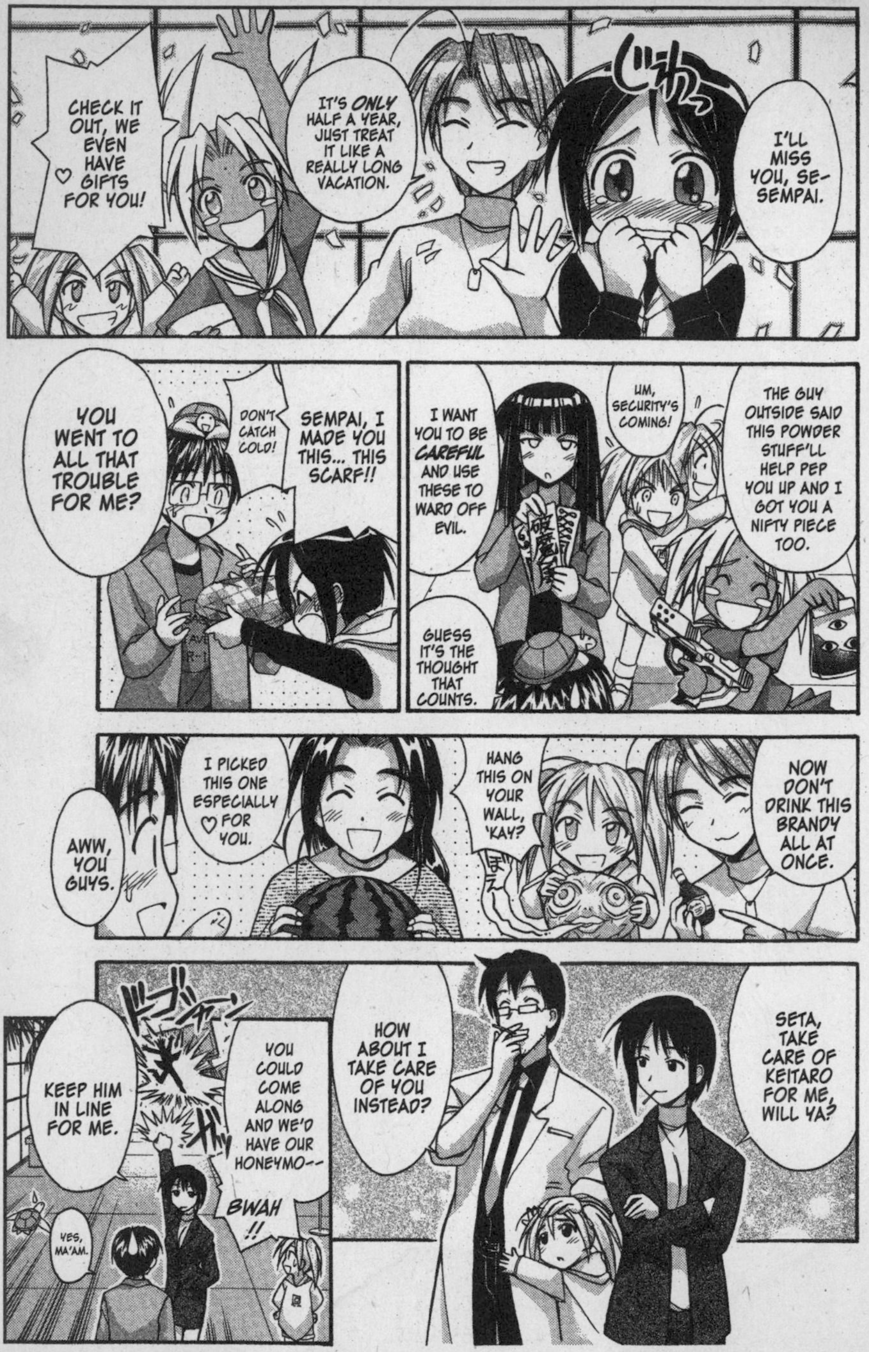
I'LL MISS YOU, SE-SEMPAI.
IT'S *ONLY* HALF A YEAR, JUST TREAT IT LIKE A REALLY LONG VACATION.
CHECK IT OUT, WE EVEN HAVE ♡ GIFTS FOR YOU!
THE GUY OUTSIDE SAID THIS POWDER STUFF'LL HELP PEP YOU UP AND I GOT YOU A NIFTY PIECE TOO.
UM, SECURITY'S COMING!
I WANT YOU TO BE *CAREFUL* AND USE THESE TO WARD OFF EVIL.
GUESS IT'S THE THOUGHT THAT COUNTS.
SEMPAI, I MADE YOU THIS... THIS SCARF!!
DON'T CATCH COLD!
YOU WENT TO ALL THAT TROUBLE FOR ME?
NOW DON'T DRINK THIS BRANDY ALL AT ONCE.
HANG THIS ON YOUR WALL, 'KAY?
I PICKED THIS ONE ESPECIALLY ♡ FOR YOU.
AWW, YOU GUYS.
SETA, TAKE CARE OF KEITARO FOR ME, WILL YA?
HOW ABOUT I TAKE CARE OF YOU INSTEAD?
YOU COULD COME ALONG AND WE'D HAVE OUR HONEYMO--
BWAH!!
KEEP HIM IN LINE FOR ME.
YES, MA'AM.

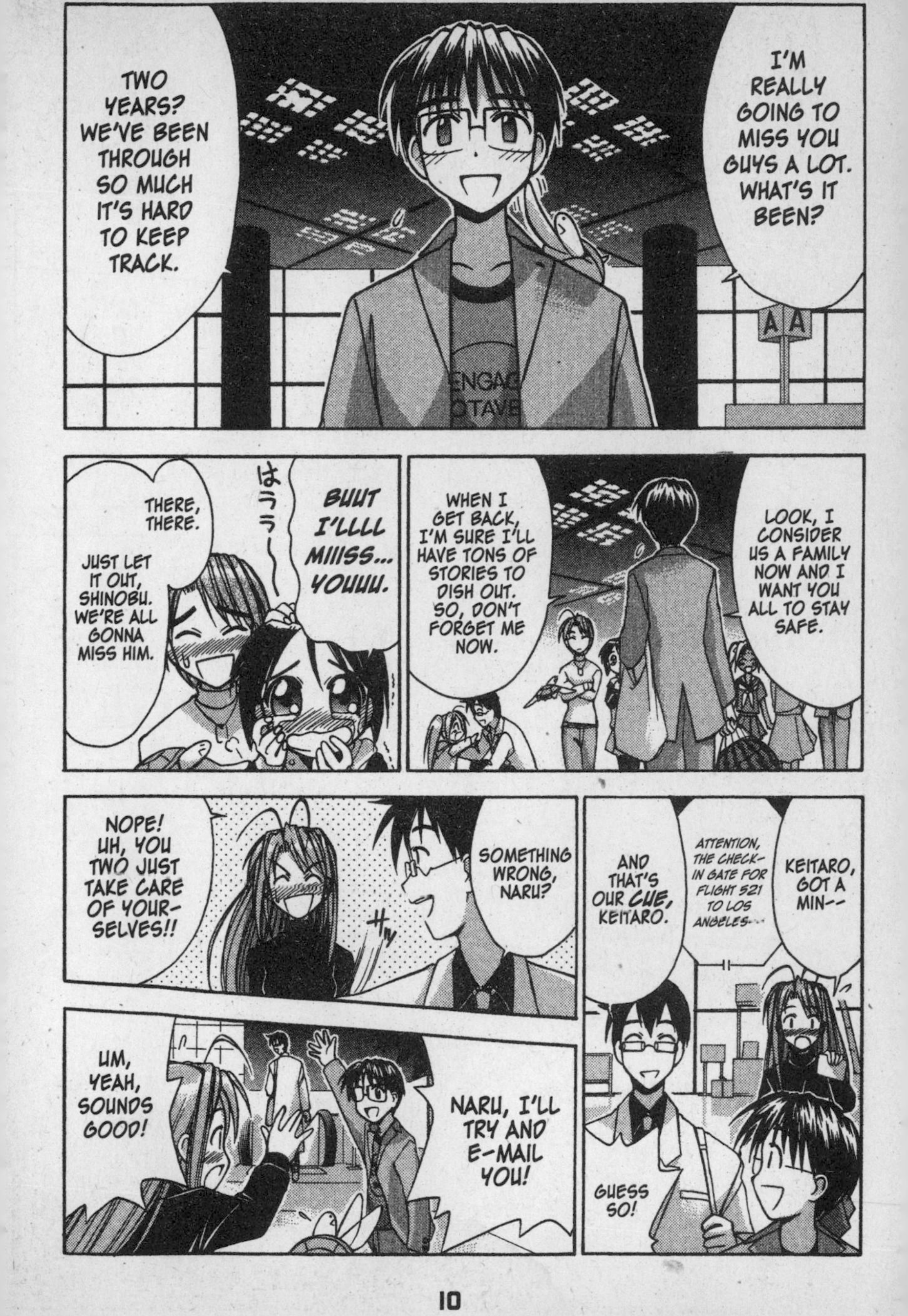

I'M REALLY GOING TO MISS YOU GUYS A LOT. WHAT'S IT BEEN?
TWO YEARS? WE'VE BEEN THROUGH SO MUCH IT'S HARD TO KEEP TRACK.
AA
LOOK, I CONSIDER US A FAMILY NOW AND I WANT YOU ALL TO STAY SAFE.
WHEN I GET BACK, I'M SURE I'LL HAVE TONS OF STORIES TO DISH OUT. SO, DON'T FORGET ME NOW.
はうう～
BUUT I'LLLL MIIISS... YOUUU.
THERE, THERE.
JUST LET IT OUT, SHINOBU. WE'RE ALL GONNA MISS HIM.
KEITARO, GOT A MIN--
ATTENTION, THE CHECK-IN GATE FOR FLIGHT 521 TO LOS ANGELES...
AND THAT'S OUR CUE, KEITARO.
GUESS SO!
SOMETHING WRONG, NARU?
NOPE! UH, YOU TWO JUST TAKE CARE OF YOURSELVES!!
NARU, I'LL TRY AND E-MAIL YOU!
UM, YEAH, SOUNDS GOOD!

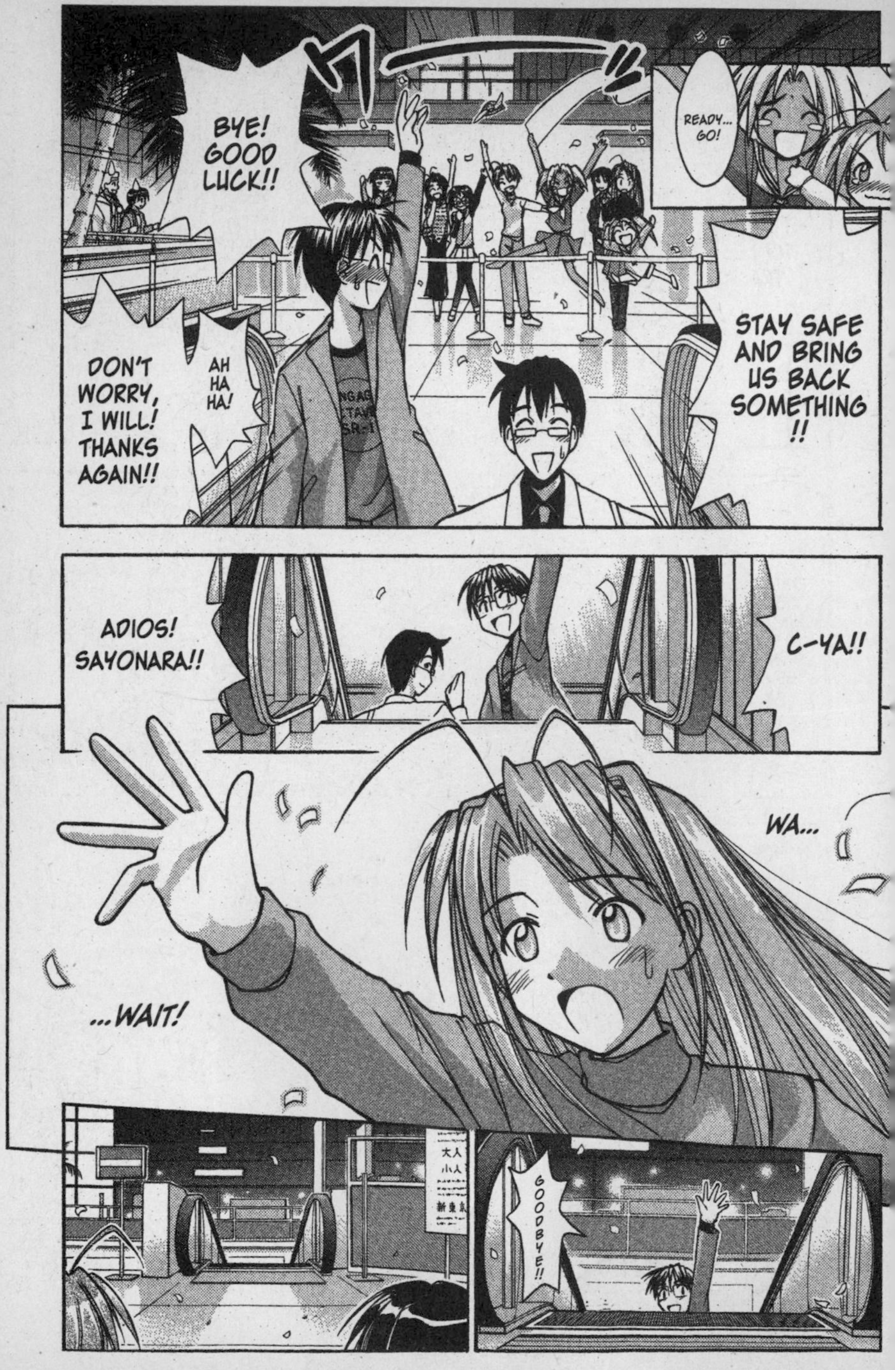
READY... GO!
STAY SAFE AND BRING US BACK SOMETHING!!
BYE! GOOD LUCK!!
AH HA HA!
DON'T WORRY, I WILL! THANKS AGAIN!!
C-YA!!
ADIOS! SAYONARA!!
WA...
...WAIT!
GOODBYE!!
大人
小人

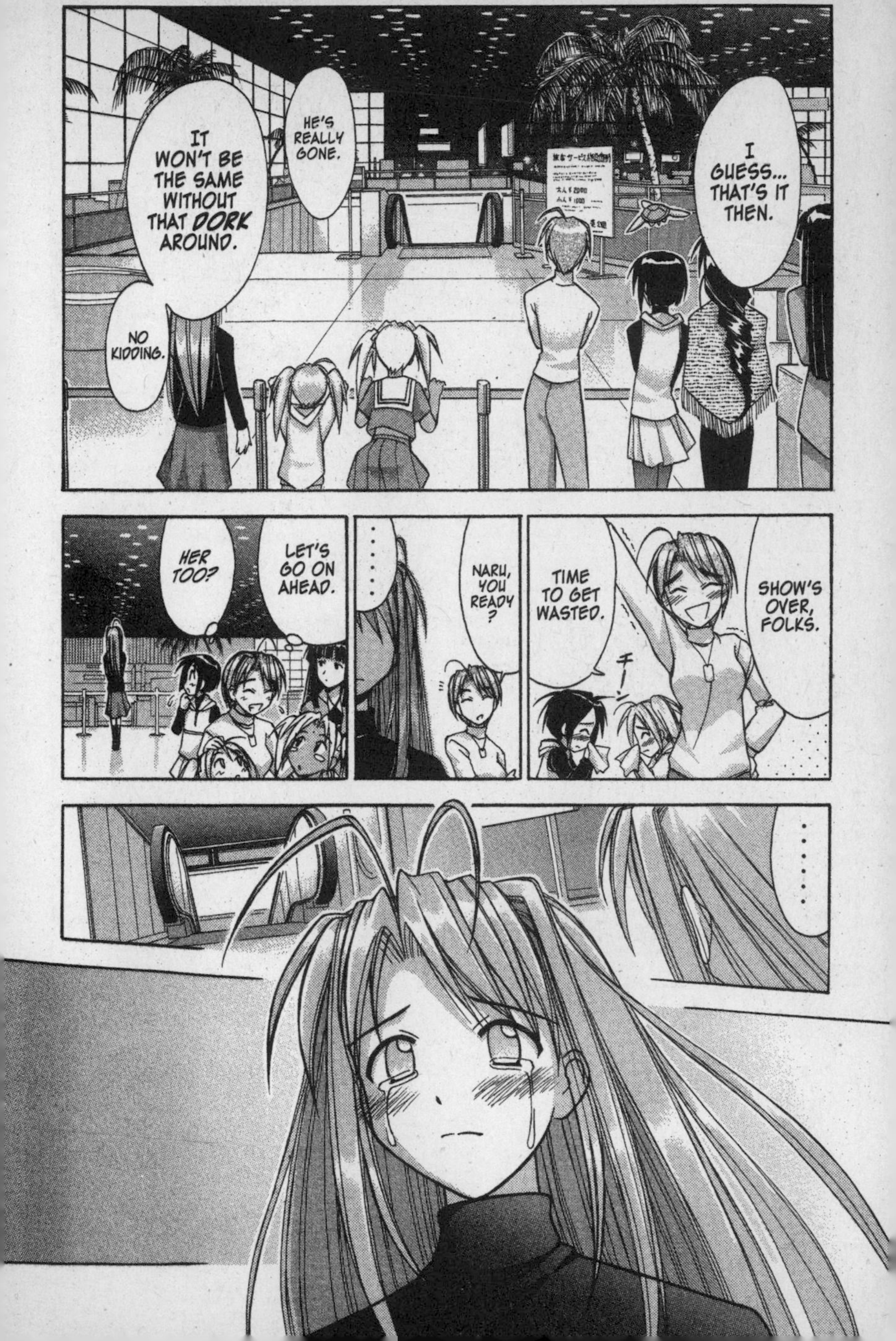
I GUESS... THAT'S IT THEN.
HE'S REALLY GONE.
IT WON'T BE THE SAME WITHOUT THAT DORK AROUND.
NO KIDDING.
SHOW'S OVER, FOLKS.
TIME TO GET WASTED.
チーン
NARU, YOU READY?
......
LET'S GO ON AHEAD.
HER TOO?
......

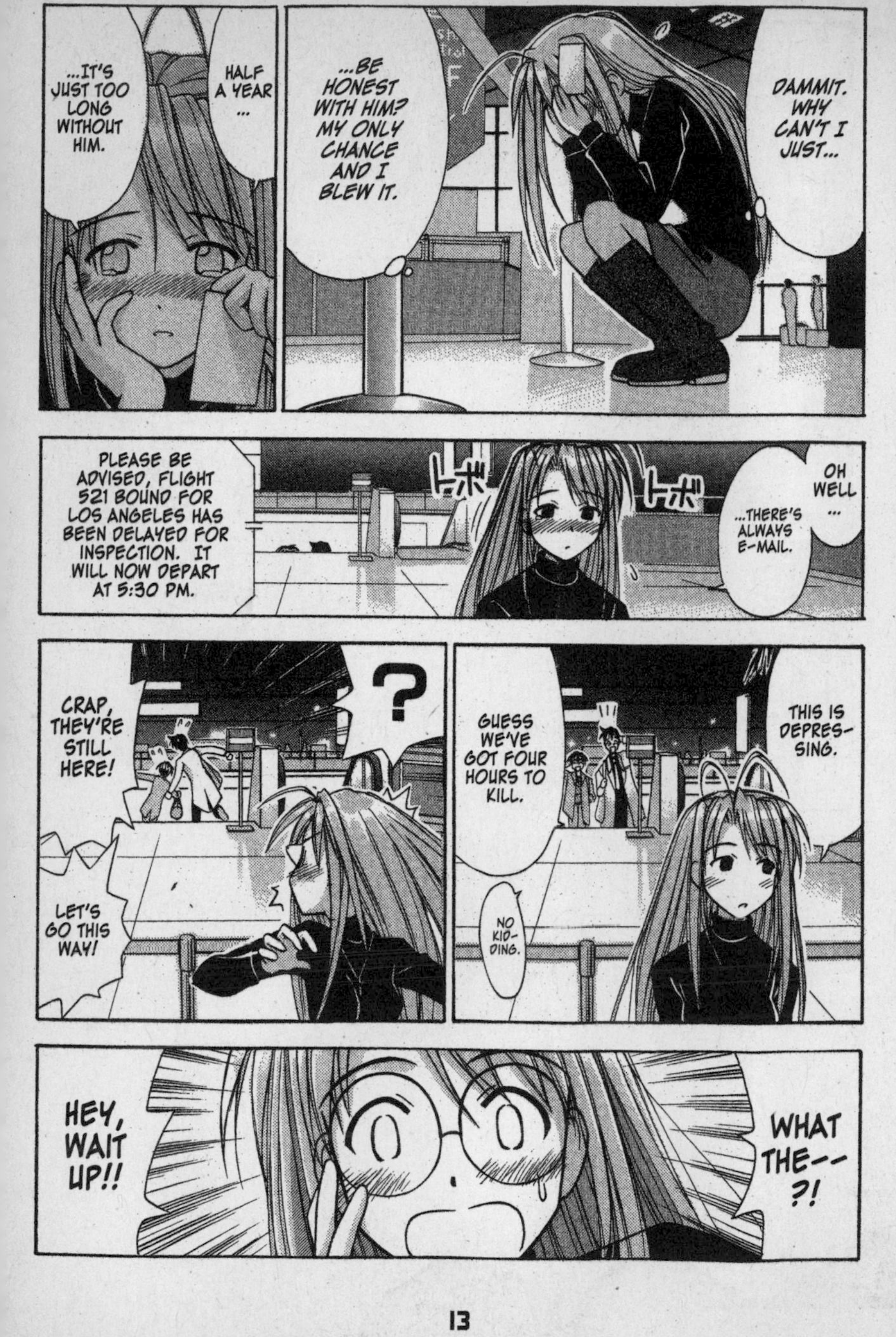
DAMMIT. WHY CAN'T I JUST...
...BE HONEST WITH HIM? MY ONLY CHANCE AND I BLEW IT.
HALF A YEAR...
...IT'S JUST TOO LONG WITHOUT HIM.
OH WELL...
...THERE'S ALWAYS E-MAIL.
トボ
トボ
PLEASE BE ADVISED, FLIGHT 521 BOUND FOR LOS ANGELES HAS BEEN DELAYED FOR INSPECTION. IT WILL NOW DEPART AT 5:30 PM.
THIS IS DEPRES-SING.
GUESS WE'VE GOT FOUR HOURS TO KILL.
NO KID-DING.
?
CRAP, THEY'RE STILL HERE!
LET'S GO THIS WAY!
WHAT THE--?!
HEY, WAIT UP!!

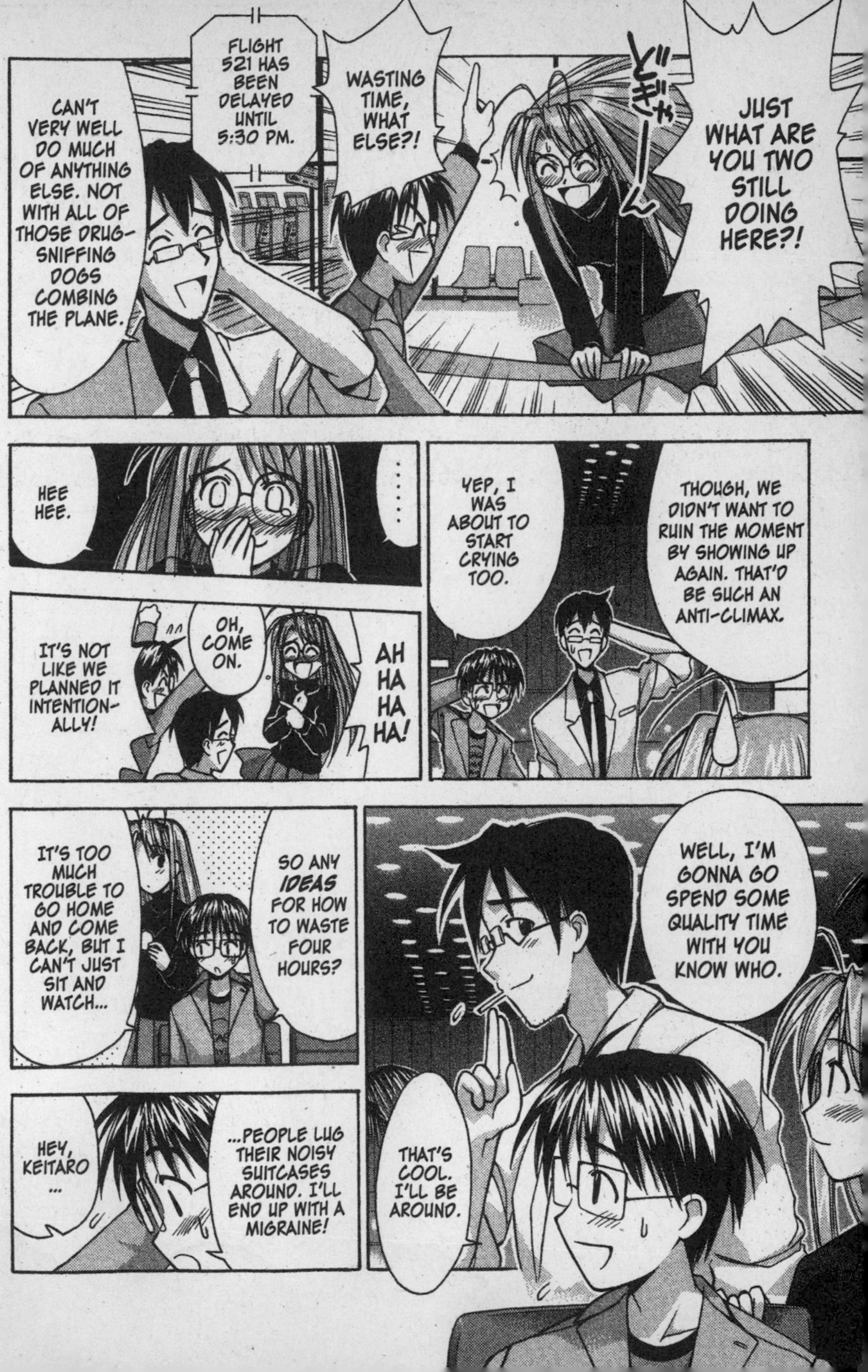
どぎゃーん
JUST WHAT ARE YOU TWO STILL DOING HERE?!
WASTING TIME, WHAT ELSE?!
FLIGHT 521 HAS BEEN DELAYED UNTIL 5:30 PM.
CAN'T VERY WELL DO MUCH OF ANYTHING ELSE. NOT WITH ALL OF THOSE DRUG-SNIFFING DOGS COMBING THE PLANE.
THOUGH, WE DIDN'T WANT TO RUIN THE MOMENT BY SHOWING UP AGAIN. THAT'D BE SUCH AN ANTI-CLIMAX.
YEP, I WAS ABOUT TO START CRYING TOO.
......
HEE HEE.
AH HA HA HA!
OH, COME ON.
IT'S NOT LIKE WE PLANNED IT INTENTION-ALLY!
WELL, I'M GONNA GO SPEND SOME QUALITY TIME WITH YOU KNOW WHO.
THAT'S COOL. I'LL BE AROUND.
SO ANY *IDEAS* FOR HOW TO WASTE FOUR HOURS?
IT'S TOO MUCH TROUBLE TO GO HOME AND COME BACK, BUT I CAN'T JUST SIT AND WATCH...
...PEOPLE LUG THEIR NOISY SUITCASES AROUND. I'LL END UP WITH A MIGRAINE!
HEY, KEITARO ...

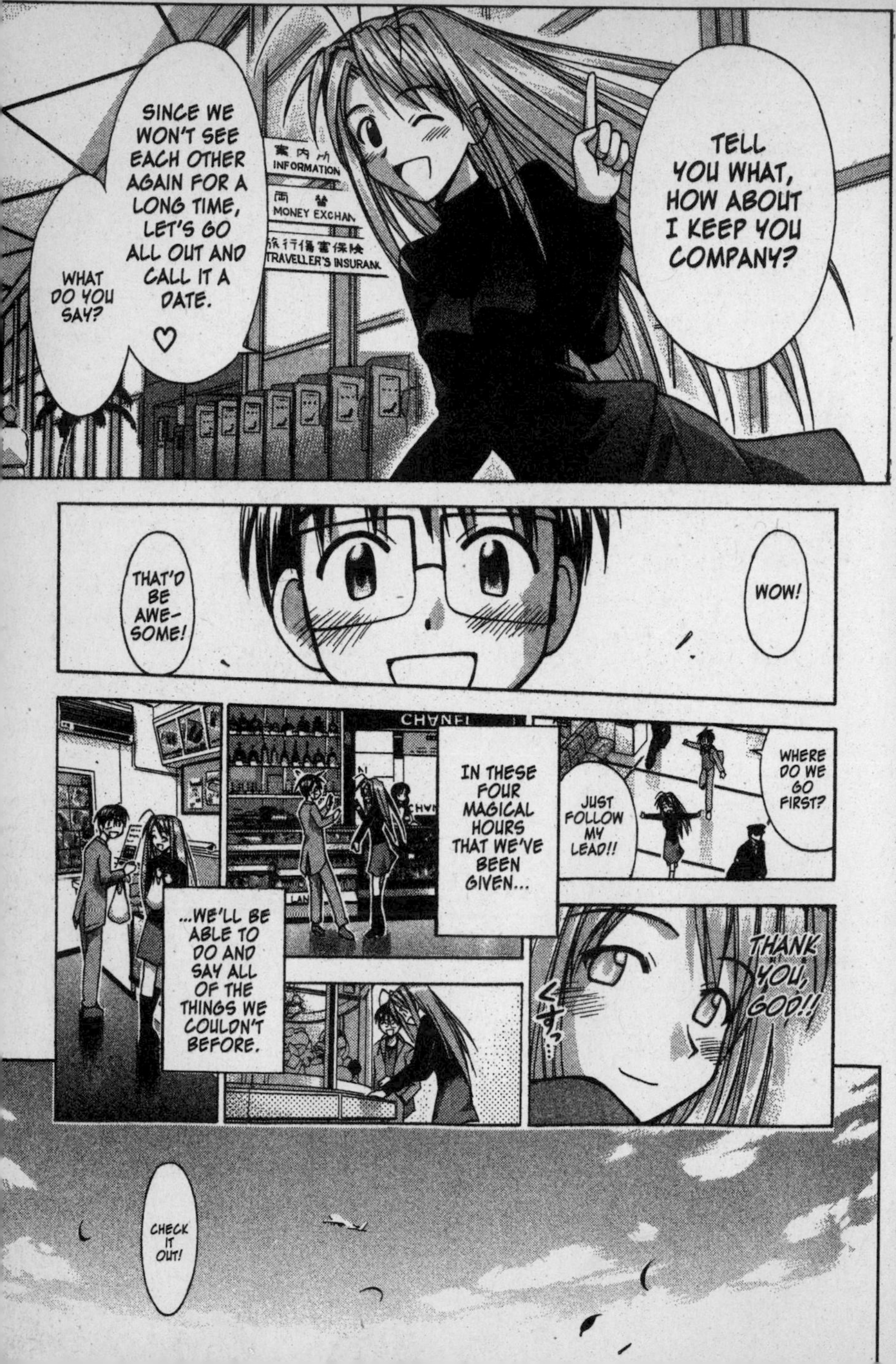

TELL YOU WHAT, HOW ABOUT I KEEP YOU COMPANY?
SINCE WE WON'T SEE EACH OTHER AGAIN FOR A LONG TIME, LET'S GO ALL OUT AND CALL IT A DATE. ♡
WHAT DO YOU SAY?
案内所 INFORMATION
両替 MONEY EXCHAN
旅行傷害保険 TRAVELLER'S INSURANK
WOW!
THAT'D BE AWESOME!
WHERE DO WE GO FIRST?
JUST FOLLOW MY LEAD!!
CHANEL
IN THESE FOUR MAGICAL HOURS THAT WE'VE BEEN GIVEN...
...WE'LL BE ABLE TO DO AND SAY ALL OF THE THINGS WE COULDN'T BEFORE.
THANK YOU, GOD!!
くすっ
CHECK IT OUT!

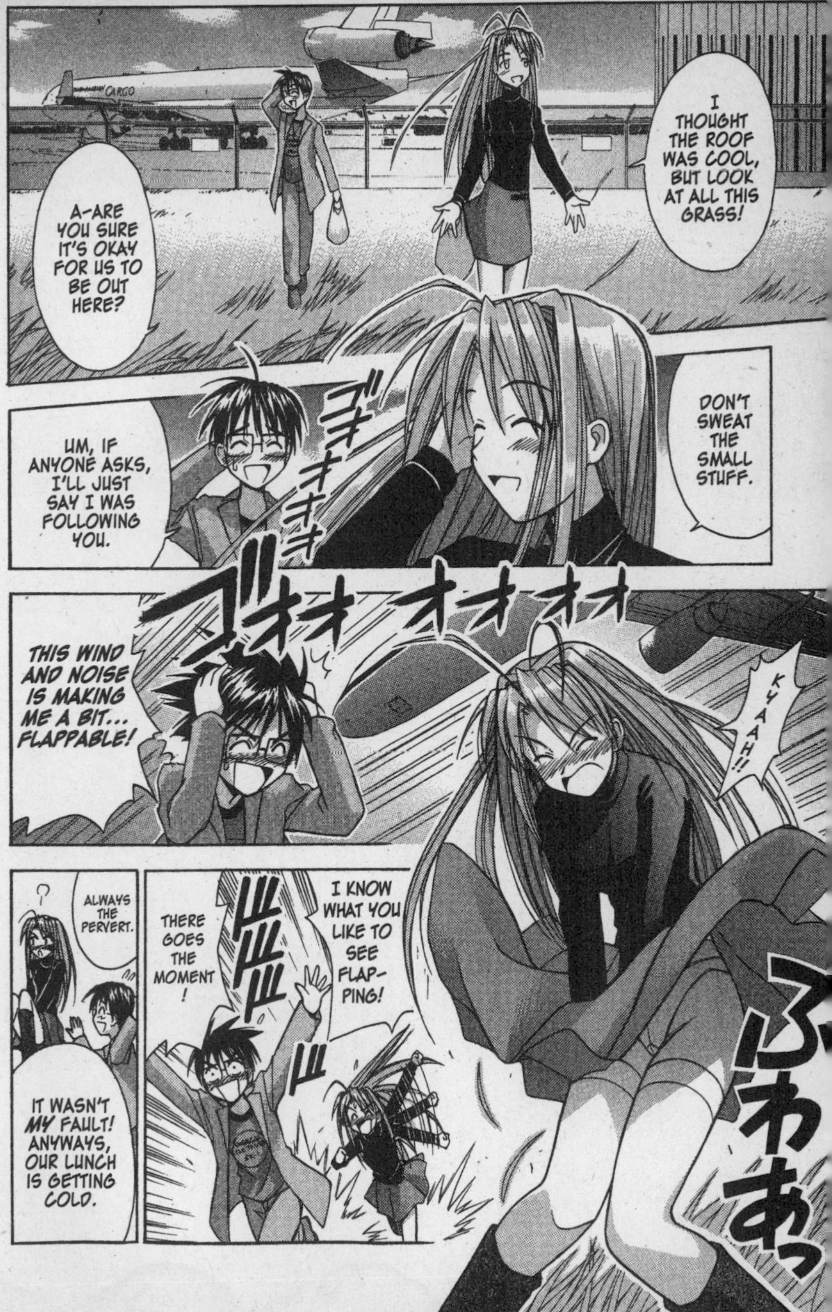

I THOUGHT THE ROOF WAS COOL, BUT LOOK AT ALL THIS GRASS!
A-ARE YOU SURE IT'S OKAY FOR US TO BE OUT HERE?
DON'T SWEAT THE SMALL STUFF.
UM, IF ANYONE ASKS, I'LL JUST SAY I WAS FOLLOWING YOU.
ゴォォォォ
ゴオオ オオオオ
KYAAAH!!
THIS WIND AND NOISE IS MAKING ME A BIT... FLAPPABLE!
ふわあっ
I KNOW WHAT YOU LIKE TO SEE FLAP-PING!
THERE GOES THE MOMENT!
ドドドド
ALWAYS THE PERVERT.
?
IT WASN'T MY FAULT! ANYWAYS, OUR LUNCH IS GETTING COLD.

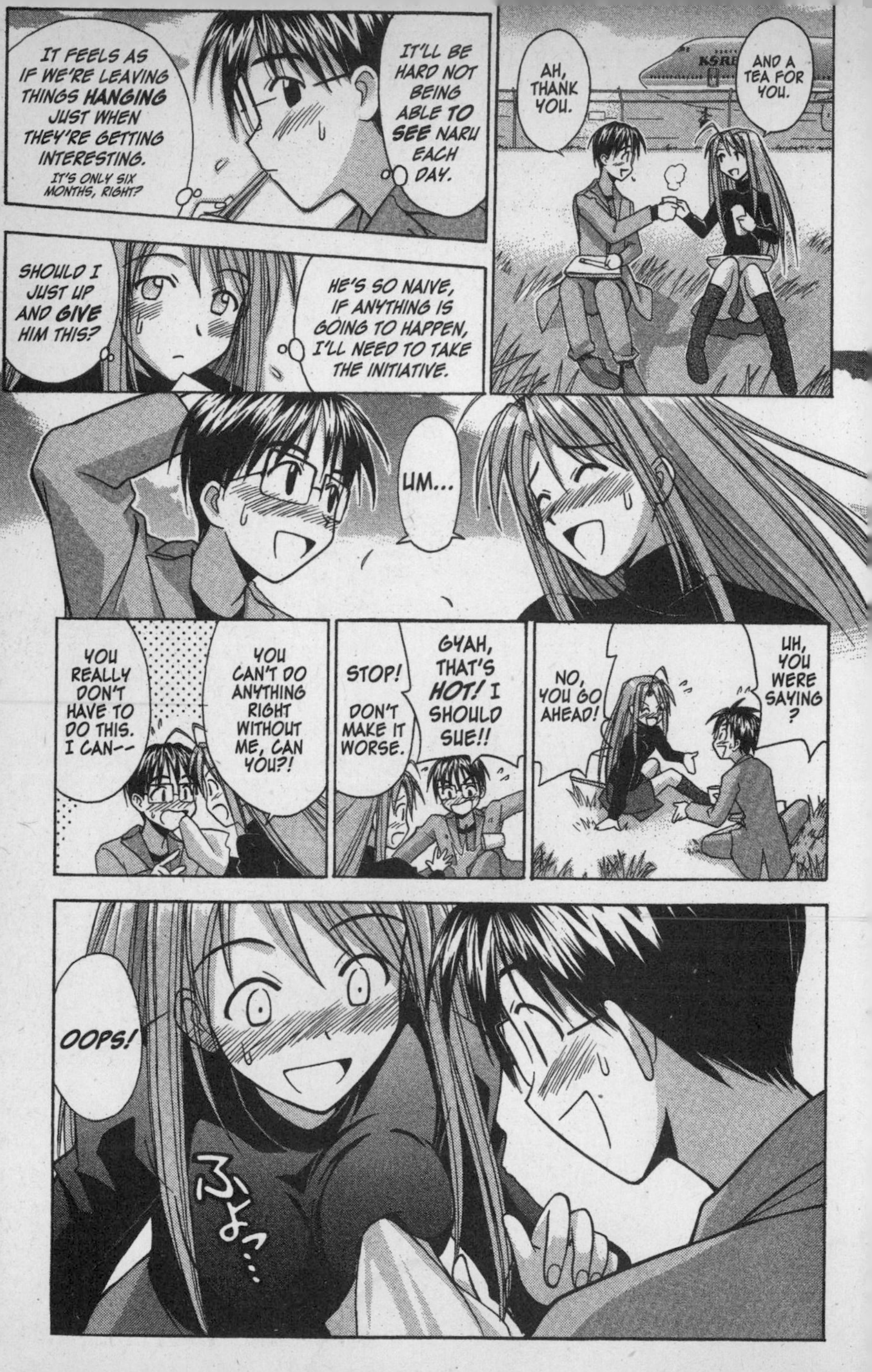
AND A TEA FOR YOU.
AH, THANK YOU.
IT'LL BE HARD NOT BEING ABLE TO SEE NARU EACH DAY.
IT FEELS AS IF WE'RE LEAVING THINGS HANGING JUST WHEN THEY'RE GETTING INTERESTING.
IT'S ONLY SIX MONTHS, RIGHT?
HE'S SO NAIVE, IF ANYTHING IS GOING TO HAPPEN, I'LL NEED TO TAKE THE INITIATIVE.
SHOULD I JUST UP AND GIVE HIM THIS?
UM...
UH, YOU WERE SAYING?
NO, YOU GO AHEAD!
GYAH, THAT'S HOT! I SHOULD SUE!!
STOP! DON'T MAKE IT WORSE.
YOU CAN'T DO ANYTHING RIGHT WITHOUT ME, CAN YOU?!
YOU REALLY DON'T HAVE TO DO THIS. I CAN--
OOPS!
ふよっ...

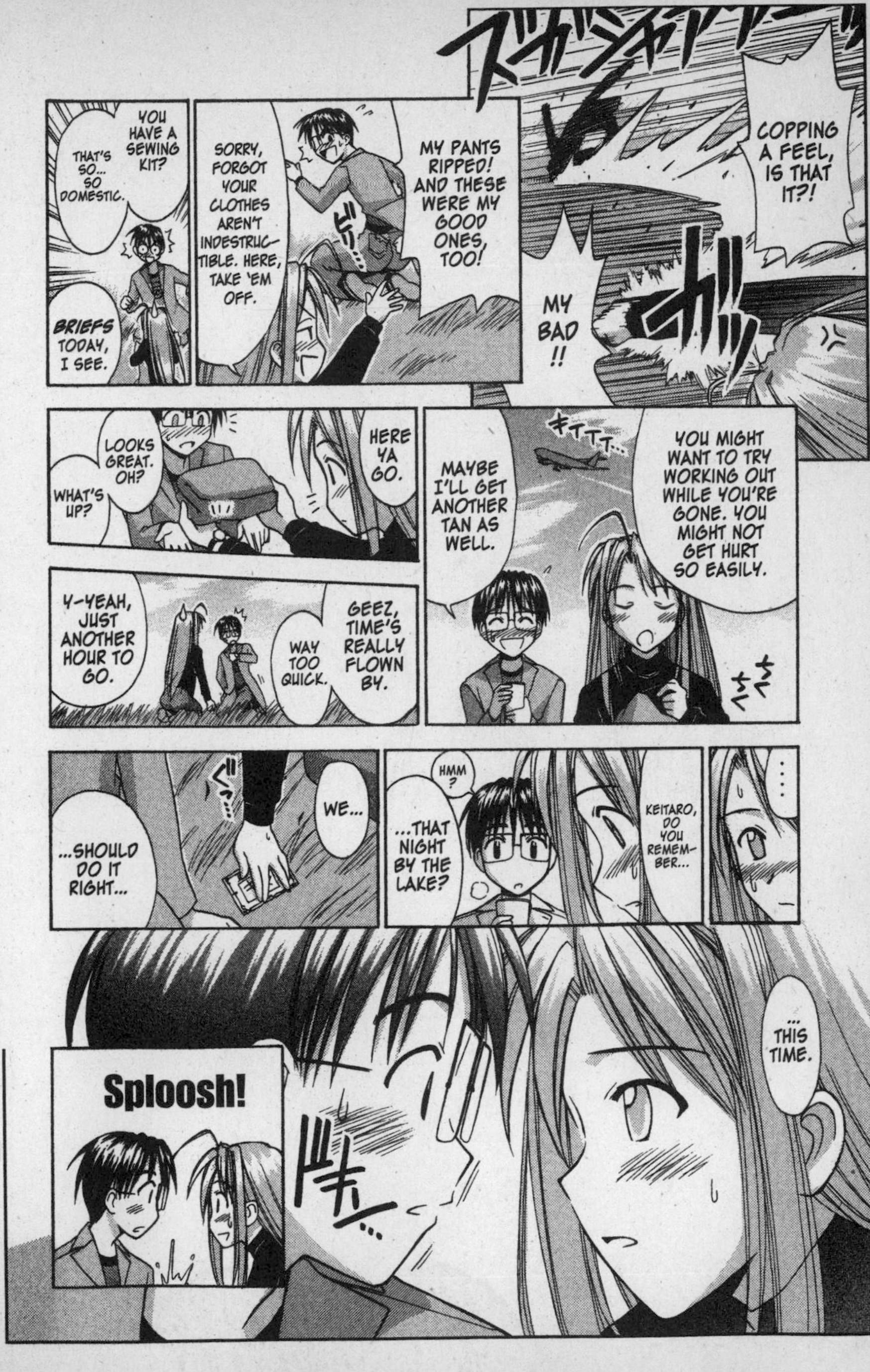
COPPING A FEEL, IS THAT IT?!
MY BAD!!
MY PANTS RIPPED! AND THESE WERE MY GOOD ONES, TOO!
SORRY, FORGOT YOUR CLOTHES AREN'T INDESTRUC-TIBLE. HERE, TAKE 'EM OFF.
YOU HAVE A SEWING KIT?
THAT'S SO... SO DOMESTIC.
BRIEFS TODAY, I SEE.
YOU MIGHT WANT TO TRY WORKING OUT WHILE YOU'RE GONE. YOU MIGHT NOT GET HURT SO EASILY.
MAYBE I'LL GET ANOTHER TAN AS WELL.
HERE YA GO.
LOOKS GREAT. OH?
WHAT'S UP?
GEEZ, TIME'S REALLY FLOWN BY.
WAY TOO QUICK.
Y-YEAH, JUST ANOTHER HOUR TO GO.
....
KEITARO, DO YOU REMEM-BER...
HMM?
...THAT NIGHT BY THE LAKE?
WE...
...SHOULD DO IT RIGHT...
... THIS TIME.
Sploosh!

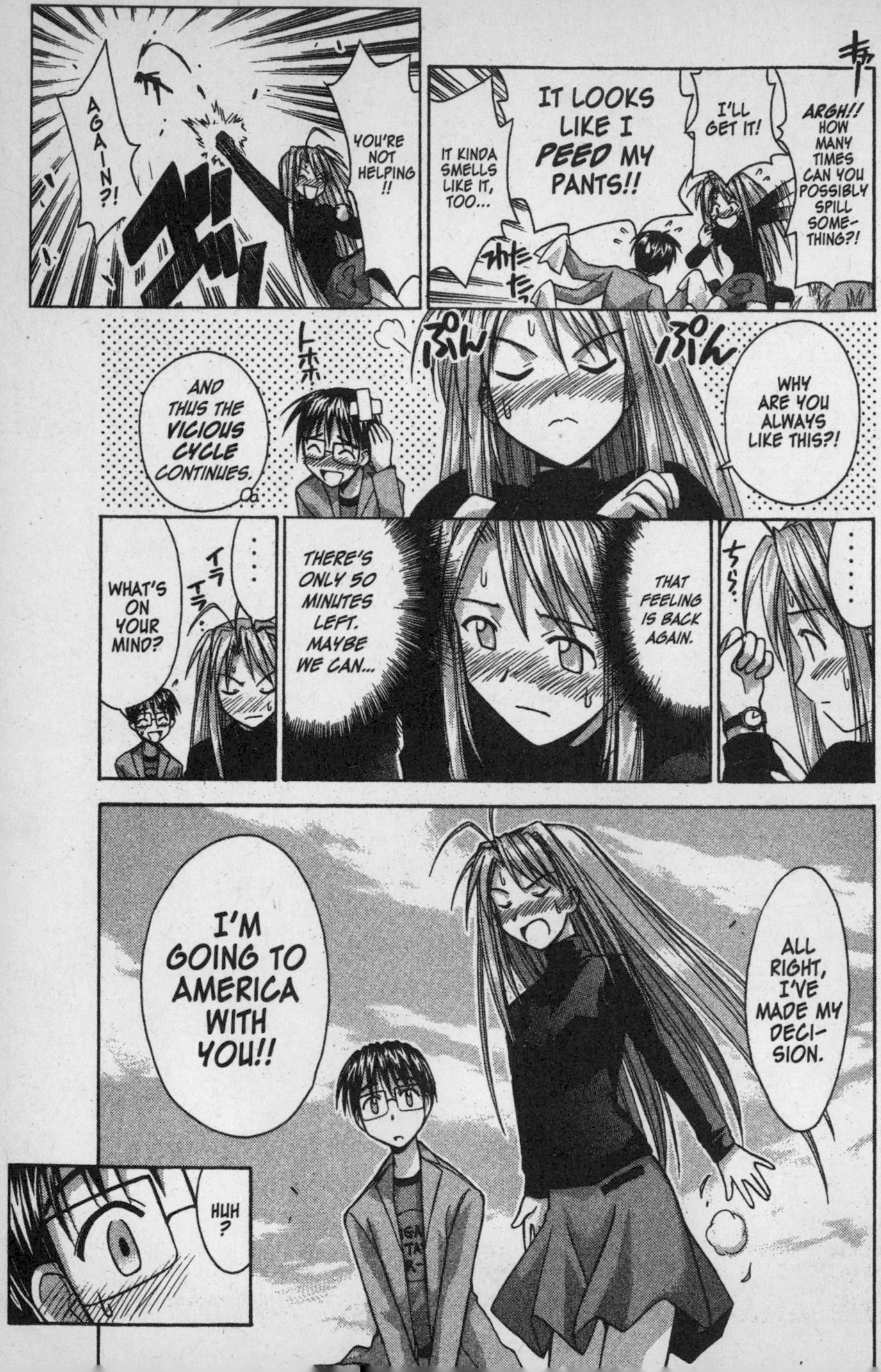
ARGH!! HOW MANY TIMES CAN YOU POSSIBLY SPILL SOME-THING?!
I'LL GET IT!
IT LOOKS LIKE I PEED MY PANTS!!
IT KINDA SMELLS LIKE IT, TOO...
YOU'RE NOT HELPING !!
AGAIN?!
ぷん
ぷん
WHY ARE YOU ALWAYS LIKE THIS?!
AND THUS THE VICIOUS CYCLE CONTINUES.
......
THAT FEELING IS BACK AGAIN.
THERE'S ONLY 50 MINUTES LEFT. MAYBE WE CAN...
......
WHAT'S ON YOUR MIND?
ALL RIGHT, I'VE MADE MY DECISION.
I'M GOING TO AMERICA WITH YOU!!
HUH?

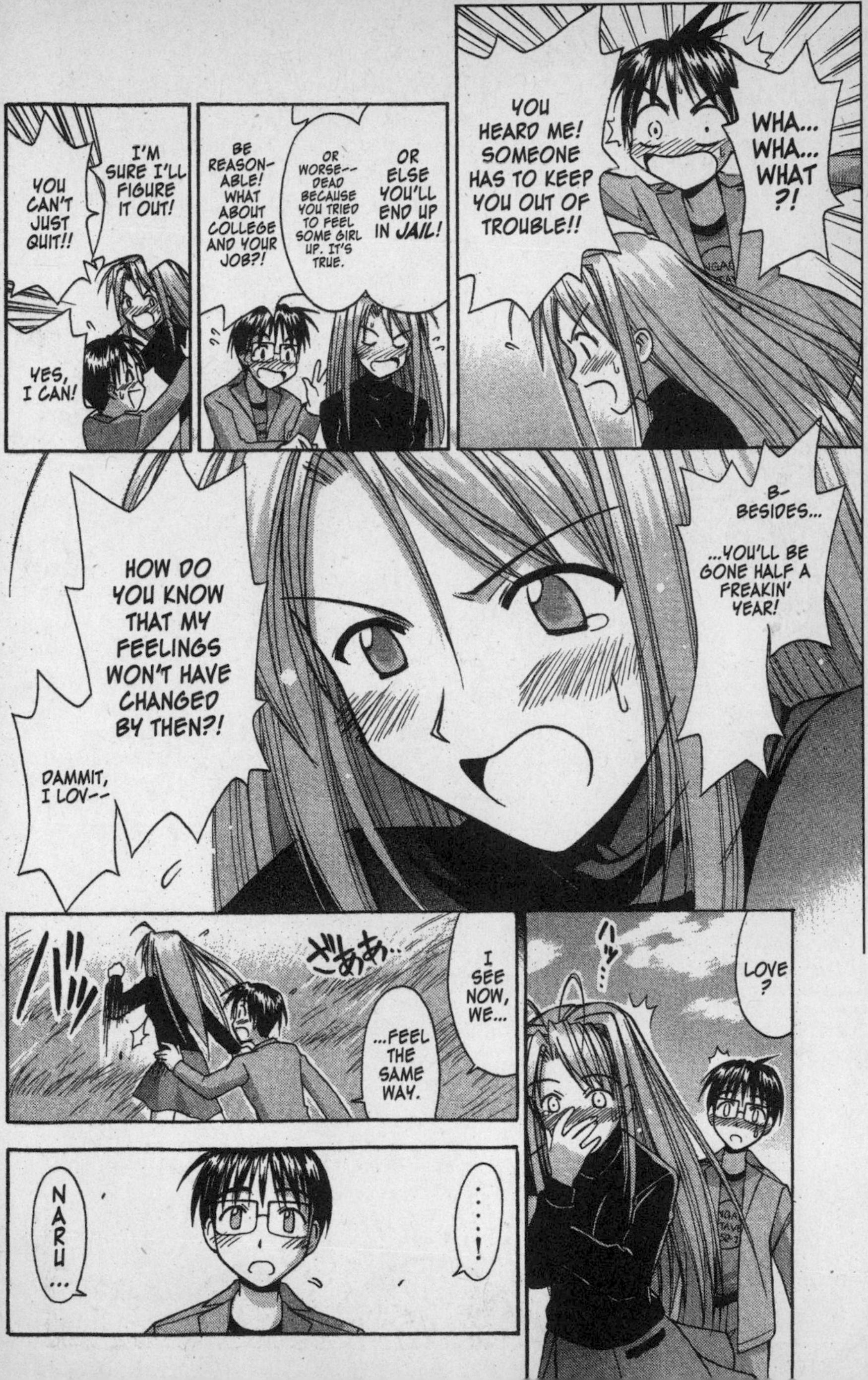
WHA... WHA... WHAT?!
YOU HEARD ME! SOMEONE HAS TO KEEP YOU OUT OF TROUBLE!!
OR ELSE YOU'LL END UP IN JAIL!
OR WORSE--DEAD BECAUSE YOU TRIED TO FEEL SOME GIRL UP. IT'S TRUE.
BE REASONABLE! WHAT ABOUT COLLEGE AND YOUR JOB?!
I'M SURE I'LL FIGURE IT OUT!
YOU CAN'T JUST QUIT!!
YES, I CAN!
B-BESIDES...
...YOU'LL BE GONE HALF A FREAKIN' YEAR!
HOW DO YOU KNOW THAT MY FEELINGS WON'T HAVE CHANGED BY THEN?!
DAMMIT, I LOV--
LOVE?
ハッ…
I SEE NOW, WE...
...FEEL THE SAME WAY.
ざああ…
バッ
....!
NARU...

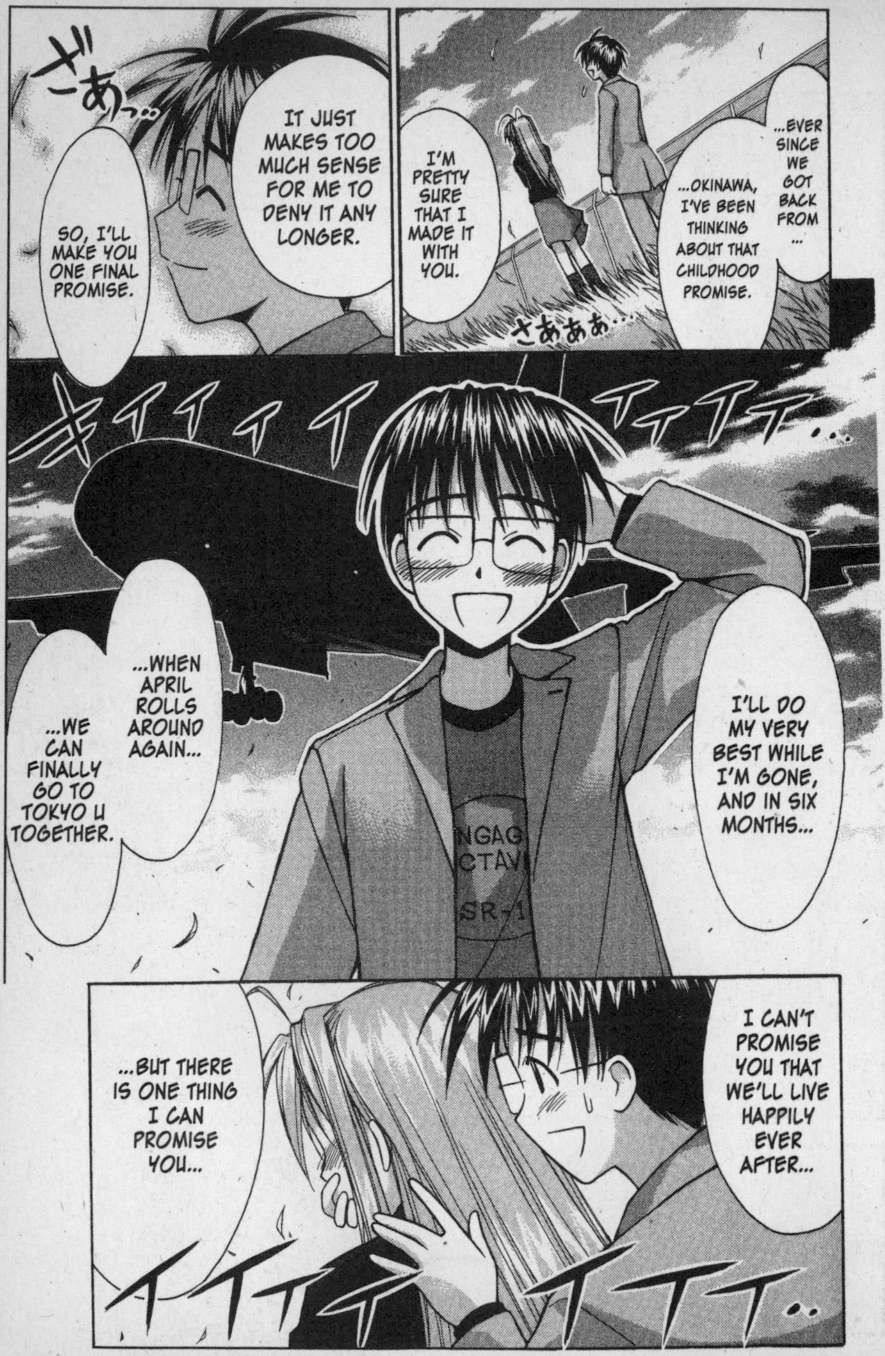
...EVER SINCE WE GOT BACK FROM ...
...OKINAWA, I'VE BEEN THINKING ABOUT THAT CHILDHOOD PROMISE.
I'M PRETTY SURE THAT I MADE IT WITH YOU.
さあああ...
ざあっ...
IT JUST MAKES TOO MUCH SENSE FOR ME TO DENY IT ANY LONGER.
SO, I'LL MAKE YOU ONE FINAL PROMISE.
キイイイイ
イイイイ...
I'LL DO MY VERY BEST WHILE I'M GONE, AND IN SIX MONTHS...
...WHEN APRIL ROLLS AROUND AGAIN...
...WE CAN FINALLY GO TO TOKYO U TOGETHER.
I CAN'T PROMISE YOU THAT WE'LL LIVE HAPPILY EVER AFTER...
...BUT THERE IS ONE THING I CAN PROMISE YOU...
イイイイ イイイ..

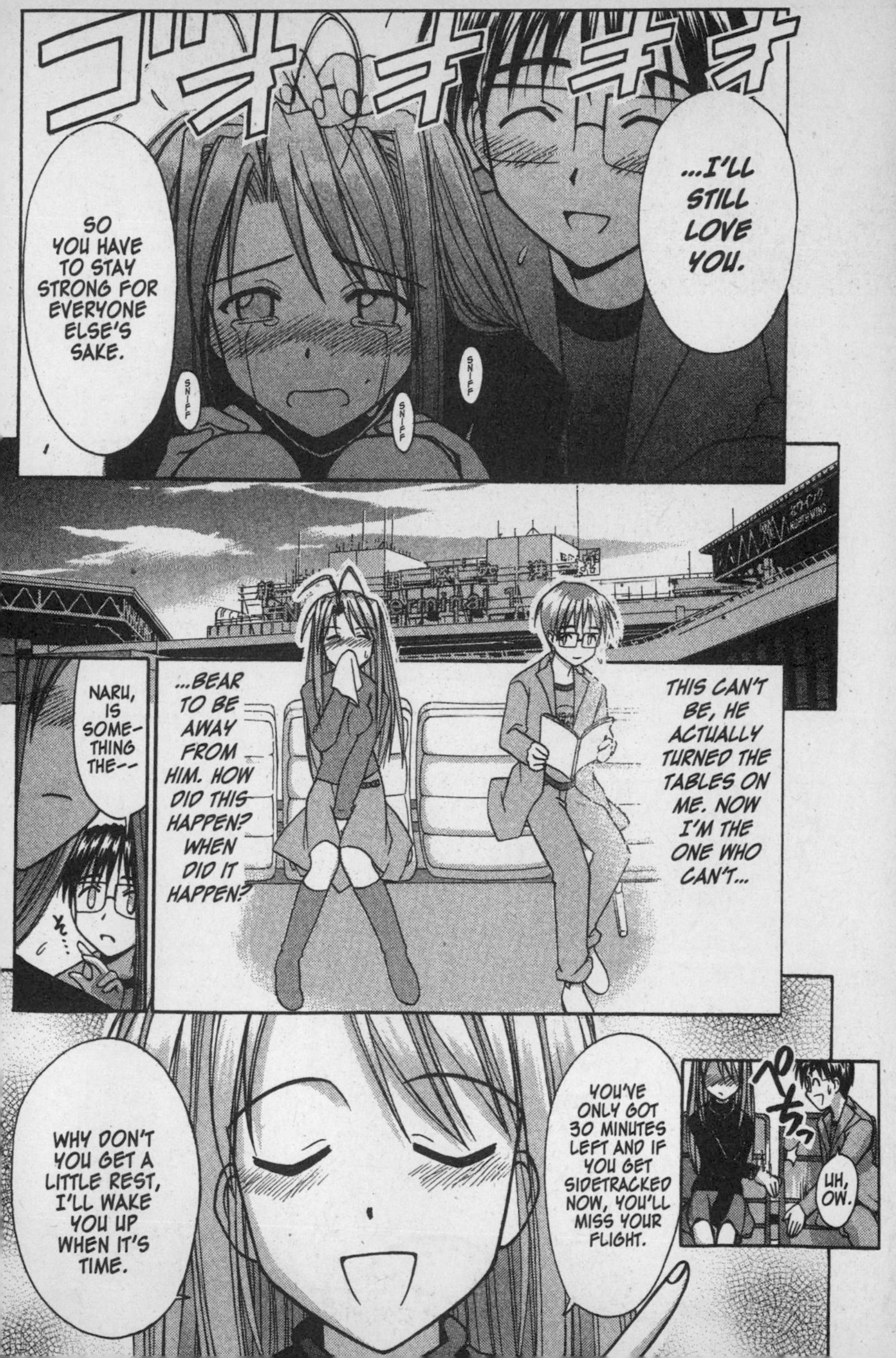
...I'LL STILL LOVE YOU.
SO YOU HAVE TO STAY STRONG FOR EVERYONE ELSE'S SAKE.
SNIFF
SNIFF
SNIFF
THIS CAN'T BE, HE ACTUALLY TURNED THE TABLES ON ME. NOW I'M THE ONE WHO CAN'T...
...BEAR TO BE AWAY FROM HIM. HOW DID THIS HAPPEN? WHEN DID IT HAPPEN?
NARU, IS SOMETHING THE--
え…
ぺちっ
UH, OW.
YOU'VE ONLY GOT 30 MINUTES LEFT AND IF YOU GET SIDETRACKED NOW, YOU'LL MISS YOUR FLIGHT.
WHY DON'T YOU GET A LITTLE REST, I'LL WAKE YOU UP WHEN IT'S TIME.

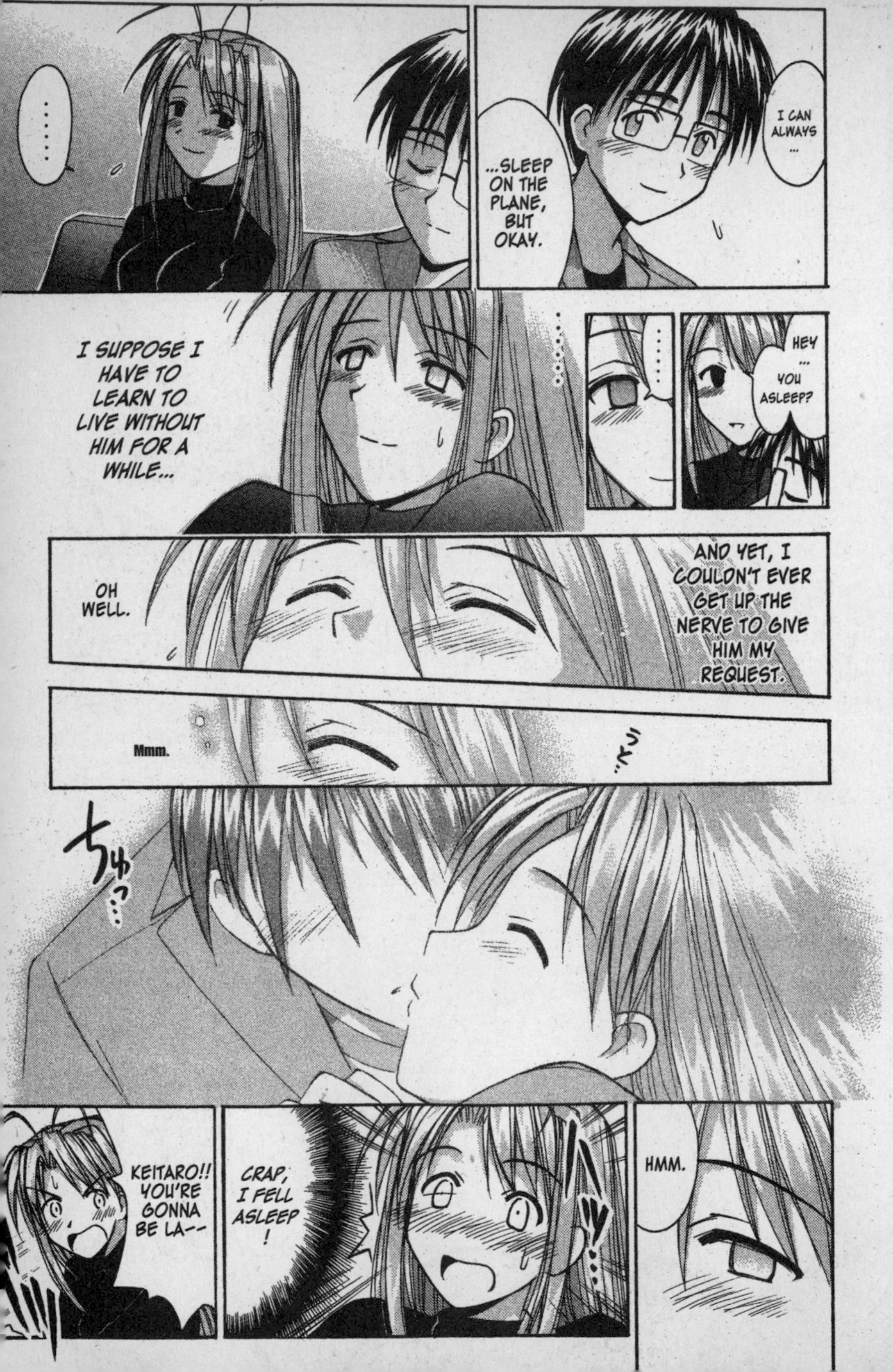
I CAN ALWAYS ...
...SLEEP ON THE PLANE, BUT OKAY.
......
HEY ... YOU ASLEEP?
......
I SUPPOSE I HAVE TO LEARN TO LIVE WITHOUT HIM FOR A WHILE...
AND YET, I COULDN'T EVER GET UP THE NERVE TO GIVE HIM MY REQUEST.
OH WELL.
うと…
Mmm.
ちゅっ…
HMM.
CRAP, I FELL ASLEEP!
KEITARO!! YOU'RE GONNA BE LA--

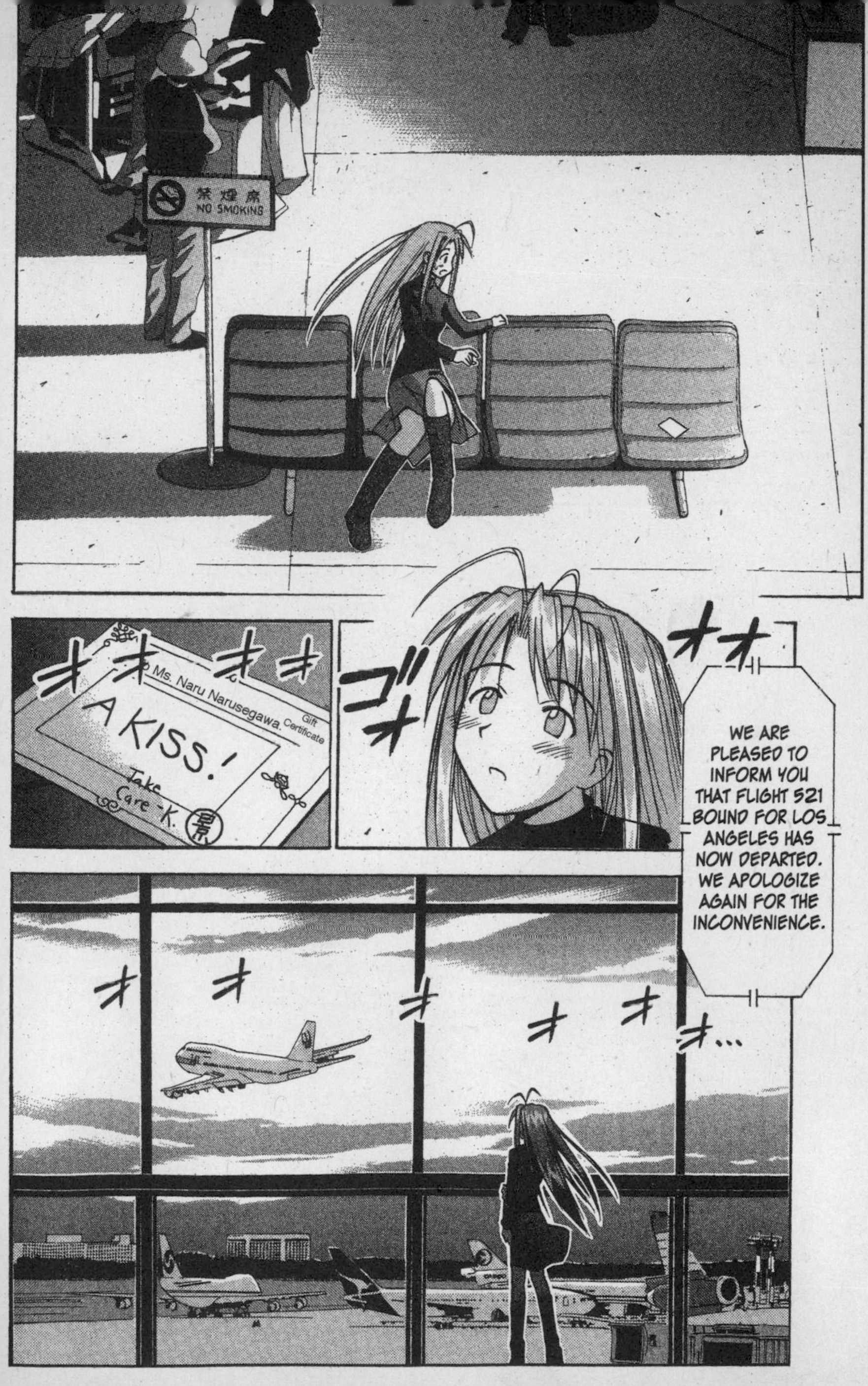
禁煙席
NO SMOKING
ゴオオ
WE ARE PLEASED TO INFORM YOU THAT FLIGHT 521 BOUND FOR LOS ANGELES HAS NOW DEPARTED. WE APOLOGIZE AGAIN FOR THE INCONVENIENCE.
オオオオ
Ms. Naru Narusegawa.
Gift Certificate
A KISS!
Take Care -K.
景
オオオオオオ…

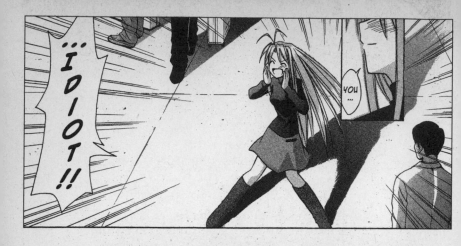

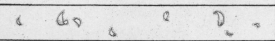

AND
SO, SIX
MONTHS
PASSED.

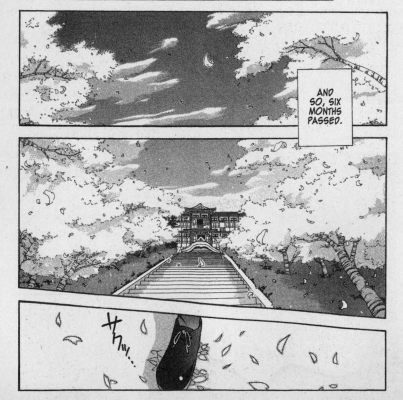

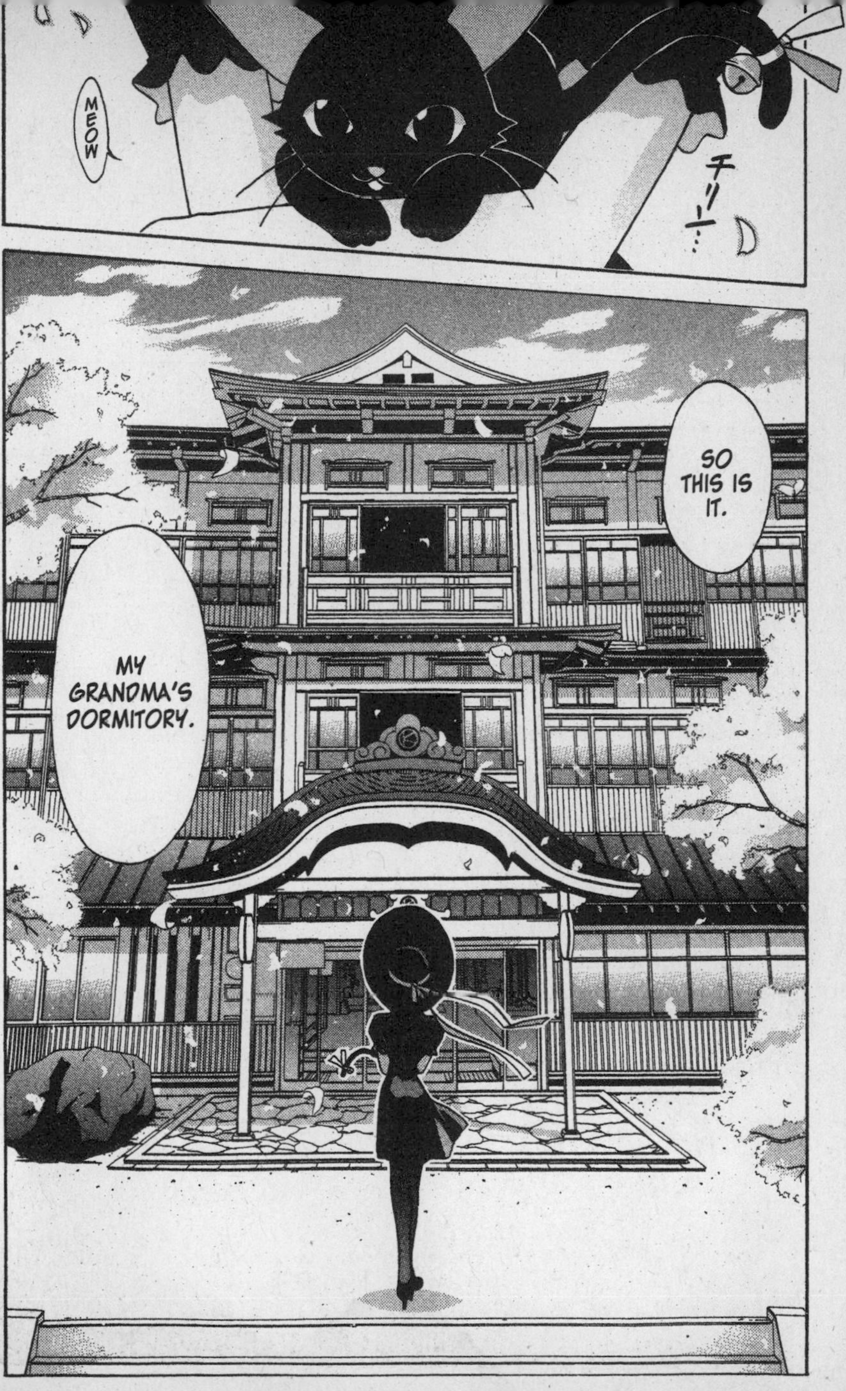

チリン…
MEOW
SO THIS IS IT.
MY GRANDMA'S DORMITORY.

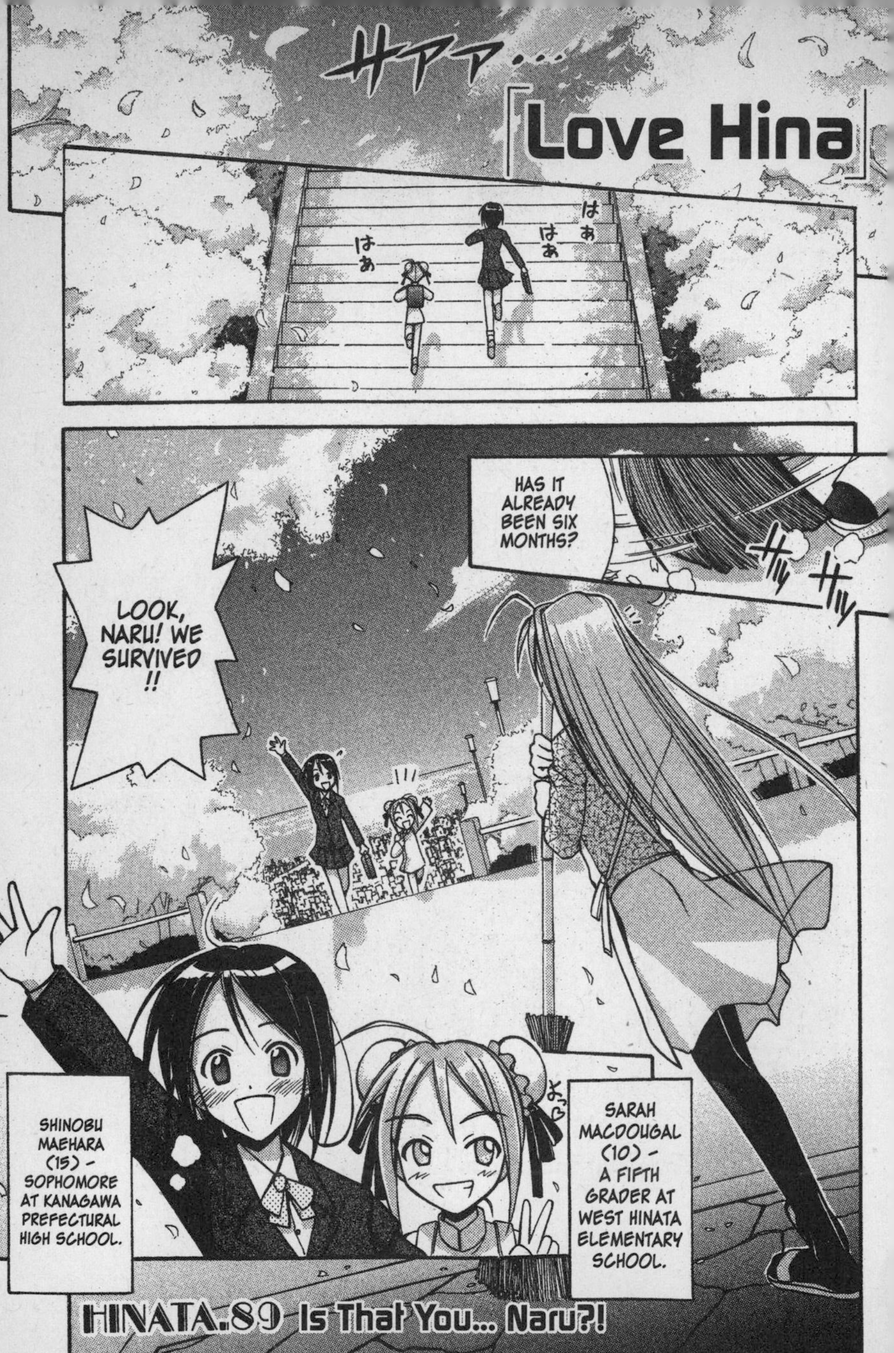
サァァ…
「Love Hina」
はぁ はぁ
はぁ
HAS IT ALREADY BEEN SIX MONTHS?
LOOK, NARU! WE SURVIVED!!
SARAH MACDOUGAL (10) - A FIFTH GRADER AT WEST HINATA ELEMENTARY SCHOOL.
SHINOBU MAEHARA (15) - SOPHOMORE AT KANAGAWA PREFECTURAL HIGH SCHOOL.
HINATA.89 Is That You... Naru?!

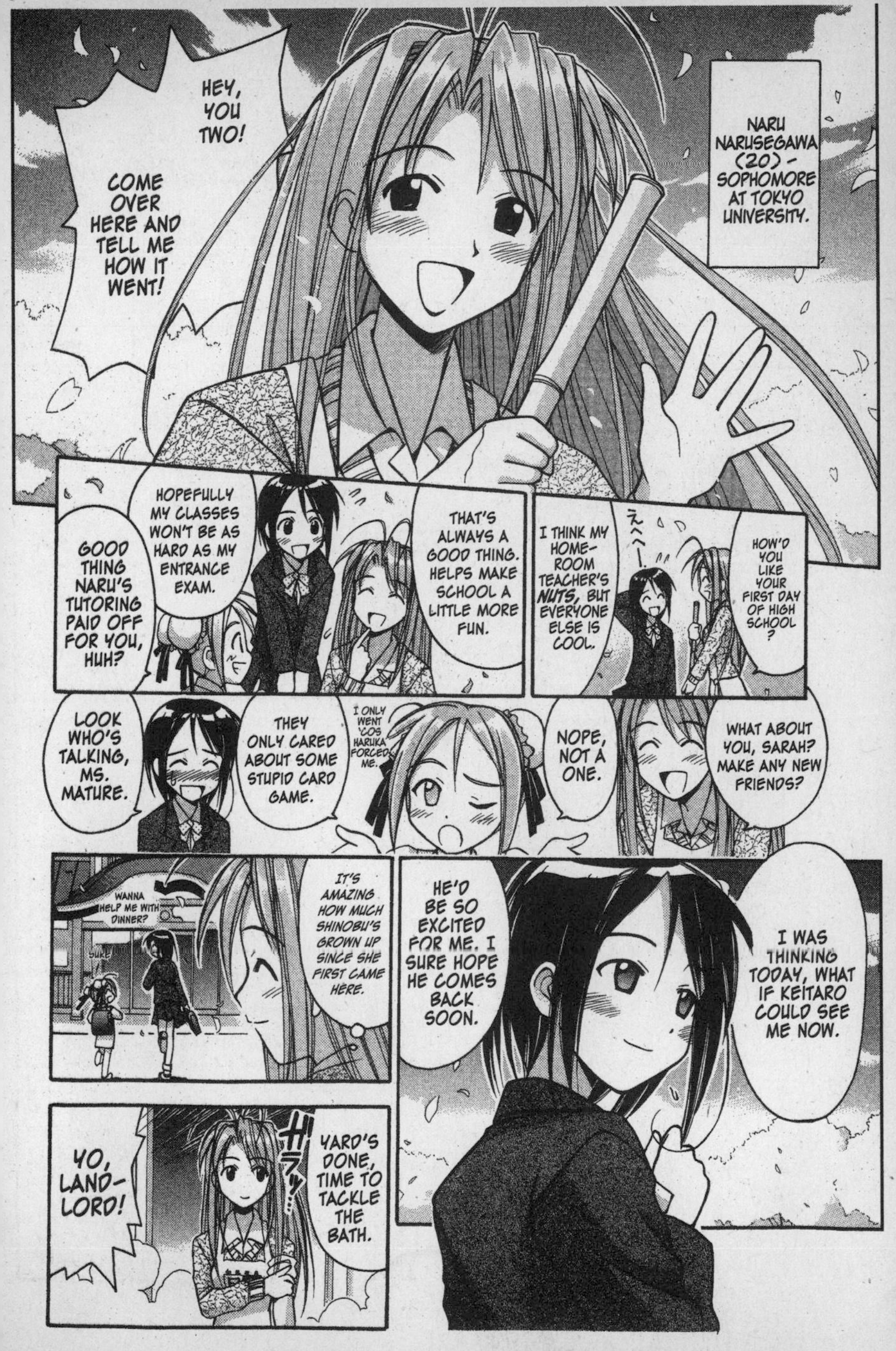
NARU NARUSEGAWA (20) - SOPHOMORE AT TOKYO UNIVERSITY.
HEY, YOU TWO!
COME OVER HERE AND TELL ME HOW IT WENT!
HOW'D YOU LIKE YOUR FIRST DAY OF HIGH SCHOOL?
えへへ…
I THINK MY HOME-ROOM TEACHER'S NUTS, BUT EVERYONE ELSE IS COOL.
THAT'S ALWAYS A GOOD THING. HELPS MAKE SCHOOL A LITTLE MORE FUN.
HOPEFULLY MY CLASSES WON'T BE AS HARD AS MY ENTRANCE EXAM.
GOOD THING NARU'S TUTORING PAID OFF FOR YOU, HUH?
WHAT ABOUT YOU, SARAH? MAKE ANY NEW FRIENDS?
NOPE, NOT A ONE.
I ONLY WENT 'COS HARUKA FORCED ME.
THEY ONLY CARED ABOUT SOME STUPID CARD GAME.
LOOK WHO'S TALKING, MS. MATURE.
I WAS THINKING TODAY, WHAT IF KEITARO COULD SEE ME NOW.
HE'D BE SO EXCITED FOR ME. I SURE HOPE HE COMES BACK SOON.
IT'S AMAZING HOW MUCH SHINOBU'S GROWN UP SINCE SHE FIRST CAME HERE.
WANNA HELP ME WITH DINNER?
SURE
YARD'S DONE, TIME TO TACKLE THE BATH.
ガラッ
YO, LANDLORD!

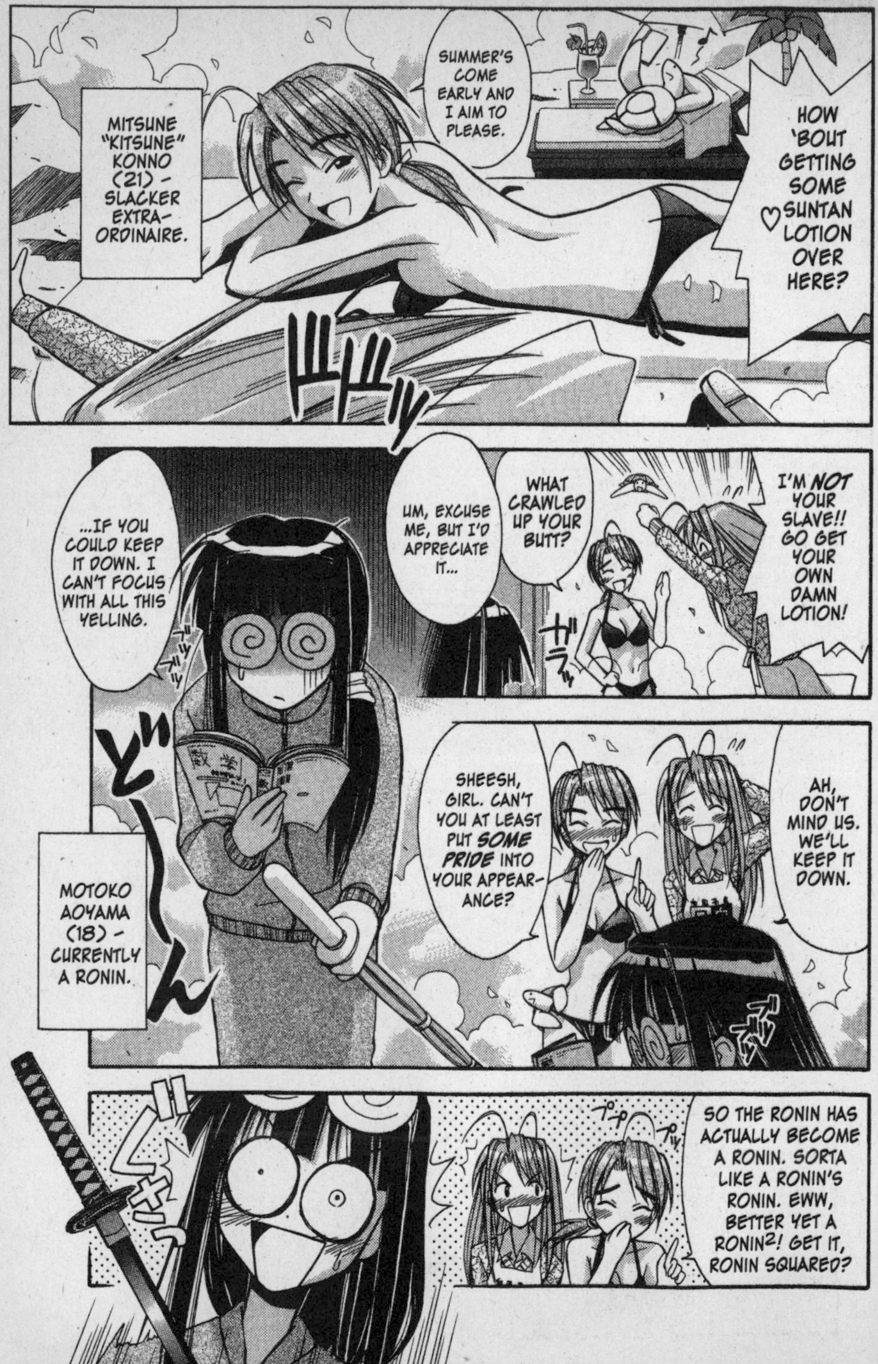
SUMMER'S COME EARLY AND I AIM TO PLEASE.
HOW 'BOUT GETTING SOME ♡ SUNTAN LOTION OVER HERE?
MITSUNE "KITSUNE" KONNO (21) - SLACKER EXTRA-ORDINAIRE.
I'M NOT YOUR SLAVE!! GO GET YOUR OWN DAMN LOTION!
WHAT CRAWLED UP YOUR BUTT?
UM, EXCUSE ME, BUT I'D APPRECIATE IT...
AH, DON'T MIND US. WE'LL KEEP IT DOWN.
SHEESH, GIRL. CAN'T YOU AT LEAST PUT SOME PRIDE INTO YOUR APPEARANCE?
...IF YOU COULD KEEP IT DOWN. I CAN'T FOCUS WITH ALL THIS YELLING.
MOTOKO AOYAMA (18) - CURRENTLY A RONIN.
SO THE RONIN HAS ACTUALLY BECOME A RONIN. SORTA LIKE A RONIN'S RONIN. EWW, BETTER YET A RONIN²! GET IT, RONIN SQUARED?

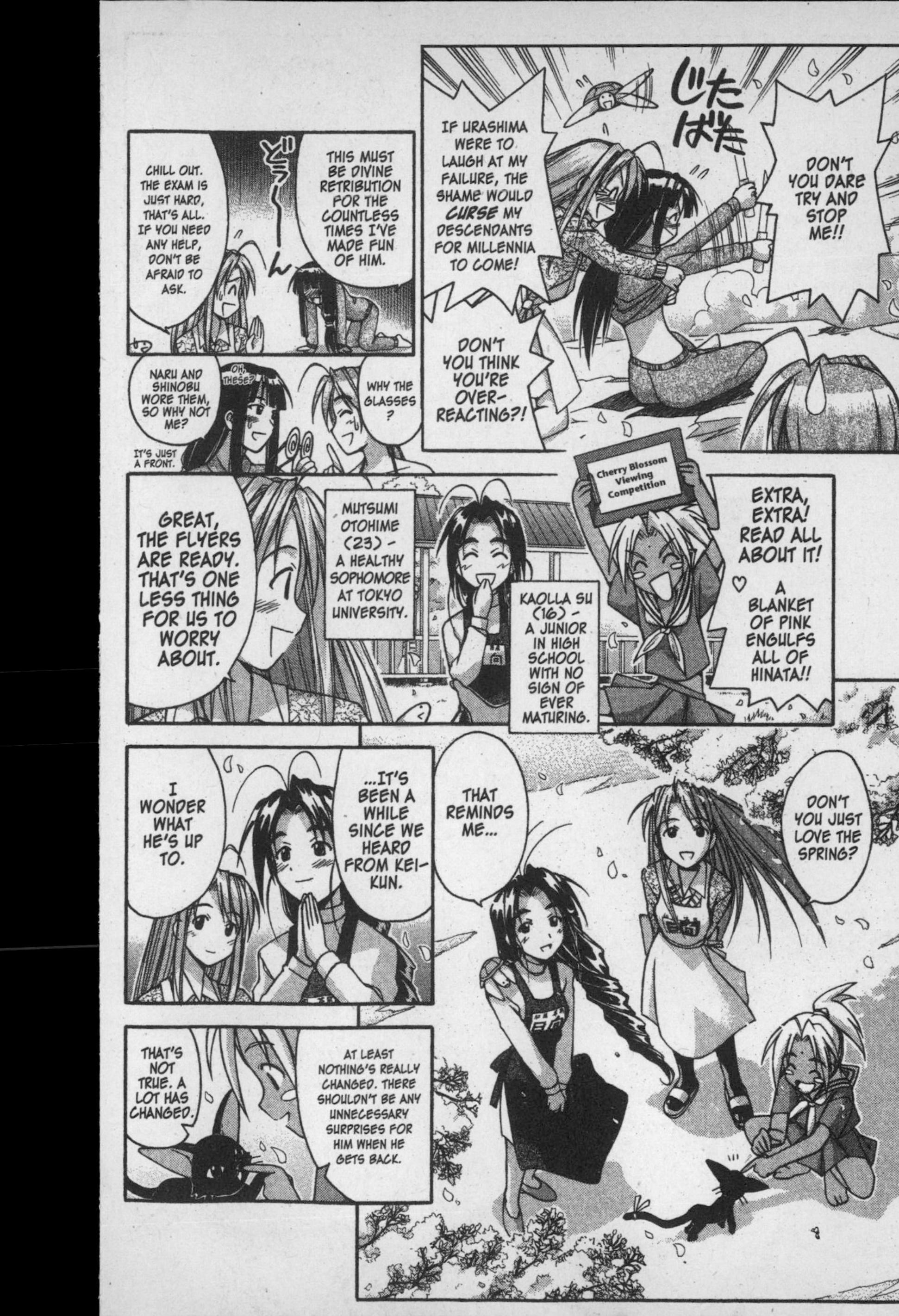
じたばた
DON'T YOU DARE TRY AND STOP ME!!
IF URASHIMA WERE TO LAUGH AT MY FAILURE, THE SHAME WOULD ***CURSE*** MY DESCENDANTS FOR MILLENNIA TO COME!
DON'T YOU THINK YOU'RE OVER-REACTING?!
どろ〜ん
THIS MUST BE DIVINE RETRIBUTION FOR THE COUNTLESS TIMES I'VE MADE FUN OF HIM.
CHILL OUT. THE EXAM IS JUST HARD, THAT'S ALL. IF YOU NEED ANY HELP, DON'T BE AFRAID TO ASK.
WHY THE GLASSES?
OH, THESE?
NARU AND SHINOBU WORE THEM, SO WHY NOT ME?
IT'S JUST A FRONT.
EXTRA, EXTRA! READ ALL ABOUT IT! ♡ A BLANKET OF PINK ENGULFS ALL OF HINATA!!
Cherry Blossom Viewing Competition
KAOLLA SU (16) - A JUNIOR IN HIGH SCHOOL WITH NO SIGN OF EVER MATURING.
MUTSUMI OTOHIME (23) - A HEALTHY SOPHOMORE AT TOKYO UNIVERSITY.
GREAT, THE FLYERS ARE READY. THAT'S ONE LESS THING FOR US TO WORRY ABOUT.
DON'T YOU JUST LOVE THE SPRING?
THAT REMINDS ME...
...IT'S BEEN A WHILE SINCE WE HEARD FROM KEI-KUN.
I WONDER WHAT HE'S UP TO.
AT LEAST NOTHING'S REALLY CHANGED. THERE SHOULDN'T BE ANY UNNECESSARY SURPRISES FOR HIM WHEN HE GETS BACK.
THAT'S NOT TRUE. A LOT HAS CHANGED.

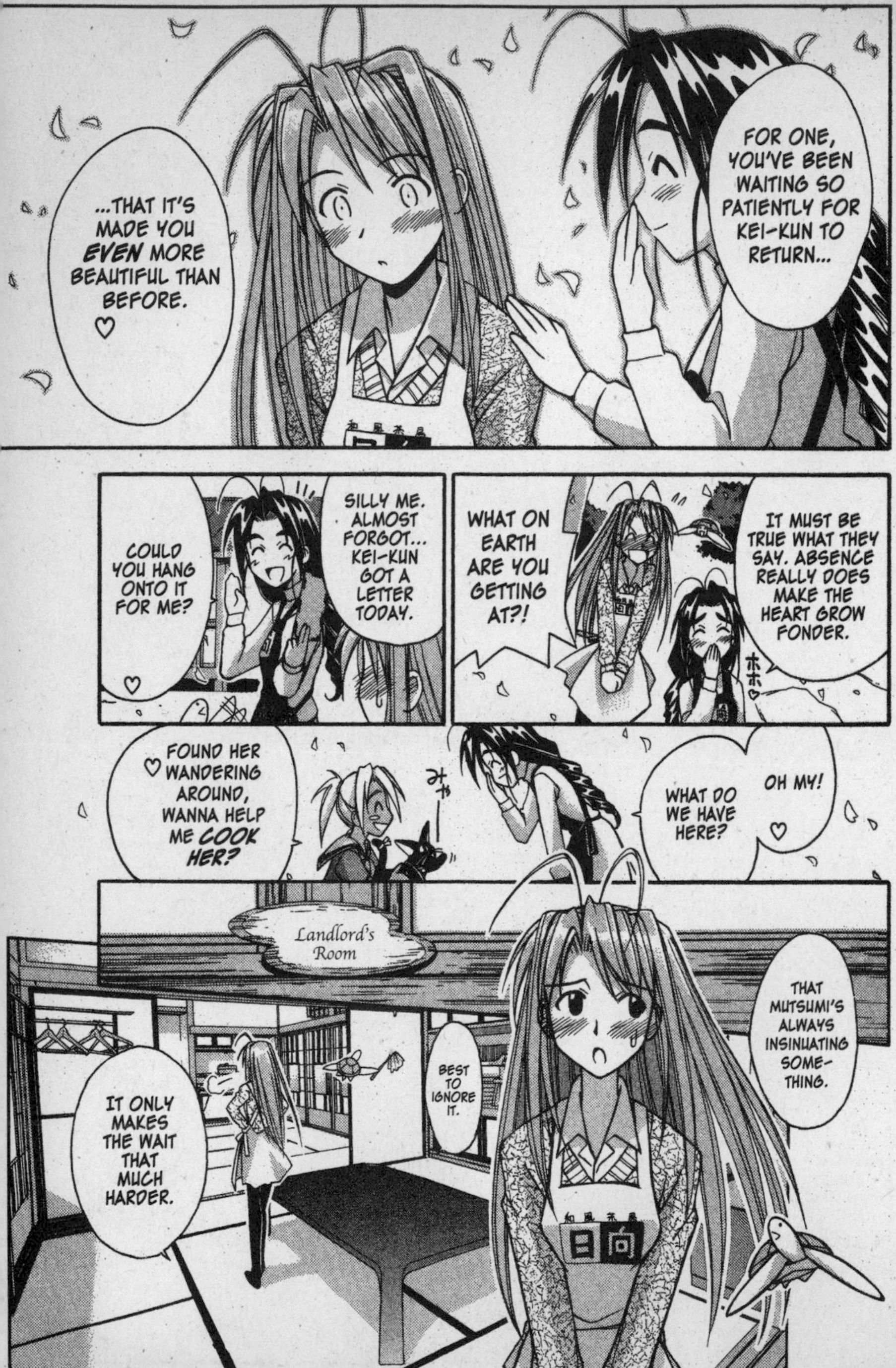
FOR ONE, YOU'VE BEEN WAITING SO PATIENTLY FOR KEI-KUN TO RETURN...
...THAT IT'S MADE YOU EVEN MORE BEAUTIFUL THAN BEFORE. ♡
IT MUST BE TRUE WHAT THEY SAY. ABSENCE REALLY DOES MAKE THE HEART GROW FONDER.
ホホ♡
WHAT ON EARTH ARE YOU GETTING AT?!
SILLY ME. ALMOST FORGOT... KEI-KUN GOT A LETTER TODAY.
COULD YOU HANG ONTO IT FOR ME? ♡
OH MY! ♡
WHAT DO WE HAVE HERE?
みゃー
FOUND HER WANDERING AROUND, WANNA HELP ME COOK HER? ♡
Landlord's Room
THAT MUTSUMI'S ALWAYS INSINUATING SOME-THING.
BEST TO IGNORE IT.
IT ONLY MAKES THE WAIT THAT MUCH HARDER.

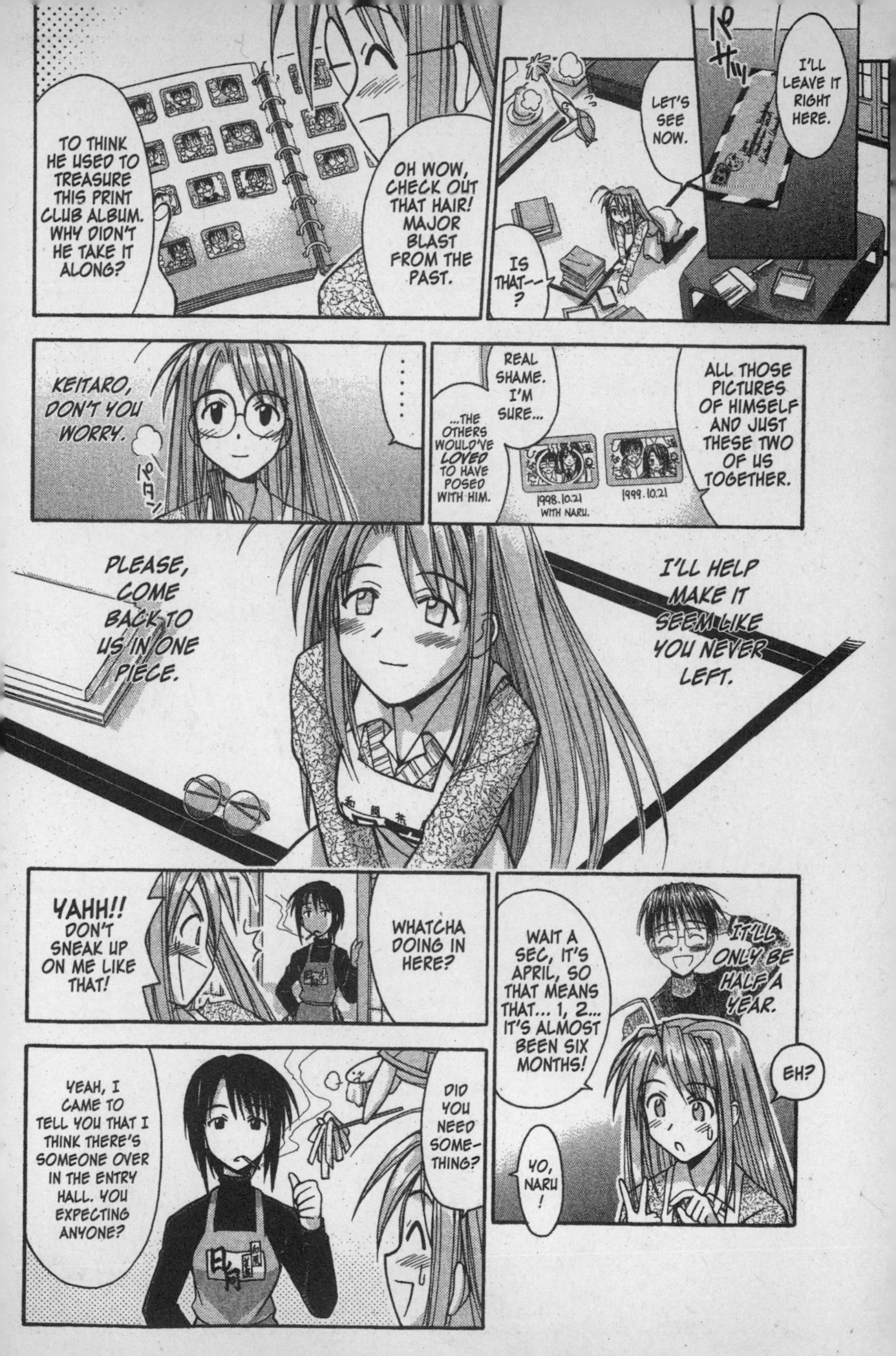
I'LL LEAVE IT RIGHT HERE.
LET'S SEE NOW.
IS THAT--?
OH WOW, CHECK OUT THAT HAIR! MAJOR BLAST FROM THE PAST.
TO THINK HE USED TO TREASURE THIS PRINT CLUB ALBUM. WHY DIDN'T HE TAKE IT ALONG?
ALL THOSE PICTURES OF HIMSELF AND JUST THESE TWO OF US TOGETHER.
REAL SHAME. I'M SURE...
...THE OTHERS WOULD'VE LOVED TO HAVE POSED WITH HIM.
1999.10.21
1998.10.21 WITH NARU.
......
KEITARO, DON'T YOU WORRY.
I'LL HELP MAKE IT SEEM LIKE YOU NEVER LEFT.
PLEASE, COME BACK TO US IN ONE PIECE.
IT'LL ONLY BE HALF A YEAR.
WAIT A SEC, IT'S APRIL, SO THAT MEANS THAT... 1, 2... IT'S ALMOST BEEN SIX MONTHS!
EH?
YO, NARU!
WHATCHA DOING IN HERE?
YAHH!! DON'T SNEAK UP ON ME LIKE THAT!
DID YOU NEED SOMETHING?
YEAH, I CAME TO TELL YOU THAT I THINK THERE'S SOMEONE OVER IN THE ENTRY HALL. YOU EXPECTING ANYONE?

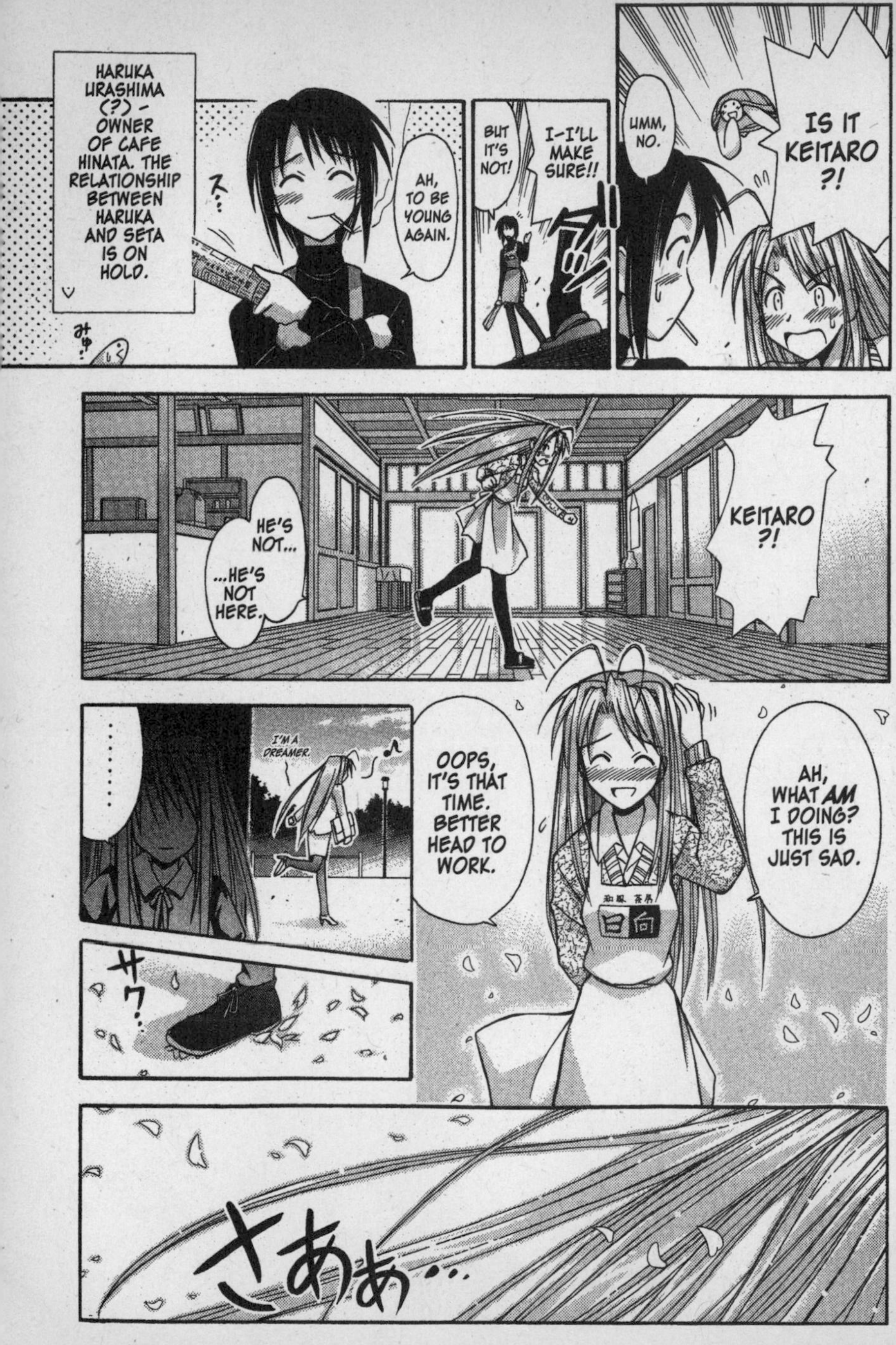
IS IT KEITARO?!
UMM, NO.
I-I'LL MAKE SURE!!
BUT IT'S NOT!
AH, TO BE YOUNG AGAIN.
ス…
HARUKA URASHIMA (?) - OWNER OF CAFE HINATA. THE RELATIONSHIP BETWEEN HARUKA AND SETA IS ON HOLD.
みゅ
KEITARO?!
HE'S NOT...
...HE'S NOT HERE.
AH, WHAT AM I DOING? THIS IS JUST SAD.
OOPS, IT'S THAT TIME. BETTER HEAD TO WORK.
I'M A DREAMER.
......
サワ…
さあぁ…

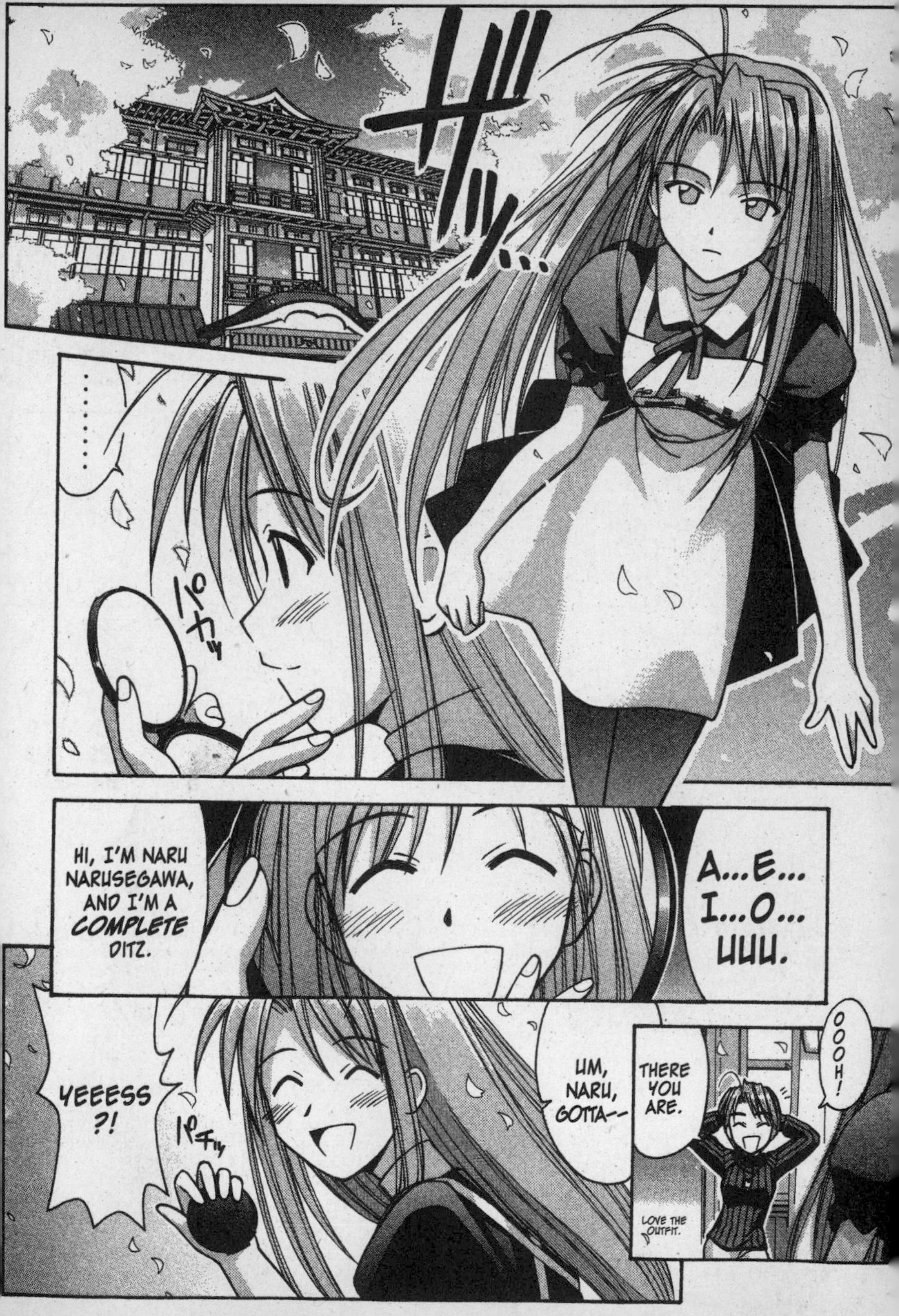

ザッ…
......
パカッ
A...E... I...O... UUU.
HI, I'M NARU NARUSEGAWA, AND I'M A COMPLETE DITZ.
OOOH!
THERE YOU ARE.
LOVE THE OUTFIT.
UM, NARU, GOTTA--
YEEESS?!
パチッ

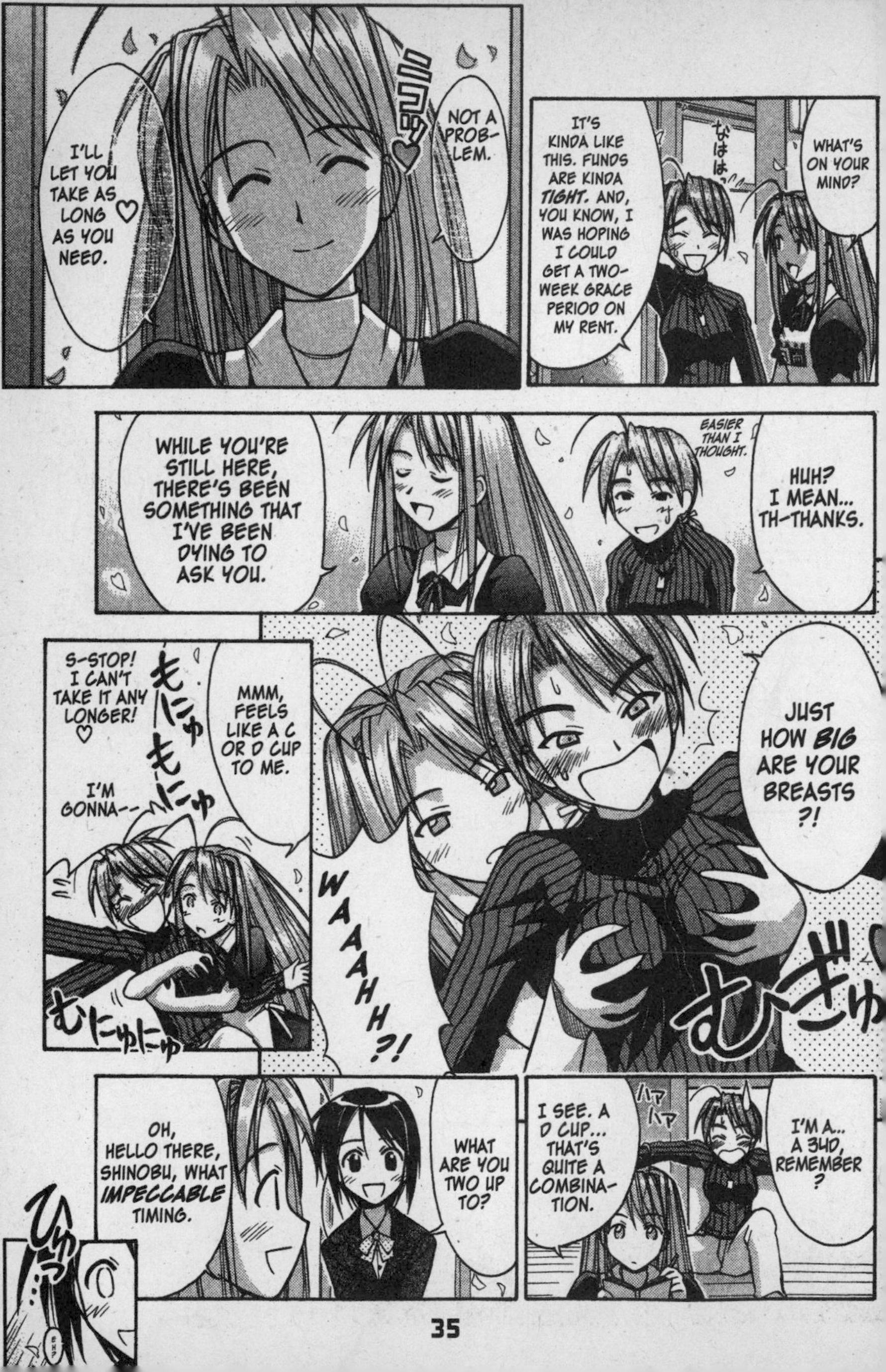
WHAT'S ON YOUR MIND?
なははっ
IT'S KINDA LIKE THIS. FUNDS ARE KINDA TIGHT. AND, YOU KNOW, I WAS HOPING I COULD GET A TWO-WEEK GRACE PERIOD ON MY RENT.
NOT A PROB-LEM.
ニコッ
I'LL LET YOU TAKE AS LONG AS YOU NEED. ♡
HUH? I MEAN... TH-THANKS.
EASIER THAN I THOUGHT.
WHILE YOU'RE STILL HERE, THERE'S BEEN SOMETHING THAT I'VE BEEN DYING TO ASK YOU.
JUST HOW BIG ARE YOUR BREASTS?!
むぎゅ
WAAAHH?!
MMM, FEELS LIKE A C OR D CUP TO ME.
S-STOP! I CAN'T TAKE IT ANY LONGER! ♡
もにゅ もにゅ
I'M GONNA--
むにゅにゅ
I'M A... A 34D, REMEMBER?
ハァ ハァ
I SEE. A D CUP... THAT'S QUITE A COMBINA-TION.
WHAT ARE YOU TWO UP TO?
OH, HELLO THERE, SHINOBU, WHAT IMPECCABLE TIMING.
ひゅっ

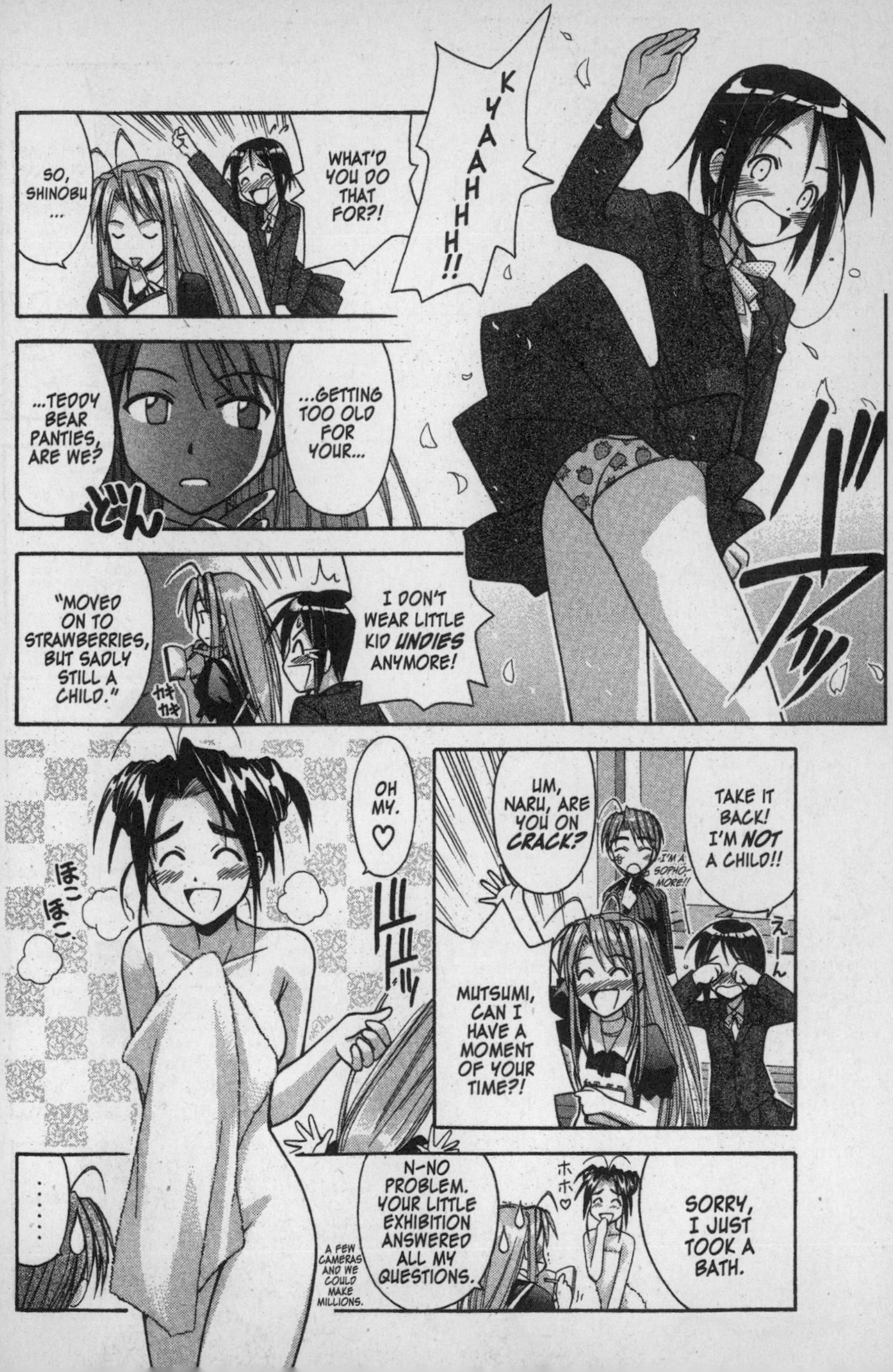
KYAAHHH!!
ブワッ
WHAT'D YOU DO THAT FOR?!
SO, SHINOBU...
...GETTING TOO OLD FOR YOUR...
...TEDDY BEAR PANTIES, ARE WE?
どん
I DON'T WEAR LITTLE KID UNDIES ANYMORE!
"MOVED ON TO STRAWBERRIES, BUT SADLY STILL A CHILD."
カキカキ
TAKE IT BACK! I'M NOT A CHILD!!
えーん
I'M A SOPHOMORE!!
UM, NARU, ARE YOU ON CRACK?
MUTSUMI, CAN I HAVE A MOMENT OF YOUR TIME?!
OH MY. ♡
ほこほこ
SORRY, I JUST TOOK A BATH.
ホホ
N-NO PROBLEM. YOUR LITTLE EXHIBITION ANSWERED ALL MY QUESTIONS.
A FEW CAMERAS AND WE COULD MAKE MILLIONS.
......

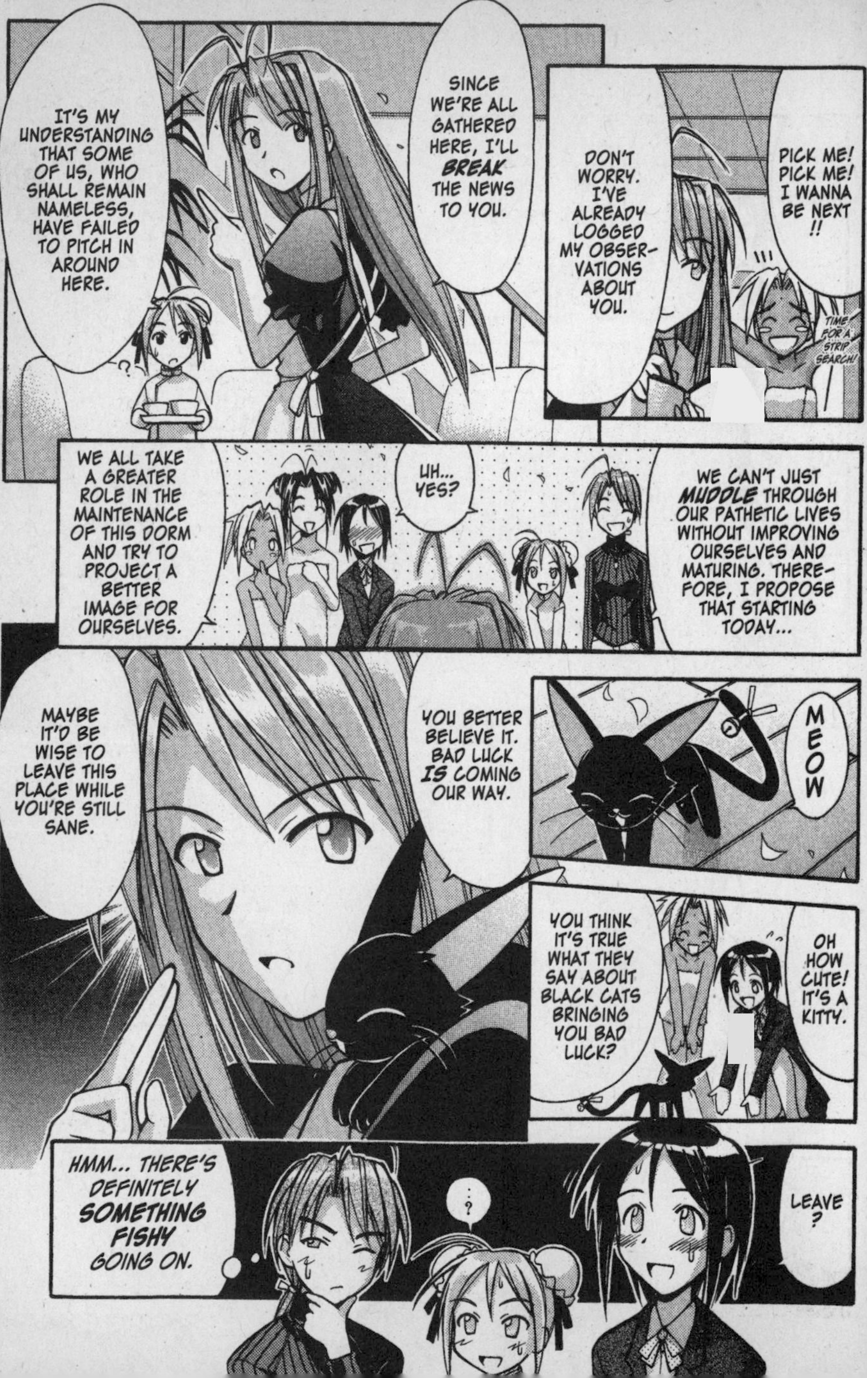
PICK ME! PICK ME! I WANNA BE NEXT !!
TIME FOR A STRIP SEARCH!
DON'T WORRY. I'VE ALREADY LOGGED MY OBSERVATIONS ABOUT YOU.
SINCE WE'RE ALL GATHERED HERE, I'LL BREAK THE NEWS TO YOU.
IT'S MY UNDERSTANDING THAT SOME OF US, WHO SHALL REMAIN NAMELESS, HAVE FAILED TO PITCH IN AROUND HERE.
WE CAN'T JUST MUDDLE THROUGH OUR PATHETIC LIVES WITHOUT IMPROVING OURSELVES AND MATURING. THEREFORE, I PROPOSE THAT STARTING TODAY...
UH... YES?
WE ALL TAKE A GREATER ROLE IN THE MAINTENANCE OF THIS DORM AND TRY TO PROJECT A BETTER IMAGE FOR OURSELVES.
MEOW
OH HOW CUTE! IT'S A KITTY.
YOU THINK IT'S TRUE WHAT THEY SAY ABOUT BLACK CATS BRINGING YOU BAD LUCK?
YOU BETTER BELIEVE IT. BAD LUCK IS COMING OUR WAY.
MAYBE IT'D BE WISE TO LEAVE THIS PLACE WHILE YOU'RE STILL SANE.
LEAVE ?
...?
HMM... THERE'S DEFINITELY SOMETHING FISHY GOING ON.

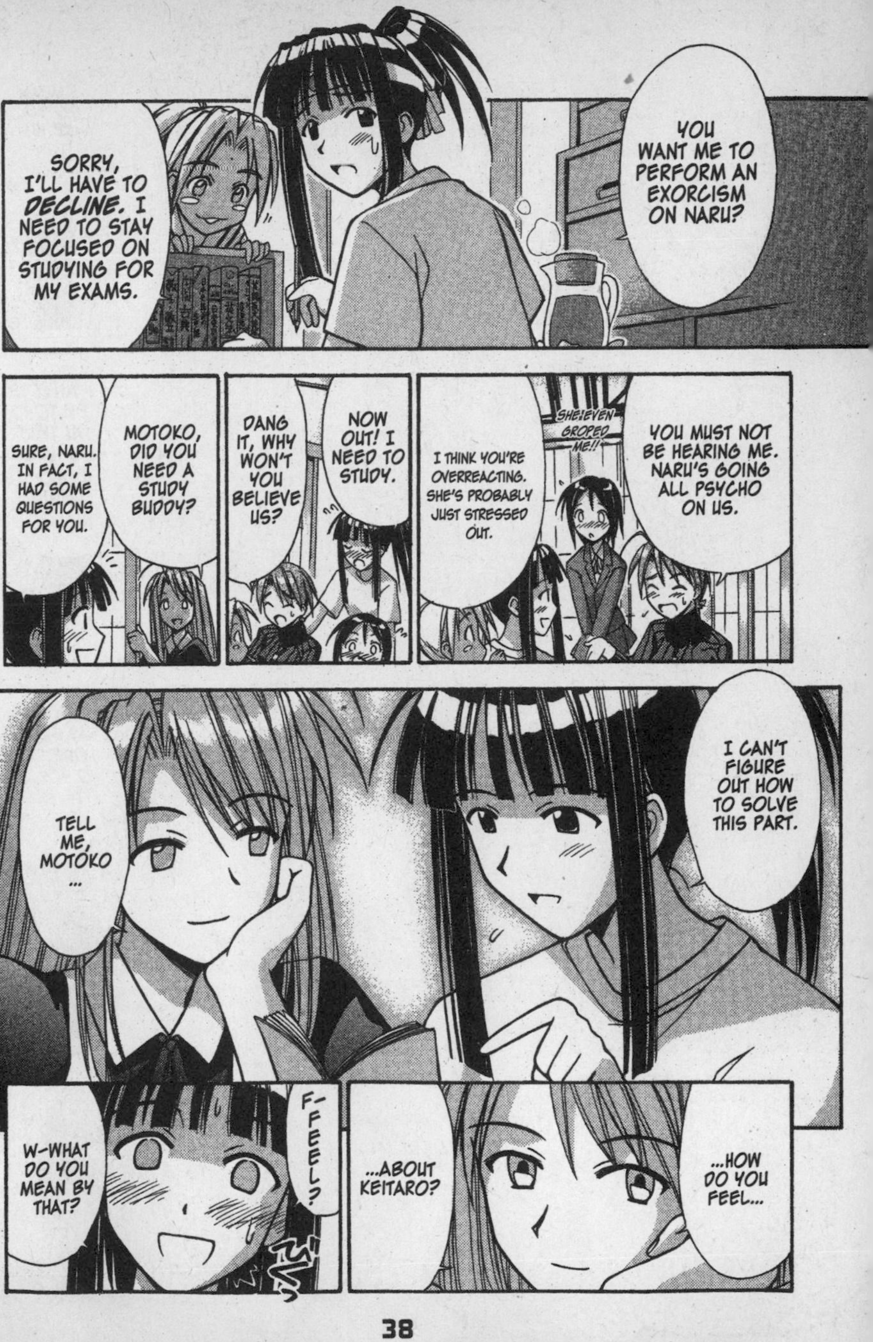

YOU WANT ME TO PERFORM AN EXORCISM ON NARU?
SORRY, I'LL HAVE TO DECLINE. I NEED TO STAY FOCUSED ON STUDYING FOR MY EXAMS.
YOU MUST NOT BE HEARING ME. NARU'S GOING ALL PSYCHO ON US.
SHE EVEN GROPED ME!!
I THINK YOU'RE OVERREACTING. SHE'S PROBABLY JUST STRESSED OUT.
NOW OUT! I NEED TO STUDY.
DANG IT, WHY WON'T YOU BELIEVE US?
MOTOKO, DID YOU NEED A STUDY BUDDY?
SURE, NARU. IN FACT, I HAD SOME QUESTIONS FOR YOU.
I CAN'T FIGURE OUT HOW TO SOLVE THIS PART.
TELL ME, MOTOKO ...
...HOW DO YOU FEEL...
...ABOUT KEITARO?
F-FEEL?
W-WHAT DO YOU MEAN BY THAT?

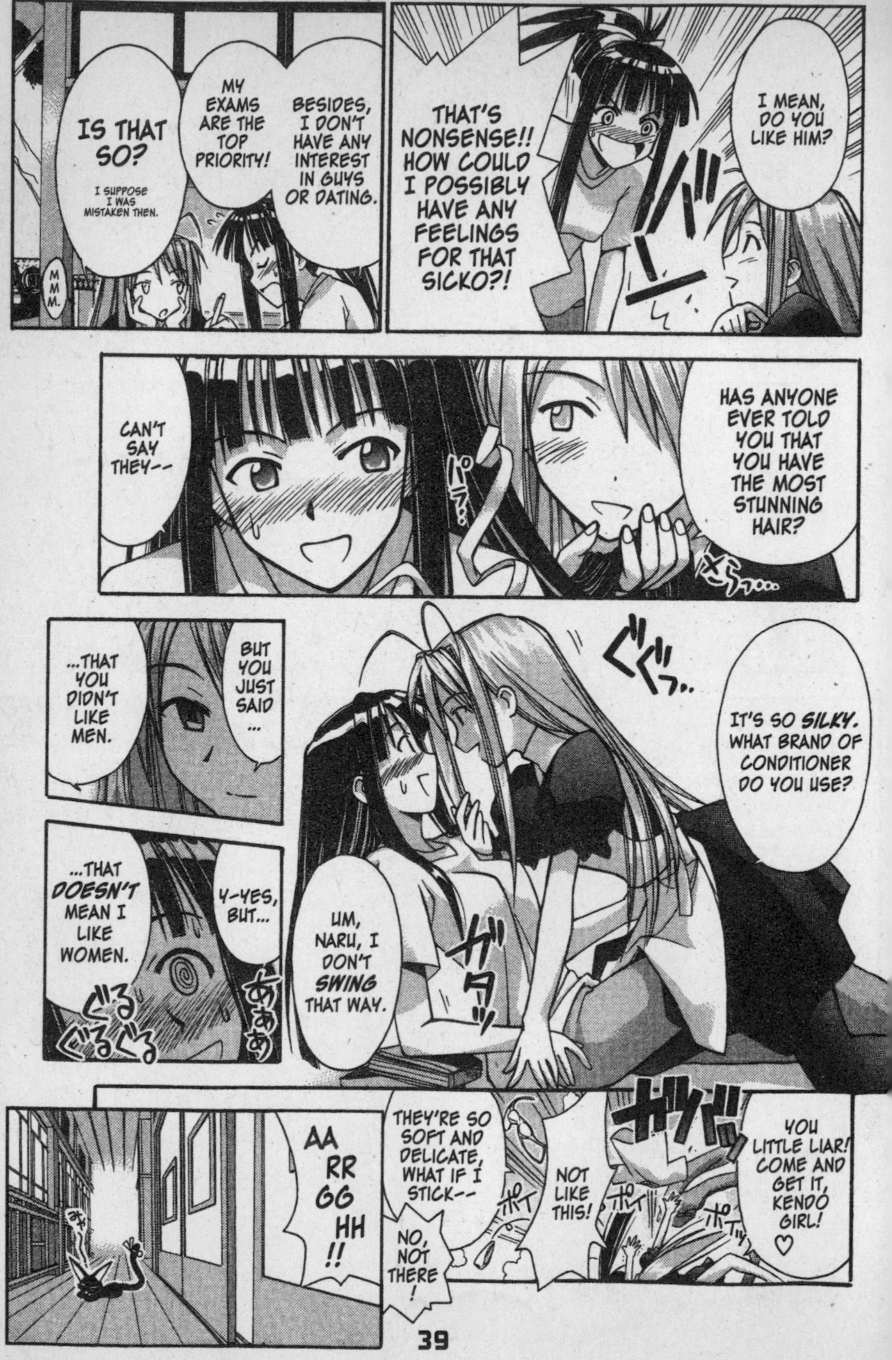
I MEAN, DO YOU LIKE HIM?
THAT'S NONSENSE!! HOW COULD I POSSIBLY HAVE ANY FEELINGS FOR THAT SICKO?!
BESIDES, I DON'T HAVE ANY INTEREST IN GUYS OR DATING.
MY EXAMS ARE THE TOP PRIORITY!
IS THAT SO?
I SUPPOSE I WAS MISTAKEN THEN.
MMM.
HAS ANYONE EVER TOLD YOU THAT YOU HAVE THE MOST STUNNING HAIR?
CAN'T SAY THEY--
IT'S SO *SILKY*. WHAT BRAND OF CONDITIONER DO YOU USE?
UM, NARU, I DON'T *SWING* THAT WAY.
BUT YOU JUST SAID...
...THAT YOU DIDN'T LIKE MEN.
Y-YES, BUT...
...THAT *DOESN'T* MEAN I LIKE WOMEN.
YOU LITTLE LIAR! COME AND GET IT, KENDO GIRL! ♡
NOT LIKE THIS!
THEY'RE SO SOFT AND DELICATE, WHAT IF I STICK--
NO, NOT THERE!
AARRGGHH!!

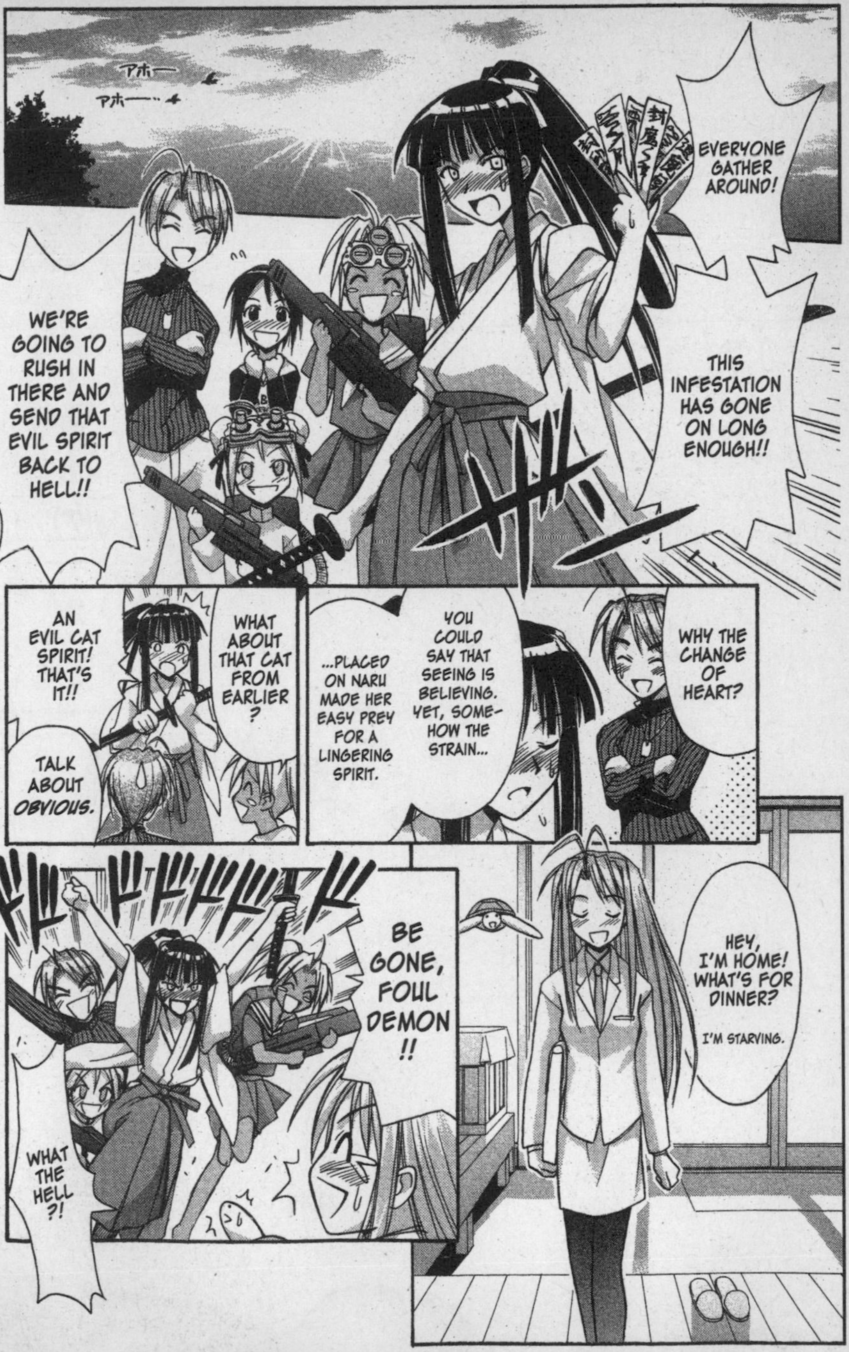
EVERYONE GATHER AROUND!
THIS INFESTATION HAS GONE ON LONG ENOUGH!!
アホー
アホー…
WE'RE GOING TO RUSH IN THERE AND SEND THAT EVIL SPIRIT BACK TO HELL!!
WHY THE CHANGE OF HEART?
YOU COULD SAY THAT SEEING IS BELIEVING. YET, SOMEHOW THE STRAIN...
...PLACED ON NARU MADE HER EASY PREY FOR A LINGERING SPIRIT.
WHAT ABOUT THAT CAT FROM EARLIER?
AN EVIL CAT SPIRIT! THAT'S IT!!
TALK ABOUT OBVIOUS.
HEY, I'M HOME! WHAT'S FOR DINNER?
I'M STARVING.
BE GONE, FOUL DEMON!!
WHAT THE HELL?!

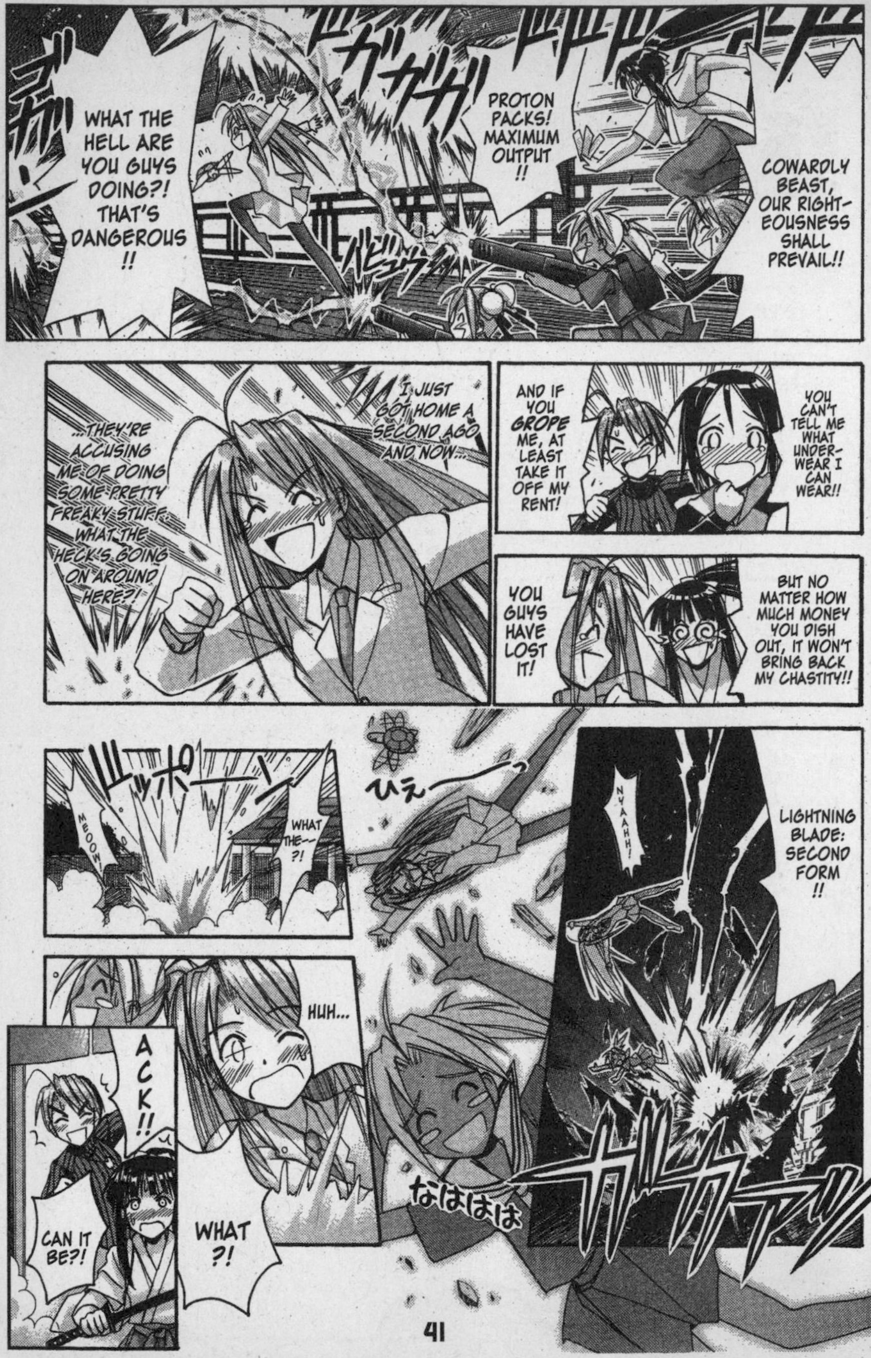
COWARDLY BEAST, OUR RIGHTEOUSNESS SHALL PREVAIL!!
PROTON PACKS! MAXIMUM OUTPUT!!
WHAT THE HELL ARE YOU GUYS DOING?! THAT'S DANGEROUS!!
YOU CAN'T TELL ME WHAT UNDERWEAR I CAN WEAR!!
AND IF YOU GROPE ME, AT LEAST TAKE IT OFF MY RENT!
BUT NO MATTER HOW MUCH MONEY YOU DISH OUT, IT WON'T BRING BACK MY CHASTITY!!
YOU GUYS HAVE LOST IT!
I JUST GOT HOME A SECOND AGO AND NOW...
...THEY'RE ACCUSING ME OF DOING SOME PRETTY FREAKY STUFF. WHAT THE HECK'S GOING ON AROUND HERE?!
LIGHTNING BLADE: SECOND FORM!!
NYAAHH!
ひえーーっ
WHAT THE--?!
MEOOOW!
HUH...
なははは
WHAT?!
ACK!!
CAN IT BE?!

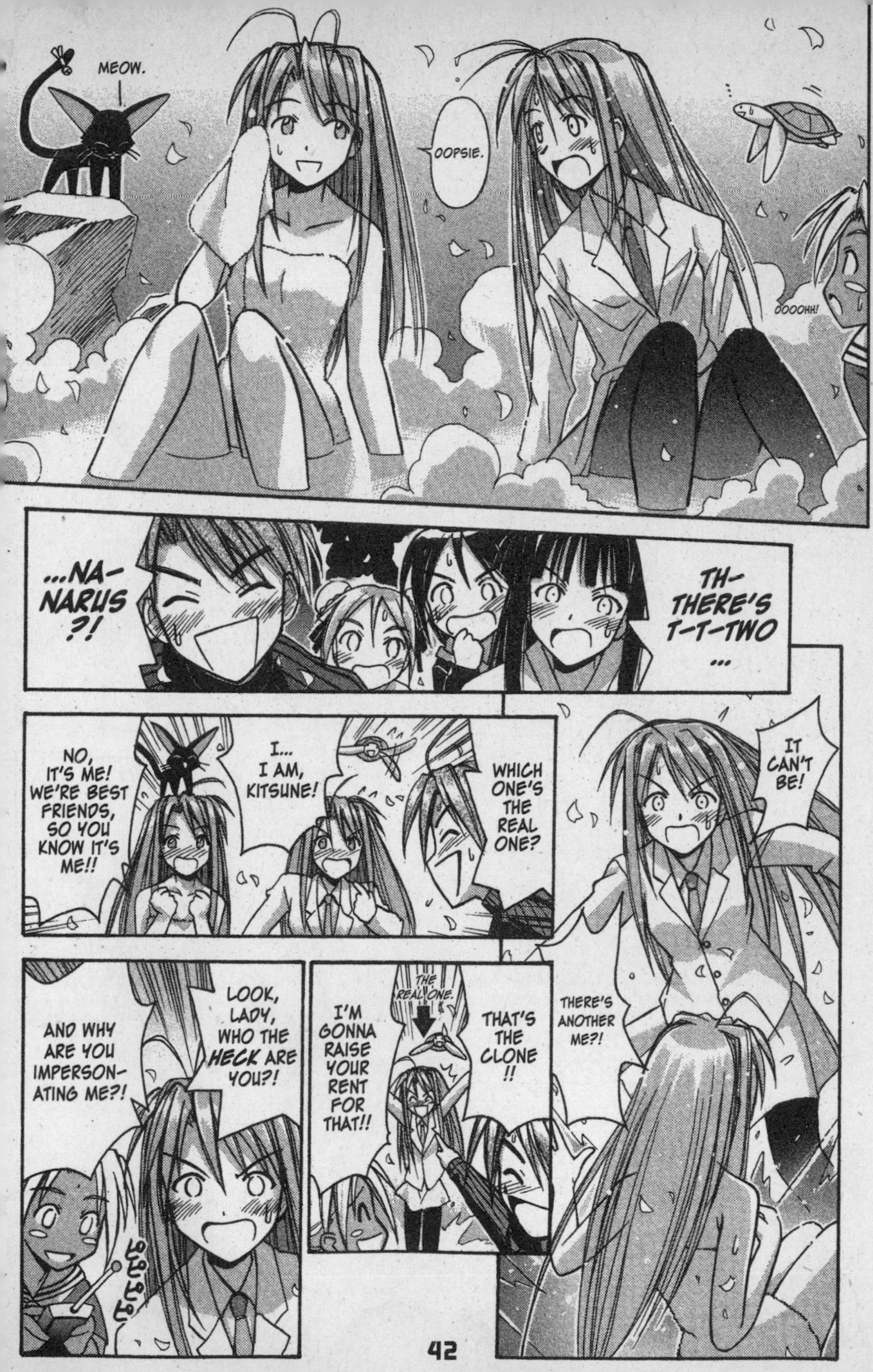
OOOOHH!
OOPSIE.
MEOW.
TH-THERE'S T-T-TWO...
...NA-NARUS?!
IT CAN'T BE!
THERE'S ANOTHER ME?!
WHICH ONE'S THE REAL ONE?
I... I AM, KITSUNE!
NO, IT'S ME! WE'RE BEST FRIENDS, SO YOU KNOW IT'S ME!!
THAT'S THE CLONE!!
THE REAL ONE.
I'M GONNA RAISE YOUR RENT FOR THAT!!
LOOK, LADY, WHO THE HECK ARE YOU?!
AND WHY ARE YOU IMPERSONATING ME?!

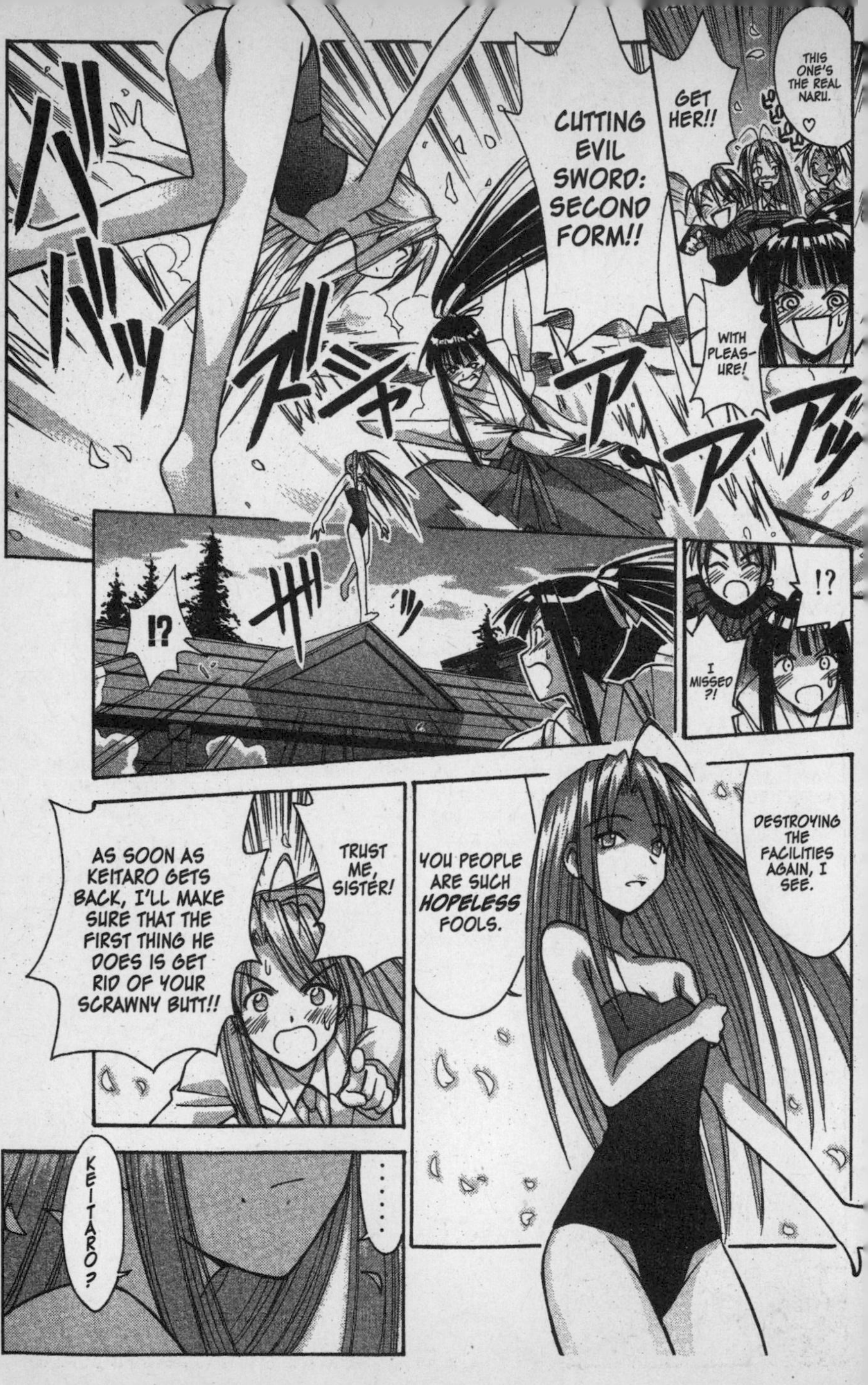
THIS ONE'S THE REAL NARU. ♥
GET HER!!
WITH PLEASURE!
CUTTING EVIL SWORD: SECOND FORM!!
!?
I MISSED?!
!?
DESTROYING THE FACILITIES AGAIN, I SEE.
YOU PEOPLE ARE SUCH *HOPELESS* FOOLS.
TRUST ME, SISTER!
AS SOON AS KEITARO GETS BACK, I'LL MAKE SURE THAT THE FIRST THING HE DOES IS GET RID OF YOUR SCRAWNY BUTT!!
......
KEITARO?

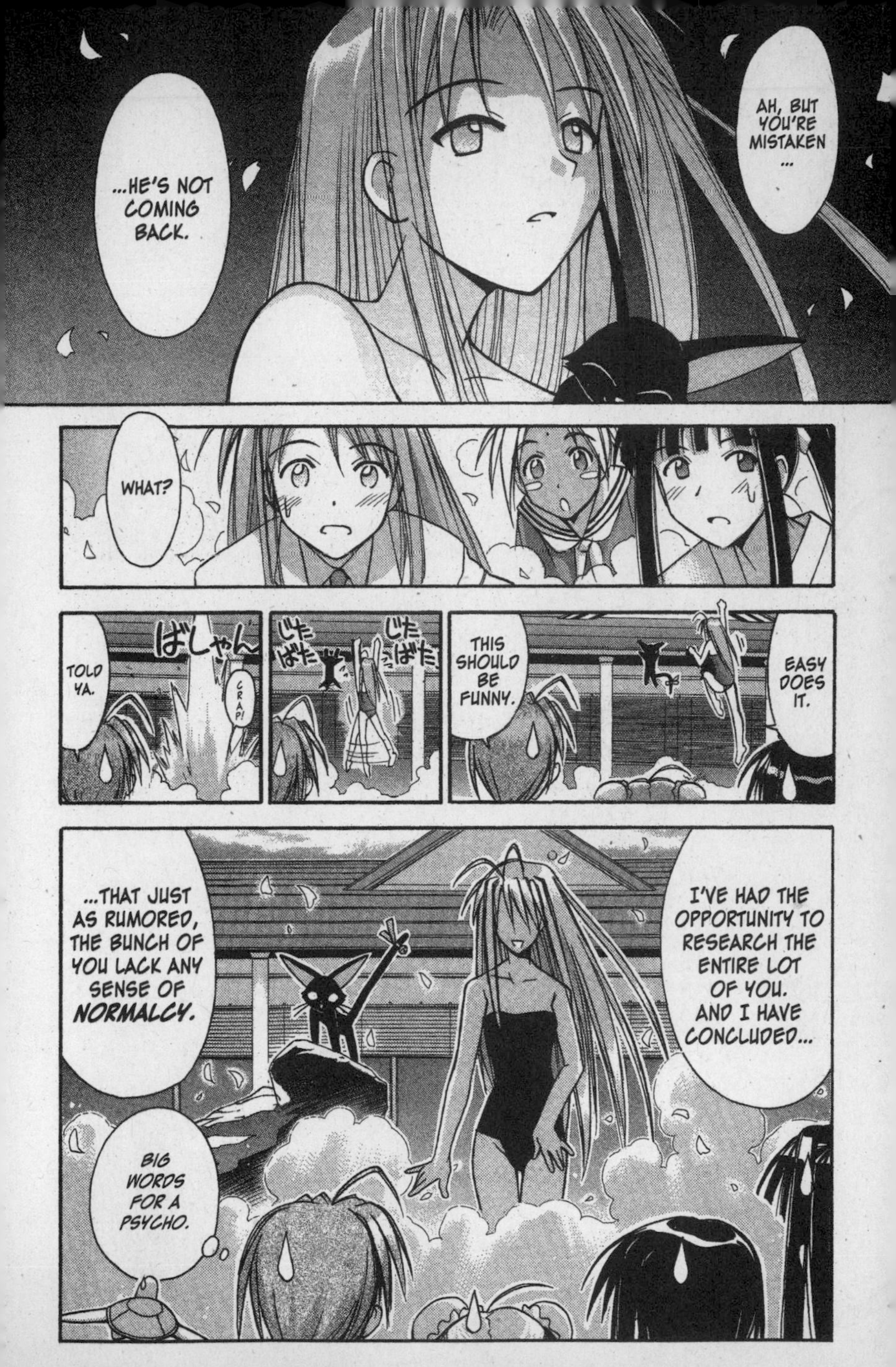
AH, BUT YOU'RE MISTAKEN ...
...HE'S NOT COMING BACK.
WHAT?
EASY DOES IT.
THIS SHOULD BE FUNNY.
じたばた
じたばた
ばしゃん
CRAP!
TOLD YA.
I'VE HAD THE OPPORTUNITY TO RESEARCH THE ENTIRE LOT OF YOU. AND I HAVE CONCLUDED...
...THAT JUST AS RUMORED, THE BUNCH OF YOU LACK ANY SENSE OF NORMALCY.
BIG WORDS FOR A PSYCHO.

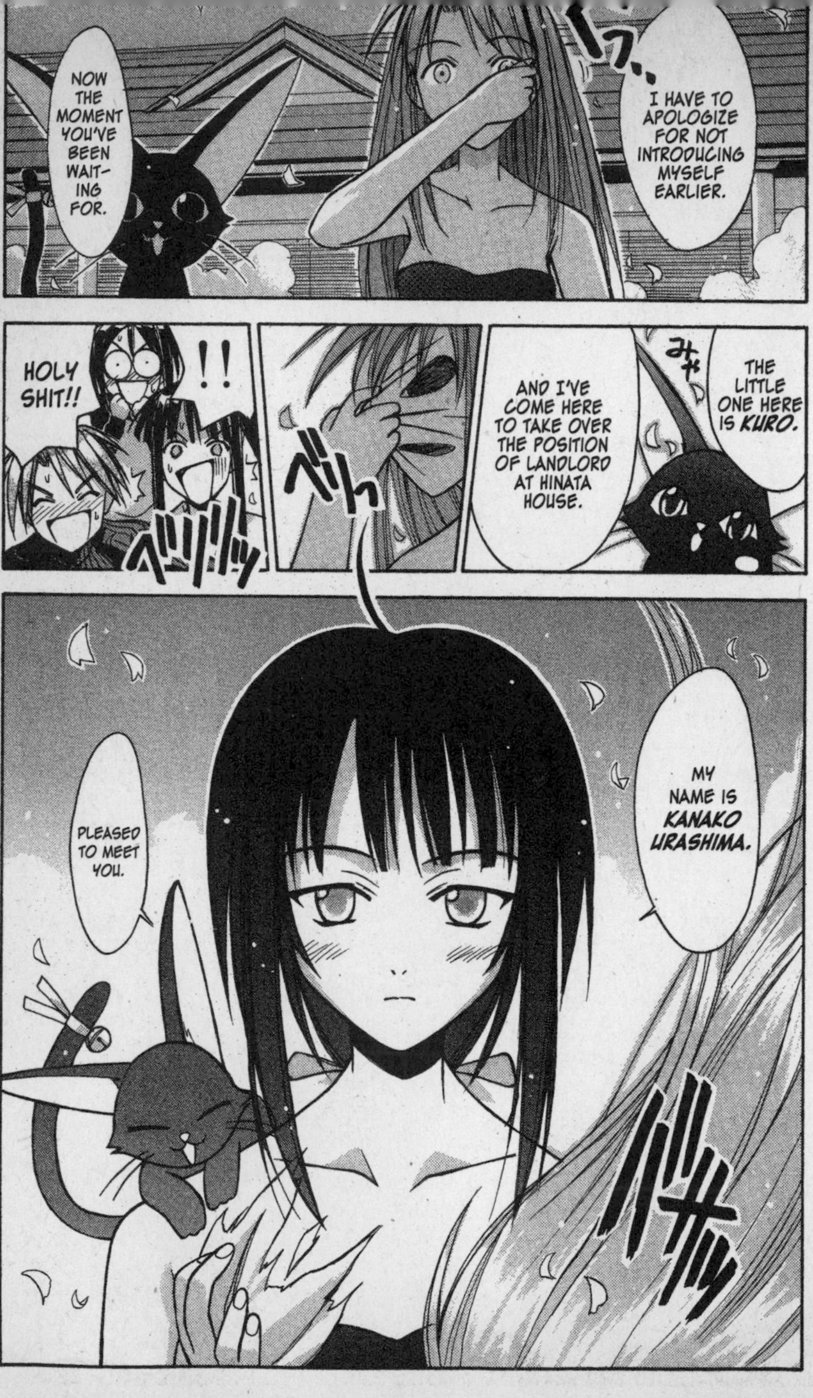
I HAVE TO APOLOGIZE FOR NOT INTRODUCING MYSELF EARLIER.
NOW THE MOMENT YOU'VE BEEN WAIT-ING FOR.
THE LITTLE ONE HERE IS KURO.
AND I'VE COME HERE TO TAKE OVER THE POSITION OF LANDLORD AT HINATA HOUSE.
!!
HOLY SHIT!!
MY NAME IS KANAKO URASHIMA.
PLEASED TO MEET YOU.

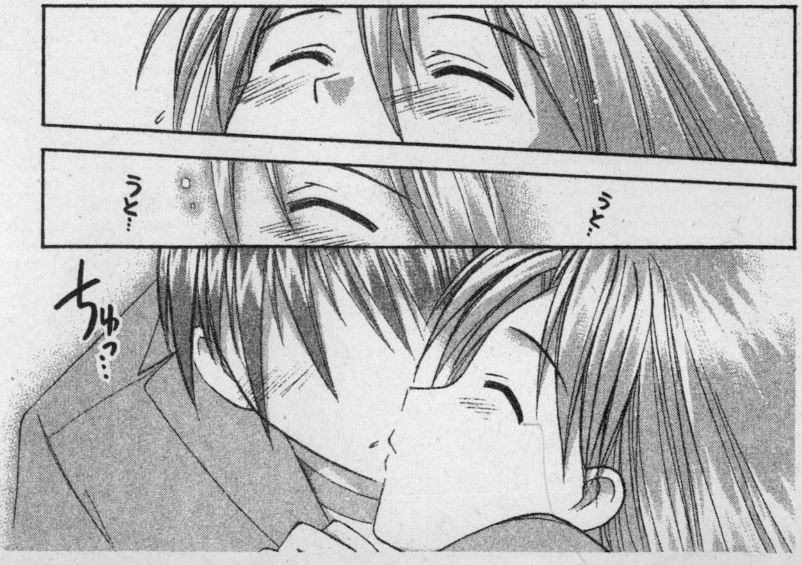
うと…
うと…
ちゅっ…

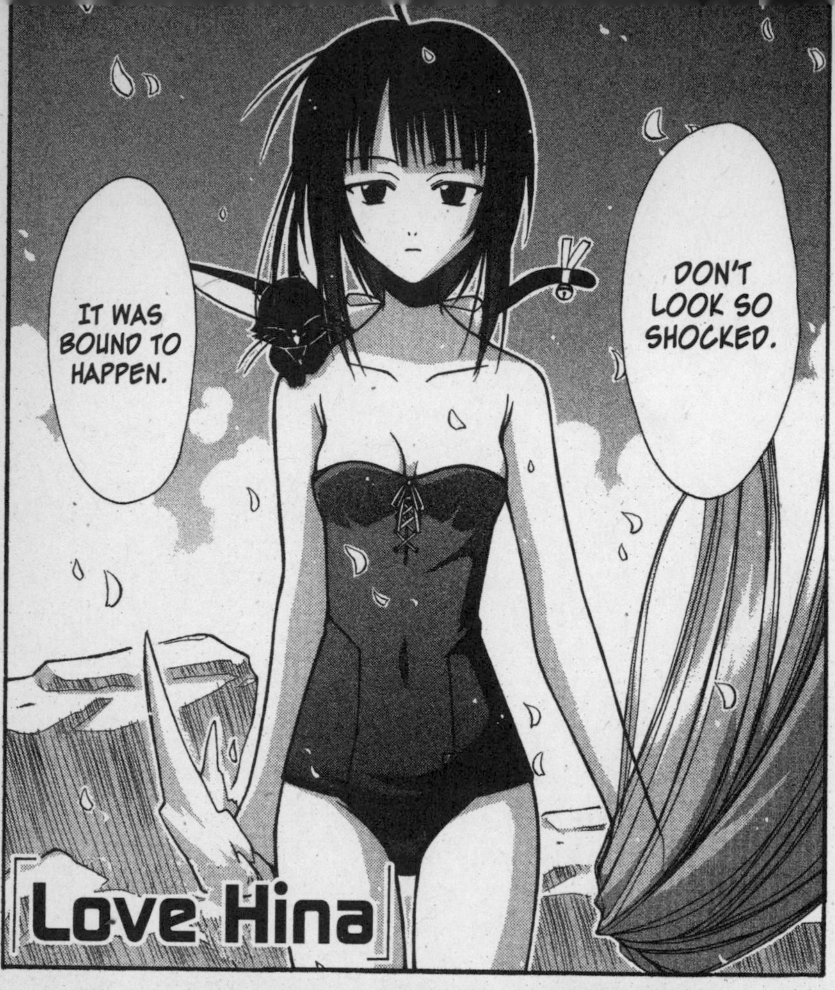
DON'T LOOK SO SHOCKED.
IT WAS BOUND TO HAPPEN.
Love Hina

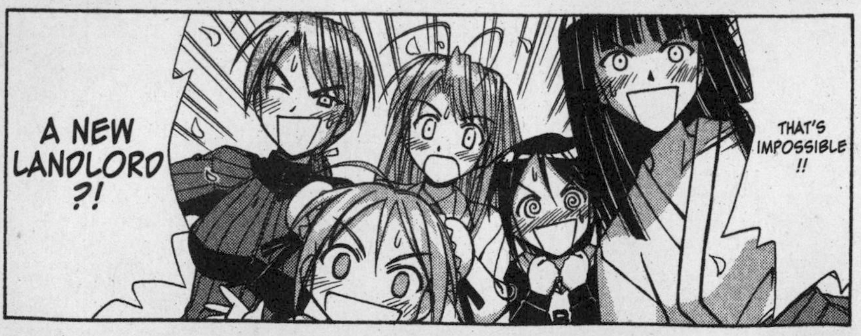
THAT'S IMPOSSIBLE !!
A NEW LANDLORD ?!

HINATA.90 Hinata House's Last Stand?!

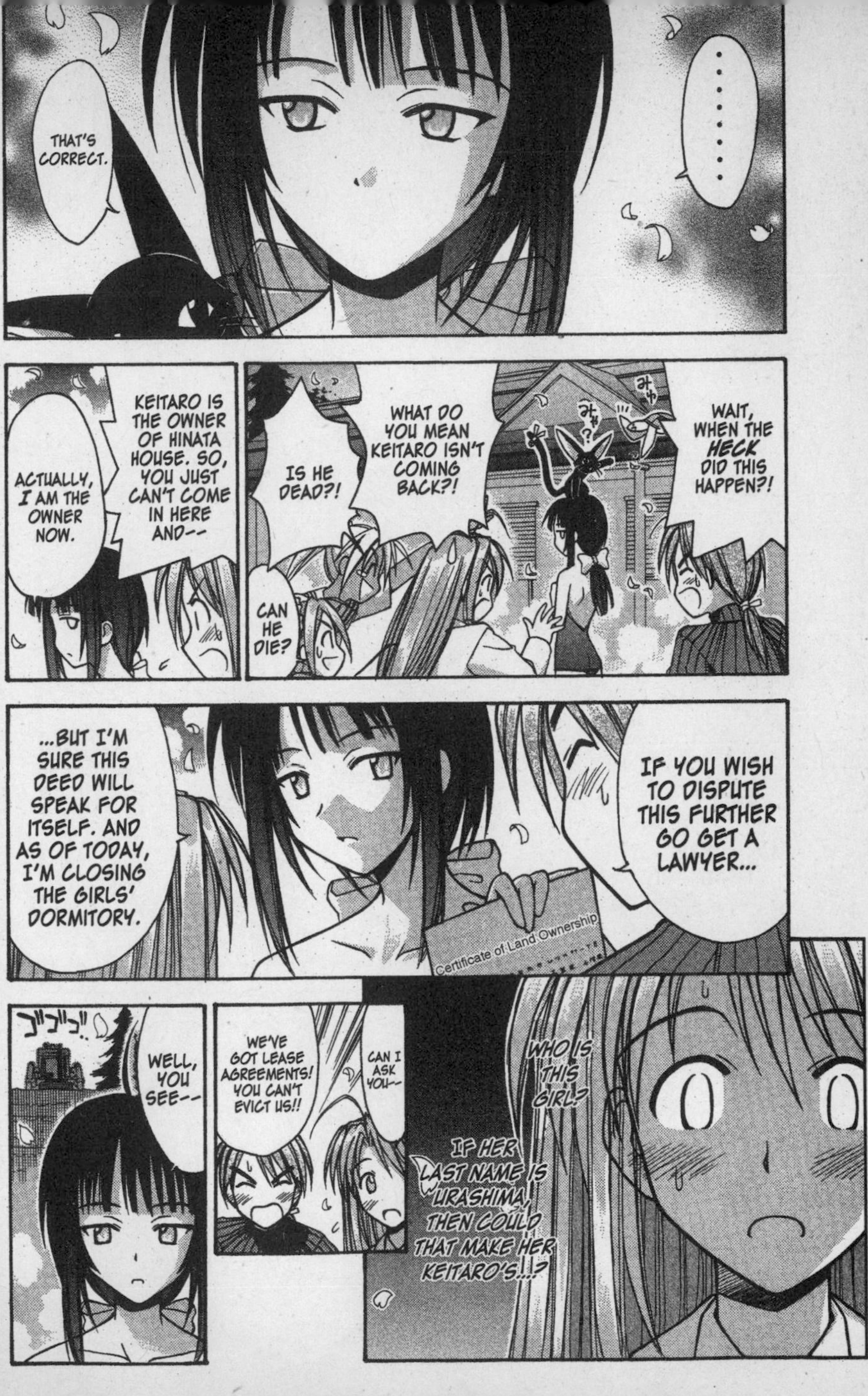
......
THAT'S CORRECT.
みゅ
みゅ
WAIT, WHEN THE HECK DID THIS HAPPEN?!
WHAT DO YOU MEAN KEITARO ISN'T COMING BACK?!
IS HE DEAD?!
CAN HE DIE?
KEITARO IS THE OWNER OF HINATA HOUSE. SO, YOU JUST CAN'T COME IN HERE AND--
ACTUALLY, I AM THE OWNER NOW.
IF YOU WISH TO DISPUTE THIS FURTHER GO GET A LAWYER...
...BUT I'M SURE THIS DEED WILL SPEAK FOR ITSELF. AND AS OF TODAY, I'M CLOSING THE GIRLS' DORMITORY.
Certificate of Land Ownership
WHO IS THIS GIRL?
IF HER LAST NAME IS URASHIMA, THEN COULD THAT MAKE HER KEITARO'S...!?
CAN I ASK YOU--
WE'VE GOT LEASE AGREEMENTS! YOU CAN'T EVICT US!!
WELL, YOU SEE--
ゴゴゴッ

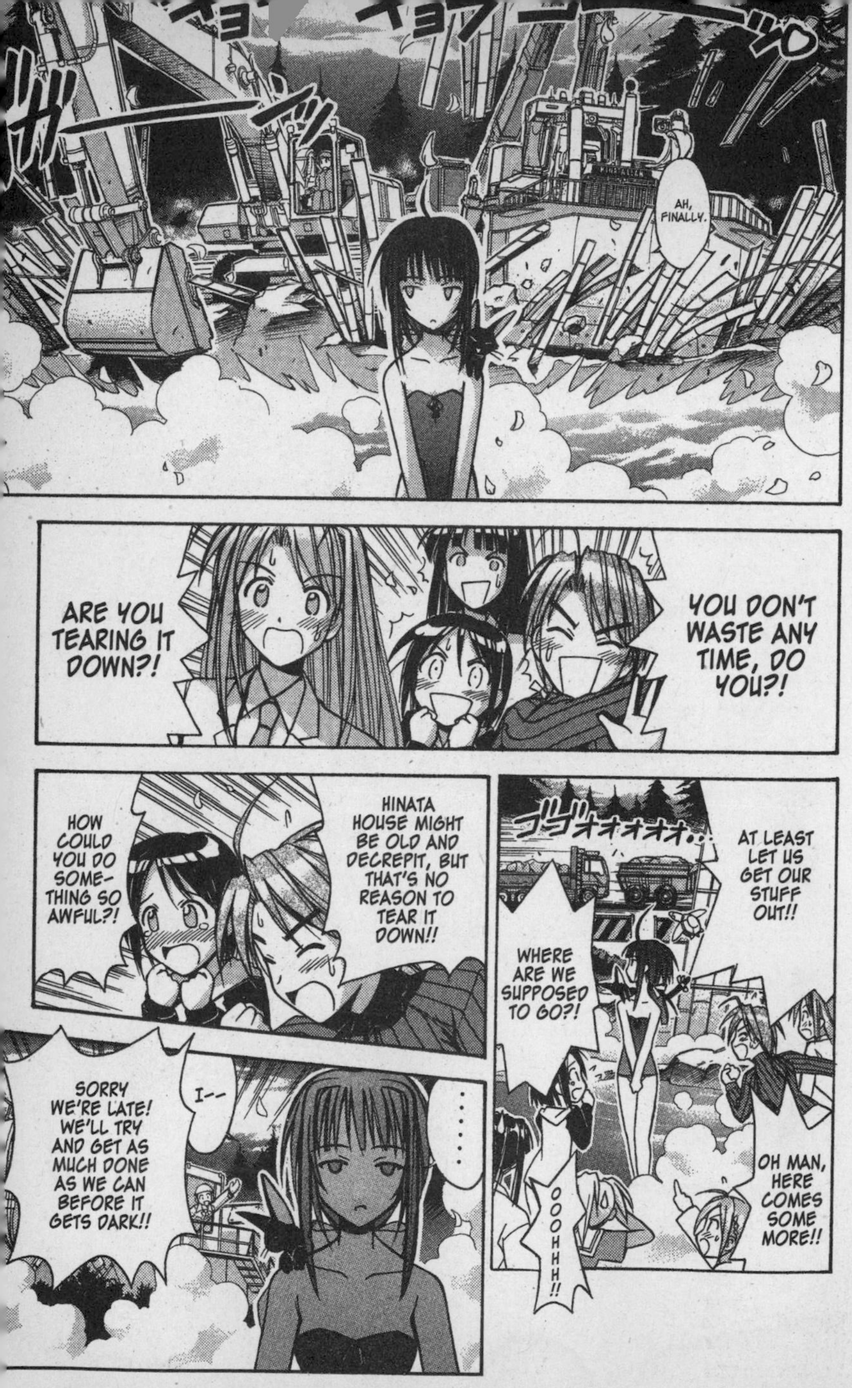
AH, FINALLY.
YOU DON'T WASTE ANY TIME, DO YOU?!
ARE YOU TEARING IT DOWN?!
ゴゴオオオオオ…
AT LEAST LET US GET OUR STUFF OUT!!
WHERE ARE WE SUPPOSED TO GO?!
OH MAN, HERE COMES SOME MORE!!
OOOOHHH!!
HINATA HOUSE MIGHT BE OLD AND DECREPIT, BUT THAT'S NO REASON TO TEAR IT DOWN!!
HOW COULD YOU DO SOME-THING SO AWFUL?!
......
I--
SORRY WE'RE LATE! WE'LL TRY AND GET AS MUCH DONE AS WE CAN BEFORE IT GETS DARK!!

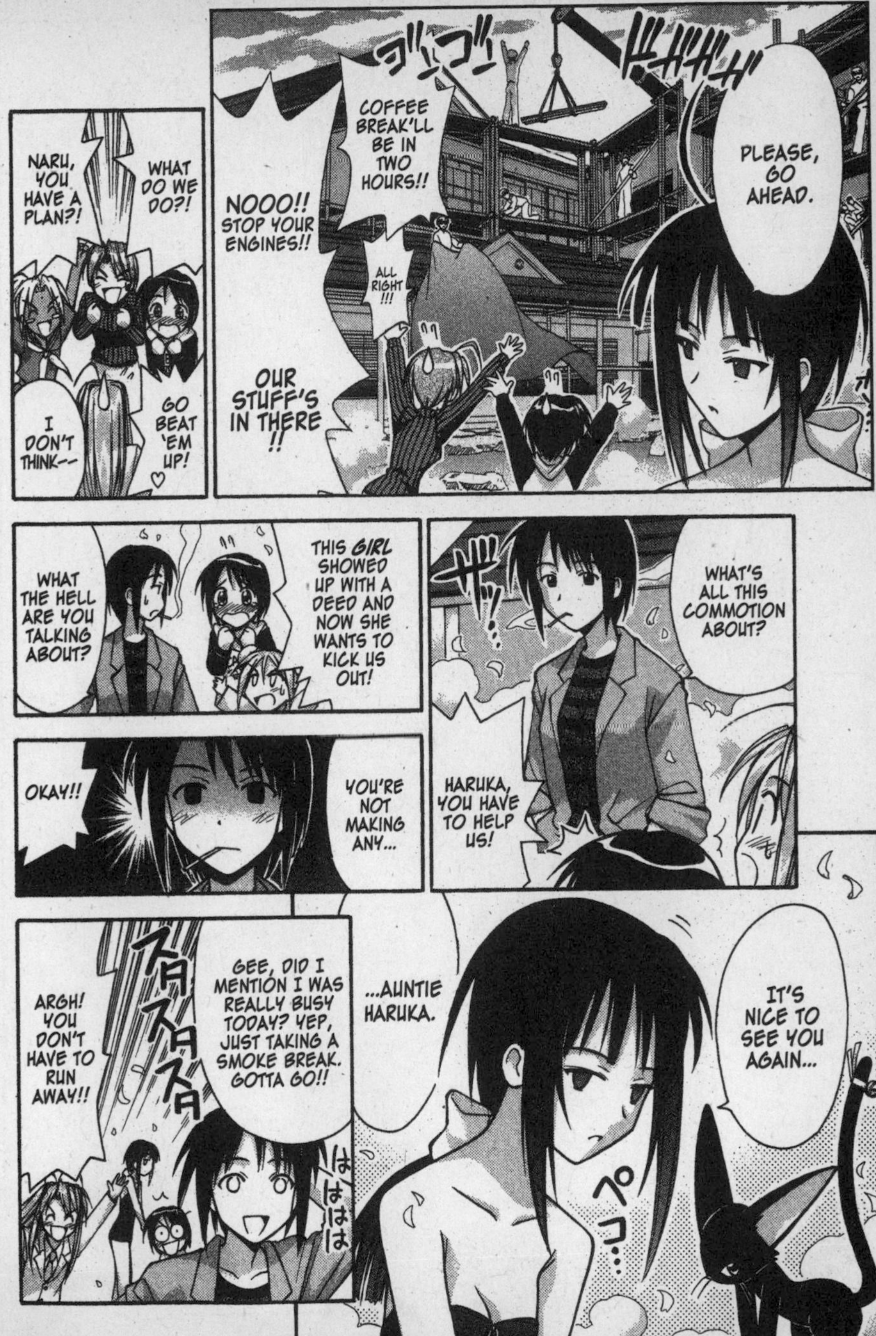
PLEASE, GO AHEAD.
COFFEE BREAK'LL BE IN TWO HOURS!!
NOOO!! STOP YOUR ENGINES!!
ALL RIGHT!!!
OUR STUFF'S IN THERE!!
WHAT DO WE DO?!
NARU, YOU HAVE A PLAN?!
GO BEAT 'EM UP!
I DON'T THINK--
WHAT'S ALL THIS COMMOTION ABOUT?
HARUKA, YOU HAVE TO HELP US!
THIS GIRL SHOWED UP WITH A DEED AND NOW SHE WANTS TO KICK US OUT!
WHAT THE HELL ARE YOU TALKING ABOUT?
YOU'RE NOT MAKING ANY...
OKAY!!
IT'S NICE TO SEE YOU AGAIN...
...AUNTIE HARUKA.
GEE, DID I MENTION I WAS REALLY BUSY TODAY? YEP, JUST TAKING A SMOKE BREAK. GOTTA GO!!
ARGH! YOU DON'T HAVE TO RUN AWAY!!

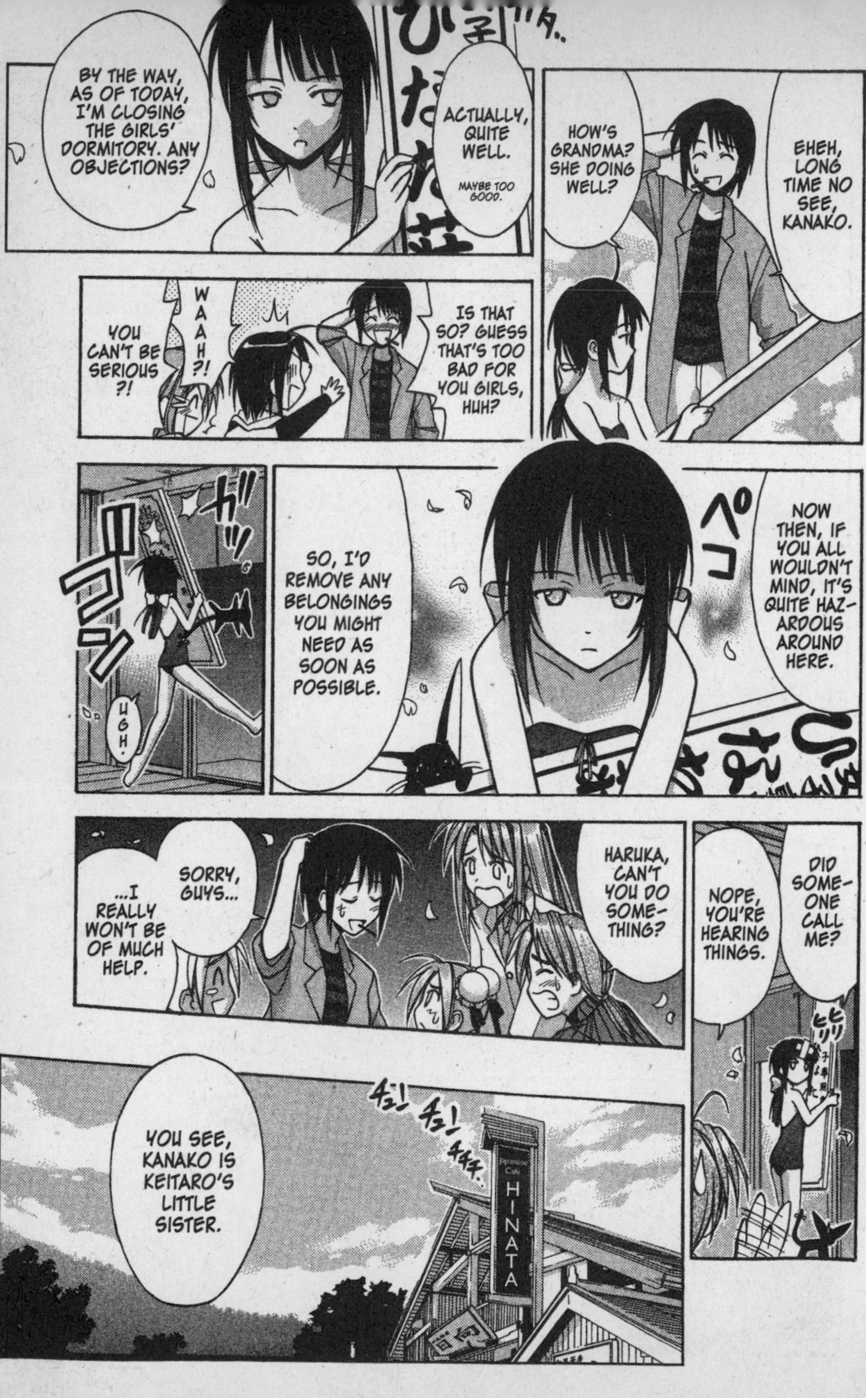

EHEH, LONG TIME NO SEE, KANAKO.
HOW'S GRANDMA? SHE DOING WELL?
ACTUALLY, QUITE WELL.
MAYBE TOO GOOD.
BY THE WAY, AS OF TODAY, I'M CLOSING THE GIRLS' DORMITORY. ANY OBJECTIONS?
IS THAT SO? GUESS THAT'S TOO BAD FOR YOU GIRLS, HUH?
WAAAH?!
YOU CAN'T BE SERIOUS?!
ペコ
NOW THEN, IF YOU ALL WOULDN'T MIND, IT'S QUITE HAZARDOUS AROUND HERE.
SO, I'D REMOVE ANY BELONGINGS YOU MIGHT NEED AS SOON AS POSSIBLE.
ガッ
UGH.
DID SOMEONE CALL ME?
NOPE, YOU'RE HEARING THINGS.
HARUKA, CAN'T YOU DO SOMETHING?
SORRY, GUYS...
...I REALLY WON'T BE OF MUCH HELP.
YOU SEE, KANAKO IS KEITARO'S LITTLE SISTER.
チュ! チュ! チチチ
Japanese Café
HINATA

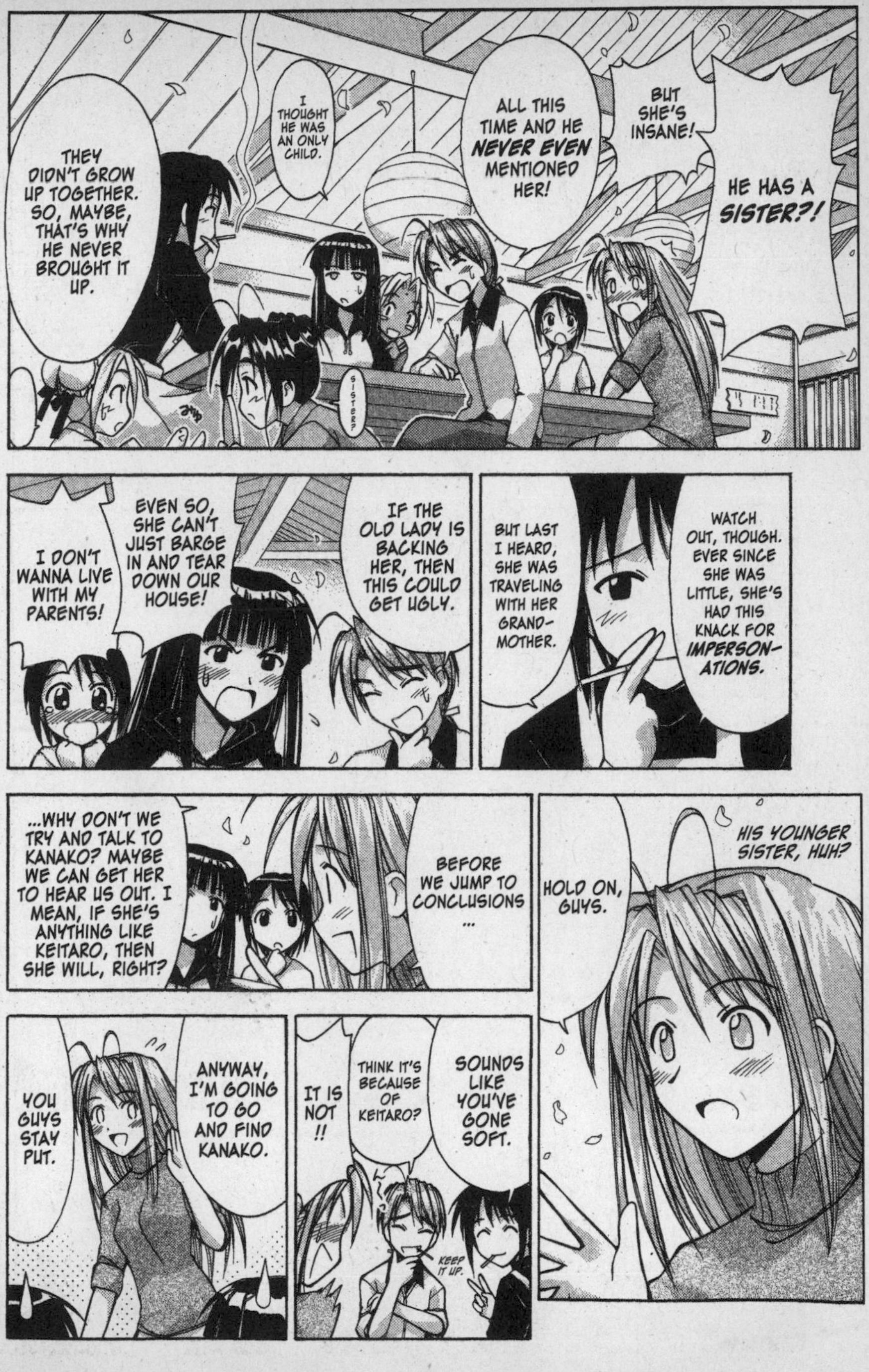
HE HAS A SISTER?!
BUT SHE'S INSANE!
ALL THIS TIME AND HE NEVER EVEN MENTIONED HER!
I THOUGHT HE WAS AN ONLY CHILD.
THEY DIDN'T GROW UP TOGETHER. SO, MAYBE, THAT'S WHY HE NEVER BROUGHT IT UP.
SISTER?
WATCH OUT, THOUGH. EVER SINCE SHE WAS LITTLE, SHE'S HAD THIS KNACK FOR IMPERSONATIONS.
BUT LAST I HEARD, SHE WAS TRAVELING WITH HER GRANDMOTHER.
IF THE OLD LADY IS BACKING HER, THEN THIS COULD GET UGLY.
EVEN SO, SHE CAN'T JUST BARGE IN AND TEAR DOWN OUR HOUSE!
I DON'T WANNA LIVE WITH MY PARENTS!
HIS YOUNGER SISTER, HUH?
HOLD ON, GUYS.
BEFORE WE JUMP TO CONCLUSIONS ...
...WHY DON'T WE TRY AND TALK TO KANAKO? MAYBE WE CAN GET HER TO HEAR US OUT. I MEAN, IF SHE'S ANYTHING LIKE KEITARO, THEN SHE WILL, RIGHT?
SOUNDS LIKE YOU'VE GONE SOFT.
THINK IT'S BECAUSE OF KEITARO?
IT IS NOT !!
KEEP IT UP.
ANYWAY, I'M GOING TO GO AND FIND KANAKO.
YOU GUYS STAY PUT.

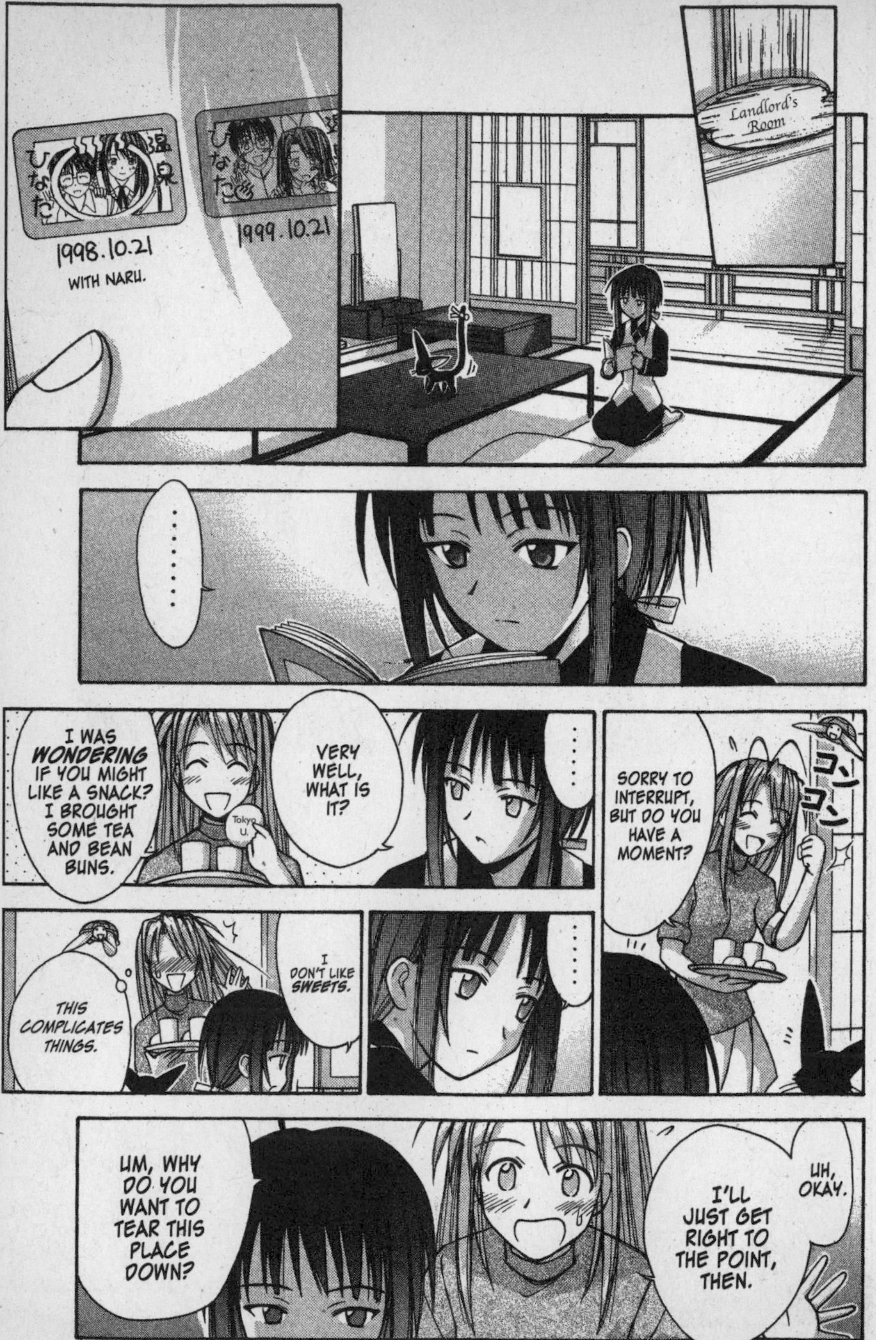
Landlord's Room
1998.10.21
WITH NARU.
1999.10.21
....
SORRY TO INTERRUPT, BUT DO YOU HAVE A MOMENT?
コン コン
......
VERY WELL, WHAT IS IT?
I WAS *WONDERING* IF YOU MIGHT LIKE A SNACK? I BROUGHT SOME TEA AND BEAN BUNS.
Tokyo U.
......
I DON'T LIKE *SWEETS.*
THIS COMPLICATES THINGS.
UH, OKAY.
I'LL JUST GET RIGHT TO THE POINT, THEN.
UM, WHY DO YOU WANT TO TEAR THIS PLACE DOWN?

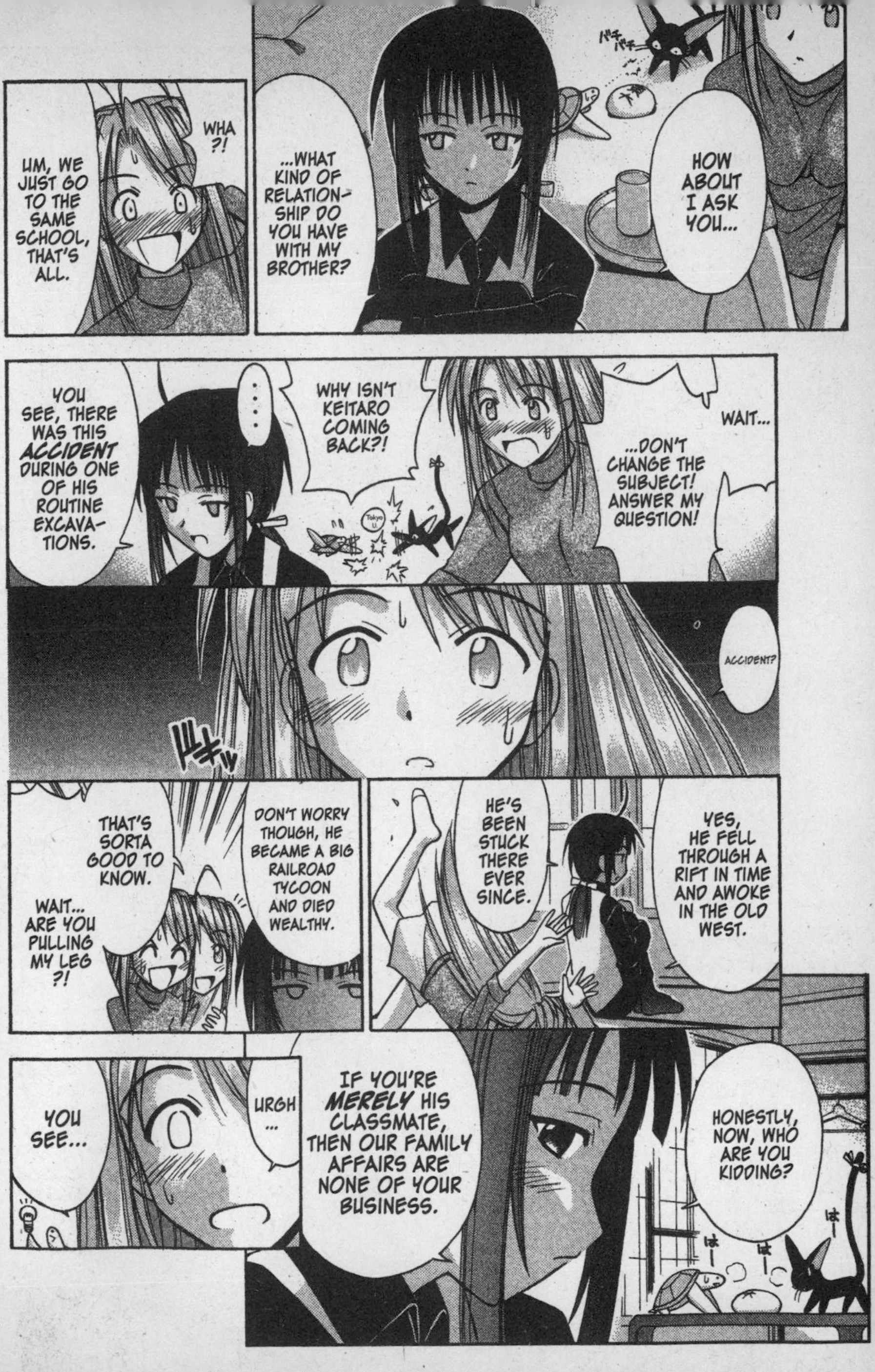
HOW ABOUT I ASK YOU...
...WHAT KIND OF RELATIONSHIP DO YOU HAVE WITH MY BROTHER?
WHA?!
UM, WE JUST GO TO THE SAME SCHOOL, THAT'S ALL.
WAIT...
...DON'T CHANGE THE SUBJECT! ANSWER MY QUESTION!
WHY ISN'T KEITARO COMING BACK?!
...
YOU SEE, THERE WAS THIS *ACCIDENT* DURING ONE OF HIS ROUTINE EXCAVATIONS.
Tokyo U.
ACCIDENT?
YES, HE FELL THROUGH A RIFT IN TIME AND AWOKE IN THE OLD WEST.
HE'S BEEN STUCK THERE EVER SINCE.
DON'T WORRY THOUGH, HE BECAME A BIG RAILROAD TYCOON AND DIED WEALTHY.
THAT'S SORTA GOOD TO KNOW.
WAIT... ARE YOU PULLING MY LEG?!
HONESTLY, NOW, WHO ARE YOU KIDDING?
IF YOU'RE *MERELY* HIS CLASSMATE, THEN OUR FAMILY AFFAIRS ARE NONE OF YOUR BUSINESS.
URGH...
YOU SEE...

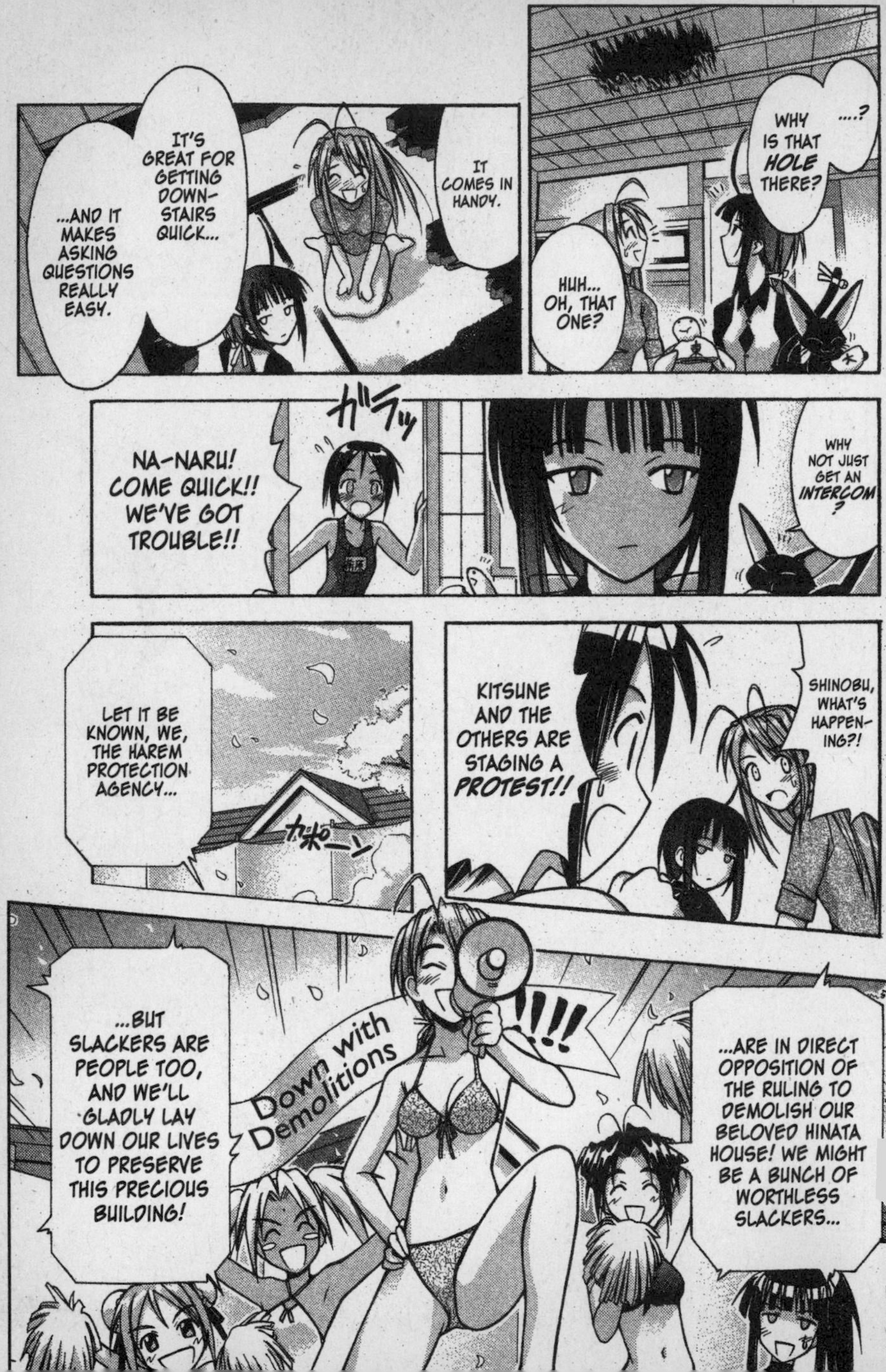
....?
WHY IS THAT HOLE THERE?
HUH... OH, THAT ONE?
IT COMES IN HANDY.
IT'S GREAT FOR GETTING DOWN-STAIRS QUICK...
...AND IT MAKES ASKING QUESTIONS REALLY EASY.
WHY NOT JUST GET AN INTERCOM?
ガラッ
NA-NARU! COME QUICK!! WE'VE GOT TROUBLE!!
SHINOBU, WHAT'S HAPPEN-ING?!
KITSUNE AND THE OTHERS ARE STAGING A PROTEST!!
LET IT BE KNOWN, WE, THE HAREM PROTECTION AGENCY...
カポーン
...ARE IN DIRECT OPPOSITION OF THE RULING TO DEMOLISH OUR BELOVED HINATA HOUSE! WE MIGHT BE A BUNCH OF WORTHLESS SLACKERS...
!!!!
Down with Demolitions
...BUT SLACKERS ARE PEOPLE TOO, AND WE'LL GLADLY LAY DOWN OUR LIVES TO PRESERVE THIS PRECIOUS BUILDING!

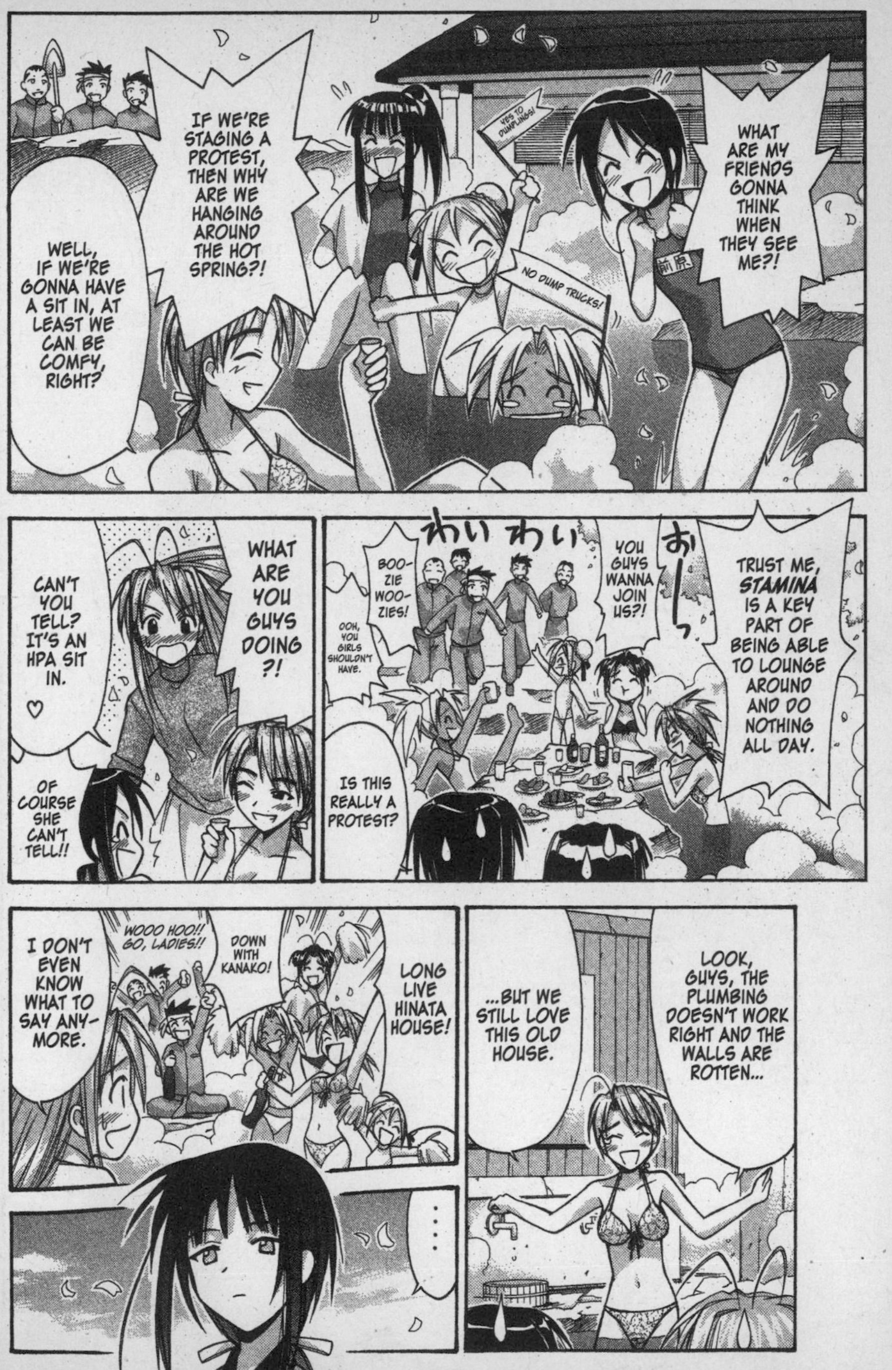
WHAT ARE MY FRIENDS GONNA THINK WHEN THEY SEE ME?!
前原
YES TO DUMPLINGS!
NO DUMP TRUCKS!
IF WE'RE STAGING A PROTEST, THEN WHY ARE WE HANGING AROUND THE HOT SPRING?!
WELL, IF WE'RE GONNA HAVE A SIT IN, AT LEAST WE CAN BE COMFY, RIGHT?
TRUST ME, STAMINA IS A KEY PART OF BEING ABLE TO LOUNGE AROUND AND DO NOTHING ALL DAY.
おーっ
YOU GUYS WANNA JOIN US?!
わいわい
BOO-ZIE WOO-ZIES!
OOH, YOU GIRLS SHOULDN'T HAVE.
IS THIS REALLY A PROTEST?
WHAT ARE YOU GUYS DOING?!
CAN'T YOU TELL? IT'S AN HPA SIT IN. ♡
OF COURSE SHE CAN'T TELL!!
LOOK, GUYS, THE PLUMBING DOESN'T WORK RIGHT AND THE WALLS ARE ROTTEN...
...BUT WE STILL LOVE THIS OLD HOUSE.
LONG LIVE HINATA HOUSE!
DOWN WITH KANAKO!
WOOO HOO!! GO, LADIES!!
I DON'T EVEN KNOW WHAT TO SAY ANYMORE.
....

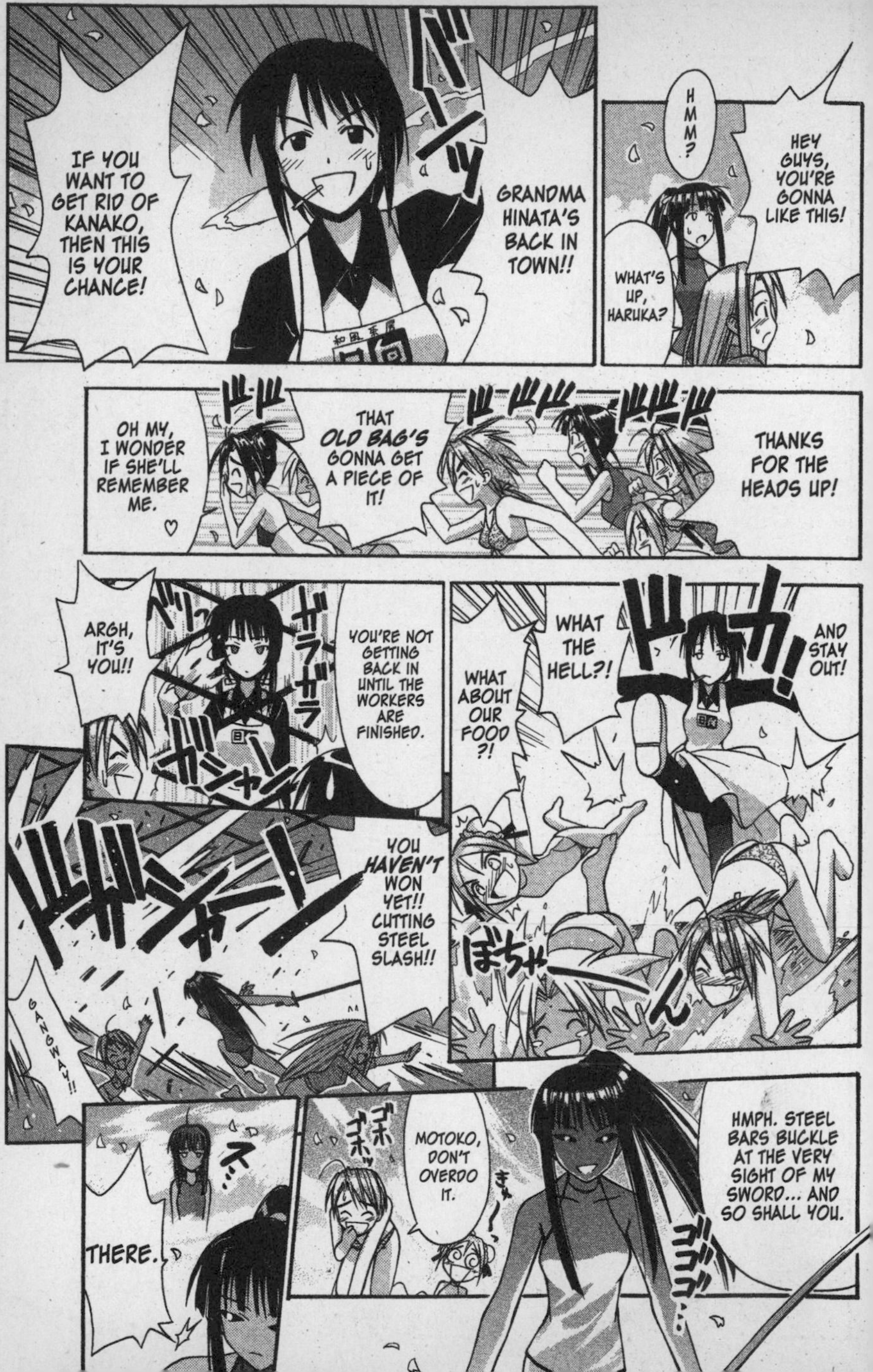
HEY GUYS, YOU'RE GONNA LIKE THIS!
HMM?
WHAT'S UP, HARUKA?
GRANDMA HINATA'S BACK IN TOWN!!
IF YOU WANT TO GET RID OF KANAKO, THEN THIS IS YOUR CHANCE!
THANKS FOR THE HEADS UP!
THAT *OLD BAG'S* GONNA GET A PIECE OF IT!
OH MY, I WONDER IF SHE'LL REMEMBER ME. ♡
AND STAY OUT!
WHAT THE HELL?!
WHAT ABOUT OUR FOOD?!
YOU'RE NOT GETTING BACK IN UNTIL THE WORKERS ARE FINISHED.
ARGH, IT'S YOU!!
YOU *HAVEN'T* WON YET!! CUTTING STEEL SLASH!!
GANGWAY!!
HMPH. STEEL BARS BUCKLE AT THE VERY SIGHT OF MY SWORD... AND SO SHALL YOU.
MOTOKO, DON'T OVERDO IT.
THERE.

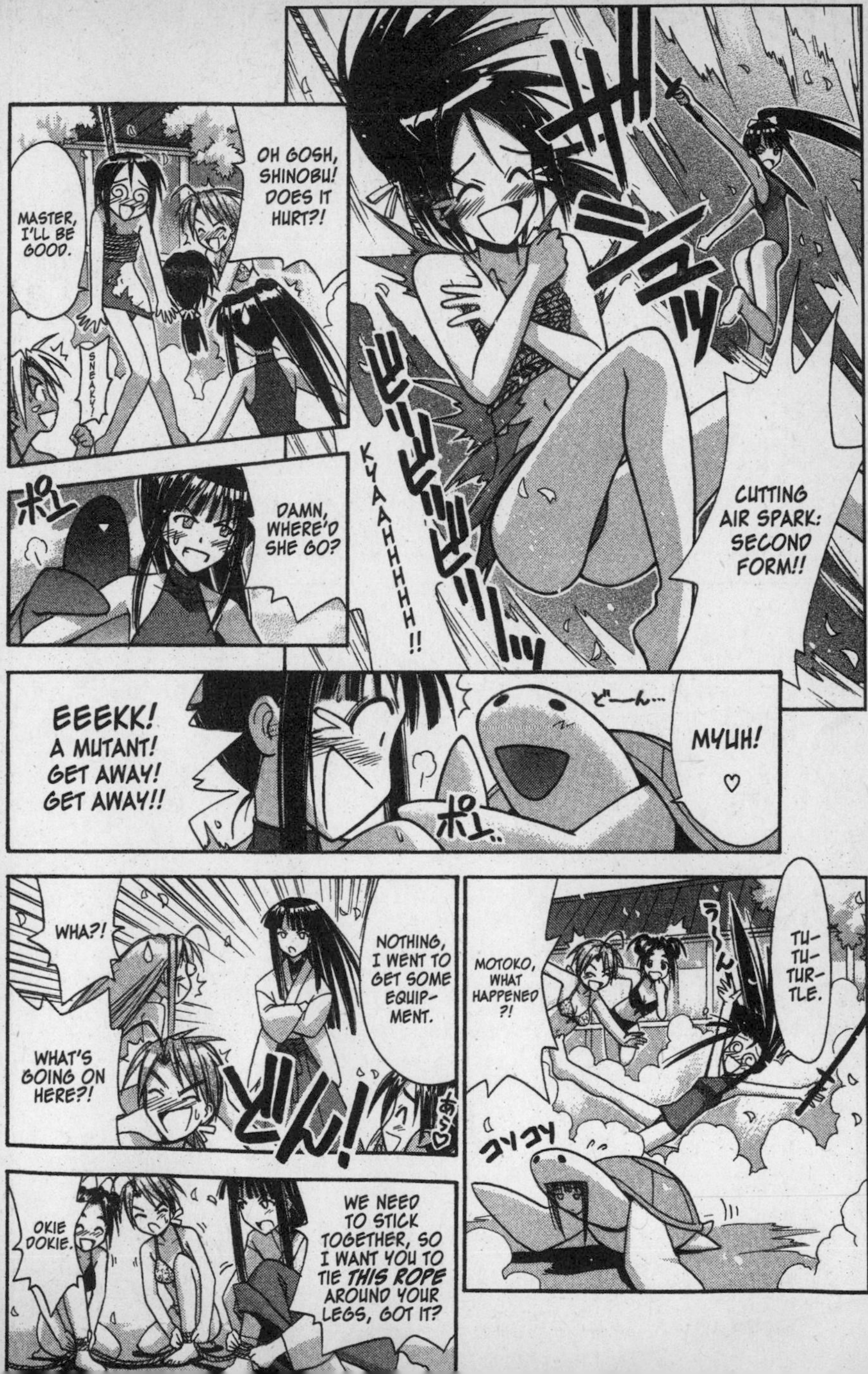
CUTTING AIR SPARK: SECOND FORM!!
KYAAHHHHHH!!
OH GOSH, SHINOBU! DOES IT HURT?!
MASTER, I'LL BE GOOD.
SNEAKY!
DAMN, WHERE'D SHE GO?
MYUH! ♡
EEEKK! A MUTANT! GET AWAY! GET AWAY!!
TU-TU-TURTLE.
MOTOKO, WHAT HAPPENED?!
NOTHING, I WENT TO GET SOME EQUIPMENT.
WHA?!
WHAT'S GOING ON HERE?!
WE NEED TO STICK TOGETHER, SO I WANT YOU TO TIE *THIS ROPE* AROUND YOUR LEGS, GOT IT?
OKIE DOKIE.

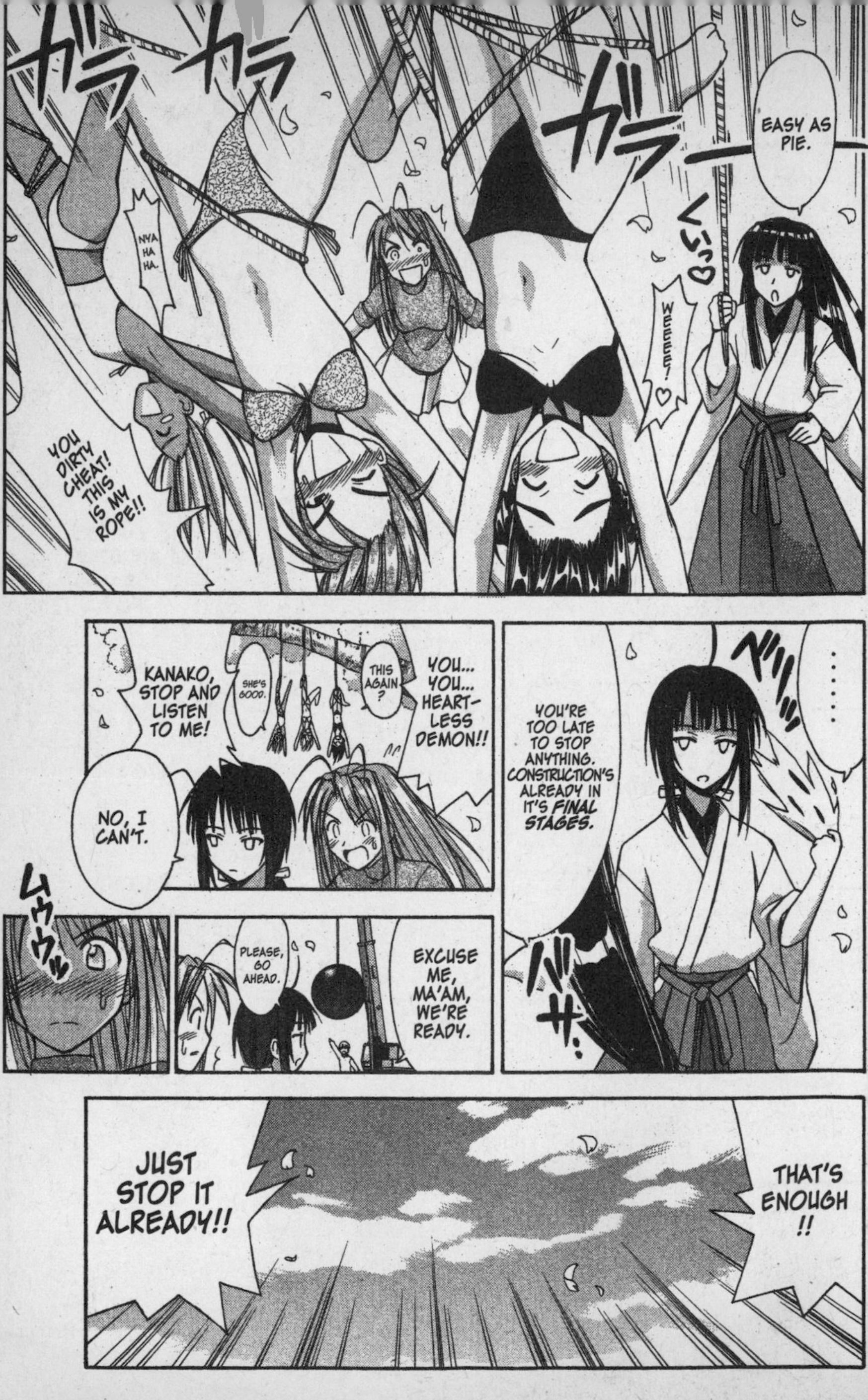
EASY AS PIE.
ガラー
くいっ♡
WEEEEE!♡
ガラ
カラ
NYA HA HA.
YOU DIRTY CHEAT! THIS IS MY ROPE!!
......
YOU'RE TOO LATE TO STOP ANYTHING. CONSTRUCTION'S ALREADY IN IT'S FINAL STAGES.
YOU... YOU... HEART-LESS DEMON!!
THIS AGAIN?
SHE'S GOOD.
KANAKO, STOP AND LISTEN TO ME!
NO, I CAN'T.
EXCUSE ME, MA'AM, WE'RE READY.
PLEASE, GO AHEAD.
THAT'S ENOUGH!!
JUST STOP IT ALREADY!!

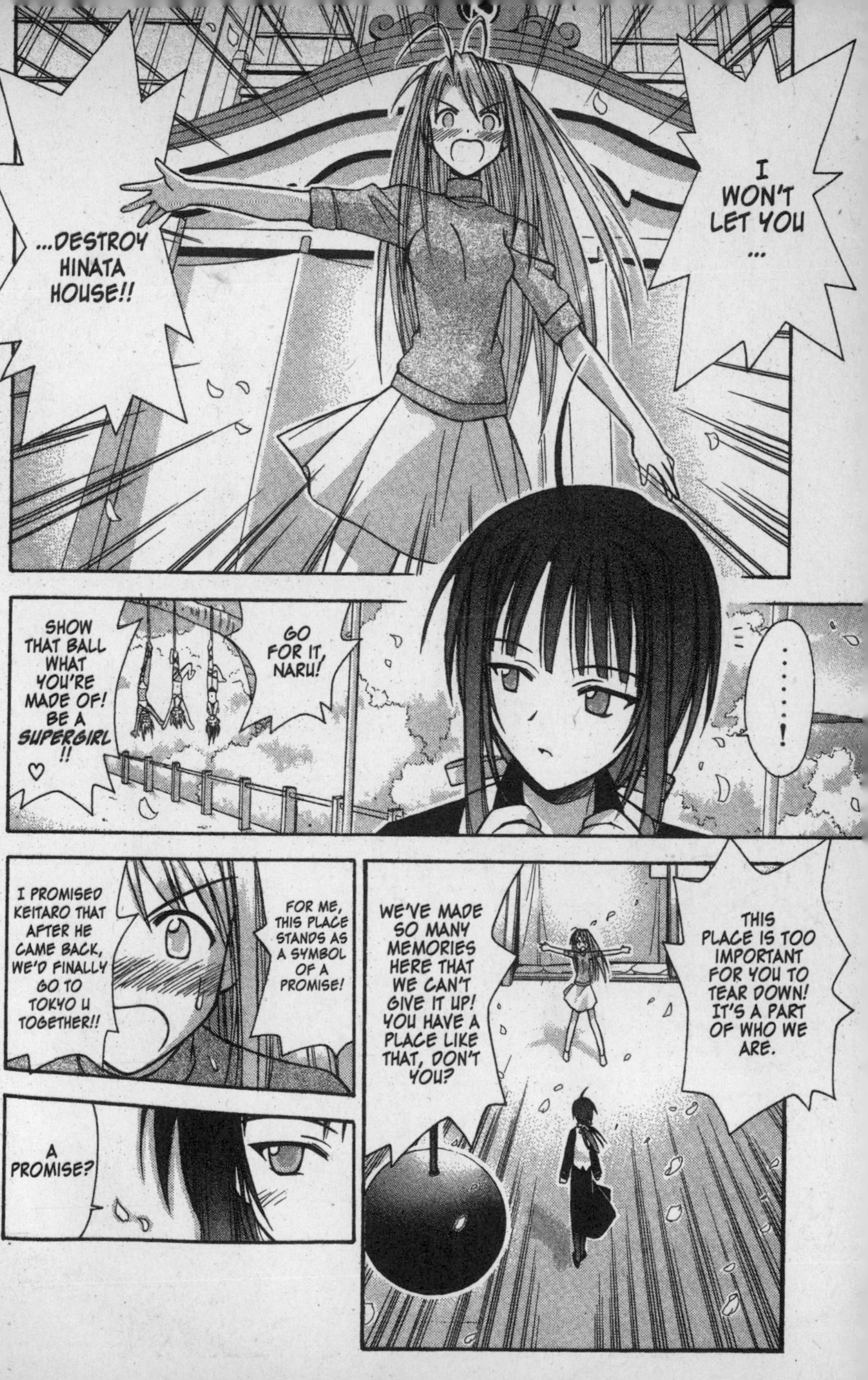
I WON'T LET YOU ...
...DESTROY HINATA HOUSE!!
......!
GO FOR IT, NARU!
SHOW THAT BALL WHAT YOU'RE MADE OF! BE A SUPERGIRL!! ♡
THIS PLACE IS TOO IMPORTANT FOR YOU TO TEAR DOWN! IT'S A PART OF WHO WE ARE.
WE'VE MADE SO MANY MEMORIES HERE THAT WE CAN'T GIVE IT UP! YOU HAVE A PLACE LIKE THAT, DON'T YOU?
FOR ME, THIS PLACE STANDS AS A SYMBOL OF A PROMISE!
I PROMISED KEITARO THAT AFTER HE CAME BACK, WE'D FINALLY GO TO TOKYO U TOGETHER!!
A PROMISE?

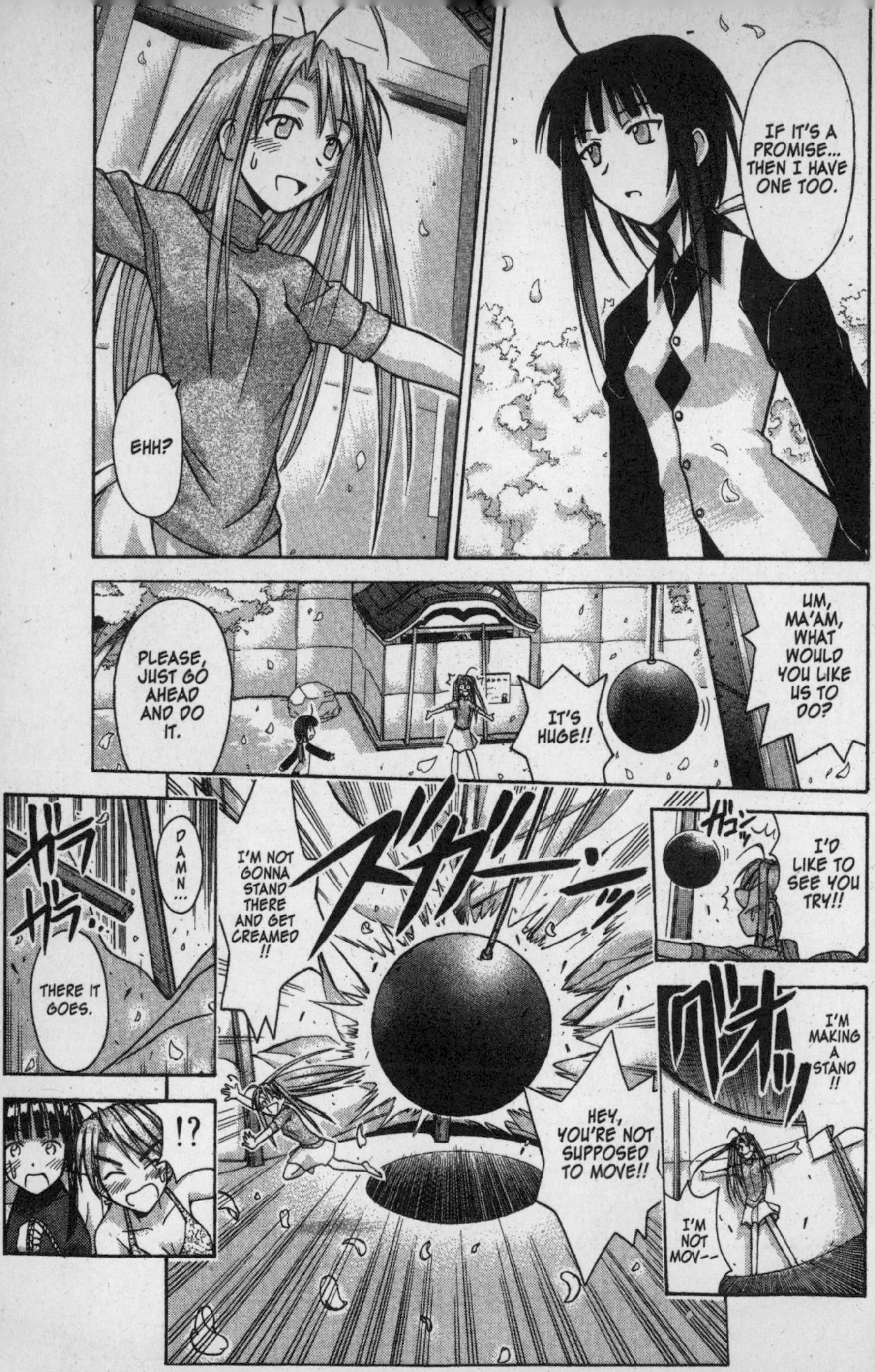

IF IT'S A PROMISE... THEN I HAVE ONE TOO.
EHH?
UM, MA'AM, WHAT WOULD YOU LIKE US TO DO?
IT'S HUGE!!
PLEASE, JUST GO AHEAD AND DO IT.
I'D LIKE TO SEE YOU TRY!!
I'M MAKING A STAND!!
I'M NOT MOV--
HEY, YOU'RE NOT SUPPOSED TO MOVE!!
I'M NOT GONNA STAND THERE AND GET CREAMED!!
DAMN...
THERE IT GOES.
!?

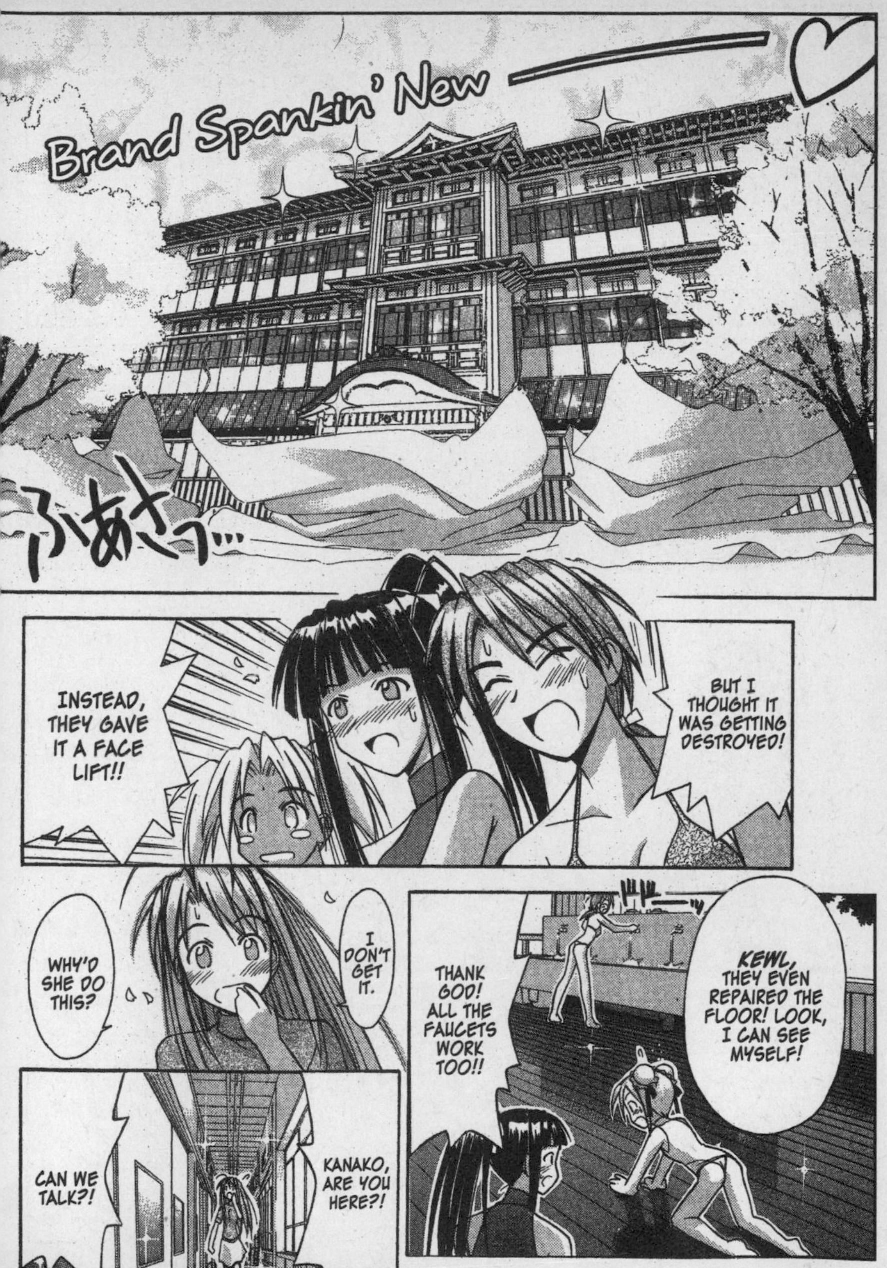
Brand Spankin' New
ふあさっ…
BUT I THOUGHT IT WAS GETTING DESTROYED!
INSTEAD, THEY GAVE IT A FACE LIFT!!
KEWL, THEY EVEN REPAIRED THE FLOOR! LOOK, I CAN SEE MYSELF!
THANK GOD! ALL THE FAUCETS WORK TOO!!
I DON'T GET IT.
WHY'D SHE DO THIS?
KANAKO, ARE YOU HERE?!
CAN WE TALK?!

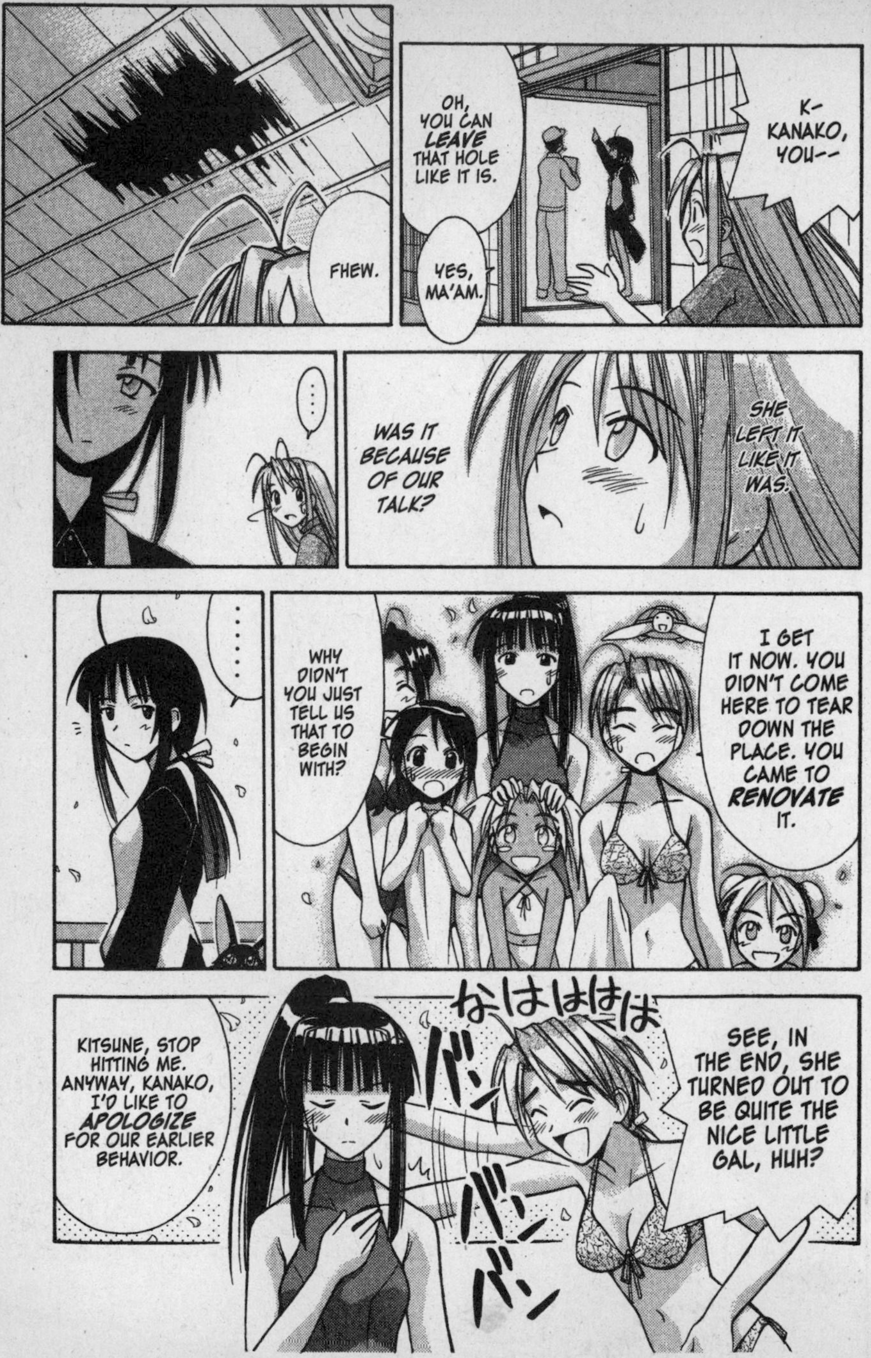

K- KANAKO, YOU--
OH, YOU CAN LEAVE THAT HOLE LIKE IT IS.
YES, MA'AM.
FHEW.
SHE LEFT IT LIKE IT WAS.
WAS IT BECAUSE OF OUR TALK?
...
I GET IT NOW. YOU DIDN'T COME HERE TO TEAR DOWN THE PLACE. YOU CAME TO RENOVATE IT.
WHY DIDN'T YOU JUST TELL US THAT TO BEGIN WITH?
......
SEE, IN THE END, SHE TURNED OUT TO BE QUITE THE NICE LITTLE GAL, HUH?
なはははは
バン
バン
バン
KITSUNE, STOP HITTING ME. ANYWAY, KANAKO, I'D LIKE TO APOLOGIZE FOR OUR EARLIER BEHAVIOR.

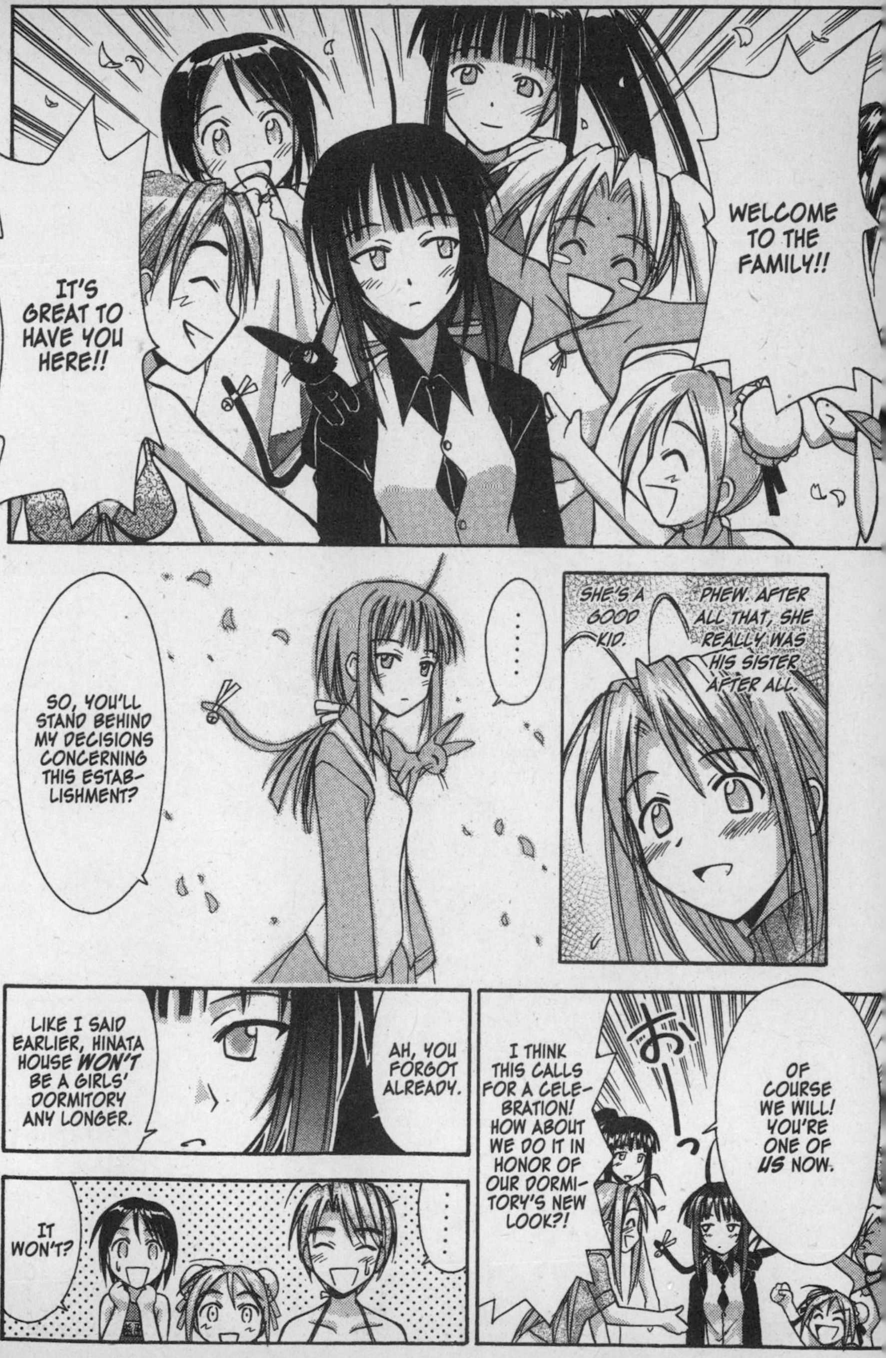
WELCOME TO THE FAMILY!!
IT'S GREAT TO HAVE YOU HERE!!
PHEW. AFTER ALL THAT, SHE REALLY WAS HIS SISTER AFTER ALL.
SHE'S A GOOD KID.
......
SO, YOU'LL STAND BEHIND MY DECISIONS CONCERNING THIS ESTAB-LISHMENT?
OF COURSE WE WILL! YOU'RE ONE OF US NOW.
おーっ
I THINK THIS CALLS FOR A CELE-BRATION! HOW ABOUT WE DO IT IN HONOR OF OUR DORMI-TORY'S NEW LOOK?!
AH, YOU FORGOT ALREADY.
LIKE I SAID EARLIER, HINATA HOUSE WON'T BE A GIRLS' DORMITORY ANY LONGER.
......
IT WON'T?

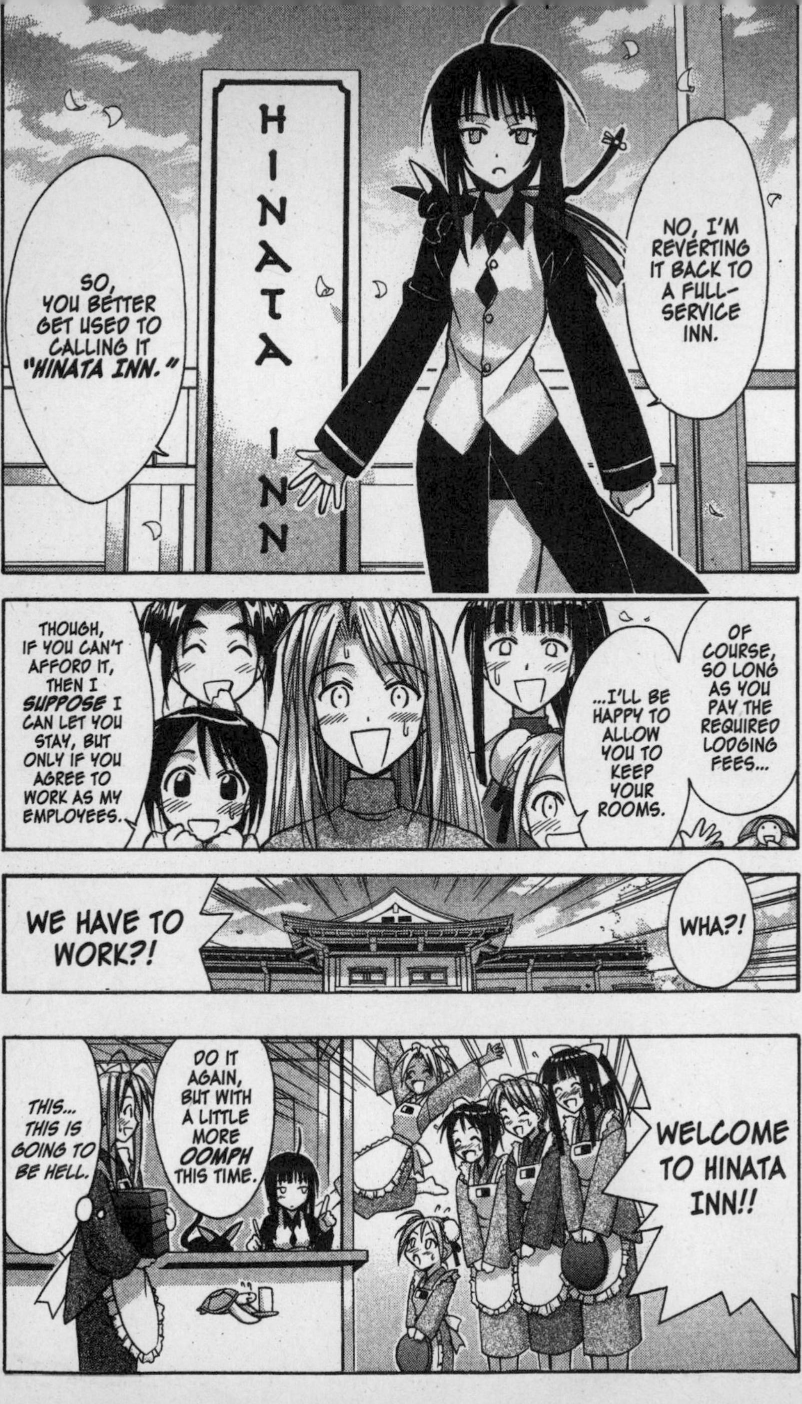
HINATA INN
NO, I'M REVERTING IT BACK TO A FULL-SERVICE INN.
SO, YOU BETTER GET USED TO CALLING IT "HINATA INN."
OF COURSE, SO LONG AS YOU PAY THE REQUIRED LODGING FEES...
...I'LL BE HAPPY TO ALLOW YOU TO KEEP YOUR ROOMS.
THOUGH, IF YOU CAN'T AFFORD IT, THEN I SUPPOSE I CAN LET YOU STAY, BUT ONLY IF YOU AGREE TO WORK AS MY EMPLOYEES.
WHA?!
WE HAVE TO WORK?!
WELCOME TO HINATA INN!!
DO IT AGAIN, BUT WITH A LITTLE MORE OOMPH THIS TIME.
THIS... THIS IS GOING TO BE HELL.

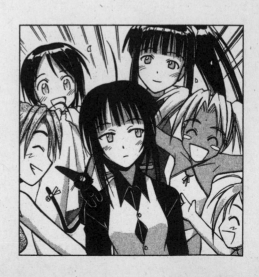

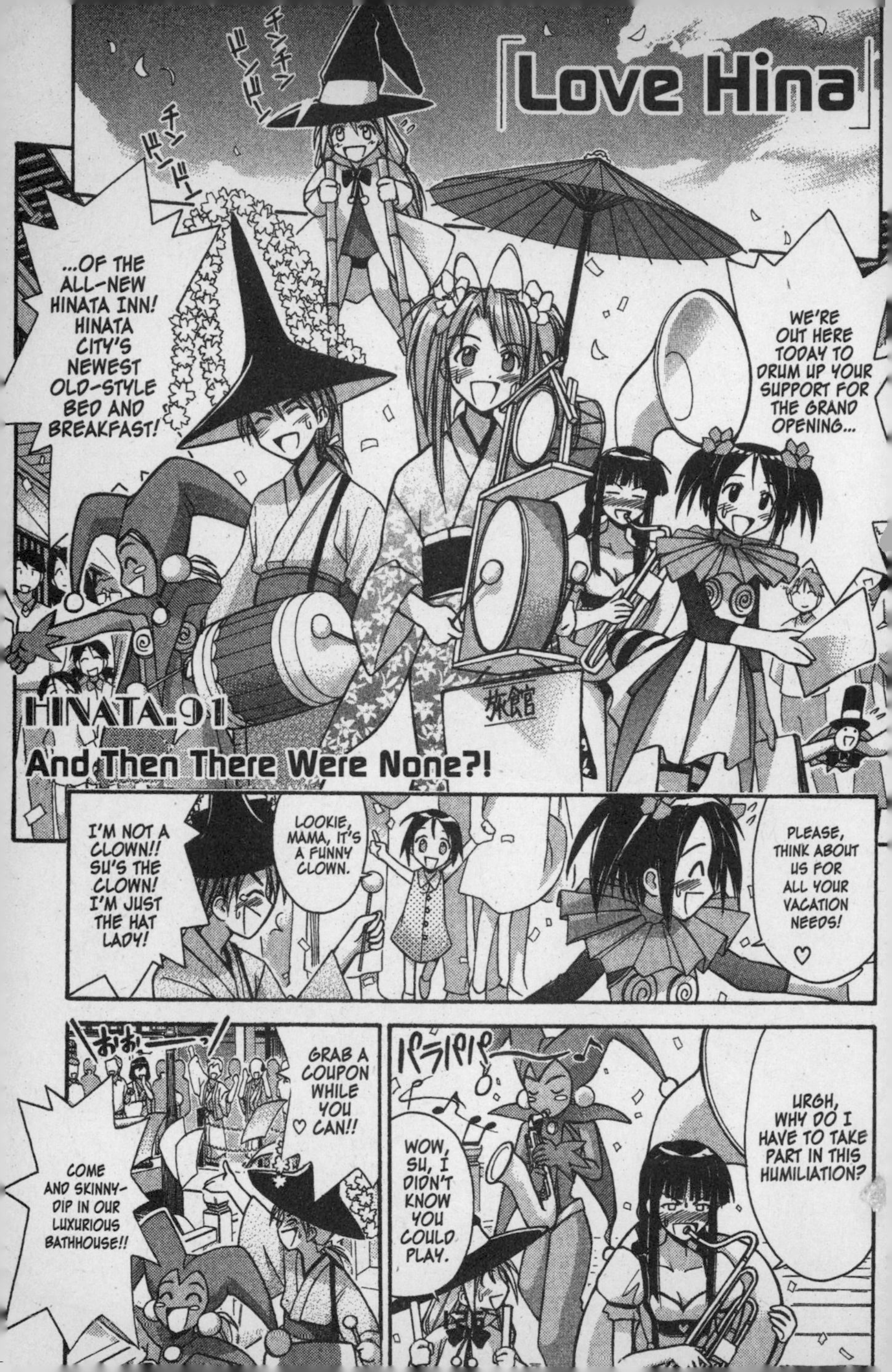
「Love Hina」
チンチン ドンドーン
チン ドンドーン
WE'RE OUT HERE TODAY TO DRUM UP YOUR SUPPORT FOR THE GRAND OPENING...
...OF THE ALL-NEW HINATA INN! HINATA CITY'S NEWEST OLD-STYLE BED AND BREAKFAST!
旅館
HINATA.91
And Then There Were None?!
PLEASE, THINK ABOUT US FOR ALL YOUR VACATION NEEDS! ♡
LOOKIE, MAMA, IT'S A FUNNY CLOWN.
I'M NOT A CLOWN!! SU'S THE CLOWN! I'M JUST THE HAT LADY!
URGH, WHY DO I HAVE TO TAKE PART IN THIS HUMILIATION?
パラパパパ
WOW, SU, I DIDN'T KNOW YOU COULD PLAY.
GRAB A COUPON WHILE YOU CAN!! ♡
おお!
COME AND SKINNY-DIP IN OUR LUXURIOUS BATHHOUSE!!

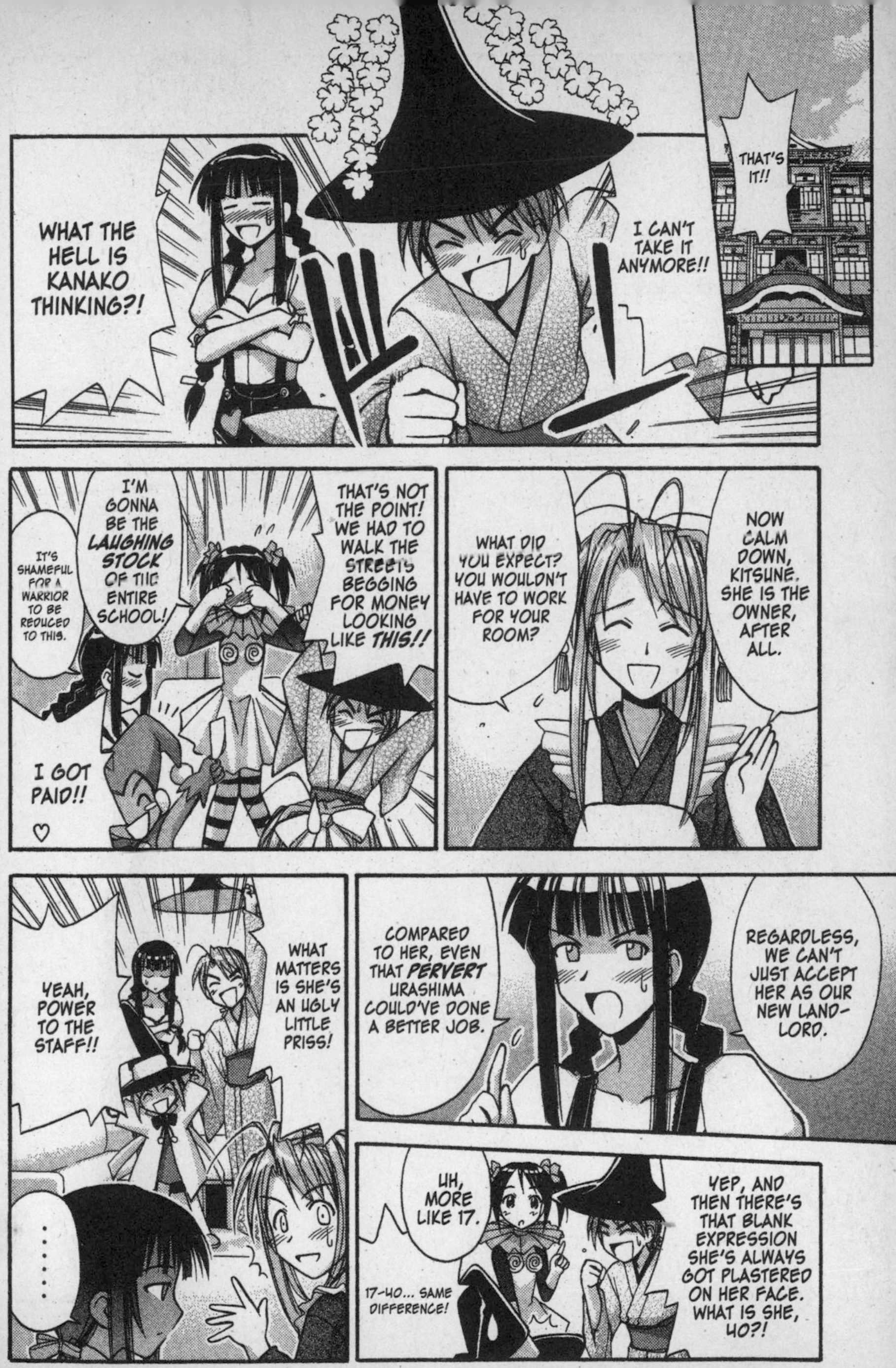
THAT'S IT!!
I CAN'T TAKE IT ANYMORE!!
WHAT THE HELL IS KANAKO THINKING?!
NOW CALM DOWN, KITSUNE. SHE IS THE OWNER, AFTER ALL.
WHAT DID YOU EXPECT? YOU WOULDN'T HAVE TO WORK FOR YOUR ROOM?
THAT'S NOT THE POINT! WE HAD TO WALK THE STREETS BEGGING FOR MONEY LOOKING LIKE *THIS!!*
I'M GONNA BE THE *LAUGHING STOCK* OF THE ENTIRE SCHOOL!
IT'S SHAMEFUL FOR A WARRIOR TO BE REDUCED TO THIS.
I GOT PAID!! ♡
REGARDLESS, WE CAN'T JUST ACCEPT HER AS OUR NEW LANDLORD.
COMPARED TO HER, EVEN THAT *PERVERT* URASHIMA COULD'VE DONE A BETTER JOB.
YEP, AND THEN THERE'S THAT BLANK EXPRESSION SHE'S ALWAYS GOT PLASTERED ON HER FACE. WHAT IS SHE, 40?!
UH, MORE LIKE 17.
17-40... SAME DIFFERENCE!
WHAT MATTERS IS SHE'S AN UGLY LITTLE PRISS!
YEAH, POWER TO THE STAFF!!
......

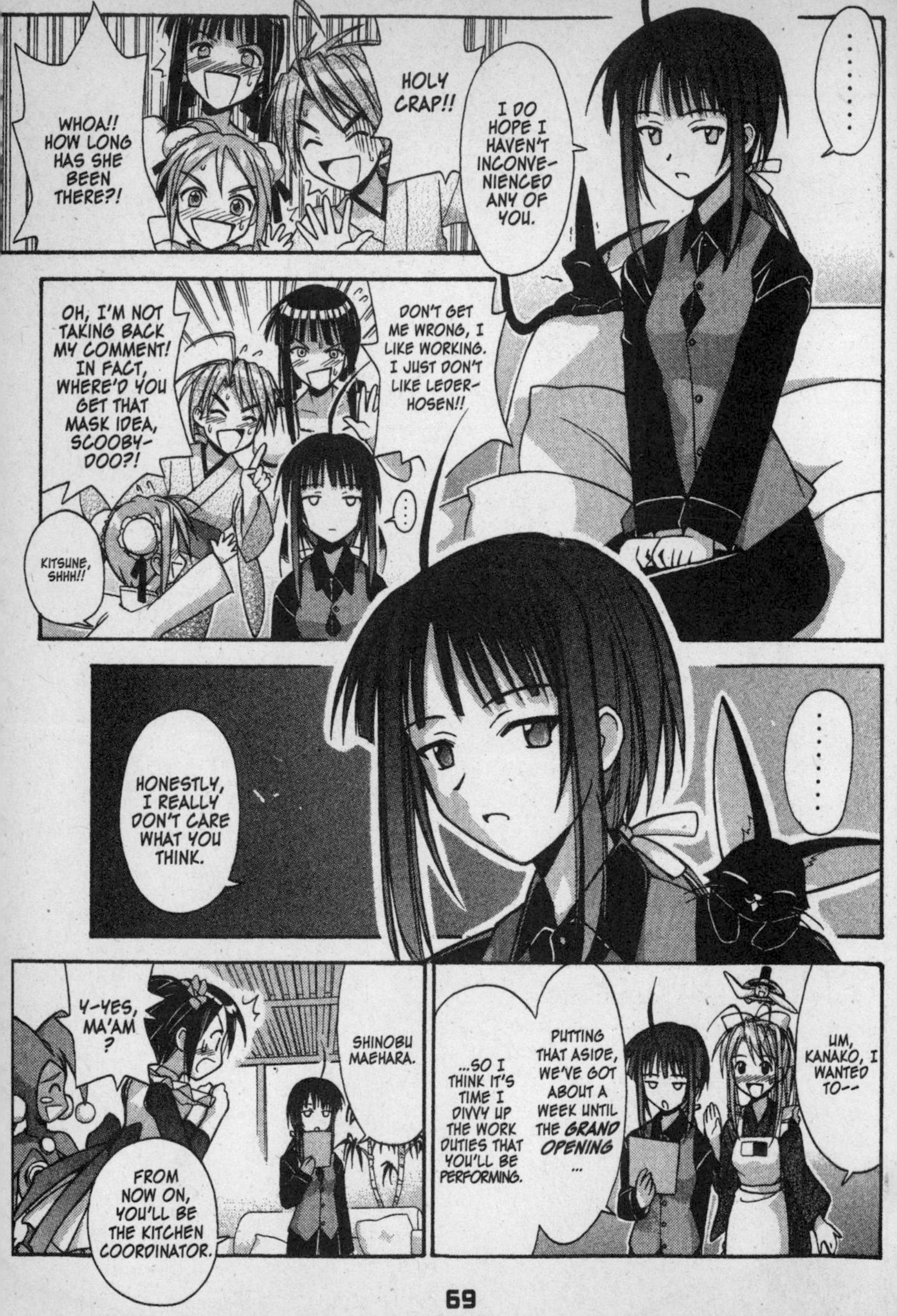
......
I DO HOPE I HAVEN'T INCONVENIENCED ANY OF YOU.
HOLY CRAP!!
WHOA!! HOW LONG HAS SHE BEEN THERE?!
DON'T GET ME WRONG, I LIKE WORKING. I JUST DON'T LIKE LEDERHOSEN!!
OH, I'M NOT TAKING BACK MY COMMENT! IN FACT, WHERE'D YOU GET THAT MASK IDEA, SCOOBY-DOO?!
...
KITSUNE, SHHH!!
......
HONESTLY, I REALLY DON'T CARE WHAT YOU THINK.
UM, KANAKO, I WANTED TO--
PUTTING THAT ASIDE, WE'VE GOT ABOUT A WEEK UNTIL THE GRAND OPENING ...
...SO I THINK IT'S TIME I DIVVY UP THE WORK DUTIES THAT YOU'LL BE PERFORMING.
SHINOBU MAEHARA.
Y-YES, MA'AM ?
FROM NOW ON, YOU'LL BE THE KITCHEN COORDINATOR.

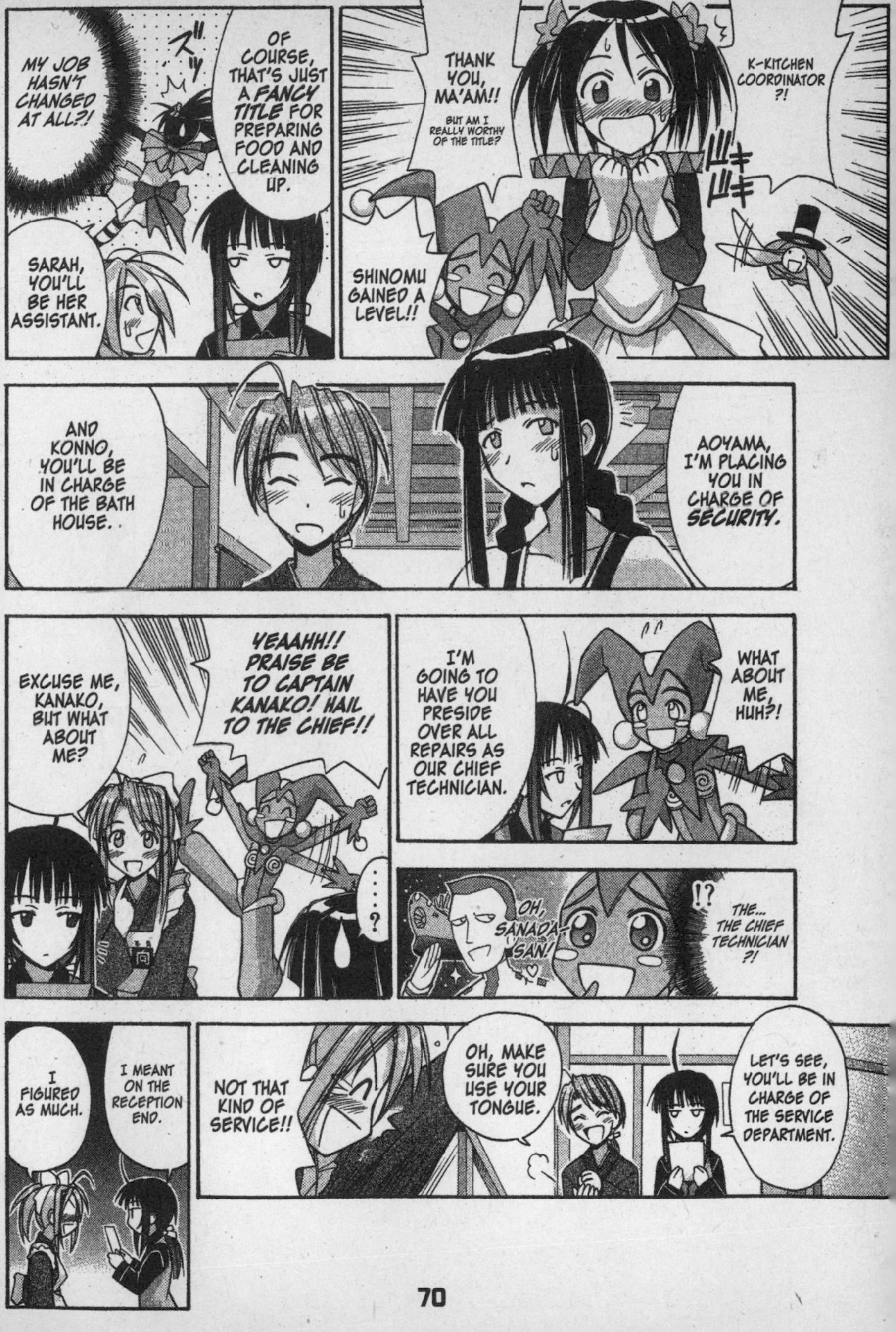
K-KITCHEN COORDINATOR ?!
ドキドキ
THANK YOU, MA'AM!!
BUT AM I REALLY WORTHY OF THE TITLE?
SHINOMU GAINED A LEVEL!!
OF COURSE, THAT'S JUST A **FANCY TITLE** FOR PREPARING FOOD AND CLEANING UP.
ズッ
MY JOB HASN'T CHANGED AT ALL?!
SARAH, YOU'LL BE HER ASSISTANT.
AOYAMA, I'M PLACING YOU IN CHARGE OF **SECURITY**.
AND KONNO, YOU'LL BE IN CHARGE OF THE BATH HOUSE.
WHAT ABOUT ME, HUH?!
I'M GOING TO HAVE YOU PRESIDE OVER ALL REPAIRS AS OUR CHIEF TECHNICIAN.
THE... THE CHIEF TECHNICIAN ?!
!?
OH, SANADA-SAN!
YEAAHH!! PRAISE BE TO CAPTAIN KANAKO! HAIL TO THE CHIEF!!
EXCUSE ME, KANAKO, BUT WHAT ABOUT ME?
....?
LET'S SEE, YOU'LL BE IN CHARGE OF THE SERVICE DEPARTMENT.
OH, MAKE SURE YOU USE YOUR TONGUE.
NOT THAT KIND OF SERVICE!!
I MEANT ON THE RECEPTION END.
I FIGURED AS MUCH.

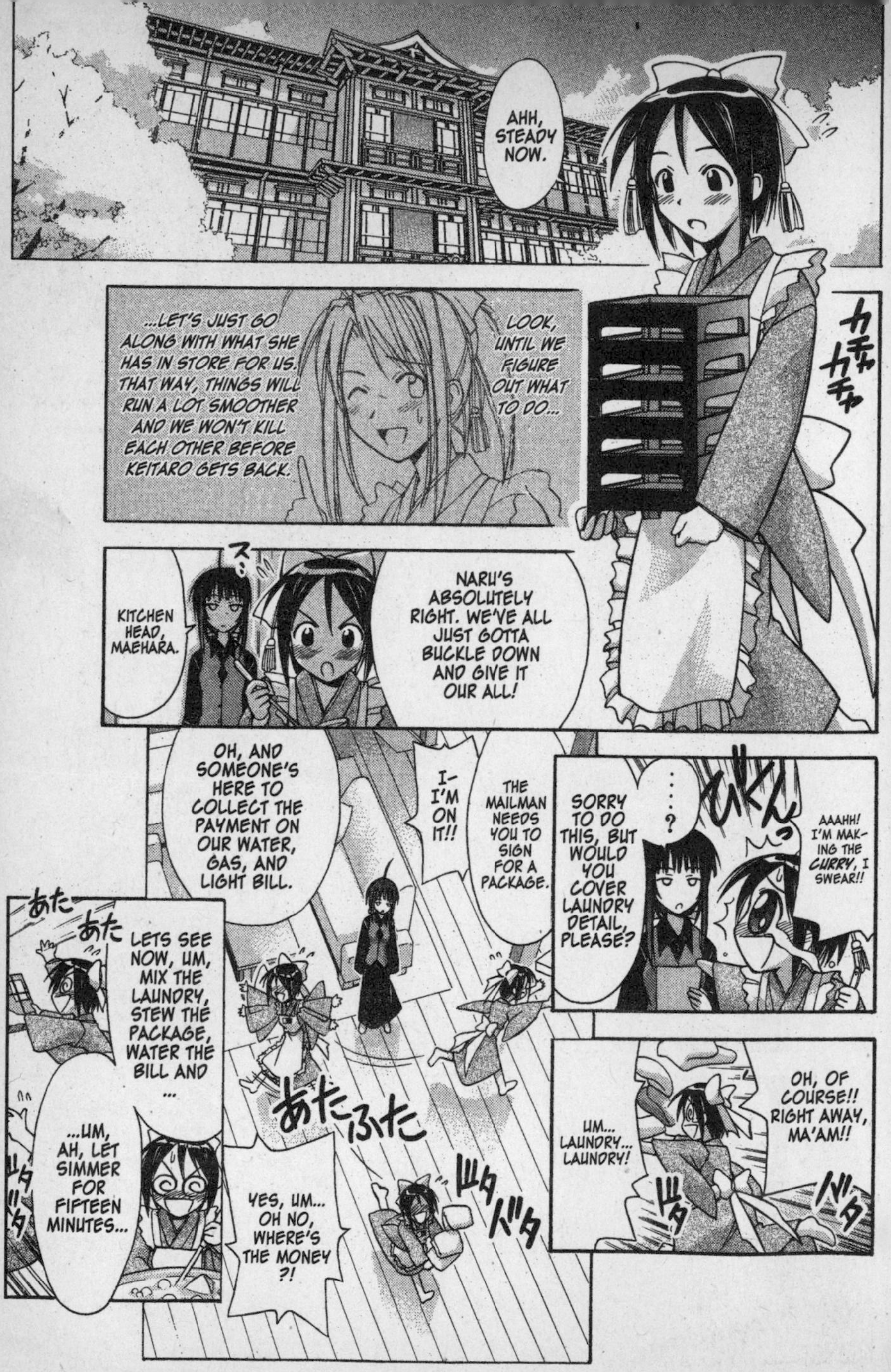
AHH, STEADY NOW.
カチャカチャ
LOOK, UNTIL WE FIGURE OUT WHAT TO DO...
...LET'S JUST GO ALONG WITH WHAT SHE HAS IN STORE FOR US. THAT WAY, THINGS WILL RUN A LOT SMOOTHER AND WE WON'T KILL EACH OTHER BEFORE KEITARO GETS BACK.
NARU'S ABSOLUTELY RIGHT. WE'VE ALL JUST GOTTA BUCKLE DOWN AND GIVE IT OUR ALL!
ス
KITCHEN HEAD, MAEHARA.
.....?
SORRY TO DO THIS, BUT WOULD YOU COVER LAUNDRY DETAIL, PLEASE?
びくんっ
AAAHH! I'M MAKING THE CURRY, I SWEAR!!
OH, OF COURSE!! RIGHT AWAY, MA'AM!!
UM... LAUNDRY... LAUNDRY!
ドタ
バタ
THE MAILMAN NEEDS YOU TO SIGN FOR A PACKAGE.
I- I'M ON IT!!
OH, AND SOMEONE'S HERE TO COLLECT THE PAYMENT ON OUR WATER, GAS, AND LIGHT BILL.
あたふた
ドタバタ
YES, UM... OH NO, WHERE'S THE MONEY ?!
あたあた
LETS SEE NOW, UM, MIX THE LAUNDRY, STEW THE PACKAGE, WATER THE BILL AND ...
...UM, AH, LET SIMMER FOR FIFTEEN MINUTES...
ドタバタ

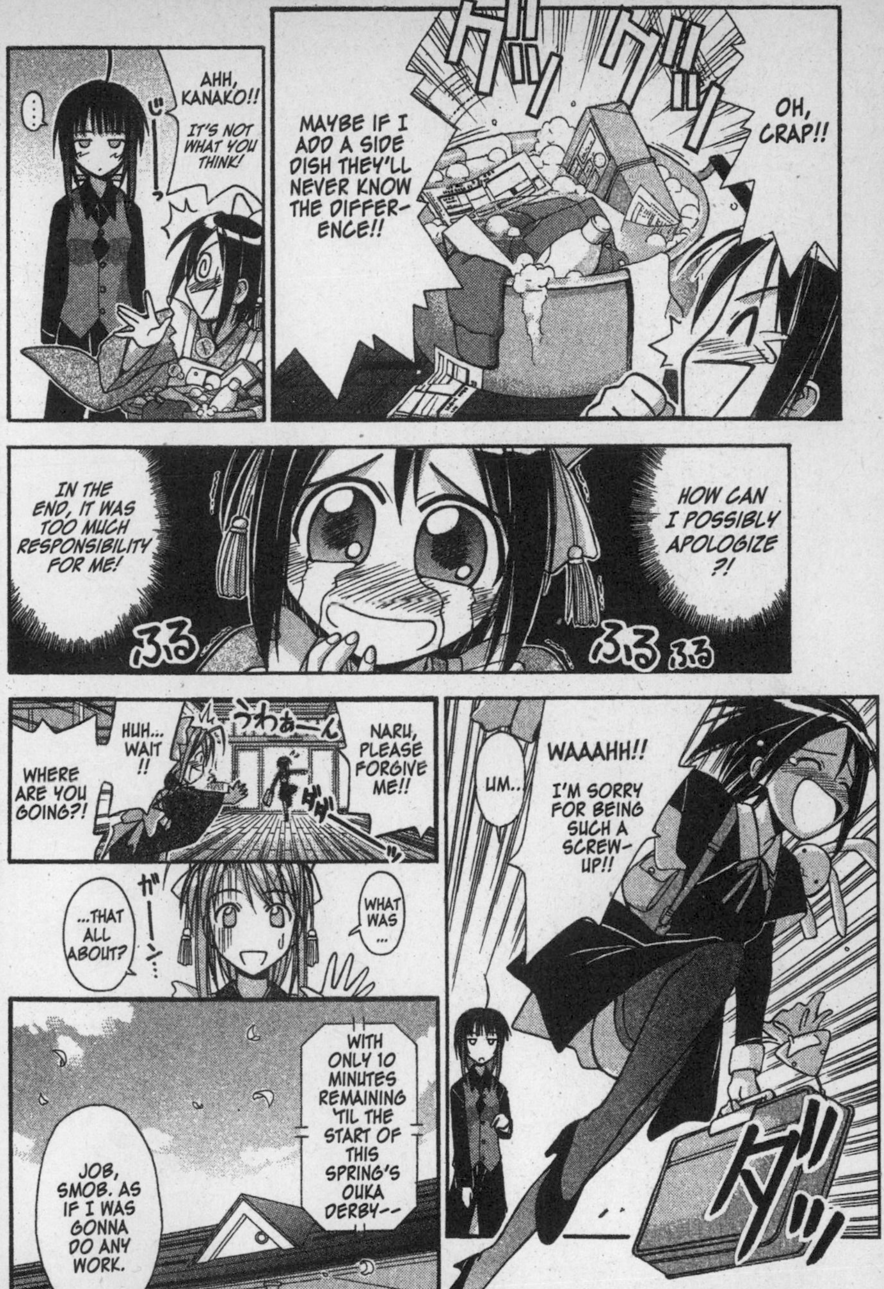
OH, CRAP!!
MAYBE IF I ADD A SIDE DISH THEY'LL NEVER KNOW THE DIFFERENCE!!
AHH, KANAKO!!
IT'S NOT WHAT YOU THINK!
...
HOW CAN I POSSIBLY APOLOGIZE ?!
IN THE END, IT WAS TOO MUCH RESPONSIBILITY FOR ME!
ふる
ふる ふる
WAAAHH!!
I'M SORRY FOR BEING SUCH A SCREW-UP!!
UM..
NARU, PLEASE FORGIVE ME!!
うわぁーん
HUH... WAIT !!
WHERE ARE YOU GOING?!
WHAT WAS ...
...THAT ALL ABOUT?
WITH ONLY 10 MINUTES REMAINING 'TIL THE START OF THIS SPRING'S OUKA DERBY--
JOB, SMOB. AS IF I WAS GONNA DO ANY WORK.

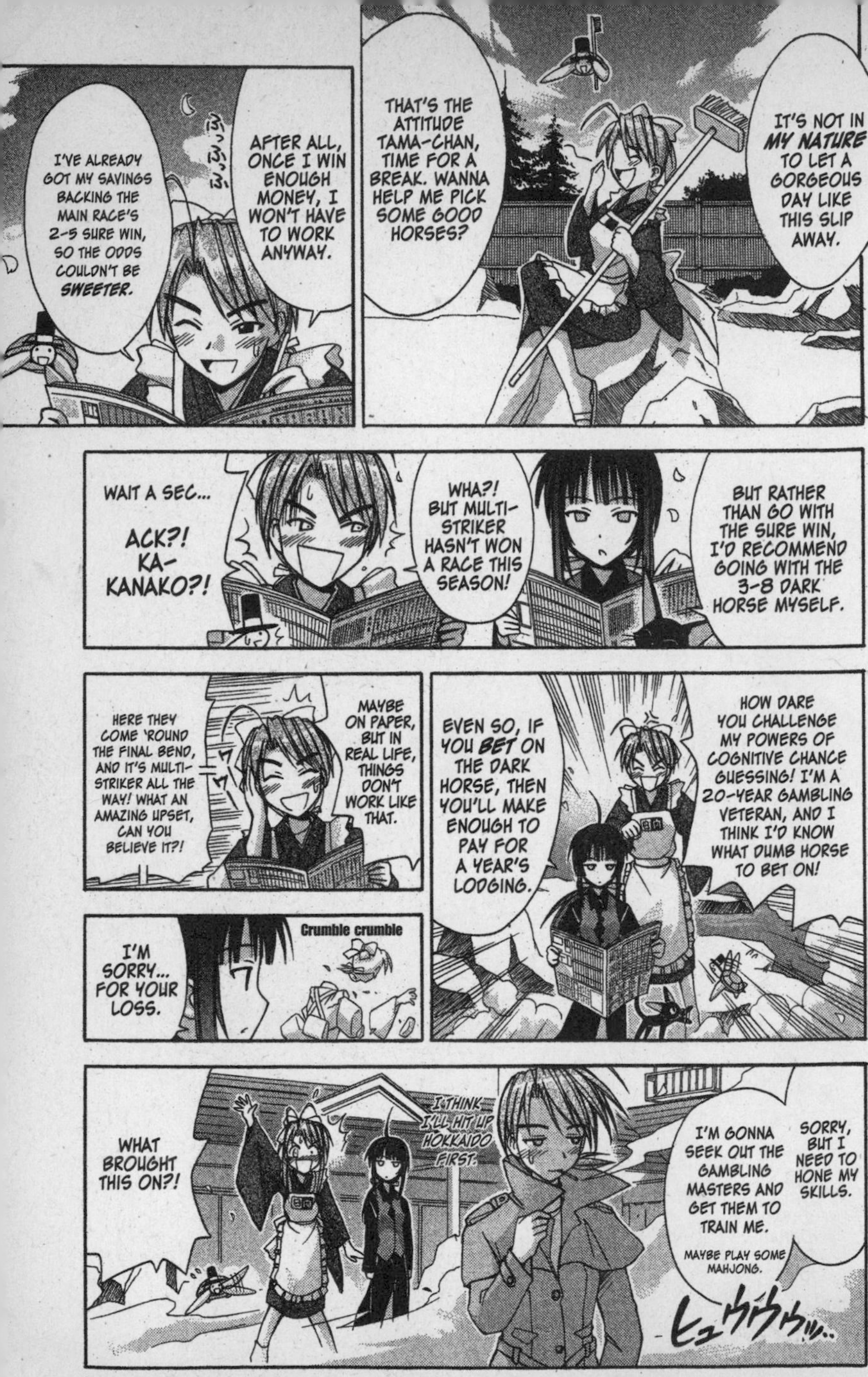
IT'S NOT IN MY NATURE TO LET A GORGEOUS DAY LIKE THIS SLIP AWAY.
THAT'S THE ATTITUDE TAMA-CHAN, TIME FOR A BREAK. WANNA HELP ME PICK SOME GOOD HORSES?
AFTER ALL, ONCE I WIN ENOUGH MONEY, I WON'T HAVE TO WORK ANYWAY.
ふっふっふ
I'VE ALREADY GOT MY SAVINGS BACKING THE MAIN RACE'S 2-5 SURE WIN, SO THE ODDS COULDN'T BE SWEETER.
BUT RATHER THAN GO WITH THE SURE WIN, I'D RECOMMEND GOING WITH THE 3-8 DARK HORSE MYSELF.
WHA?! BUT MULTI-STRIKER HASN'T WON A RACE THIS SEASON!
WAIT A SEC...
ACK?! KA-KANAKO?!
HOW DARE YOU CHALLENGE MY POWERS OF COGNITIVE CHANCE GUESSING! I'M A 20-YEAR GAMBLING VETERAN, AND I THINK I'D KNOW WHAT DUMB HORSE TO BET ON!
EVEN SO, IF YOU BET ON THE DARK HORSE, THEN YOU'LL MAKE ENOUGH TO PAY FOR A YEAR'S LODGING.
MAYBE ON PAPER, BUT IN REAL LIFE, THINGS DON'T WORK LIKE THAT.
HERE THEY COME 'ROUND THE FINAL BEND, AND IT'S MULTI-STRIKER ALL THE WAY! WHAT AN AMAZING UPSET, CAN YOU BELIEVE IT?!
Crumble crumble
I'M SORRY... FOR YOUR LOSS.
SORRY, BUT I NEED TO HONE MY SKILLS.
I'M GONNA SEEK OUT THE GAMBLING MASTERS AND GET THEM TO TRAIN ME.
MAYBE PLAY SOME MAHJONG.
I THINK I'LL HIT UP HOKKAIDO FIRST.
WHAT BROUGHT THIS ON?!
ヒュウウウ

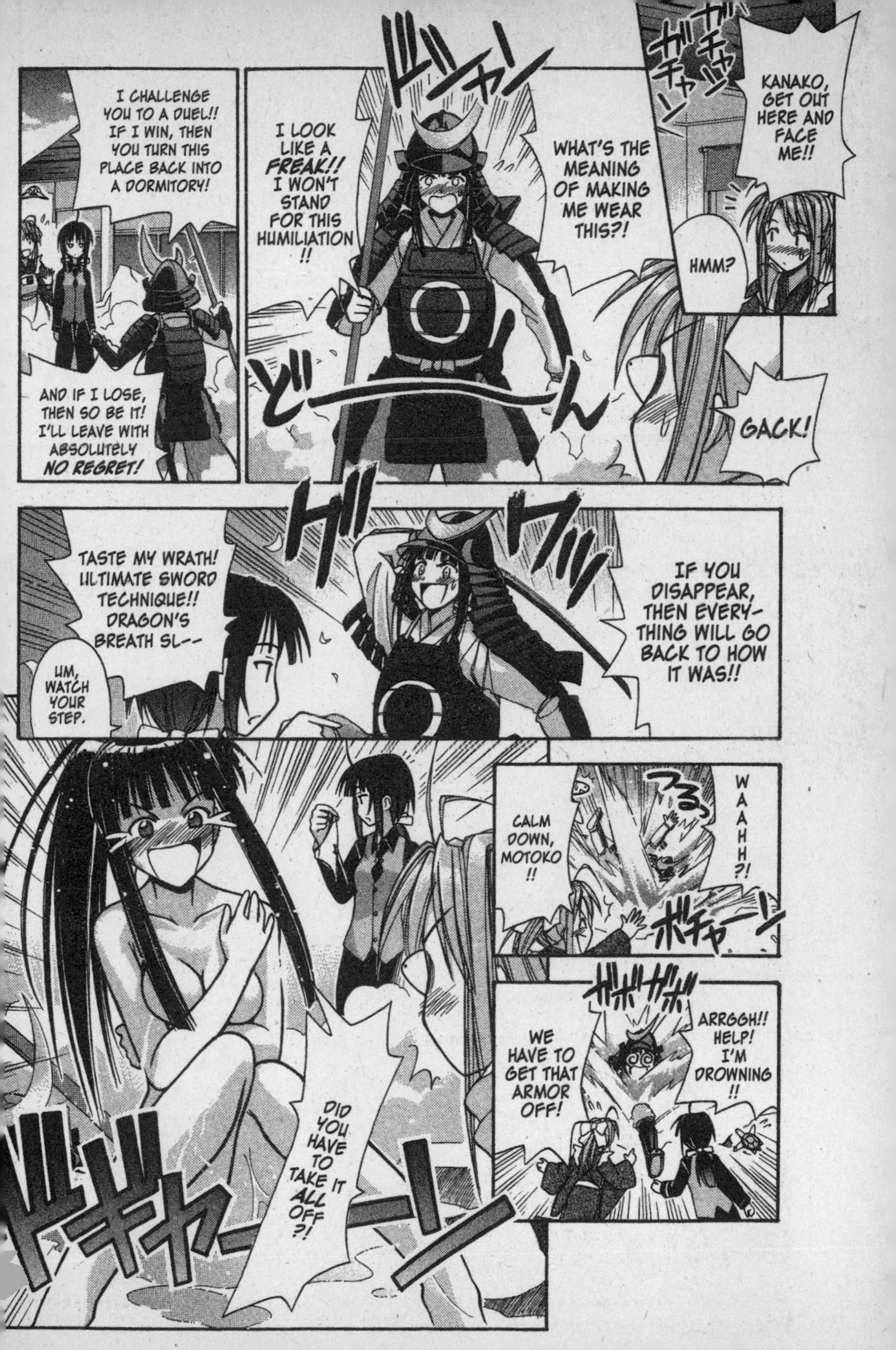
ガチャン ガチャン
KANAKO, GET OUT HERE AND FACE ME!!
HMM?
ドジャーン
WHAT'S THE MEANING OF MAKING ME WEAR THIS?!
I LOOK LIKE A FREAK!! I WON'T STAND FOR THIS HUMILIATION!!
どーーん
GACK!
I CHALLENGE YOU TO A DUEL!! IF I WIN, THEN YOU TURN THIS PLACE BACK INTO A DORMITORY!
AND IF I LOSE, THEN SO BE IT! I'LL LEAVE WITH ABSOLUTELY NO REGRET!
ガバッ
IF YOU DISAPPEAR, THEN EVERY-THING WILL GO BACK TO HOW IT WAS!!
TASTE MY WRATH! ULTIMATE SWORD TECHNIQUE!! DRAGON'S BREATH SL--
UM, WATCH YOUR STEP.
つるっ
WAAHH?!
CALM DOWN, MOTOKO!!
ボチャーン
ガボガボ
ARRGGH!! HELP! I'M DROWNING!!
WE HAVE TO GET THAT ARMOR OFF!
DID YOU HAVE TO TAKE IT ALL OFF?!
ドギャーン

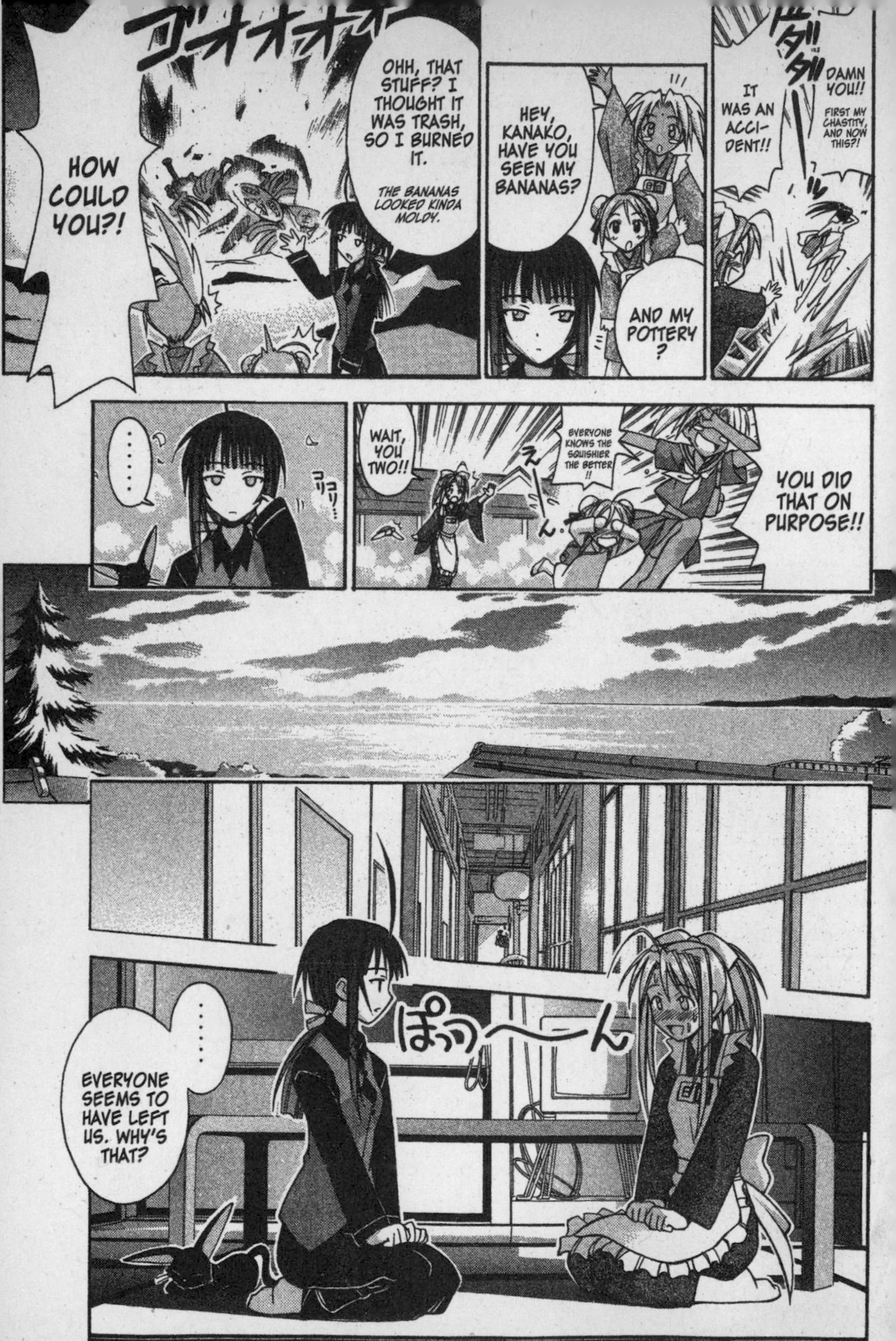
DAMN YOU!!
FIRST MY CHASTITY, AND NOW THIS?!
IT WAS AN ACCIDENT!!
HEY, KANAKO, HAVE YOU SEEN MY BANANAS?
AND MY POTTERY?
OHH, THAT STUFF? I THOUGHT IT WAS TRASH, SO I BURNED IT.
THE BANANAS LOOKED KINDA MOLDY.
HOW COULD YOU?!
ゴオオオオー
YOU DID THAT ON PURPOSE!!
EVERYONE KNOWS THE SQUISHIER THE BETTER!!
えーん
WAIT, YOU TWO!!
......
コリコリ...
......
EVERYONE SEEMS TO HAVE LEFT US. WHY'S THAT?
ぽっ～～ん

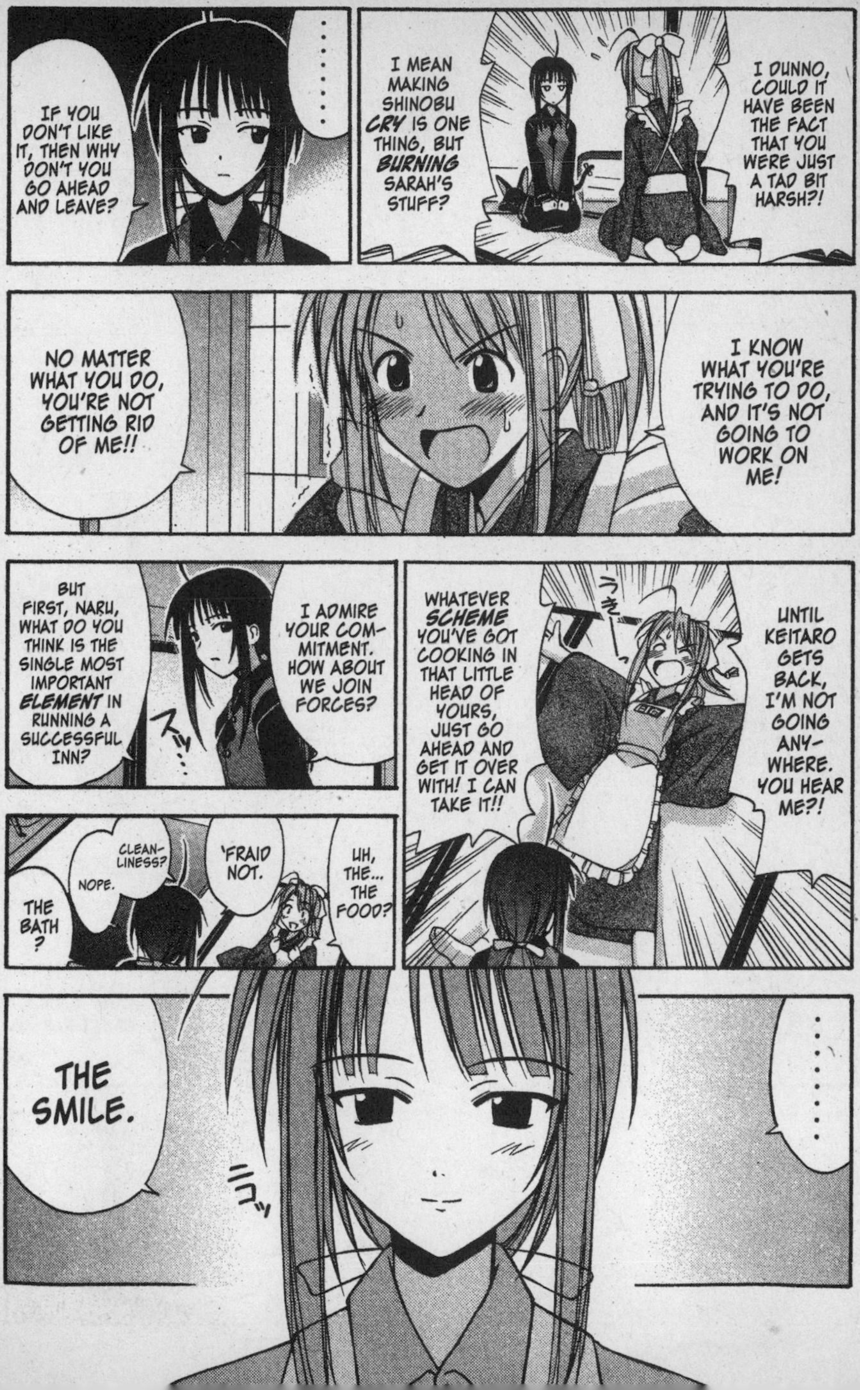
I DUNNO, COULD IT HAVE BEEN THE FACT THAT YOU WERE JUST A TAD BIT HARSH?!
I MEAN MAKING SHINOBU CRY IS ONE THING, BUT BURNING SARAH'S STUFF?
......
IF YOU DON'T LIKE IT, THEN WHY DON'T YOU GO AHEAD AND LEAVE?
I KNOW WHAT YOU'RE TRYING TO DO, AND IT'S NOT GOING TO WORK ON ME!
NO MATTER WHAT YOU DO, YOU'RE NOT GETTING RID OF ME!!
UNTIL KEITARO GETS BACK, I'M NOT GOING ANY-WHERE. YOU HEAR ME?!
WHATEVER SCHEME YOU'VE GOT COOKING IN THAT LITTLE HEAD OF YOURS, JUST GO AHEAD AND GET IT OVER WITH! I CAN TAKE IT!!
I ADMIRE YOUR COM-MITMENT. HOW ABOUT WE JOIN FORCES?
スッ
BUT FIRST, NARU, WHAT DO YOU THINK IS THE SINGLE MOST IMPORTANT ELEMENT IN RUNNING A SUCCESSFUL INN?
UH, THE... THE FOOD?
'FRAID NOT.
CLEAN-LINESS?
NOPE.
THE BATH?
....
THE SMILE.
ニコッ

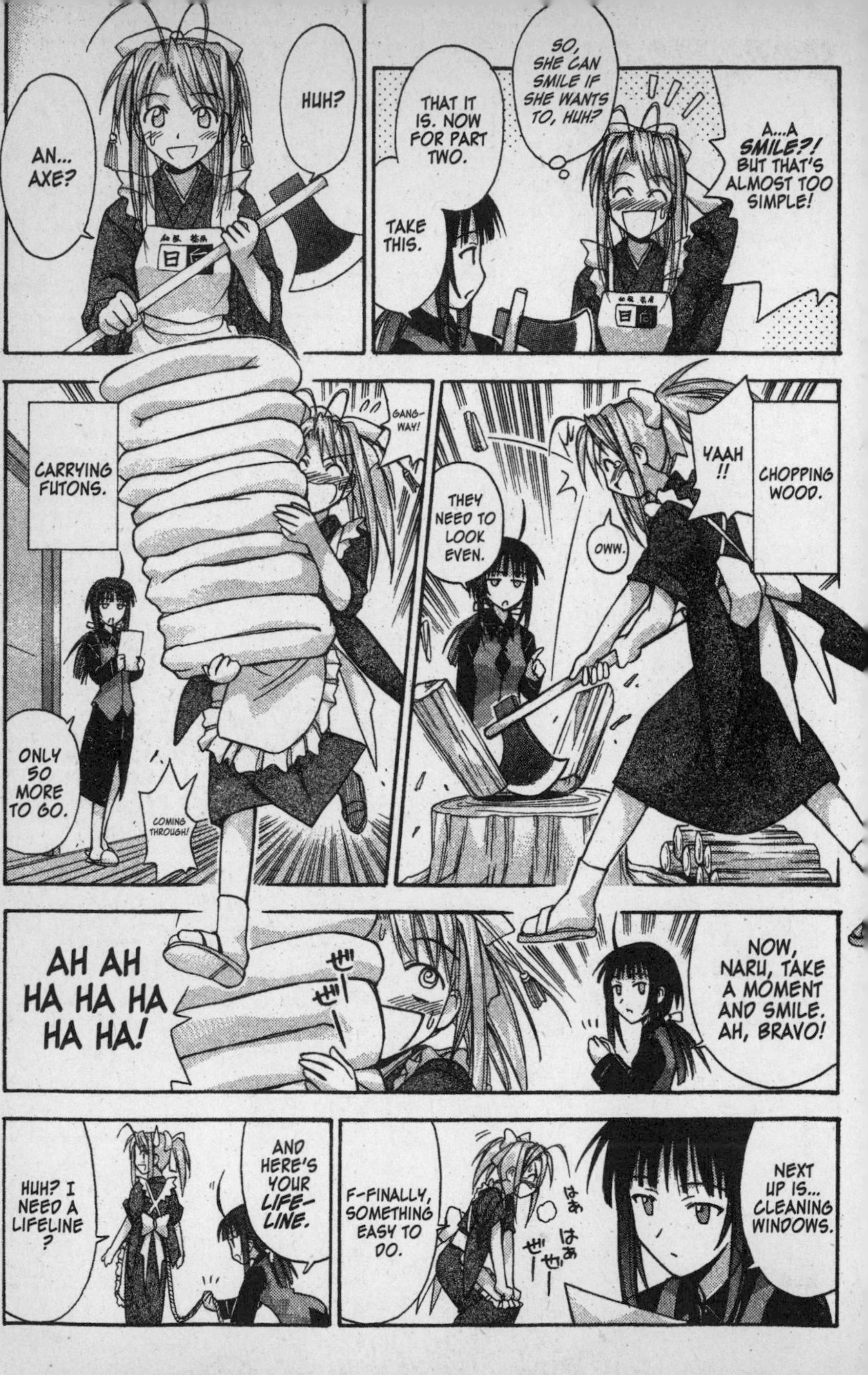
A...A SMILE?! BUT THAT'S ALMOST TOO SIMPLE!
SO, SHE CAN SMILE IF SHE WANTS TO, HUH?
THAT IT IS. NOW FOR PART TWO.
TAKE THIS.
HUH?
AN... AXE?
CHOPPING WOOD.
YAAH !!
OWW.
THEY NEED TO LOOK EVEN.
GANG-WAY!
CARRYING FUTONS.
ONLY 50 MORE TO GO.
COMING THROUGH!
NOW, NARU, TAKE A MOMENT AND SMILE. AH, BRAVO!
ゼー ゼー
AH AH HA HA HA HA HA!
NEXT UP IS... CLEANING WINDOWS.
はあ はあ ゼー ゼー
F-FINALLY, SOMETHING EASY TO DO.
AND HERE'S YOUR LIFE-LINE.
HUH? I NEED A LIFELINE?

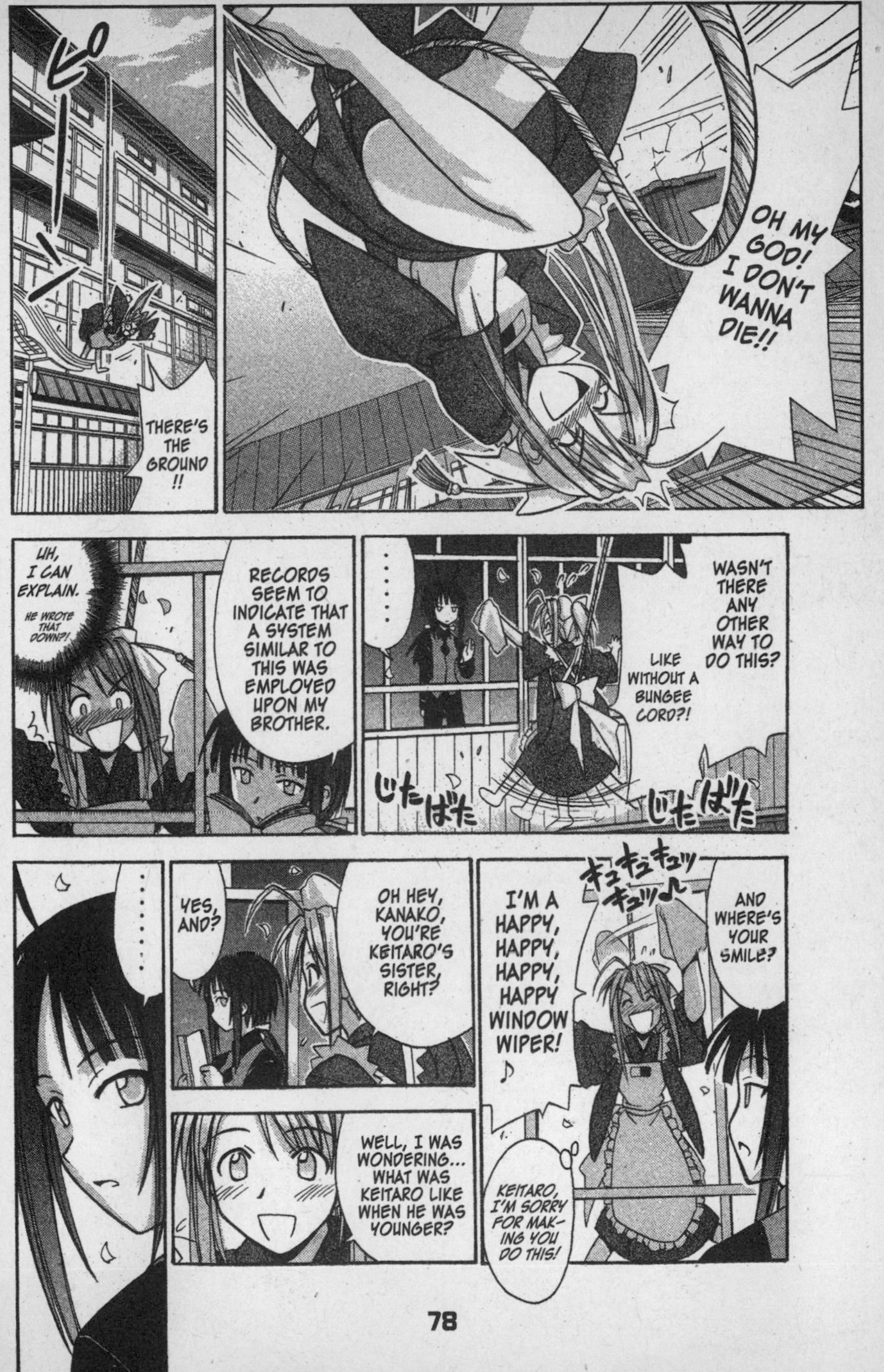
OH MY GOD! I DON'T WANNA DIE!!
ピー
THERE'S THE GROUND !!
WASN'T THERE ANY OTHER WAY TO DO THIS?
LIKE WITHOUT A BUNGEE CORD?!
......
じたばた
じたばた
RECORDS SEEM TO INDICATE THAT A SYSTEM SIMILAR TO THIS WAS EMPLOYED UPON MY BROTHER.
UH, I CAN EXPLAIN.
HE WROTE THAT DOWN?!
AND WHERE'S YOUR SMILE?
キュキュキュッ キュッ♪
I'M A HAPPY, HAPPY, HAPPY, HAPPY WINDOW WIPER! ♪
KEITARO, I'M SORRY FOR MAKING YOU DO THIS!
OH HEY, KANAKO, YOU'RE KEITARO'S SISTER, RIGHT?
YES, AND?
WELL, I WAS WONDERING... WHAT WAS KEITARO LIKE WHEN HE WAS YOUNGER?
......

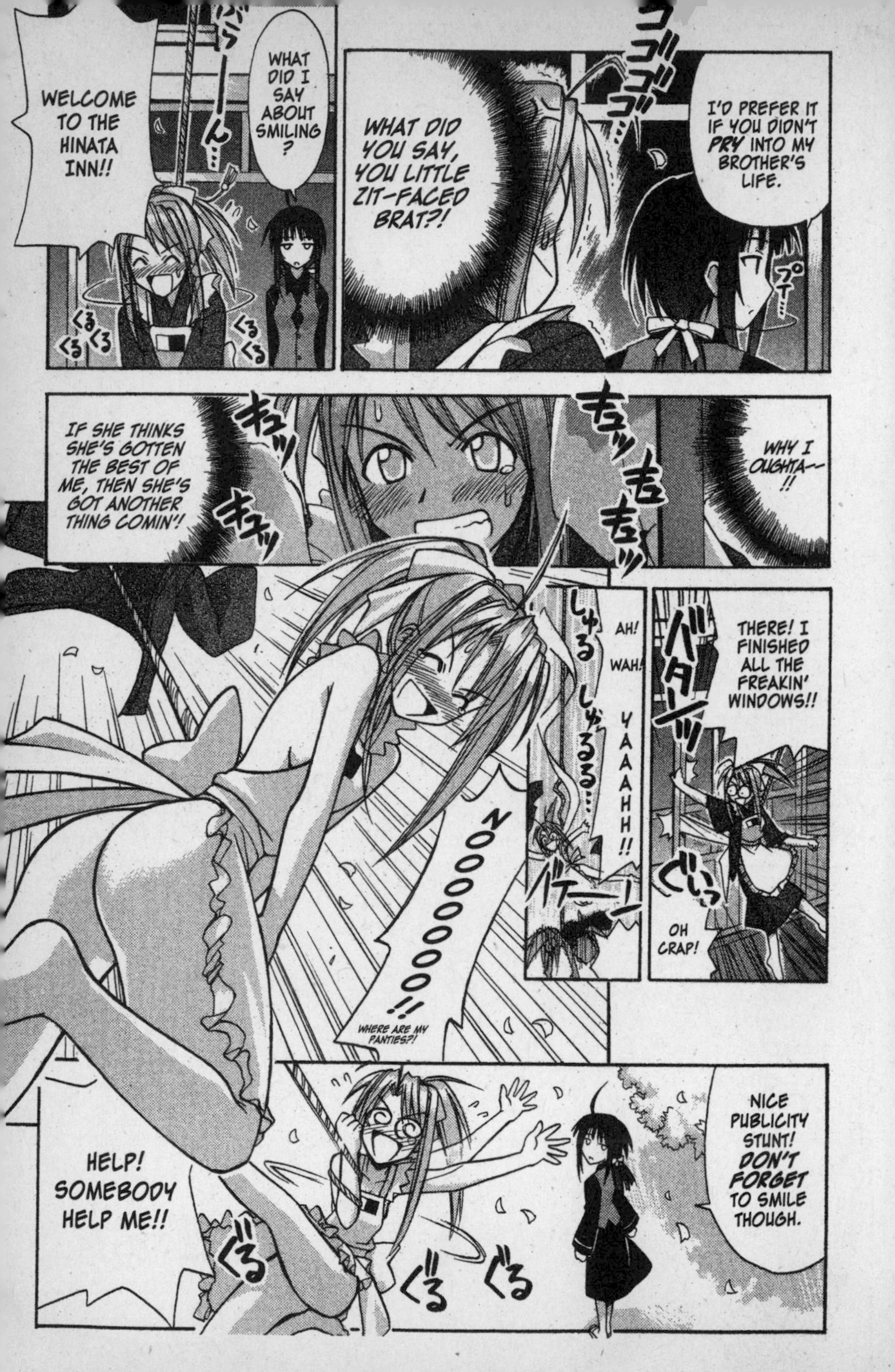
I'D PREFER IT IF YOU DIDN'T PRY INTO MY BROTHER'S LIFE.
WHAT DID YOU SAY, YOU LITTLE ZIT-FACED BRAT?!
WHAT DID I SAY ABOUT SMILING?
WELCOME TO THE HINATA INN!!
WHY I OUGHTA--!!
IF SHE THINKS SHE'S GOTTEN THE BEST OF ME, THEN SHE'S GOT ANOTHER THING COMIN'!
THERE! I FINISHED ALL THE FREAKIN' WINDOWS!!
OH CRAP!
AH!
WAH!
YAAAAHH!!
NOOOOOOOOOO!!
WHERE ARE MY PANTIES?!
NICE PUBLICITY STUNT! DON'T FORGET TO SMILE THOUGH.
HELP! SOMEBODY HELP ME!!

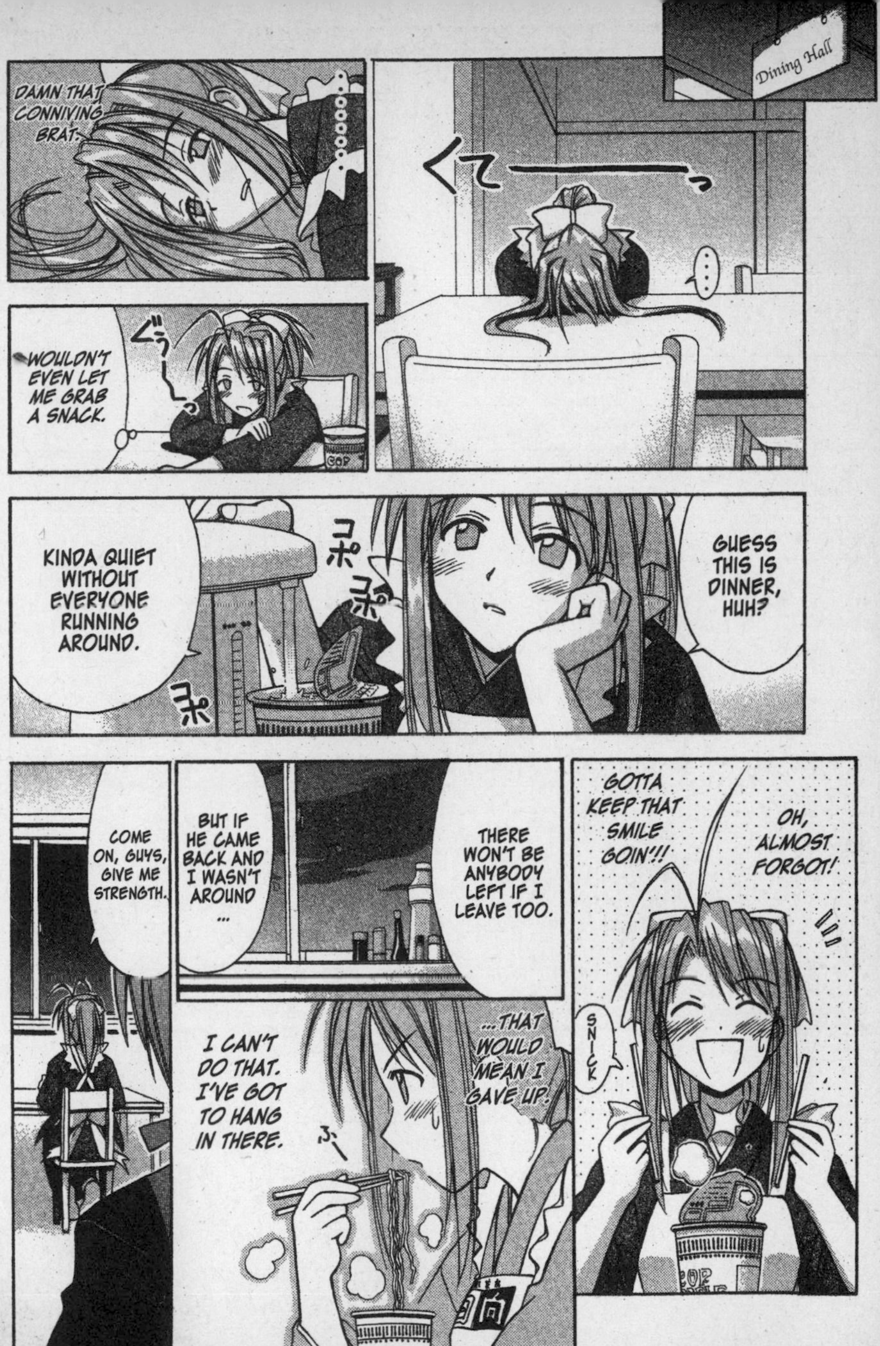

Dining Hall
くてーーっ
...
DAMN THAT CONNIVING BRAT.
ぐぅ〜っ
WOULDN'T EVEN LET ME GRAB A SNACK.
GUESS THIS IS DINNER, HUH?
コポ
コポ
KINDA QUIET WITHOUT EVERYONE RUNNING AROUND.
コポ
OH, ALMOST FORGOT!
!!!
GOTTA KEEP THAT SMILE GOIN'!!
SNICK
THERE WON'T BE ANYBODY LEFT IF I LEAVE TOO.
BUT IF HE CAME BACK AND I WASN'T AROUND ...
...THAT WOULD MEAN I GAVE UP.
I CAN'T DO THAT. I'VE GOT TO HANG IN THERE.
ふーっ
COME ON, GUYS, GIVE ME STRENGTH.

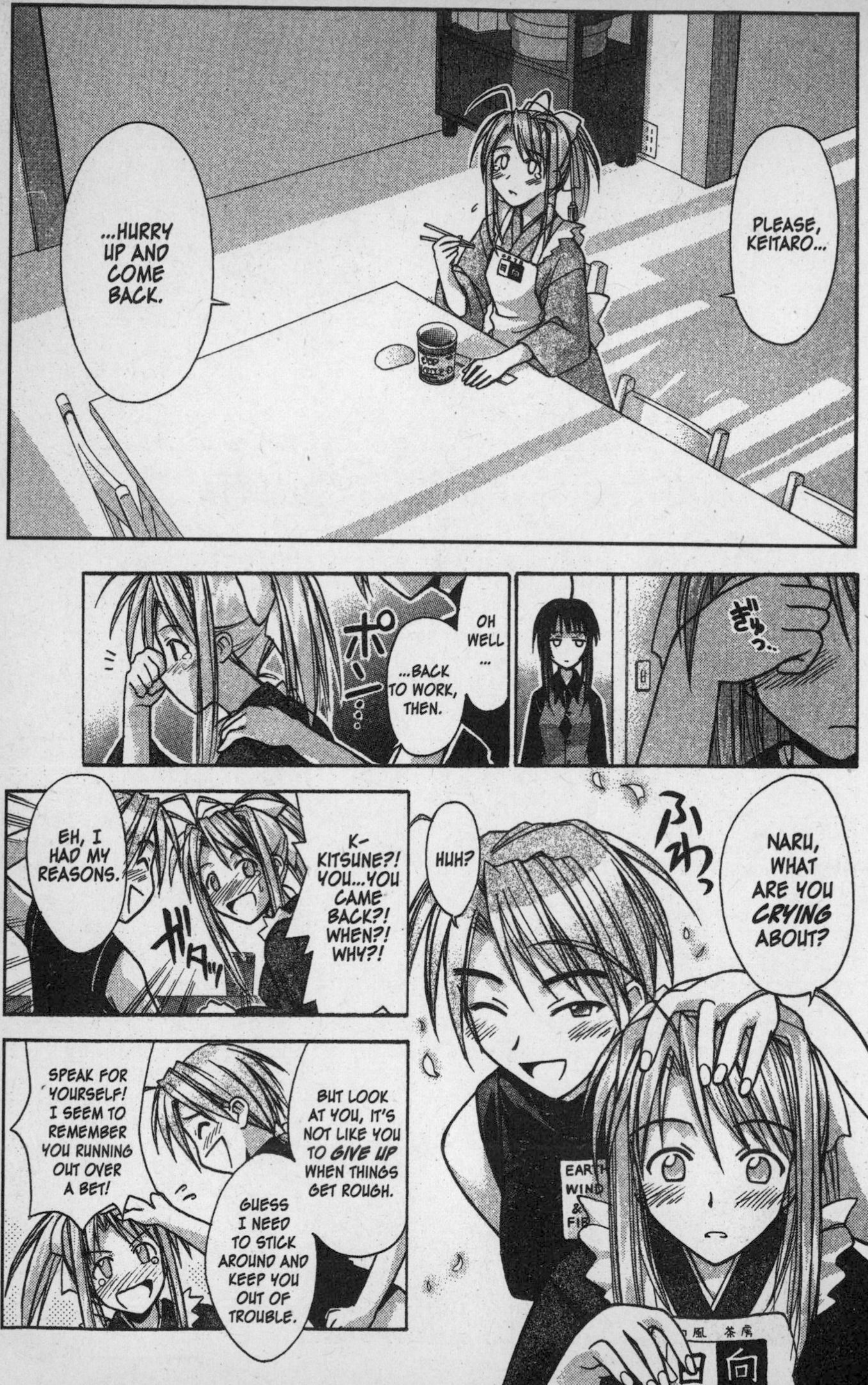
PLEASE, KEITARO...
...HURRY UP AND COME BACK.
ぎゅっ...
OH WELL ...
...BACK TO WORK, THEN.
ふわっ
NARU, WHAT ARE YOU *CRYING* ABOUT?
HUH?
K-KITSUNE?! YOU...YOU CAME BACK?! WHEN?! WHY?!
ガバッ
EH, I HAD MY REASONS.
BUT LOOK AT YOU, IT'S NOT LIKE YOU TO *GIVE UP* WHEN THINGS GET ROUGH.
SPEAK FOR YOURSELF! I SEEM TO REMEMBER YOU RUNNING OUT OVER A BET!
GUESS I NEED TO STICK AROUND AND KEEP YOU OUT OF TROUBLE.

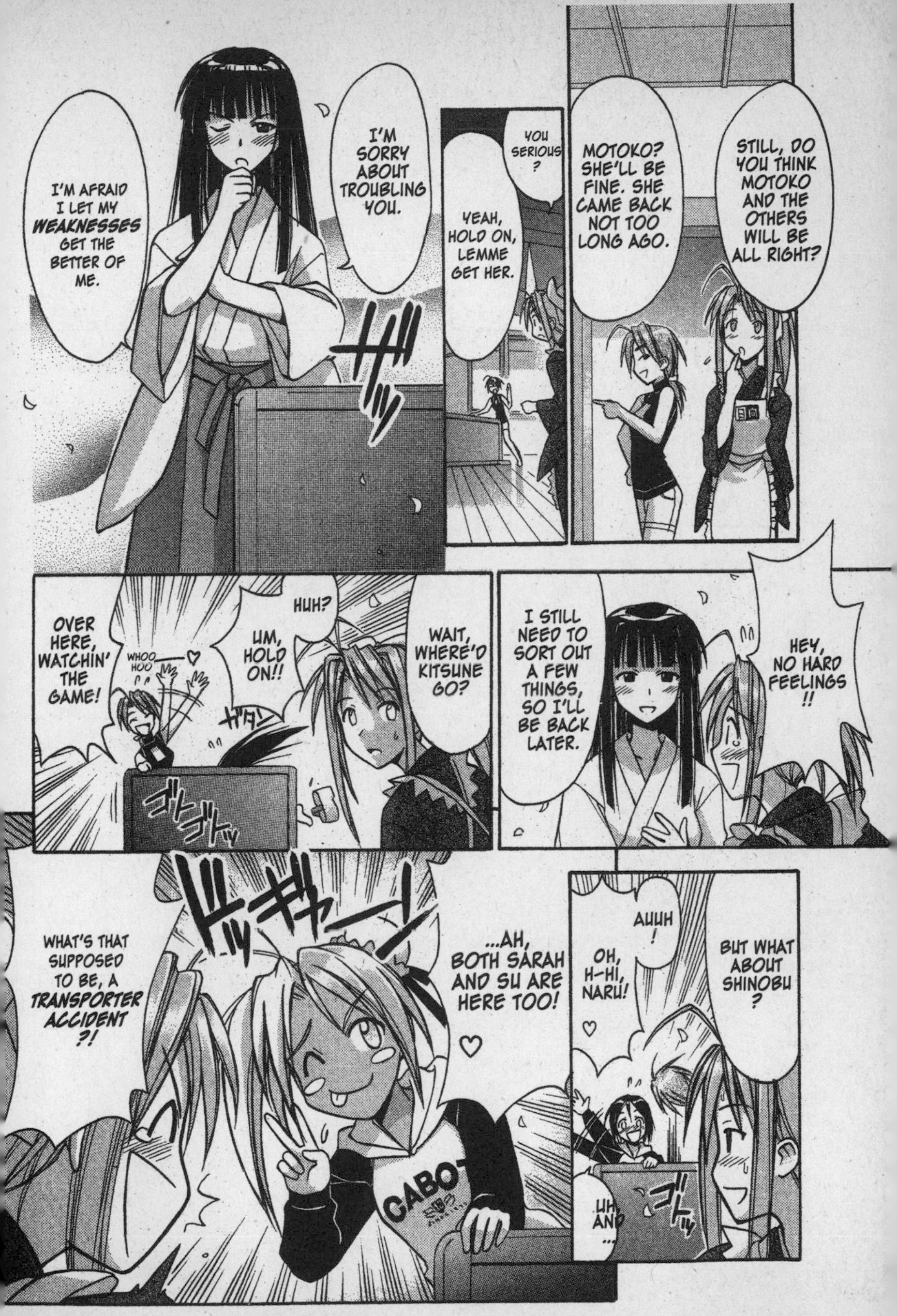
STILL, DO YOU THINK MOTOKO AND THE OTHERS WILL BE ALL RIGHT?
MOTOKO? SHE'LL BE FINE. SHE CAME BACK NOT TOO LONG AGO.
YOU SERIOUS?
YEAH, HOLD ON, LEMME GET HER.
I'M SORRY ABOUT TROUBLING YOU.
I'M AFRAID I LET MY WEAKNESSES GET THE BETTER OF ME.
HEY, NO HARD FEELINGS!!
I STILL NEED TO SORT OUT A FEW THINGS, SO I'LL BE BACK LATER.
WAIT, WHERE'D KITSUNE GO?
HUH?
UM, HOLD ON!!
WHOO HOO
OVER HERE, WATCHIN' THE GAME!
BUT WHAT ABOUT SHINOBU?
AUUH!
OH, H-HI, NARU!
UH, AND ...
...AH, BOTH SARAH AND SU ARE HERE TOO!
CABOT
WHAT'S THAT SUPPOSED TO BE, A TRANSPORTER ACCIDENT?!

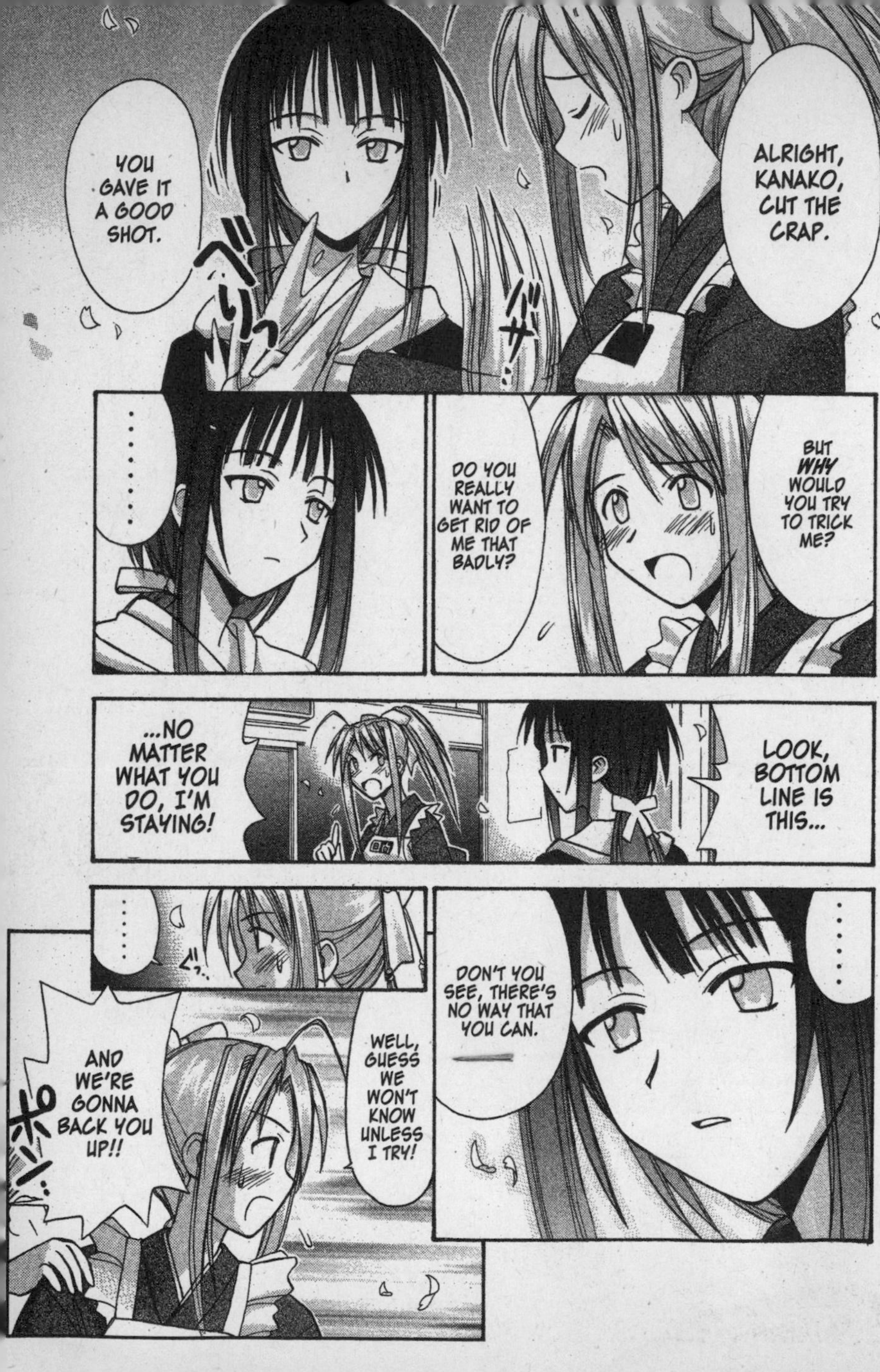

ALRIGHT, KANAKO, CUT THE CRAP.
YOU GAVE IT A GOOD SHOT.
BUT *WHY* WOULD YOU TRY TO TRICK ME?
DO YOU REALLY WANT TO GET RID OF ME THAT BADLY?
......
LOOK, BOTTOM LINE IS THIS...
...NO MATTER WHAT YOU DO, I'M STAYING!
......
DON'T YOU SEE, THERE'S NO WAY THAT YOU CAN.
......
WELL, GUESS WE WON'T KNOW UNLESS I TRY!
AND WE'RE GONNA BACK YOU UP!!

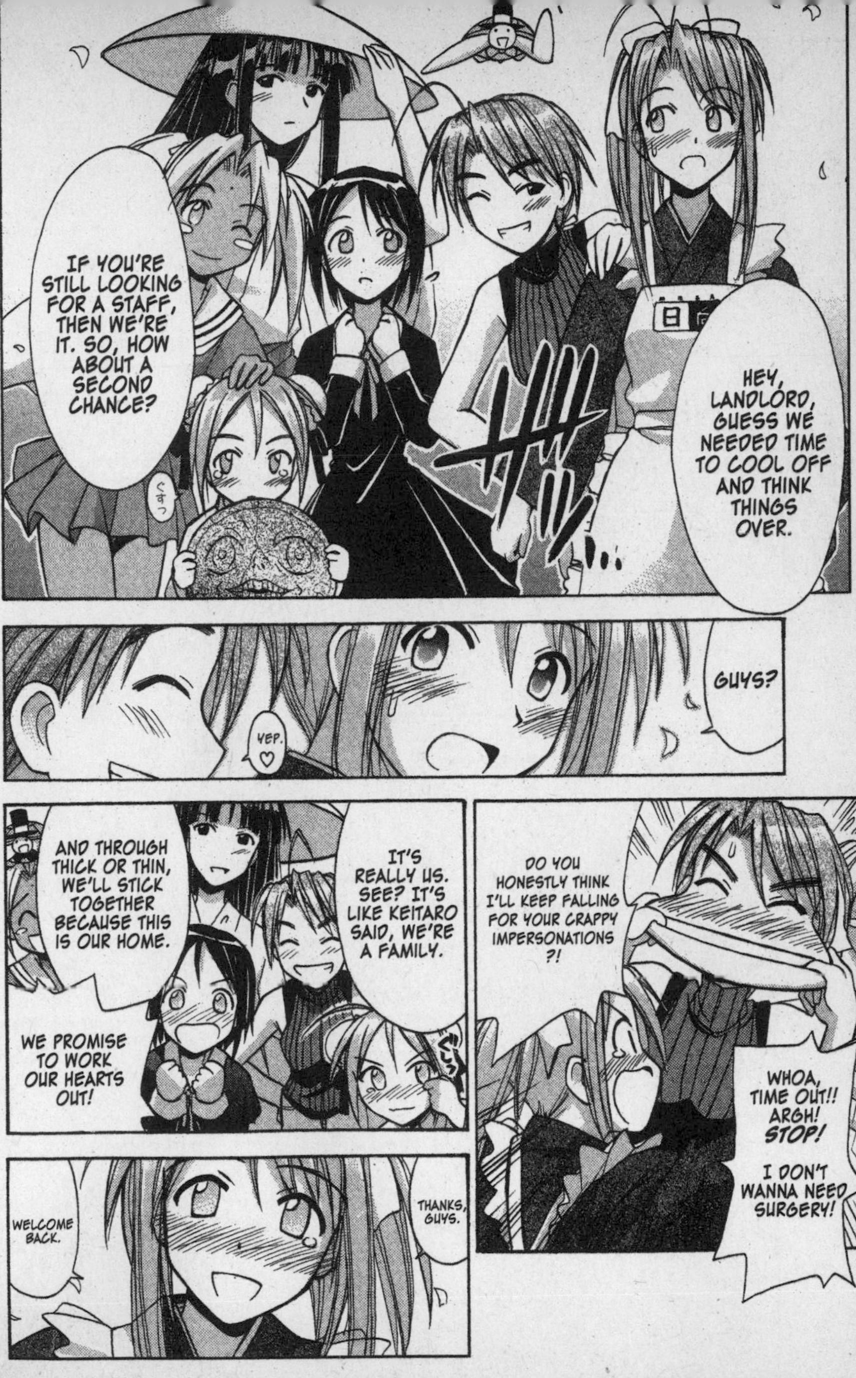
HEY, LANDLORD, GUESS WE NEEDED TIME TO COOL OFF AND THINK THINGS OVER.
IF YOU'RE STILL LOOKING FOR A STAFF, THEN WE'RE IT. SO, HOW ABOUT A SECOND CHANCE?
GUYS?
YEP. ♡
DO YOU HONESTLY THINK I'LL KEEP FALLING FOR YOUR CRAPPY IMPERSONATIONS ?!
WHOA, TIME OUT!! ARGH! STOP!
I DON'T WANNA NEED SURGERY!
IT'S REALLY US. SEE? IT'S LIKE KEITARO SAID, WE'RE A FAMILY.
AND THROUGH THICK OR THIN, WE'LL STICK TOGETHER BECAUSE THIS IS OUR HOME.
WE PROMISE TO WORK OUR HEARTS OUT!
THANKS, GUYS.
WELCOME BACK.

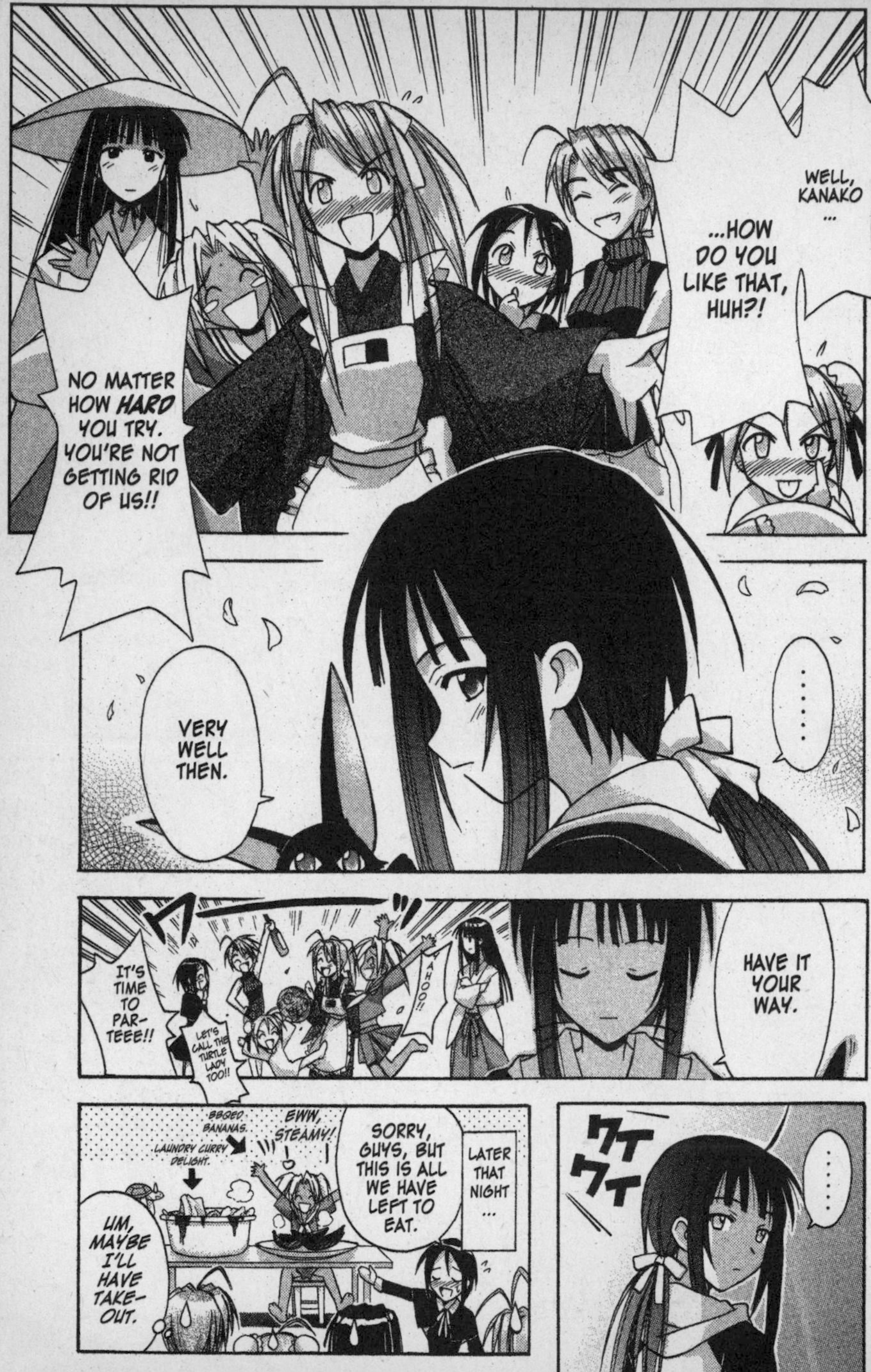
WELL, KANAKO ...
...HOW DO YOU LIKE THAT, HUH?!
NO MATTER HOW **HARD** YOU TRY. YOU'RE NOT GETTING RID OF US!!
......
VERY WELL THEN.
HAVE IT YOUR WAY.
YAHOOO!!
IT'S TIME TO PAR-TEEE!!
LET'S CALL THE TURTLE LADY TOO!!
ワイワイ
......
LATER THAT NIGHT ...
SORRY, GUYS, BUT THIS IS ALL WE HAVE LEFT TO EAT.
EWW, STEAMY!
BBQED BANANAS.
LAUNDRY CURRY DELIGHT.
UM, MAYBE I'LL HAVE TAKE-OUT.

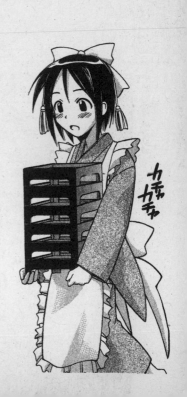

カチャ
カチャ

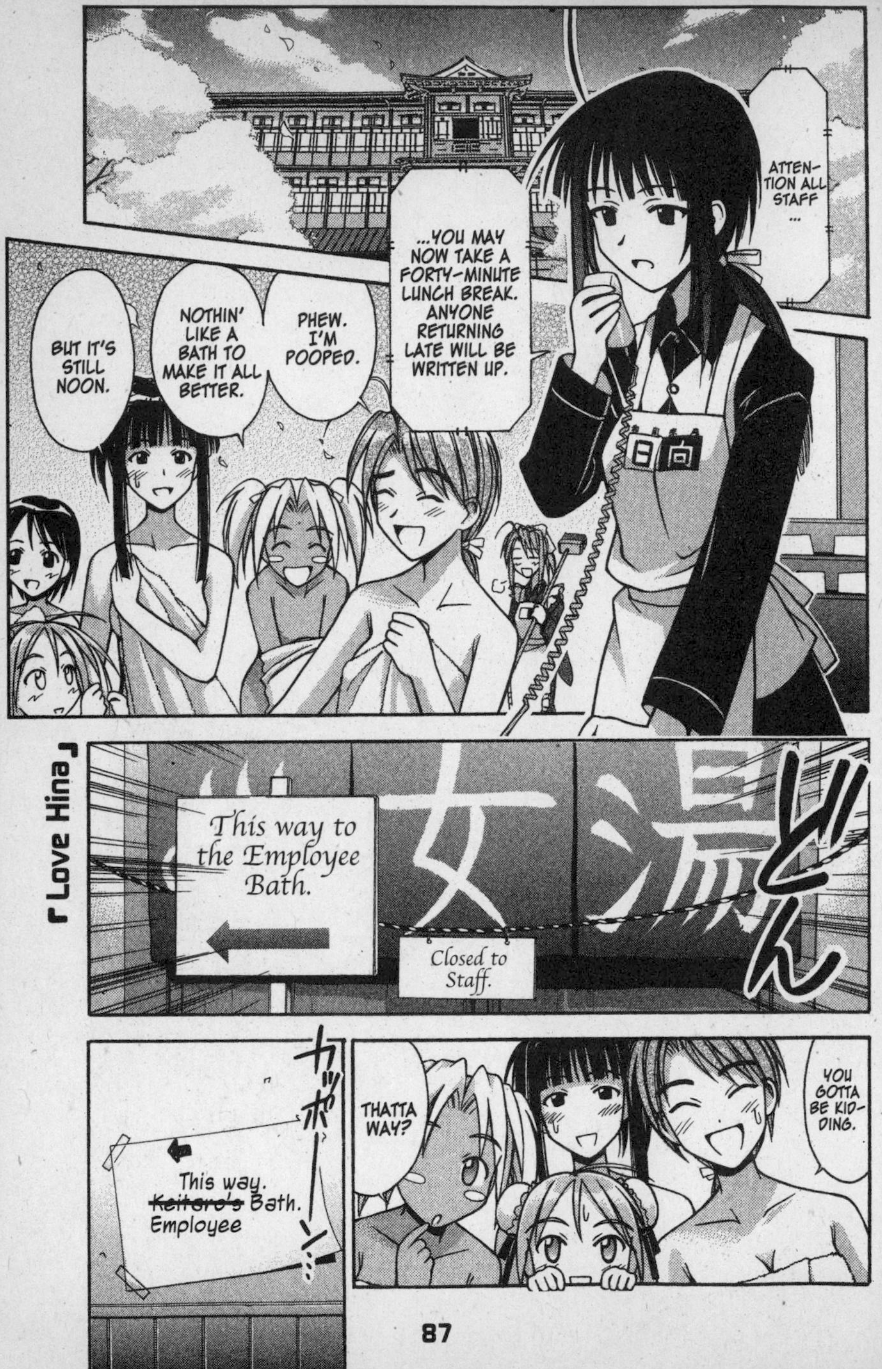
ATTEN-
TION ALL
STAFF
...
...YOU MAY NOW TAKE A FORTY-MINUTE LUNCH BREAK. ANYONE RETURNING LATE WILL BE WRITTEN UP.
日向
PHEW. I'M POOPED.
NOTHIN' LIKE A BATH TO MAKE IT ALL BETTER.
BUT IT'S STILL NOON.
どん
女湯
This way to the Employee Bath.
Closed to Staff.
YOU GOTTA BE KID-DING.
THATTA WAY?
カッポーン…
This way.
~~Keitaro's~~ Bath.
Employee

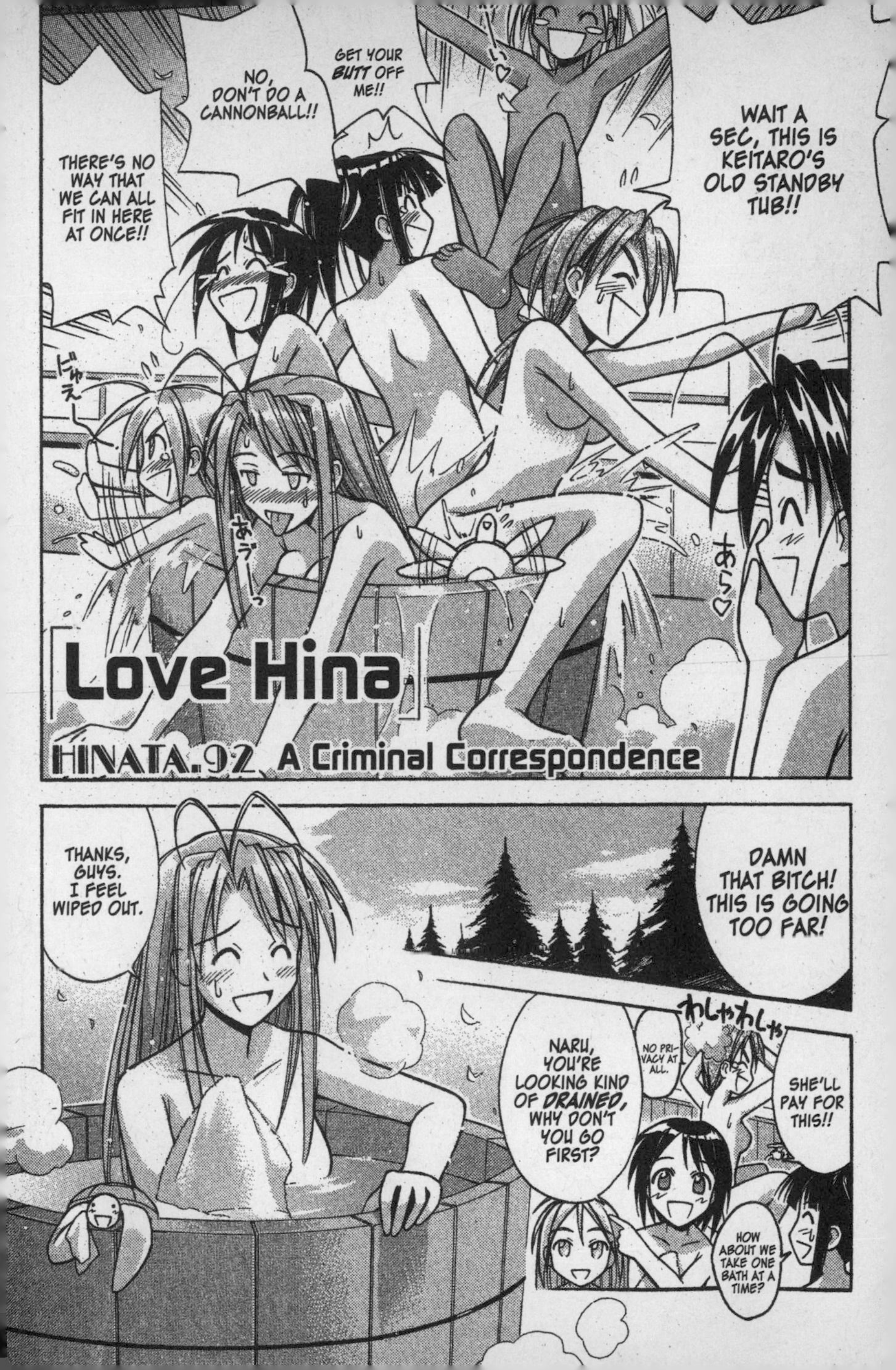

WAIT A SEC, THIS IS KEITARO'S OLD STANDBY TUB!!
GET YOUR BUTT OFF ME!!
NO, DON'T DO A CANNONBALL!!
THERE'S NO WAY THAT WE CAN ALL FIT IN HERE AT ONCE!!
あら♡
Love Hina
HINATA.92 A Criminal Correspondence
DAMN THAT BITCH! THIS IS GOING TOO FAR!
わしゃわしゃ
SHE'LL PAY FOR THIS!!
HOW ABOUT WE TAKE ONE BATH AT A TIME?
NO PRIVACY AT ALL.
NARU, YOU'RE LOOKING KIND OF DRAINED, WHY DON'T YOU GO FIRST?
THANKS, GUYS. I FEEL WIPED OUT.

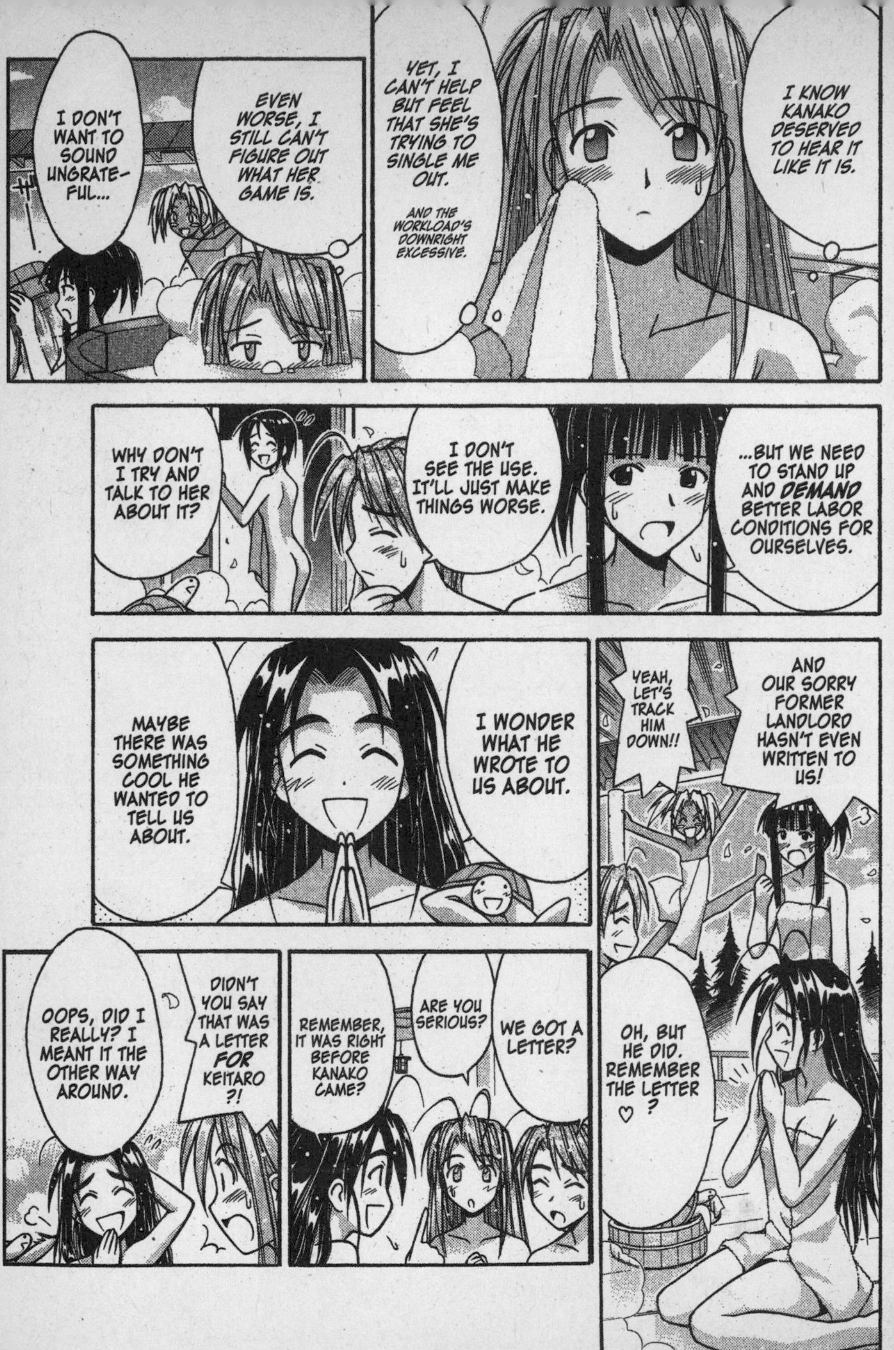
I KNOW KANAKO DESERVED TO HEAR IT LIKE IT IS.
YET, I CAN'T HELP BUT FEEL THAT SHE'S TRYING TO SINGLE ME OUT.
AND THE WORKLOAD'S DOWNRIGHT EXCESSIVE.
EVEN WORSE, I STILL CAN'T FIGURE OUT WHAT HER GAME IS.
I DON'T WANT TO SOUND UNGRATE-FUL...
...BUT WE NEED TO STAND UP AND DEMAND BETTER LABOR CONDITIONS FOR OURSELVES.
I DON'T SEE THE USE. IT'LL JUST MAKE THINGS WORSE.
WHY DON'T I TRY AND TALK TO HER ABOUT IT?
AND OUR SORRY FORMER LANDLORD HASN'T EVEN WRITTEN TO US!
YEAH, LET'S TRACK HIM DOWN!!
OH, BUT HE DID. REMEMBER THE LETTER ♡ ?
I WONDER WHAT HE WROTE TO US ABOUT.
MAYBE THERE WAS SOMETHING COOL HE WANTED TO TELL US ABOUT.
WE GOT A LETTER?
ARE YOU SERIOUS?
REMEMBER, IT WAS RIGHT BEFORE KANAKO CAME?
DIDN'T YOU SAY THAT WAS A LETTER FOR KEITARO ?!
OOPS, DID I REALLY? I MEANT IT THE OTHER WAY AROUND.

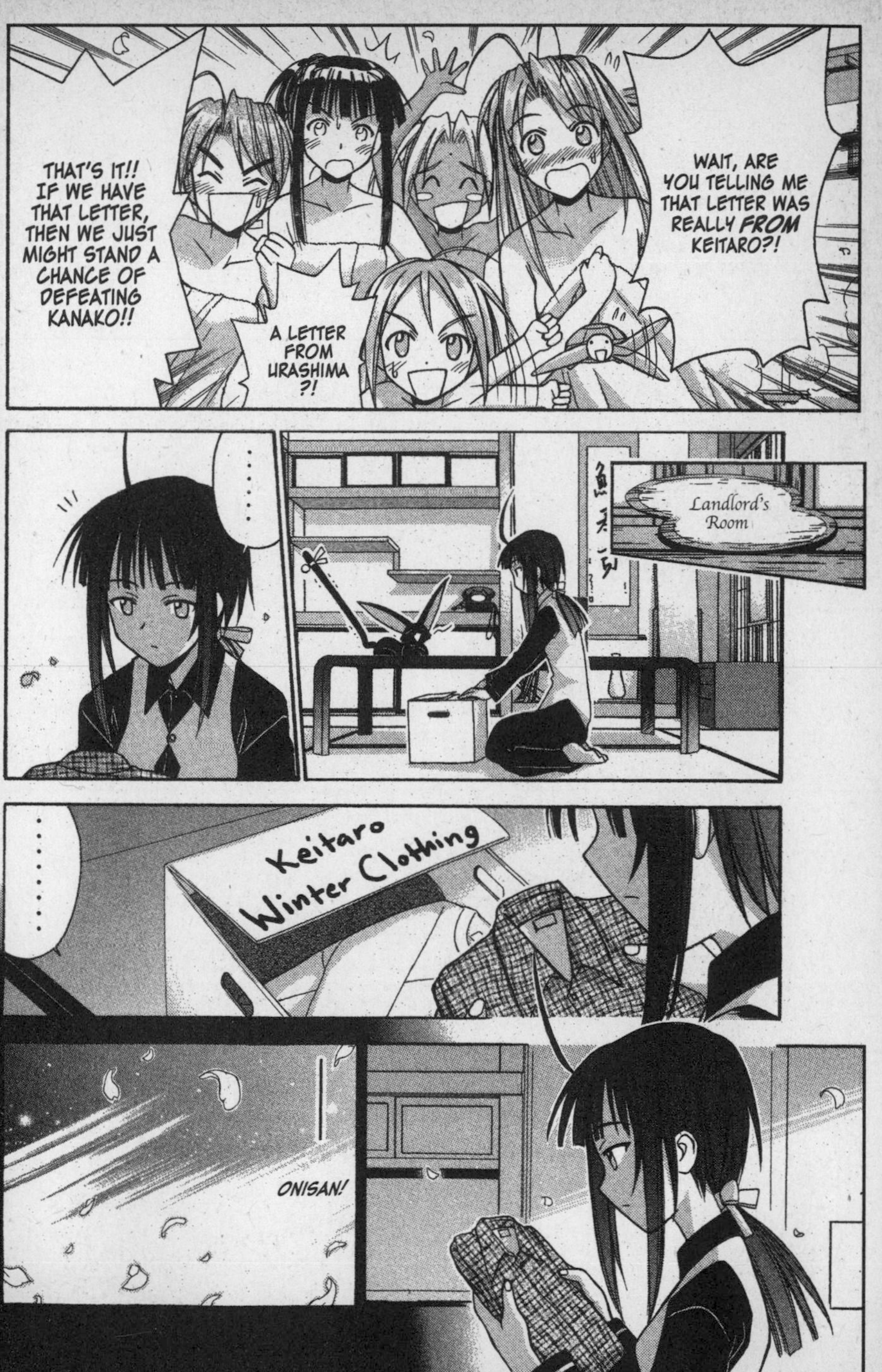
WAIT, ARE YOU TELLING ME THAT LETTER WAS REALLY *FROM* KEITARO?!
A LETTER FROM URASHIMA ?!
THAT'S IT!! IF WE HAVE THAT LETTER, THEN WE JUST MIGHT STAND A CHANCE OF DEFEATING KANAKO!!
Landlord's Room
......
Keitaro Winter Clothing
......
ONISAN!

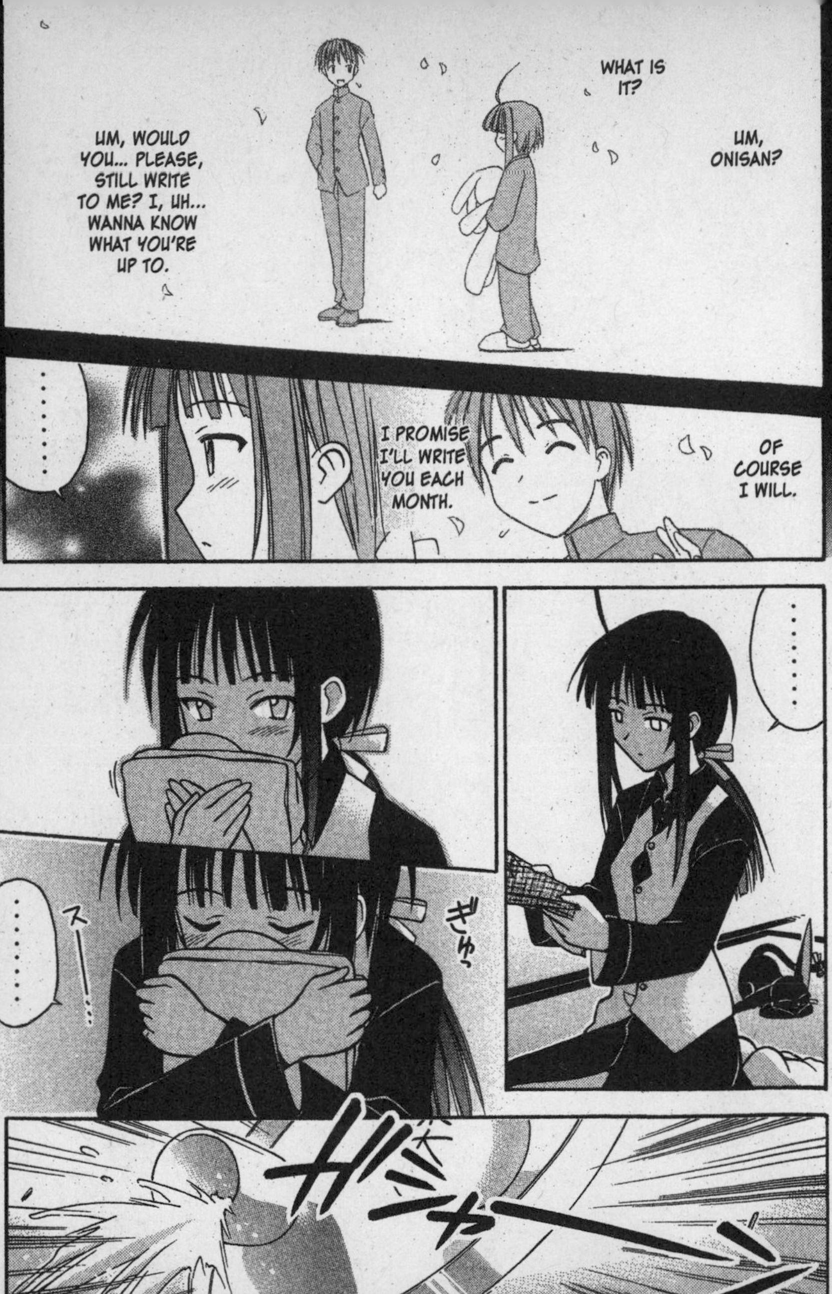
UM, ONISAN?
WHAT IS IT?
UM, WOULD YOU... PLEASE, STILL WRITE TO ME? I, UH... WANNA KNOW WHAT YOU'RE UP TO.
OF COURSE I WILL.
I PROMISE I'LL WRITE YOU EACH MONTH.
......
......
ぎゅっ
......
スー……
ガシャーン

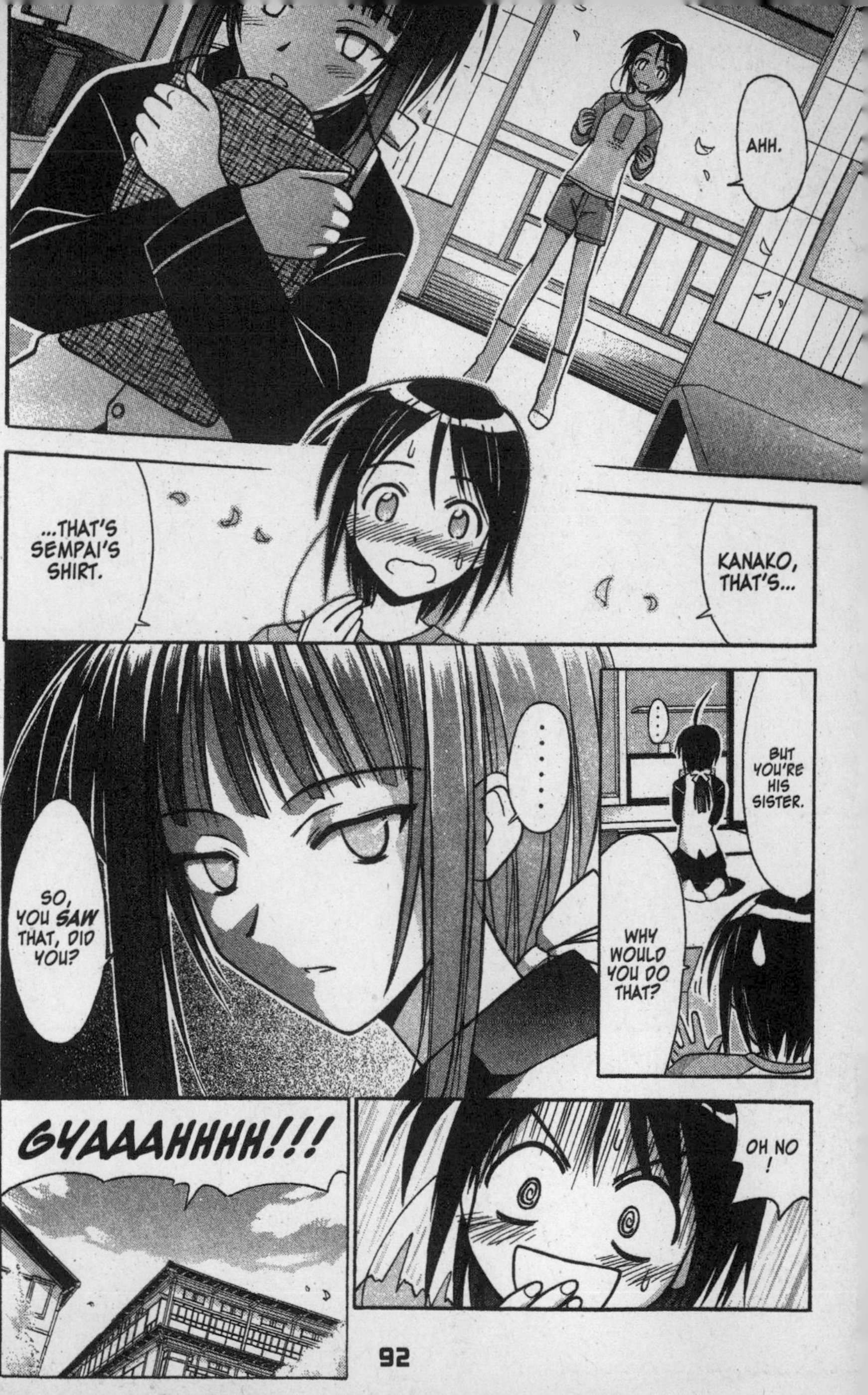
AHH.
KANAKO, THAT'S...
...THAT'S SEMPAI'S SHIRT.
BUT YOU'RE HIS SISTER.
WHY WOULD YOU DO THAT?
......
SO, YOU SAW THAT, DID YOU?
OH NO!
GYAAAHHHH!!!

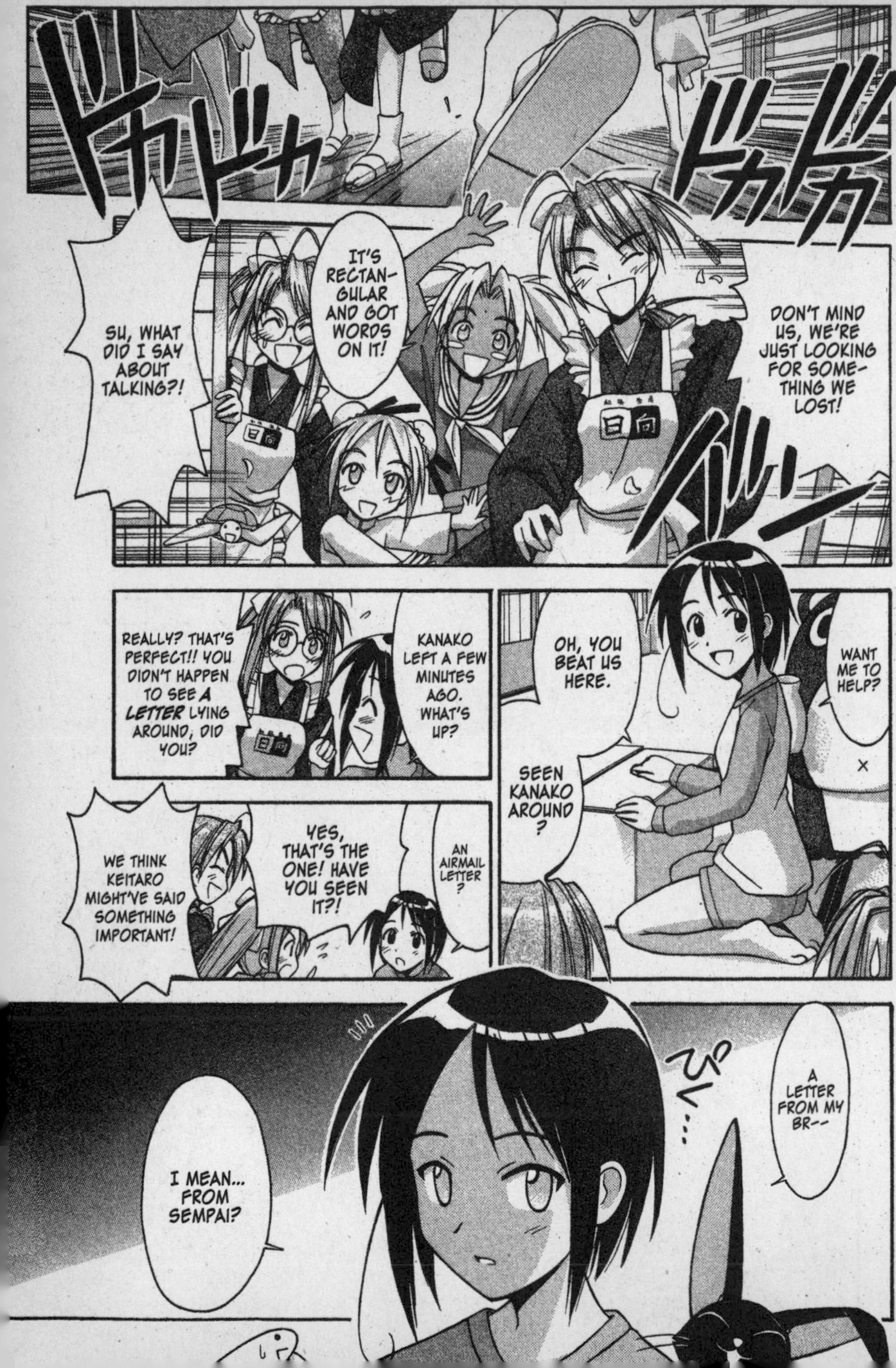
DON'T MIND US, WE'RE JUST LOOKING FOR SOMETHING WE LOST!
IT'S RECTANGULAR AND GOT WORDS ON IT!
SU, WHAT DID I SAY ABOUT TALKING?!
WANT ME TO HELP?
OH, YOU BEAT US HERE.
SEEN KANAKO AROUND?
KANAKO LEFT A FEW MINUTES AGO. WHAT'S UP?
REALLY? THAT'S PERFECT!! YOU DIDN'T HAPPEN TO SEE A LETTER LYING AROUND, DID YOU?
AN AIRMAIL LETTER?
YES, THAT'S THE ONE! HAVE YOU SEEN IT?!
WE THINK KEITARO MIGHT'VE SAID SOMETHING IMPORTANT!
A LETTER FROM MY BR--
I MEAN... FROM SEMPAI?

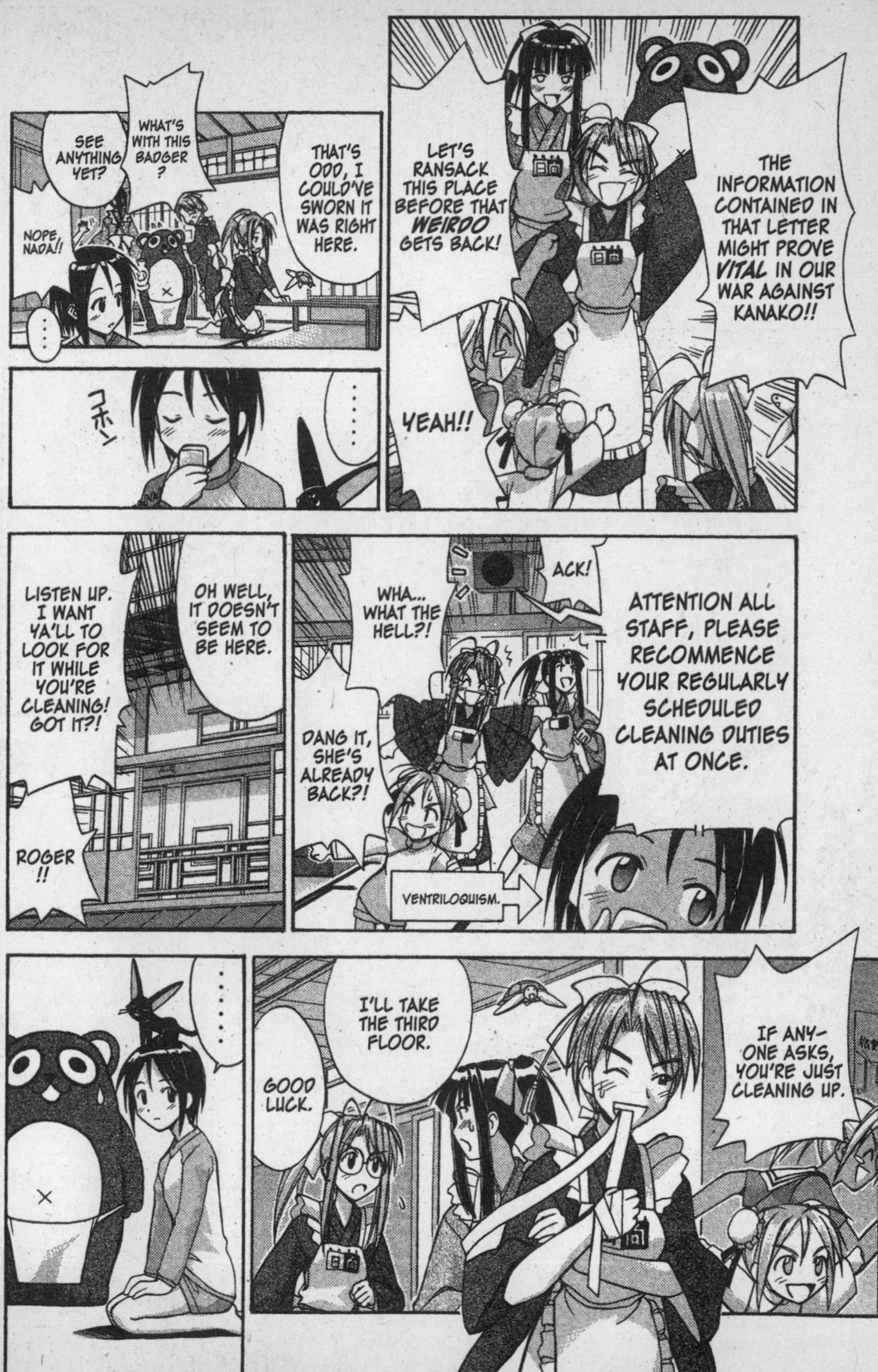
THE INFORMATION CONTAINED IN THAT LETTER MIGHT PROVE VITAL IN OUR WAR AGAINST KANAKO!!
LET'S RANSACK THIS PLACE BEFORE THAT WEIRDO GETS BACK!
YEAH!!
THAT'S ODD, I COULD'VE SWORN IT WAS RIGHT HERE.
WHAT'S WITH THIS BADGER ?
SEE ANYTHING YET?
NOPE, NADA!!
......
......
コホン
ATTENTION ALL STAFF, PLEASE RECOMMENCE YOUR REGULARLY SCHEDULED CLEANING DUTIES AT ONCE.
ACK!
WHA... WHAT THE HELL?!
DANG IT, SHE'S ALREADY BACK?!
VENTRILOQUISM.
OH WELL, IT DOESN'T SEEM TO BE HERE.
LISTEN UP. I WANT YA'LL TO LOOK FOR IT WHILE YOU'RE CLEANING! GOT IT?!
ROGER !!
IF ANY-ONE ASKS, YOU'RE JUST CLEANING UP.
I'LL TAKE THE THIRD FLOOR.
GOOD LUCK.
......

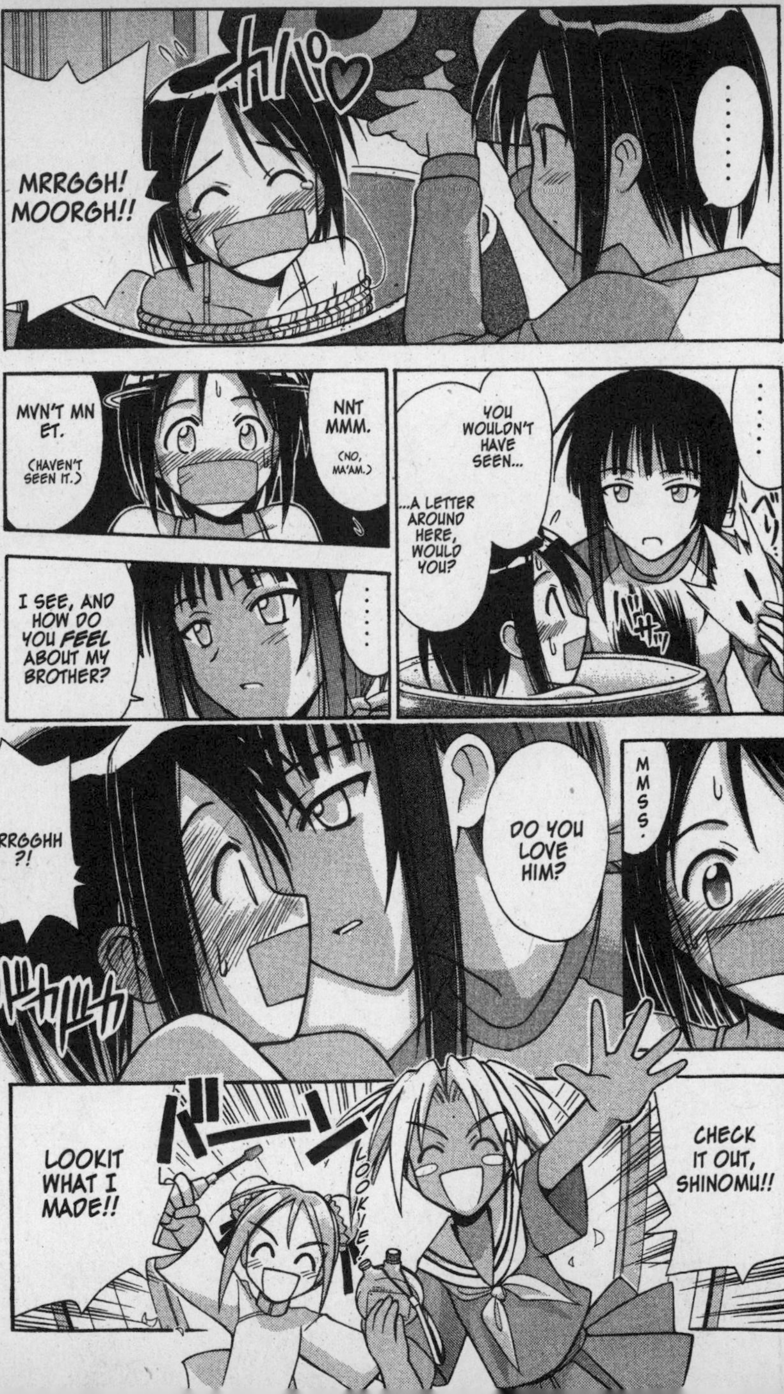
......
MRRGGH! MOORGH!!
......
YOU WOULDN'T HAVE SEEN...
...A LETTER AROUND HERE, WOULD YOU?
NNT MMM.
(NO, MA'AM.)
MVN'T MN ET.
(HAVEN'T SEEN IT.)
......
I SEE, AND HOW DO YOU FEEL ABOUT MY BROTHER?
MMSS.
DO YOU LOVE HIM?
MRRGGHH?!
CHECK IT OUT, SHINOMU!!
LOOKIE!
LOOKIT WHAT I MADE!!

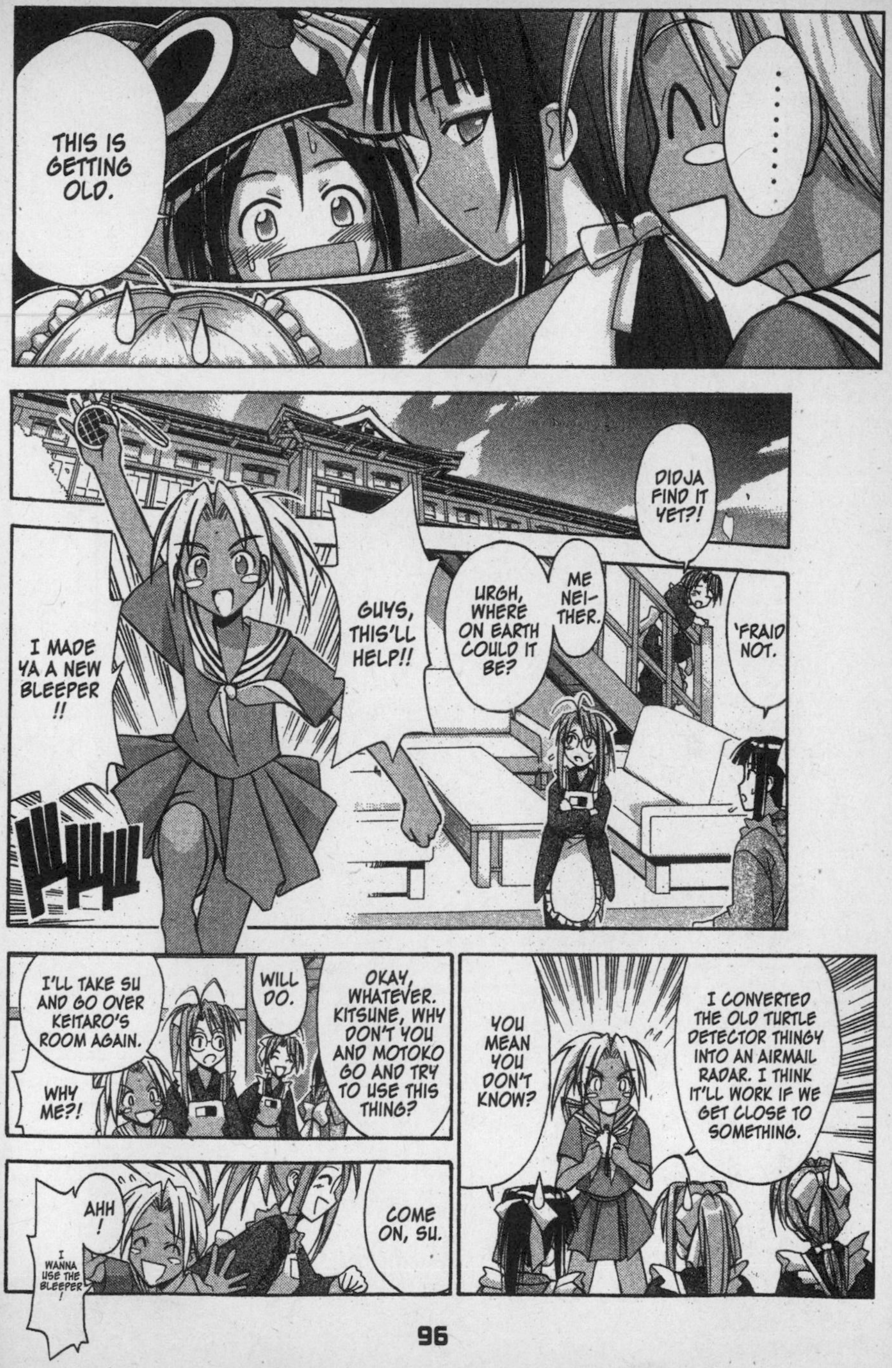
....
THIS IS GETTING OLD.
DIDJA FIND IT YET?!
'FRAID NOT.
ME NEI-THER.
URGH, WHERE ON EARTH COULD IT BE?
GUYS, THIS'LL HELP!!
I MADE YA A NEW BLEEPER!!
I CONVERTED THE OLD TURTLE DETECTOR THINGY INTO AN AIRMAIL RADAR. I THINK IT'LL WORK IF WE GET CLOSE TO SOMETHING.
YOU MEAN YOU DON'T KNOW?
OKAY, WHATEVER. KITSUNE, WHY DON'T YOU AND MOTOKO GO AND TRY TO USE THIS THING?
WILL DO.
I'LL TAKE SU AND GO OVER KEITARO'S ROOM AGAIN.
WHY ME?!
COME ON, SU.
AHH!
I WANNA USE THE BLEEPER!

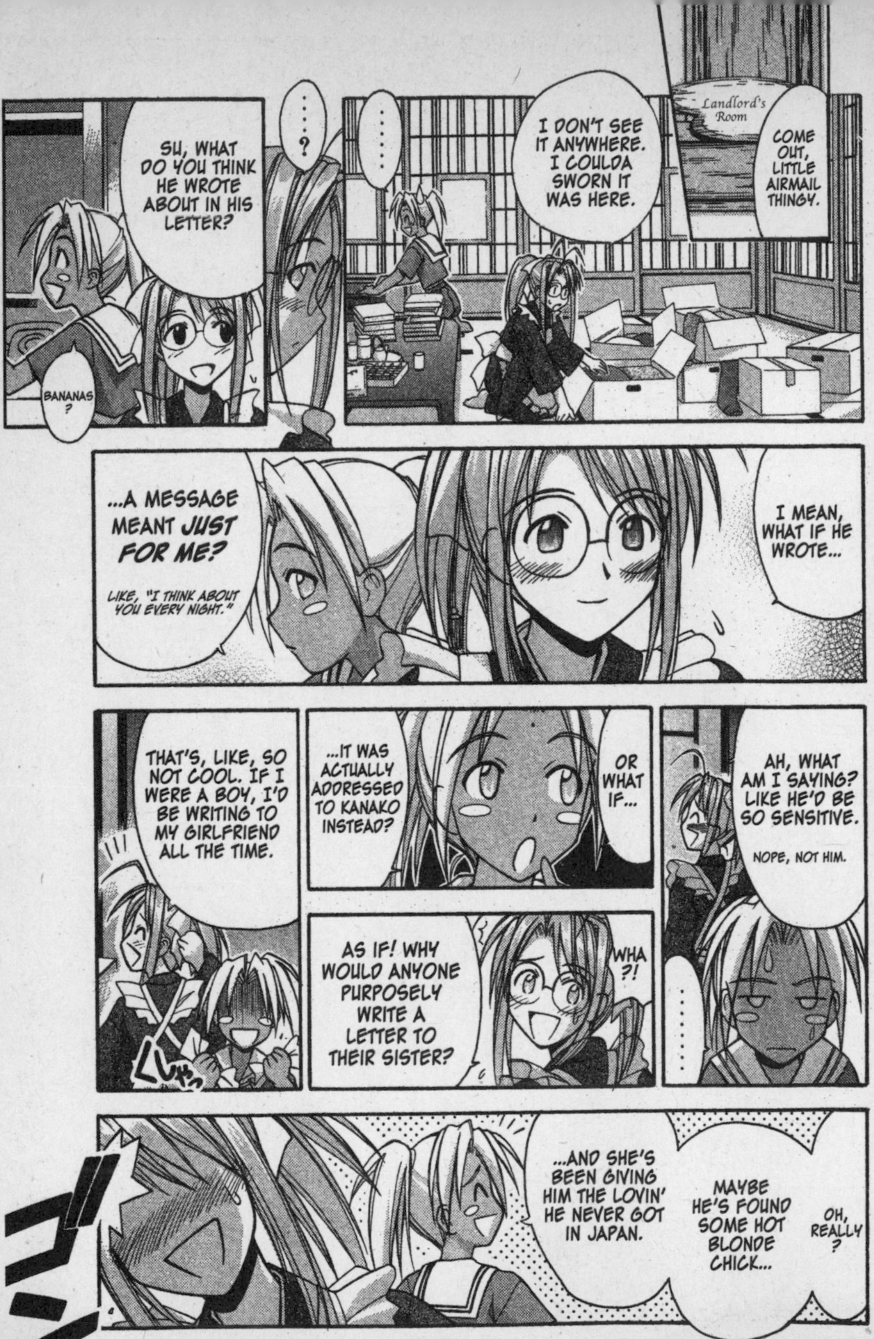
Landlord's Room
COME OUT, LITTLE AIRMAIL THINGY.
I DON'T SEE IT ANYWHERE. I COULDA SWORN IT WAS HERE.
......
...?
SU, WHAT DO YOU THINK HE WROTE ABOUT IN HIS LETTER?
BANANAS?
I MEAN, WHAT IF HE WROTE...
...A MESSAGE MEANT **JUST FOR ME?**
LIKE, "I THINK ABOUT YOU EVERY NIGHT."
AH, WHAT AM I SAYING? LIKE HE'D BE SO SENSITIVE.
NOPE, NOT HIM.
......
OR WHAT IF...
...IT WAS ACTUALLY ADDRESSED TO KANAKO INSTEAD?
WHA?!
AS IF! WHY WOULD ANYONE PURPOSELY WRITE A LETTER TO THEIR SISTER?
THAT'S, LIKE, SO NOT COOL. IF I WERE A BOY, I'D BE WRITING TO MY GIRLFRIEND ALL THE TIME.
OH, REALLY?
MAYBE HE'S FOUND SOME HOT BLONDE CHICK...
...AND SHE'S BEEN GIVING HIM THE LOVIN' HE NEVER GOT IN JAPAN.

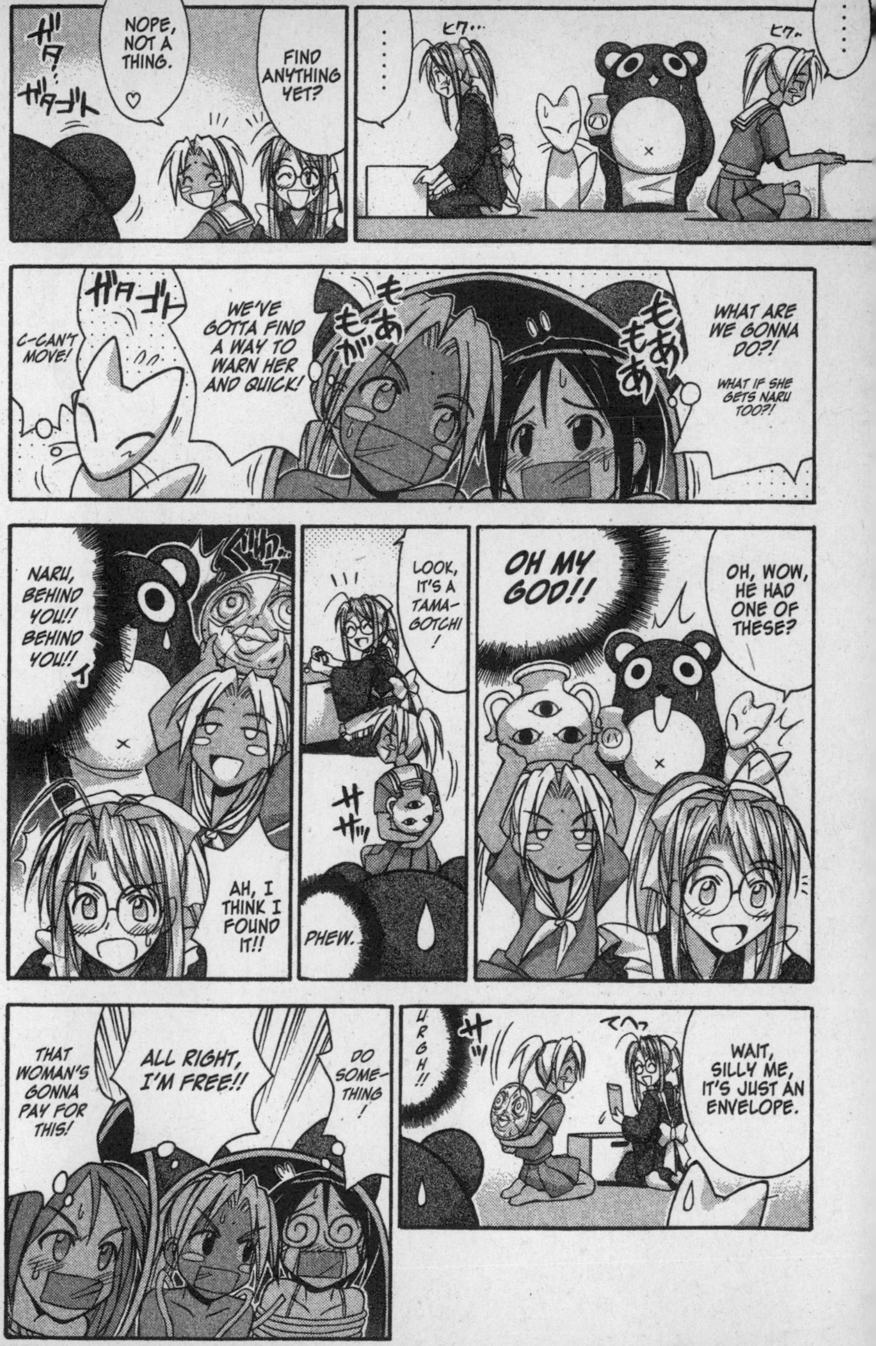
......
......
FIND ANYTHING YET?
NOPE, NOT A THING. ♡
ガタゴト
WHAT ARE WE GONNA DO?!
WHAT IF SHE GETS NARU TOO?!
WE'VE GOTTA FIND A WAY TO WARN HER AND QUICK!
C-CAN'T MOVE!
ガタゴト
OH, WOW, HE HAD ONE OF THESE?
OH MY GOD!!
LOOK, IT'S A TAMA-GOTCHI!
PHEW.
NARU, BEHIND YOU!! BEHIND YOU!!
AH, I THINK I FOUND IT!!
WAIT, SILLY ME, IT'S JUST AN ENVELOPE.
URGH!!
DO SOME-THING!
ALL RIGHT, I'M FREE!!
THAT WOMAN'S GONNA PAY FOR THIS!

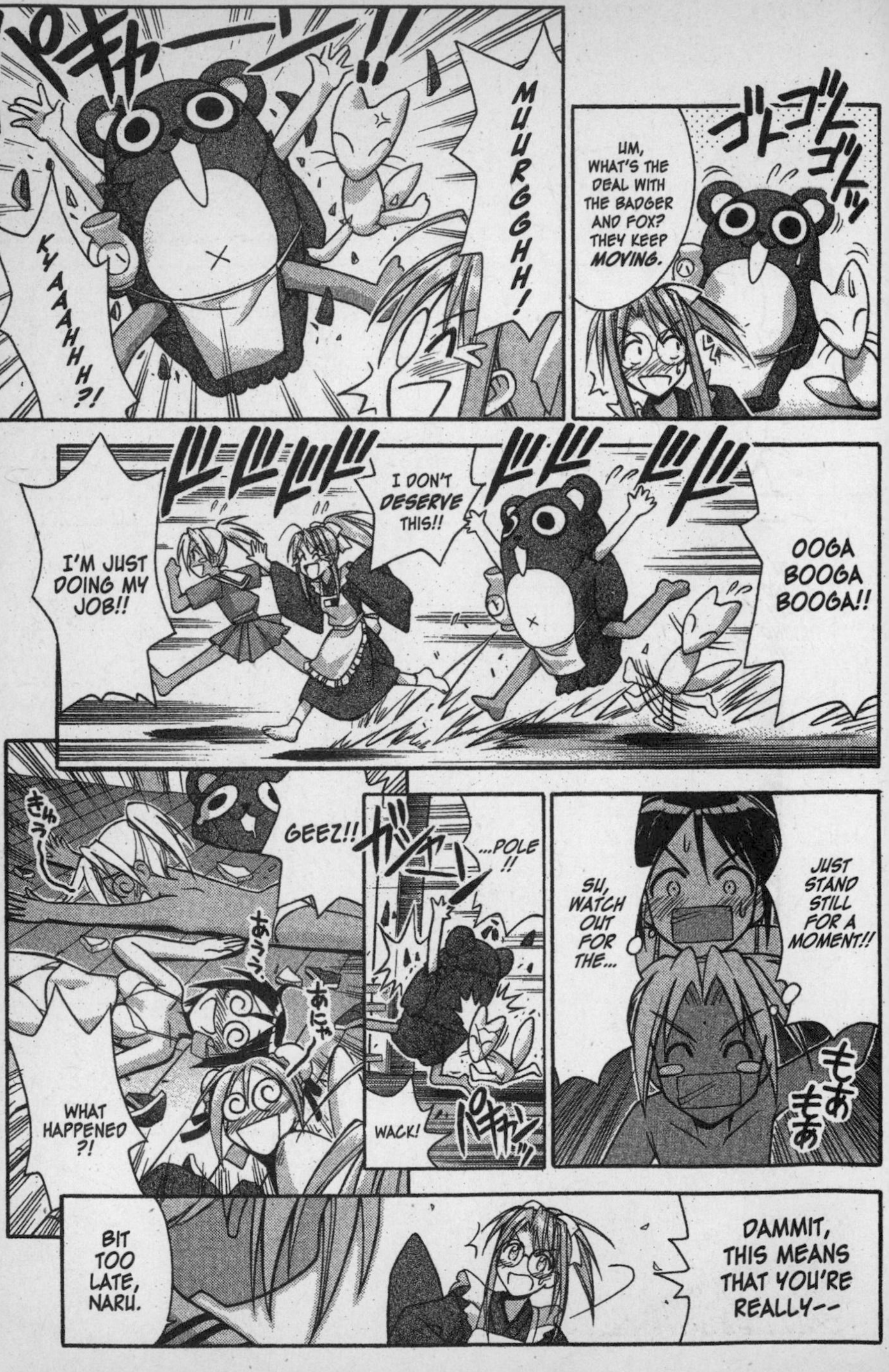
ゴトゴトゴトッ
UM, WHAT'S THE DEAL WITH THE BADGER AND FOX? THEY KEEP MOVING.
MUURGGHH!
パキャーン!!
KYAAAHHH?!
OOGA BOOGA BOOGA!!
I DON'T DESERVE THIS!!
I'M JUST DOING MY JOB!!
JUST STAND STILL FOR A MOMENT!!
SU, WATCH OUT FOR THE...
もあもあ
...POLE!!
WACK!
GEEZ!!
WHAT HAPPENED?!
DAMMIT, THIS MEANS THAT YOU'RE REALLY--
BIT TOO LATE, NARU.

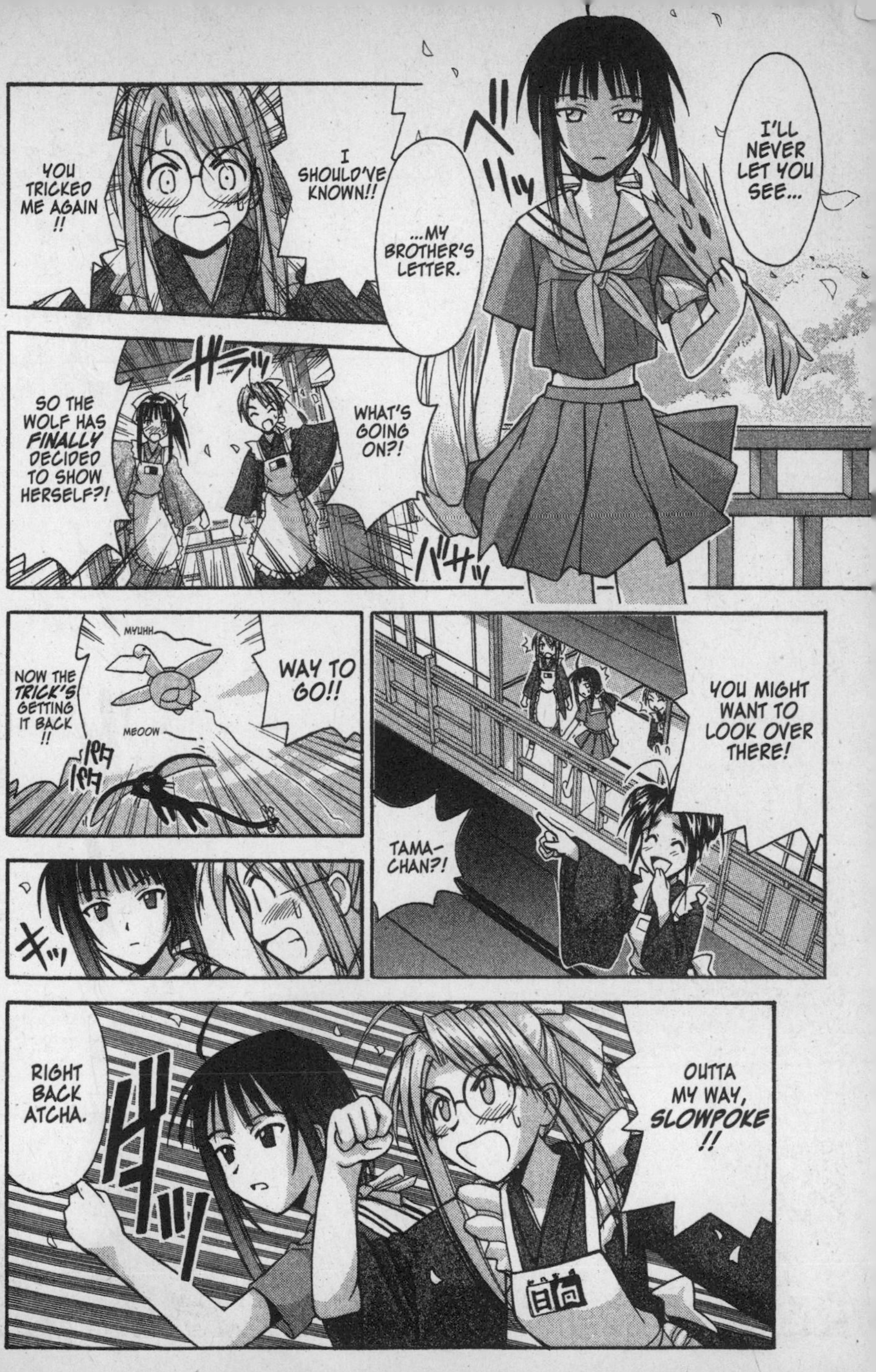
I'LL NEVER LET YOU SEE...
...MY BROTHER'S LETTER.
I SHOULD'VE KNOWN!!
YOU TRICKED ME AGAIN !!
WHAT'S GOING ON?!
SO THE WOLF HAS FINALLY DECIDED TO SHOW HERSELF?!
YOU MIGHT WANT TO LOOK OVER THERE!
TAMA-CHAN?!
WAY TO GO!!
MYUHH
NOW THE TRICK'S GETTING IT BACK !!
MEOOW
OUTTA MY WAY, SLOWPOKE !!
RIGHT BACK ATCHA.

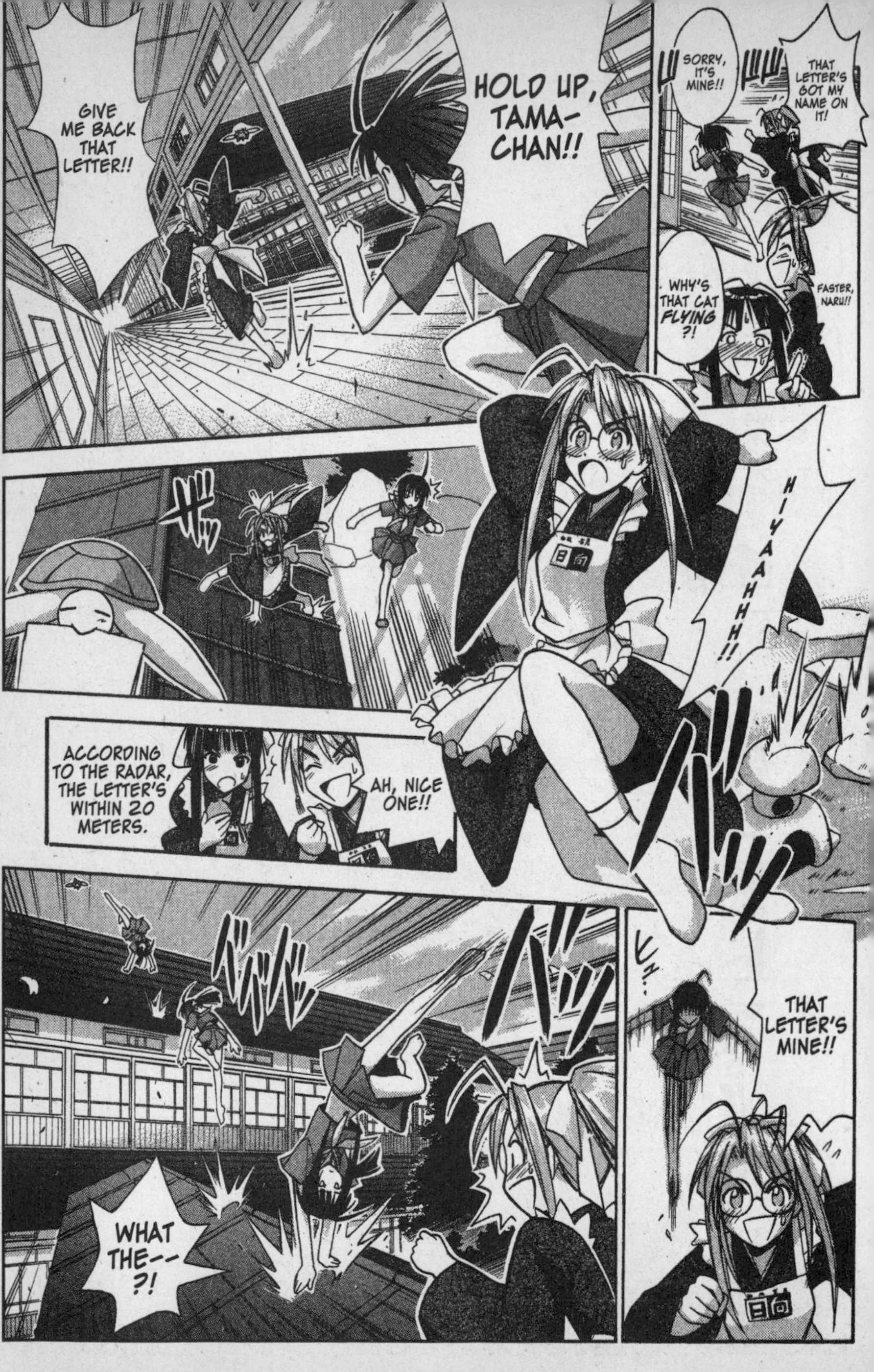
THAT LETTER'S GOT MY NAME ON IT!
SORRY, IT'S MINE!!
FASTER, NARU!!
WHY'S THAT CAT FLYING?!
HOLD UP, TAMA-CHAN!!
GIVE ME BACK THAT LETTER!!
HIYAAHHH!!
AH, NICE ONE!!
ACCORDING TO THE RADAR, THE LETTER'S WITHIN 20 METERS.
THAT LETTER'S MINE!!
WHAT THE--?!

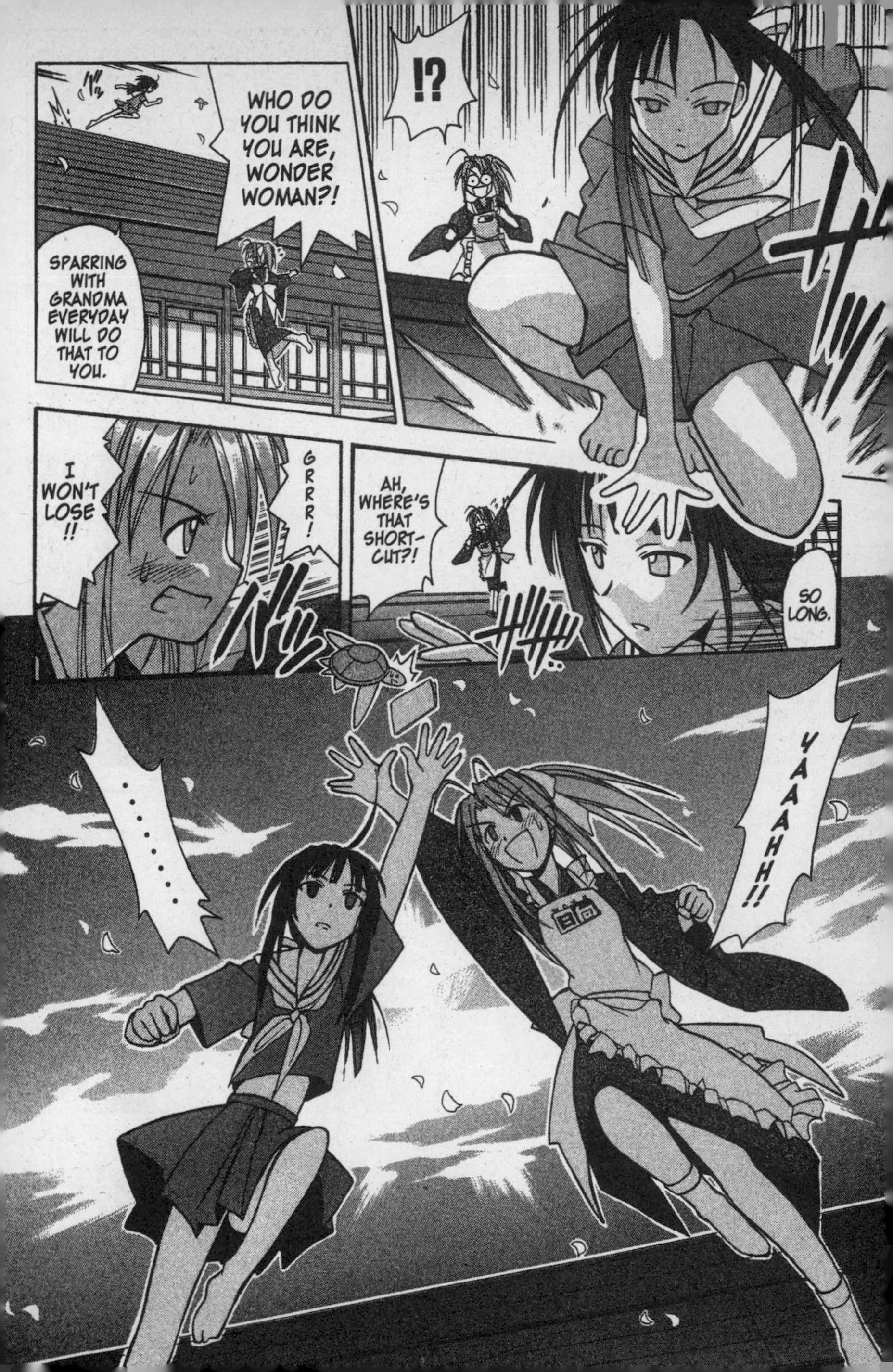
!?
WHO DO YOU THINK YOU ARE, WONDER WOMAN?!
SPARRING WITH GRANDMA EVERYDAY WILL DO THAT TO YOU.
AH, WHERE'S THAT SHORT-CUT?!
SO LONG.
GRRR!
I WON'T LOSE!!
YAAAAHH!!
......

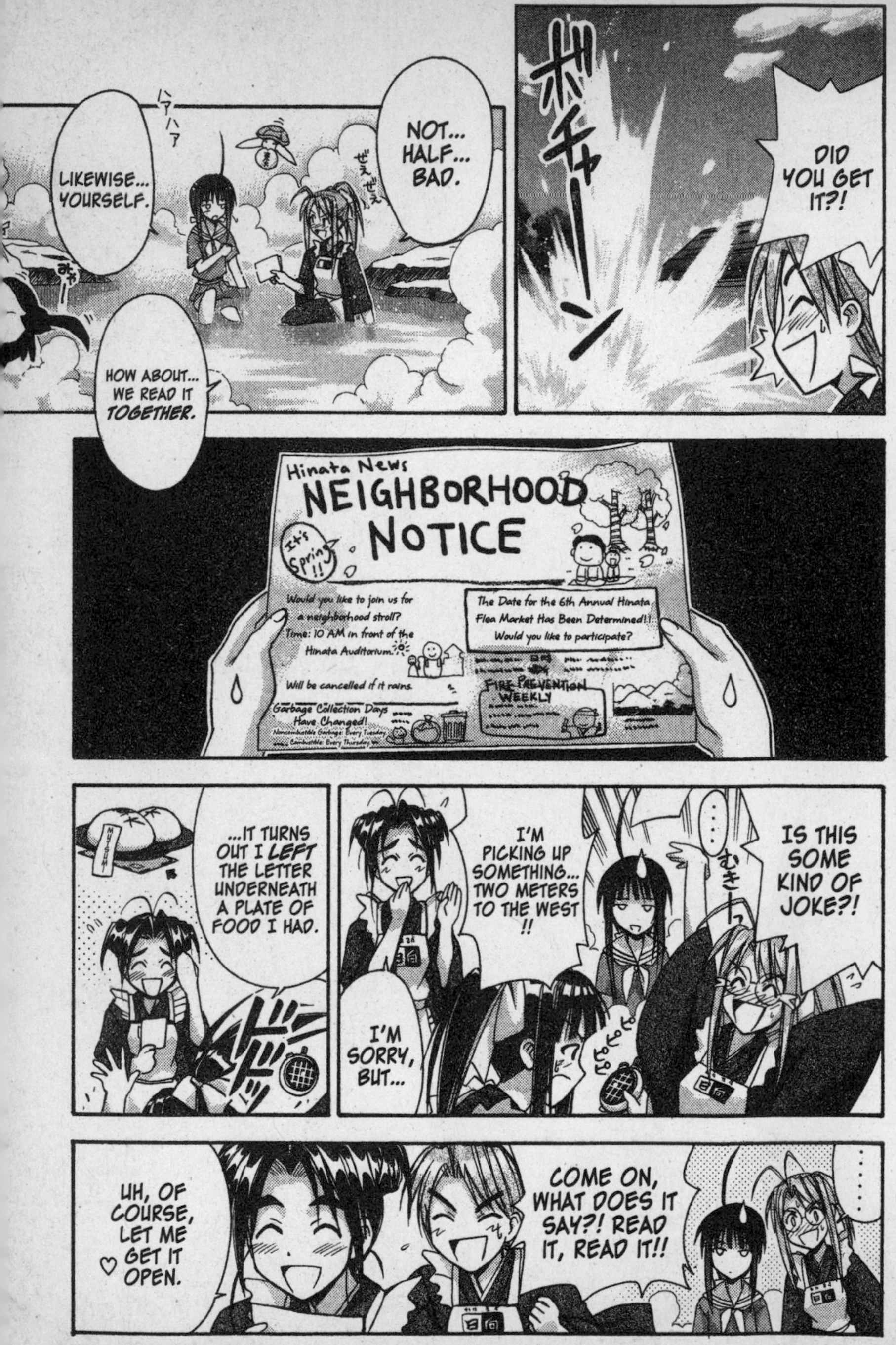
ポチャーン
DID YOU GET IT?!
NOT... HALF... BAD.
ぜぇぜぇ
ハァハァ
LIKEWISE... YOURSELF.
みゃ
HOW ABOUT... WE READ IT *TOGETHER*.
Hinata News
NEIGHBORHOOD NOTICE
It's Spring!!
Would you like to join us for a neighborhood stroll?
Time: 10 AM in front of the Hinata Auditorium.
Will be cancelled if it rains.
The Date for the 6th Annual Hinata Flea Market Has Been Determined!!
Would you like to participate?
FIRE PREVENTION WEEKLY
Garbage Collection Days Have Changed!
Noncombustible Garbage: Every Tuesday
Combustible: Every Thursday
IS THIS SOME KIND OF JOKE?!
むきーっ
....
I'M PICKING UP SOMETHING... TWO METERS TO THE WEST!!
ピピピピ
I'M SORRY, BUT...
...IT TURNS OUT I *LEFT* THE LETTER UNDERNEATH A PLATE OF FOOD I HAD.
MUTSUMI
....
COME ON, WHAT DOES IT SAY?! READ IT, READ IT!!
UH, OF COURSE, LET ME GET IT OPEN. ♡

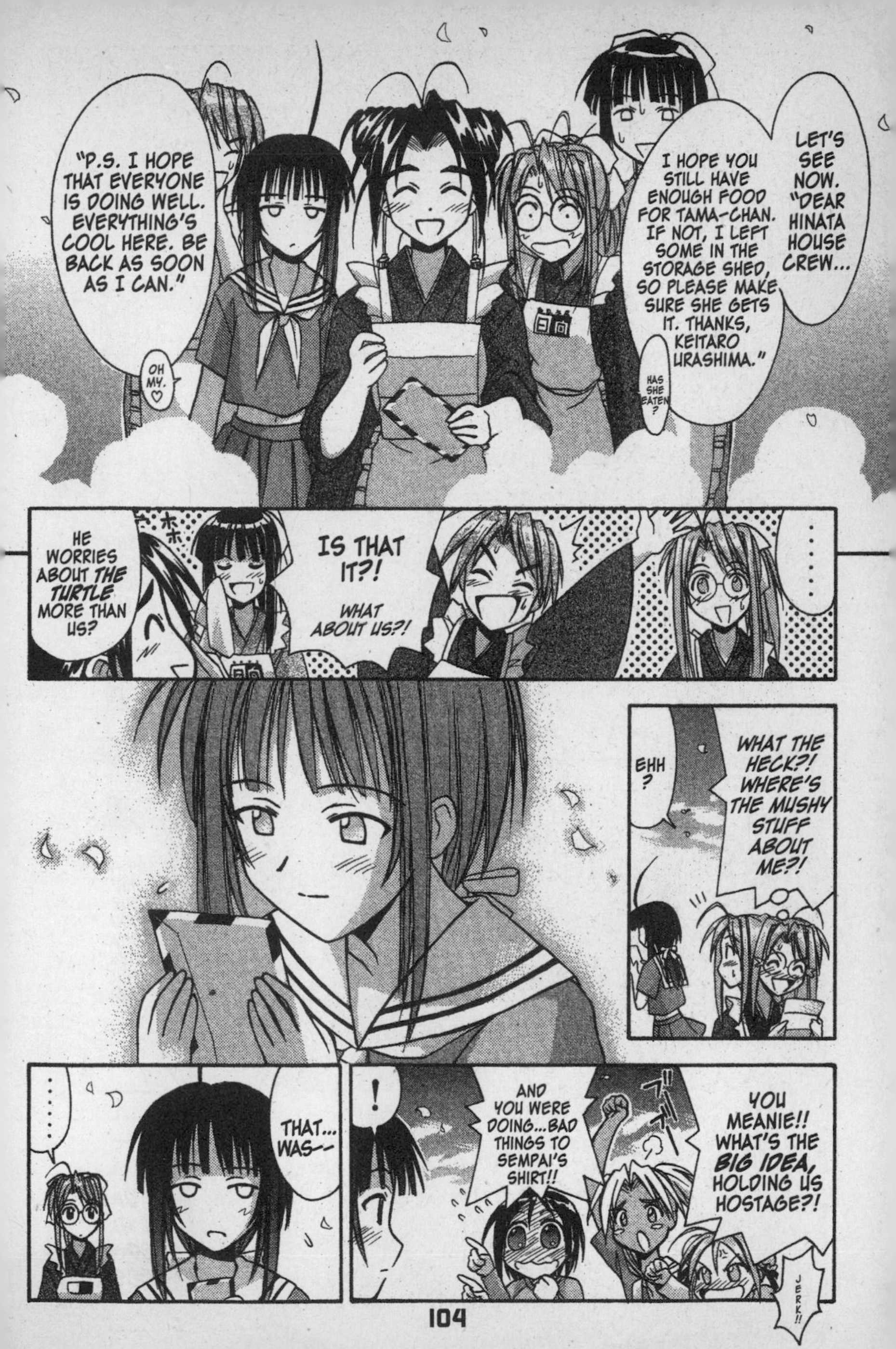
LET'S SEE NOW. "DEAR HINATA HOUSE CREW...
I HOPE YOU STILL HAVE ENOUGH FOOD FOR TAMA-CHAN. IF NOT, I LEFT SOME IN THE STORAGE SHED, SO PLEASE MAKE SURE SHE GETS IT. THANKS, KEITARO URASHIMA."
"P.S. I HOPE THAT EVERYONE IS DOING WELL. EVERYTHING'S COOL HERE. BE BACK AS SOON AS I CAN."
HAS SHE EATEN?
OH MY. ♥
......
IS THAT IT?!
WHAT ABOUT US?!
HE WORRIES ABOUT THE TURTLE MORE THAN US?
WHAT THE HECK?! WHERE'S THE MUSHY STUFF ABOUT ME?!
EHH?
YOU MEANIE!! WHAT'S THE BIG IDEA, HOLDING US HOSTAGE?!
AND YOU WERE DOING...BAD THINGS TO SEMPAI'S SHIRT!!
!
JERK!!
THAT... WAS--
......

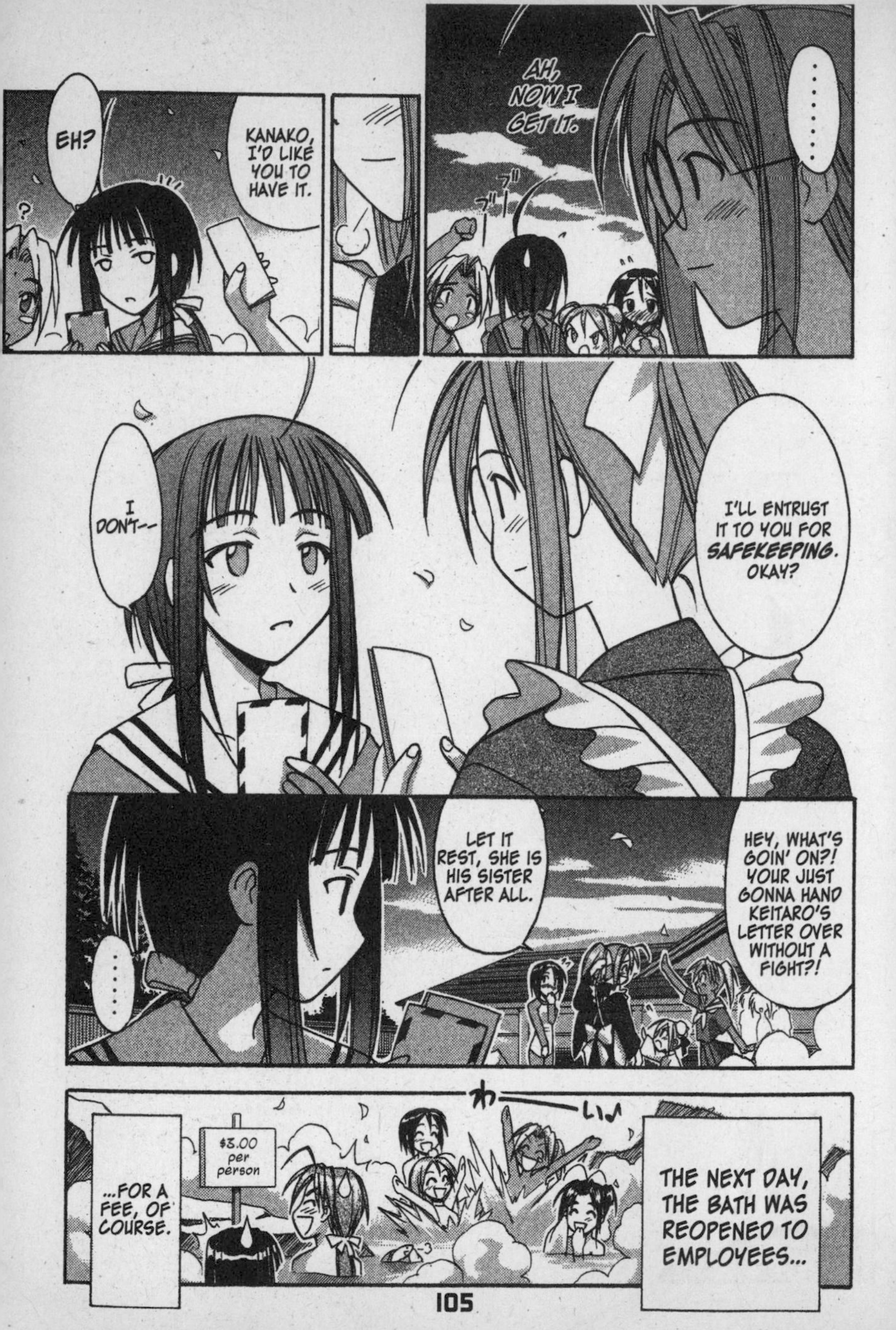

......
AH, NOW I GET IT.
KANAKO, I'D LIKE YOU TO HAVE IT.
EH?
I'LL ENTRUST IT TO YOU FOR **SAFEKEEPING.** OKAY?
I DON'T--
HEY, WHAT'S GOIN' ON?! YOUR JUST GONNA HAND KEITARO'S LETTER OVER WITHOUT A FIGHT?!
LET IT REST, SHE IS HIS SISTER AFTER ALL.
......
THE NEXT DAY, THE BATH WAS REOPENED TO EMPLOYEES...
$3.00 per person
...FOR A FEE, OF COURSE.

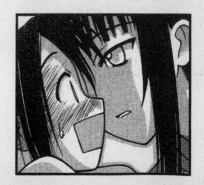

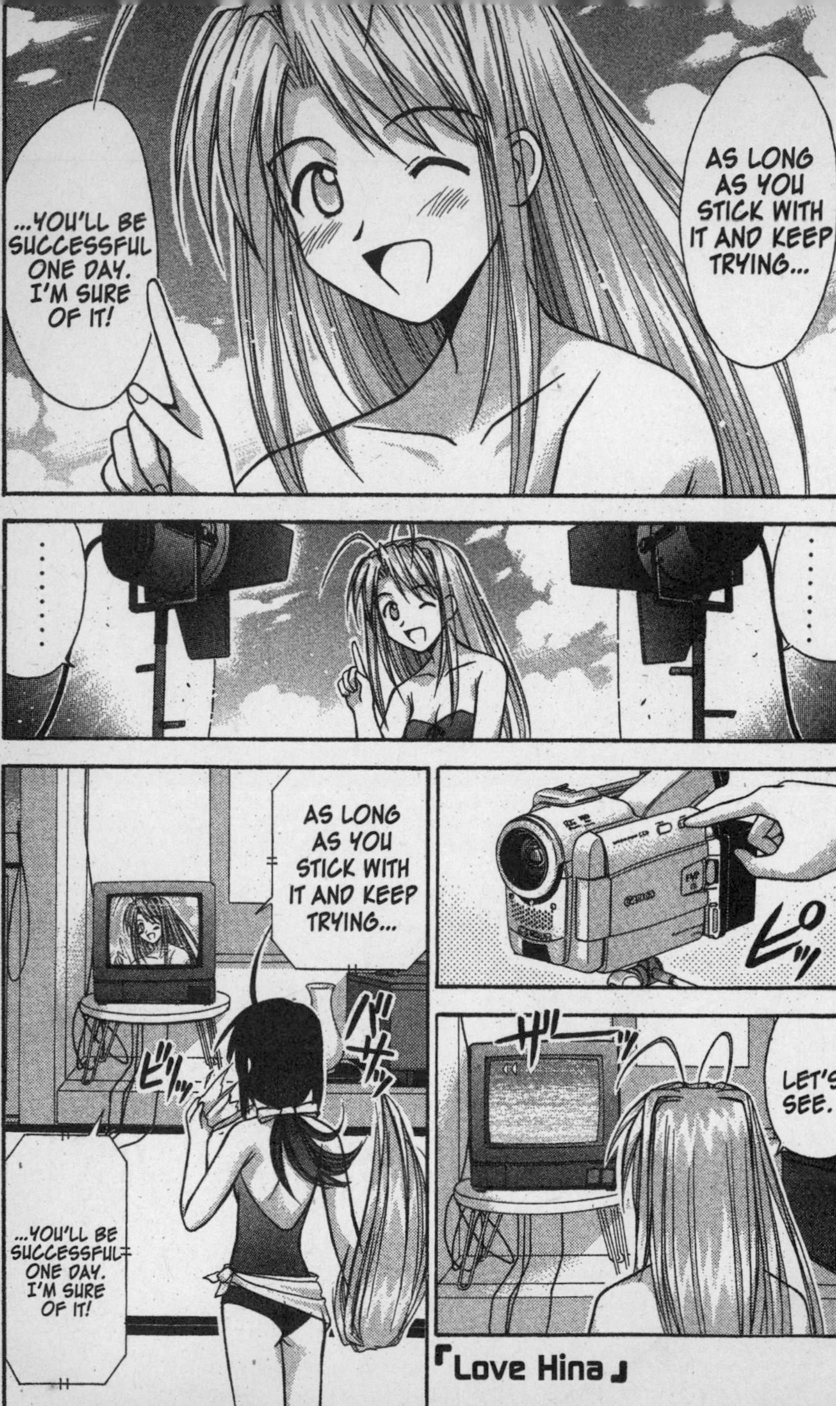
AS LONG AS YOU STICK WITH IT AND KEEP TRYING...
...YOU'LL BE SUCCESSFUL ONE DAY. I'M SURE OF IT!
......
......
ピッ
ザーッ
LET'S SEE.
AS LONG AS YOU STICK WITH IT AND KEEP TRYING...
バサッ
ビリッ
...YOU'LL BE SUCCESSFUL ONE DAY. I'M SURE OF IT!

「Love Hina」

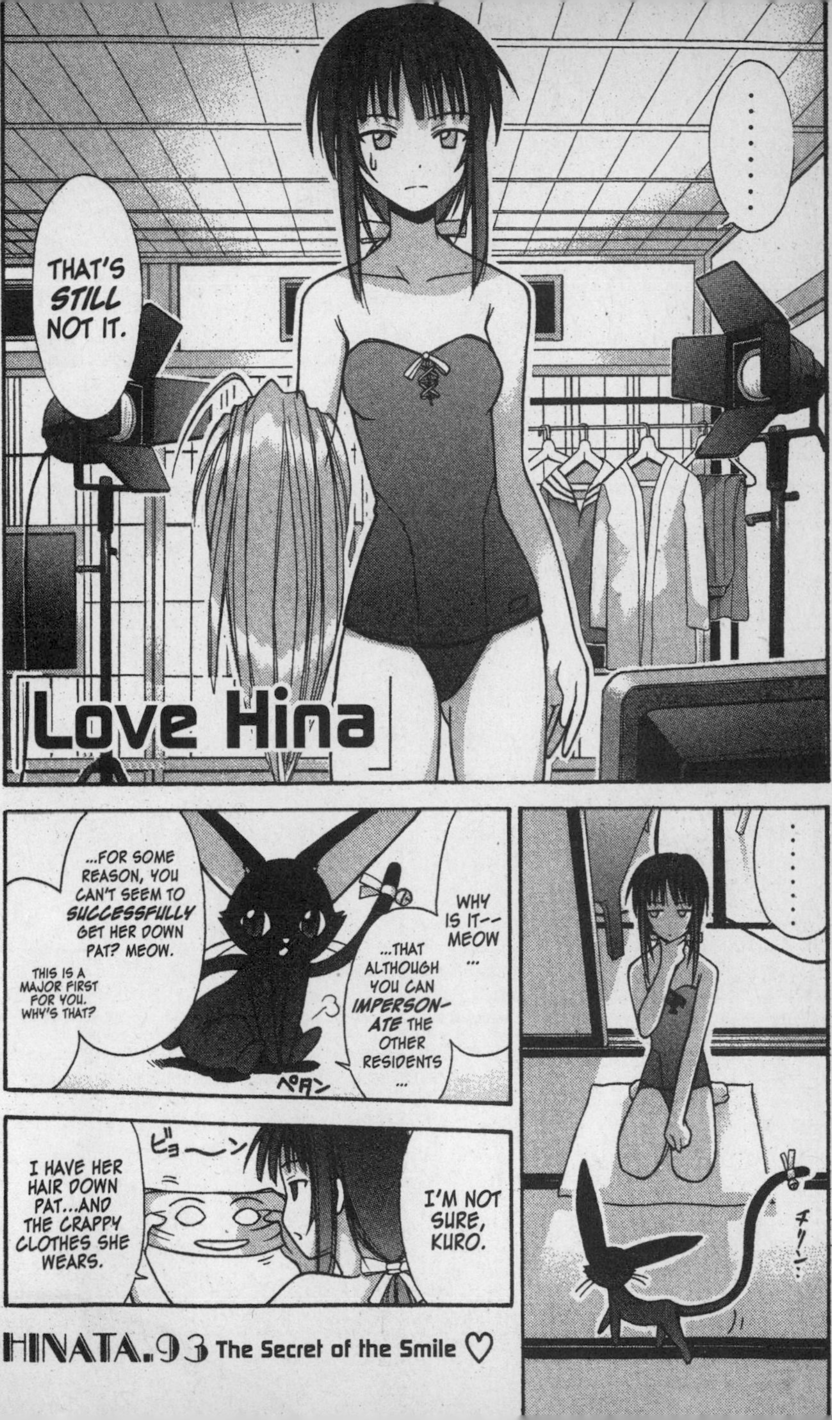
……
THAT'S STILL NOT IT.
Love Hina
……
チリーン…
WHY IS IT-- MEOW ...
...THAT ALTHOUGH YOU CAN IMPERSONATE THE OTHER RESIDENTS ...
...FOR SOME REASON, YOU CAN'T SEEM TO SUCCESSFULLY GET HER DOWN PAT? MEOW.
THIS IS A MAJOR FIRST FOR YOU. WHY'S THAT?
ペタン
I'M NOT SURE, KURO.
ビョ〜ン
I HAVE HER HAIR DOWN PAT...AND THE CRAPPY CLOTHES SHE WEARS.

HINATA.93 The Secret of the Smile ♡

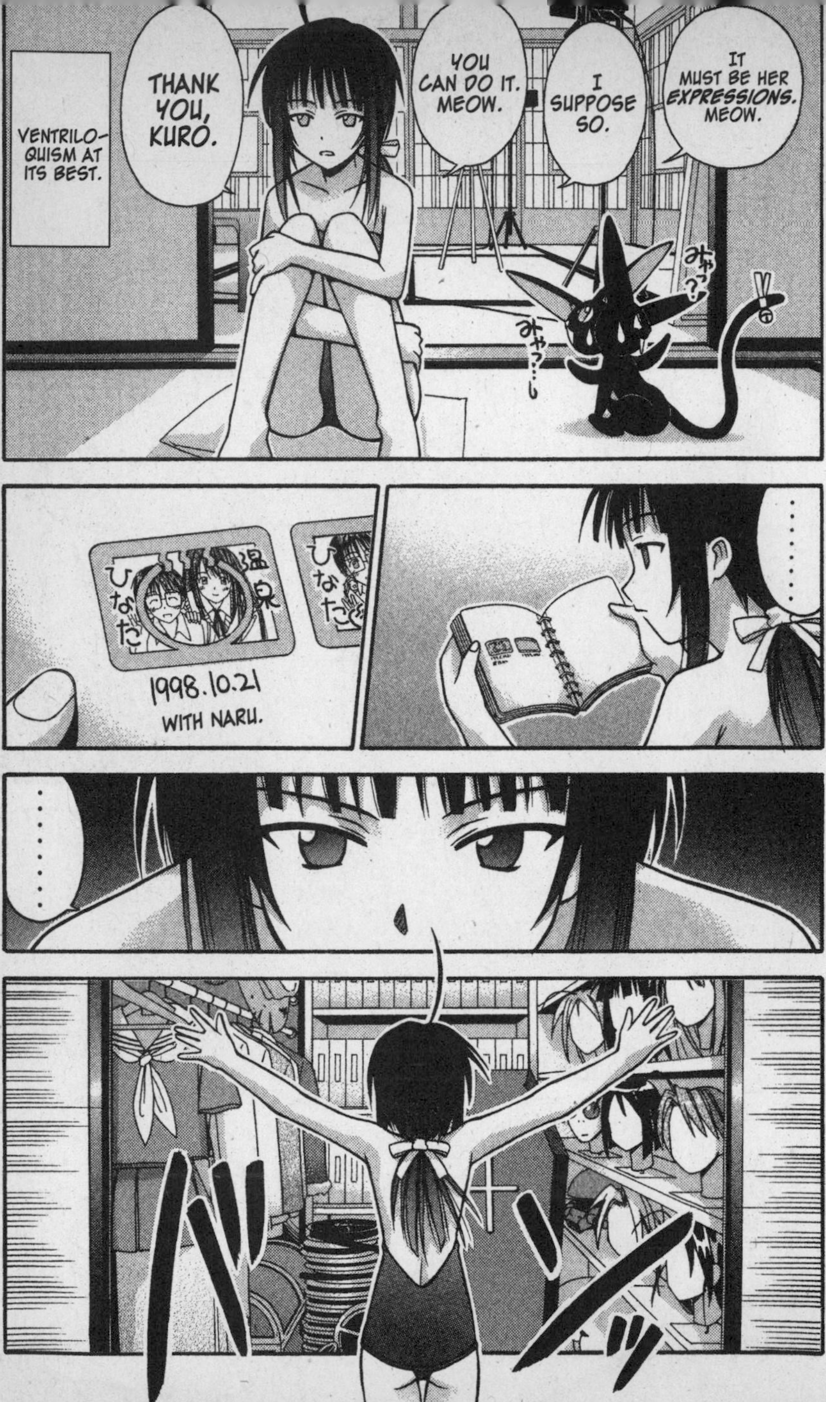
IT MUST BE HER *EXPRESSIONS.* MEOW.
I SUPPOSE SO.
YOU CAN DO IT. MEOW.
THANK YOU, KURO.
VENTRILO-QUISM AT ITS BEST.
みゃっ?
......
1998.10.21
WITH NARU.
......

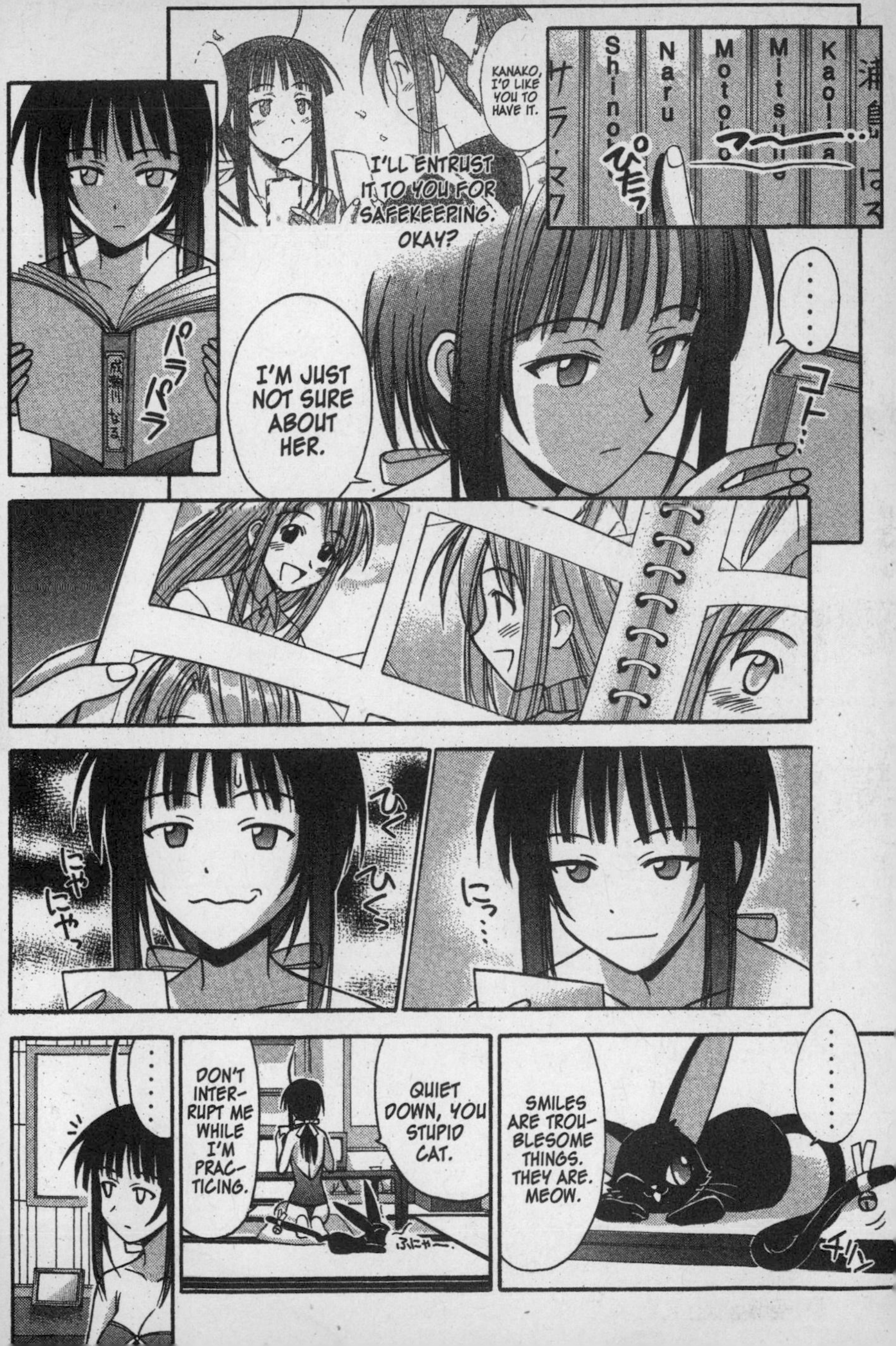

Naru
ぴたっ
KANAKO, I'D LIKE YOU TO HAVE IT.
I'LL ENTRUST IT TO YOU FOR SAFEKEEPING. OKAY?
パラパラ
......
コト…
I'M JUST NOT SURE ABOUT HER.
にっ…
ひくひくっ
にやにやっ
......
SMILES ARE TROUBLESOME THINGS. THEY ARE. MEOW.
QUIET DOWN, YOU STUPID CAT.
DON'T INTERRUPT ME WHILE I'M PRACTICING.
ふにゃー
......

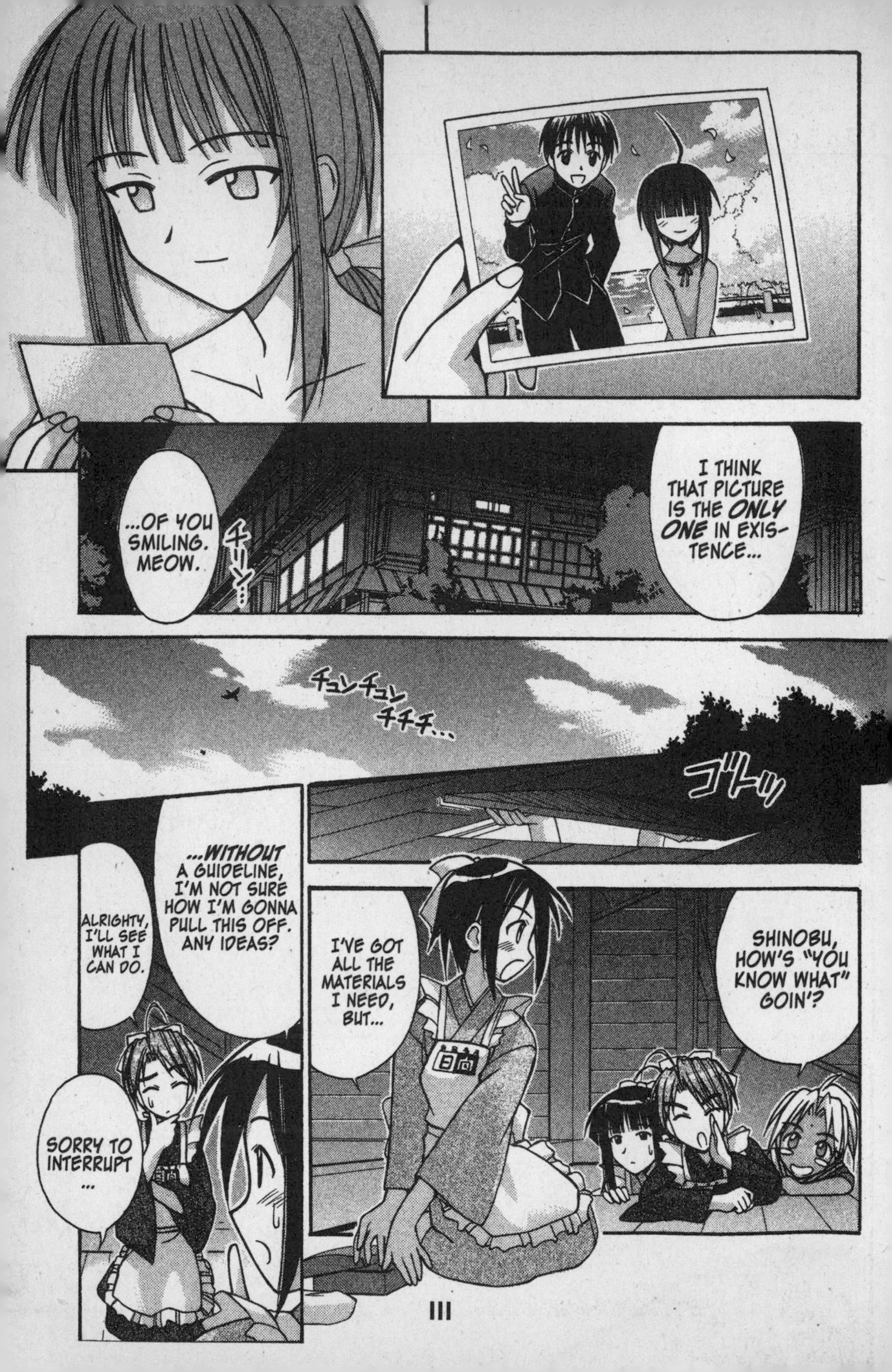
I THINK THAT PICTURE IS THE *ONLY ONE* IN EXIS-TENCE...
...OF YOU SMILING. MEOW.
チリーン…
チュンチュン チチチ…
ゴトッ
SHINOBU, HOW'S "YOU KNOW WHAT" GOIN'?
I'VE GOT ALL THE MATERIALS I NEED, BUT...
...WITHOUT A GUIDELINE, I'M NOT SURE HOW I'M GONNA PULL THIS OFF. ANY IDEAS?
ALRIGHTY, I'LL SEE WHAT I CAN DO.
SORRY TO INTERRUPT ...

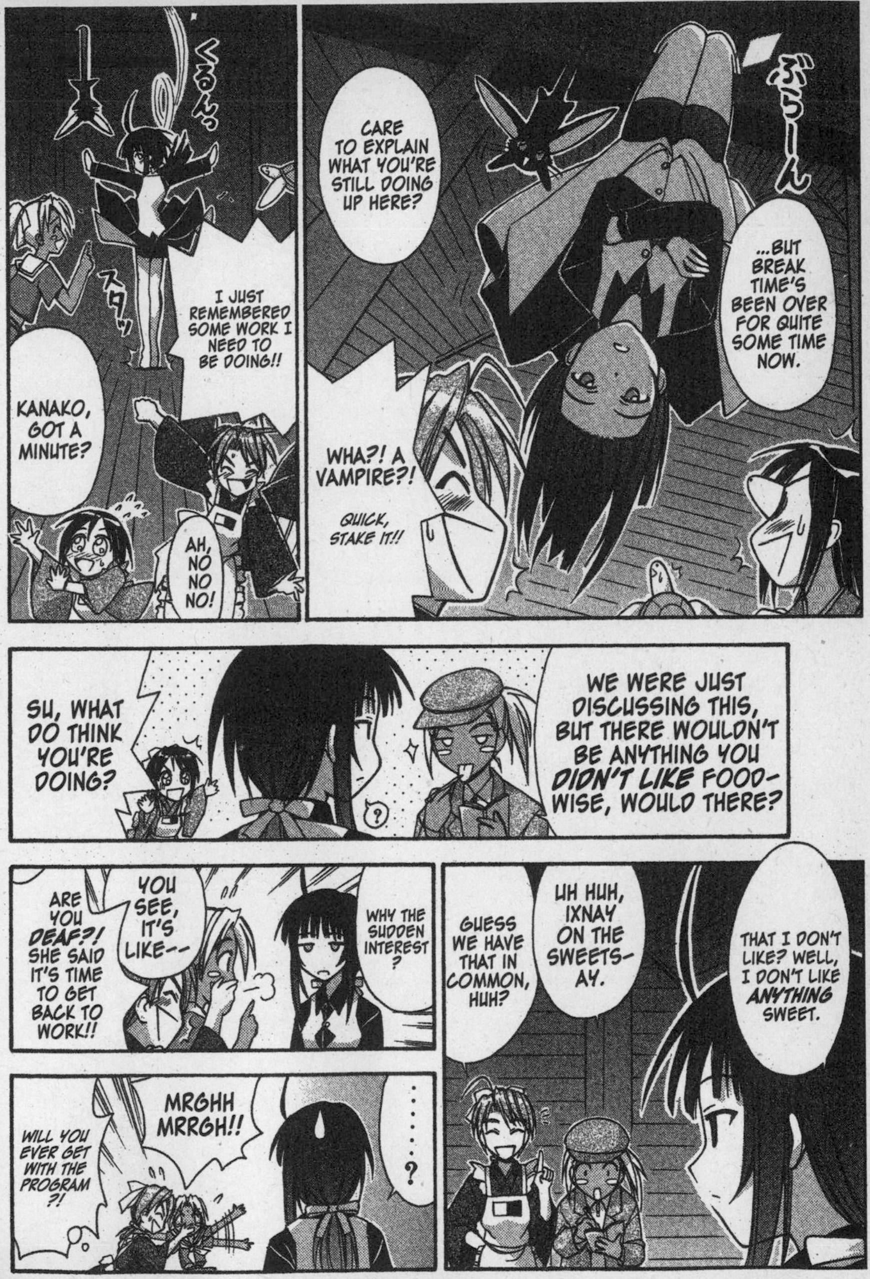
ぶらーん
...BUT BREAK TIME'S BEEN OVER FOR QUITE SOME TIME NOW.
CARE TO EXPLAIN WHAT YOU'RE STILL DOING UP HERE?
WHA?! A VAMPIRE?!
QUICK, STAKE IT!!
くるんっ
I JUST REMEMBERED SOME WORK I NEED TO BE DOING!!
スタッ
KANAKO, GOT A MINUTE?
AH, NO NO NO NO!
WE WERE JUST DISCUSSING THIS, BUT THERE WOULDN'T BE ANYTHING YOU *DIDN'T LIKE* FOOD-WISE, WOULD THERE?
?
SU, WHAT DO THINK YOU'RE DOING?
THAT I DON'T LIKE? WELL, I DON'T LIKE *ANYTHING* SWEET.
UH HUH, IXNAY ON THE SWEETS-AY.
GUESS WE HAVE THAT IN COMMON, HUH?
WHY THE SUDDEN INTEREST?
YOU SEE, IT'S LIKE--
ARE YOU *DEAF?!* SHE SAID IT'S TIME TO GET BACK TO WORK!!
......?
MRGHH MRRGH!!
WILL YOU EVER GET WITH THE PROGRAM?!

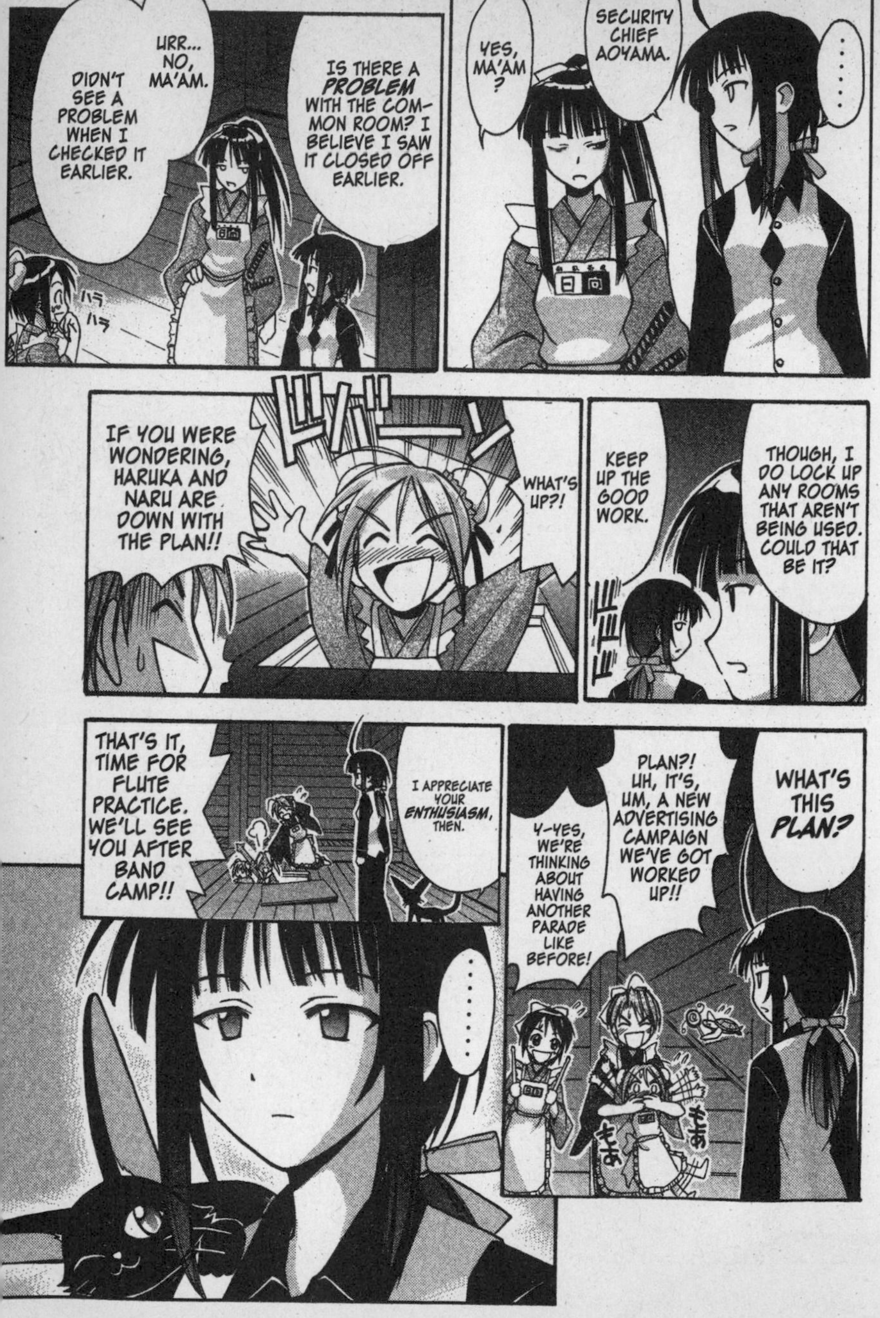
SECURITY CHIEF AOYAMA.
YES, MA'AM?
......
IS THERE A PROBLEM WITH THE COMMON ROOM? I BELIEVE I SAW IT CLOSED OFF EARLIER.
URR... NO, MA'AM.
DIDN'T SEE A PROBLEM WHEN I CHECKED IT EARLIER.
ハラ ハラ
THOUGH, I DO LOCK UP ANY ROOMS THAT AREN'T BEING USED. COULD THAT BE IT?
KEEP UP THE GOOD WORK.
WHAT'S UP?!
IF YOU WERE WONDERING, HARUKA AND NARU ARE DOWN WITH THE PLAN!!
WHAT'S THIS PLAN?
PLAN?! UH, IT'S, UM, A NEW ADVERTISING CAMPAIGN WE'VE GOT WORKED UP!!
Y-YES, WE'RE THINKING ABOUT HAVING ANOTHER PARADE LIKE BEFORE!
I APPRECIATE YOUR ENTHUSIASM, THEN.
THAT'S IT, TIME FOR FLUTE PRACTICE. WE'LL SEE YOU AFTER BAND CAMP!!
....

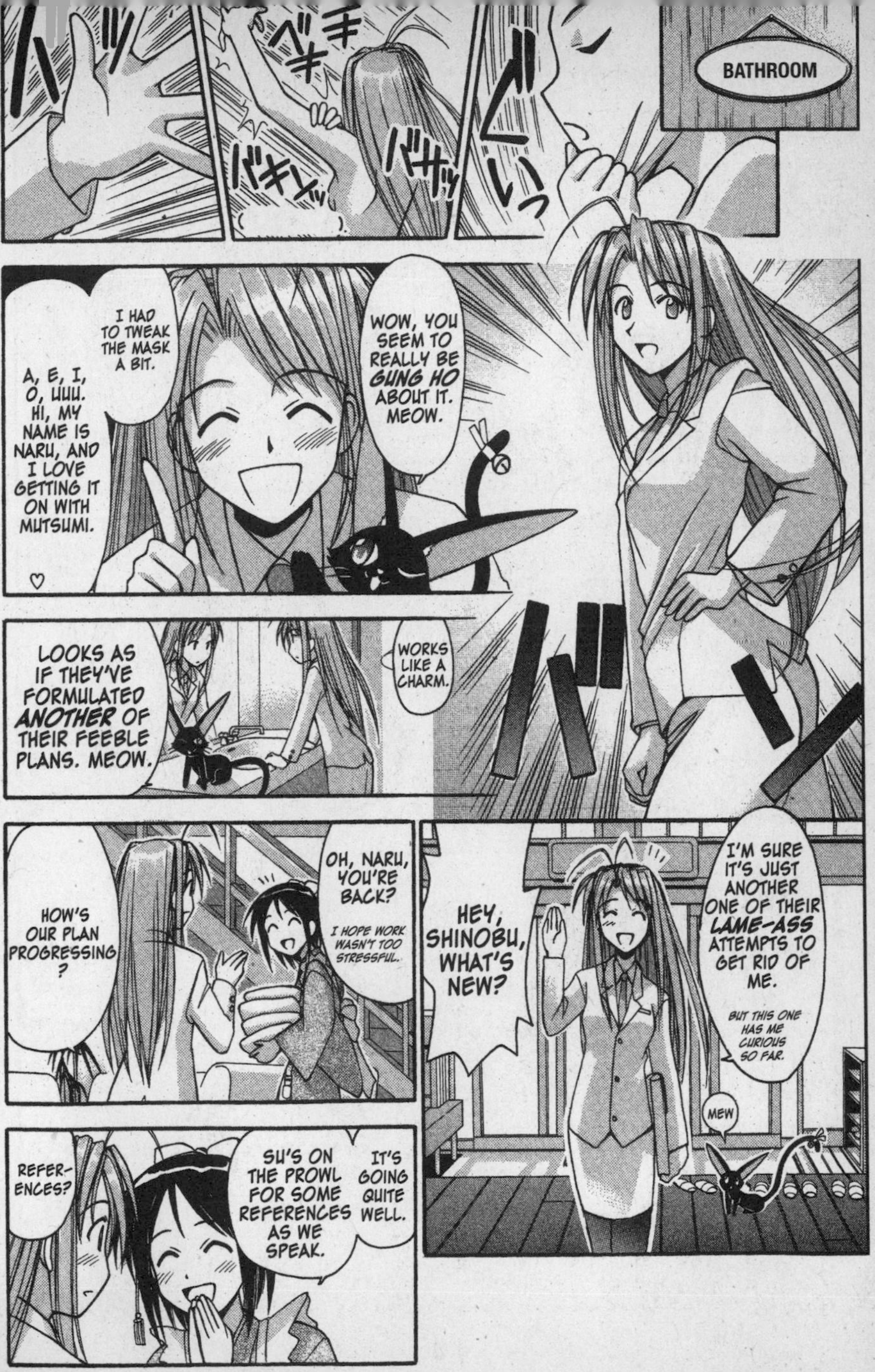
BATHROOM
WOW, YOU SEEM TO REALLY BE GUNG HO ABOUT IT. MEOW.
I HAD TO TWEAK THE MASK A BIT.
A, E, I, O, UUU. HI, MY NAME IS NARU, AND I LOVE GETTING IT ON WITH MUTSUMI. ♡
WORKS LIKE A CHARM.
LOOKS AS IF THEY'VE FORMULATED ANOTHER OF THEIR FEEBLE PLANS. MEOW.
I'M SURE IT'S JUST ANOTHER ONE OF THEIR LAME-ASS ATTEMPTS TO GET RID OF ME.
BUT THIS ONE HAS ME CURIOUS SO FAR.
HEY, SHINOBU, WHAT'S NEW?
MEW
OH, NARU, YOU'RE BACK?
I HOPE WORK WASN'T TOO STRESSFUL.
HOW'S OUR PLAN PROGRESSING?
IT'S GOING QUITE WELL.
SU'S ON THE PROWL FOR SOME REFERENCES AS WE SPEAK.
REFERENCES?

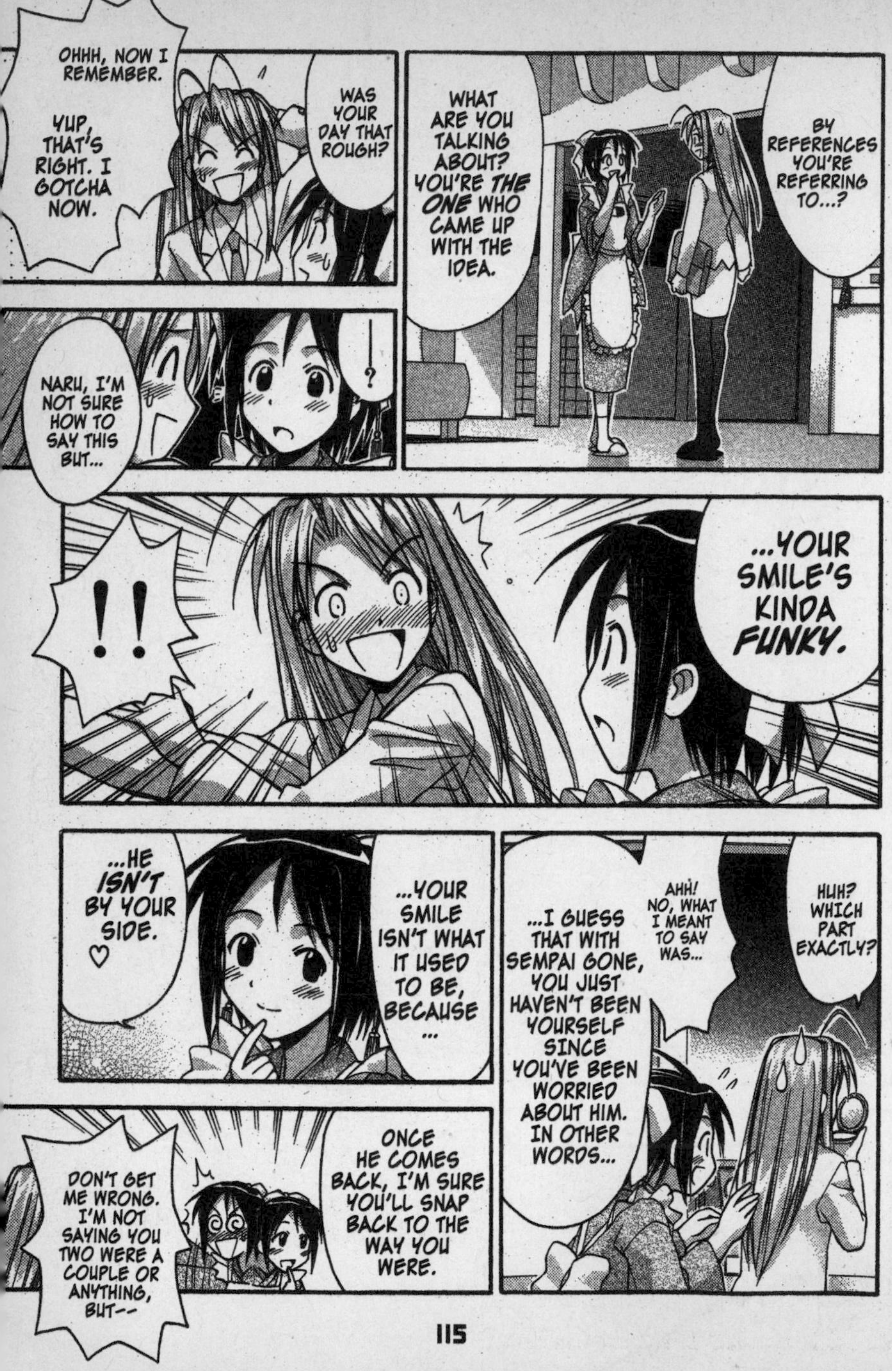
BY REFERENCES YOU'RE REFERRING TO...?
WHAT ARE YOU TALKING ABOUT? YOU'RE THE ONE WHO CAME UP WITH THE IDEA.
WAS YOUR DAY THAT ROUGH?
OHHH, NOW I REMEMBER.
YUP, THAT'S RIGHT. I GOTCHA NOW.
!?
NARU, I'M NOT SURE HOW TO SAY THIS BUT...
...YOUR SMILE'S KINDA FUNKY.
!!
HUH? WHICH PART EXACTLY?
AHH! NO, WHAT I MEANT TO SAY WAS...
...I GUESS THAT WITH SEMPAI GONE, YOU JUST HAVEN'T BEEN YOURSELF SINCE YOU'VE BEEN WORRIED ABOUT HIM. IN OTHER WORDS...
...YOUR SMILE ISN'T WHAT IT USED TO BE, BECAUSE ...
...HE ISN'T BY YOUR SIDE. ♡
ONCE HE COMES BACK, I'M SURE YOU'LL SNAP BACK TO THE WAY YOU WERE.
DON'T GET ME WRONG. I'M NOT SAYING YOU TWO WERE A COUPLE OR ANYTHING, BUT--

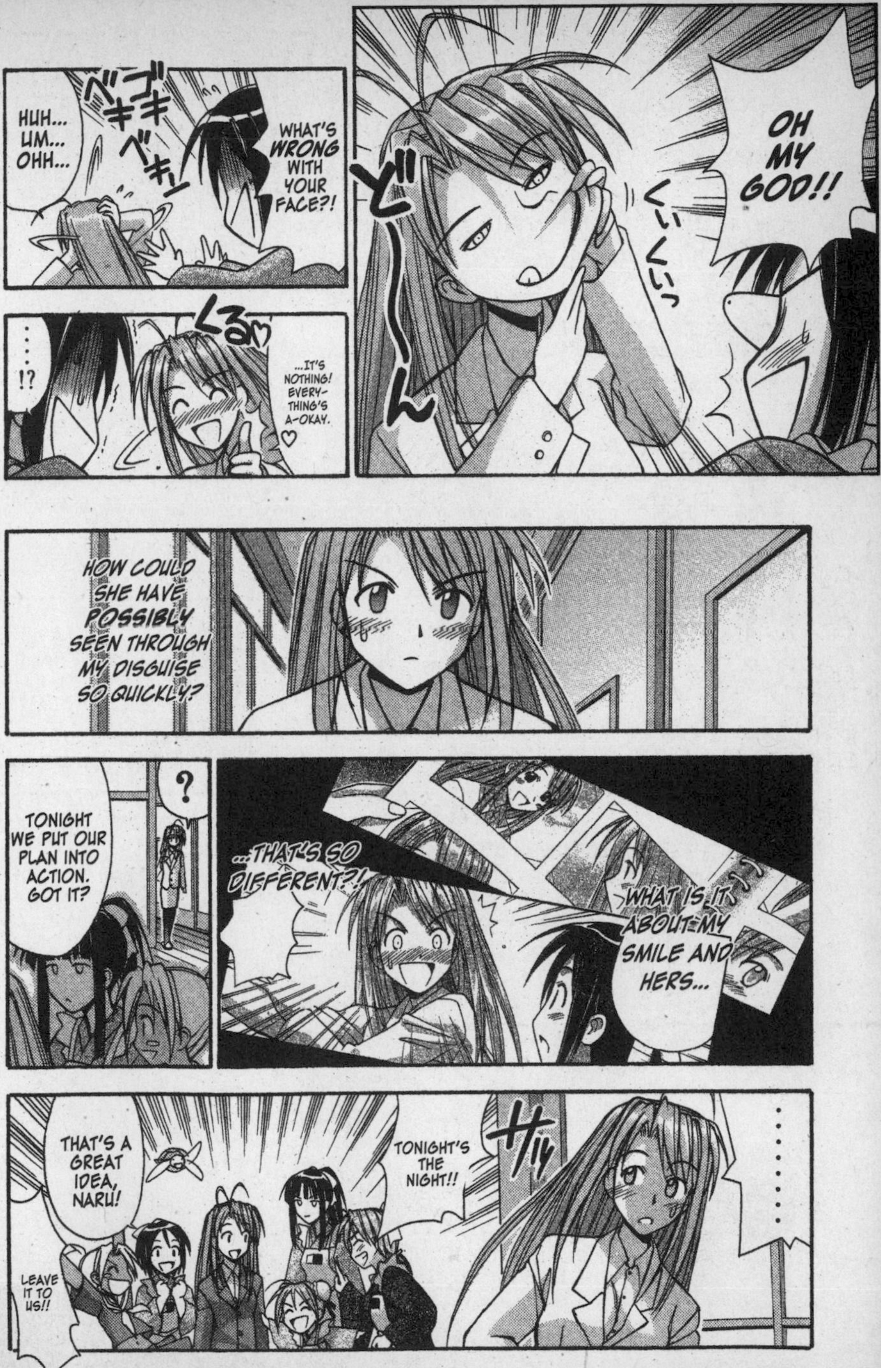
OH MY GOD!!
WHAT'S WRONG WITH YOUR FACE?!
HUH... UM... OHH...
...IT'S NOTHING! EVERY-THING'S A-OKAY. ♡
....!?
HOW COULD SHE HAVE POSSIBLY SEEN THROUGH MY DISGUISE SO QUICKLY?
WHAT IS IT ABOUT MY SMILE AND HERS...
...THAT'S SO DIFFERENT?!
?
TONIGHT WE PUT OUR PLAN INTO ACTION. GOT IT?
......
TONIGHT'S THE NIGHT!!
THAT'S A GREAT IDEA, NARU!
LEAVE IT TO US!!

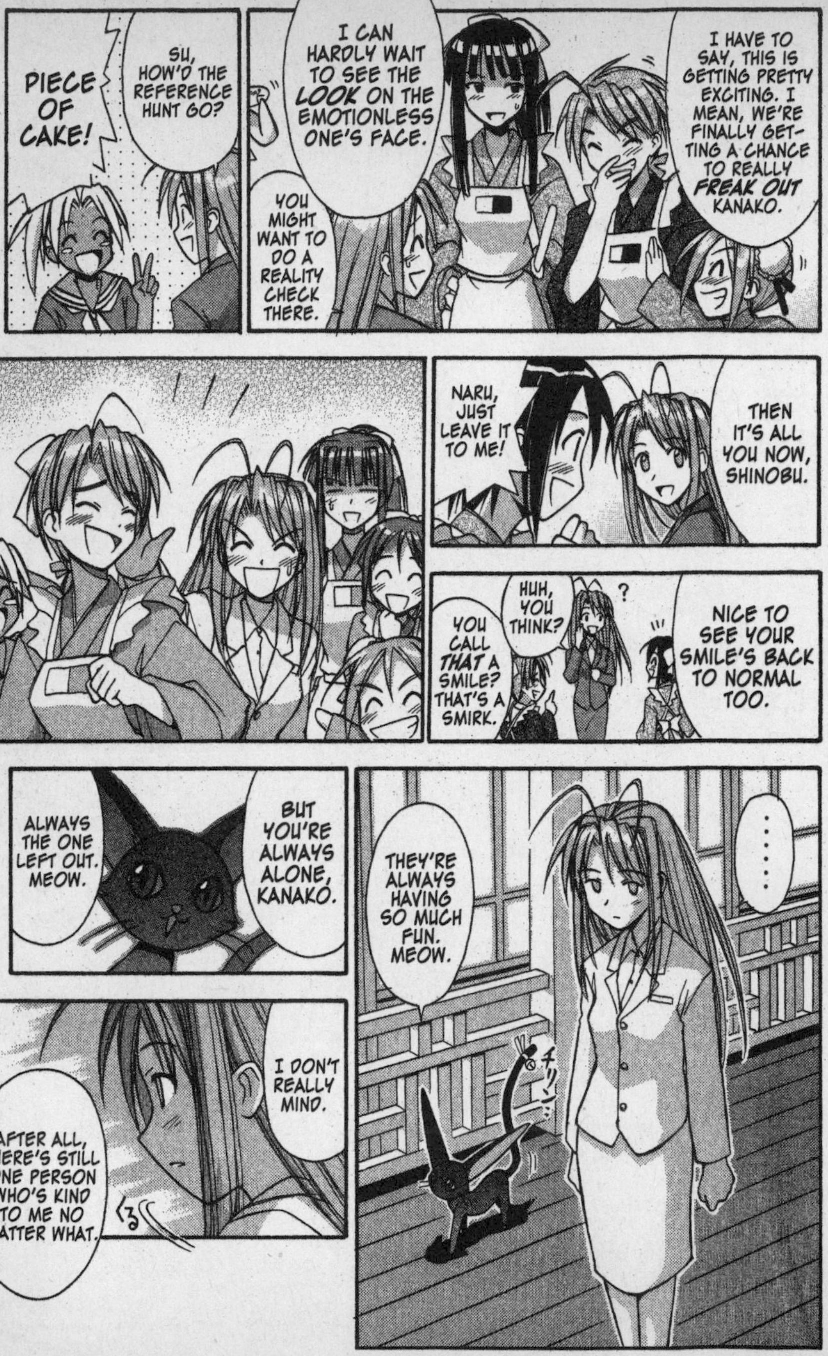
I HAVE TO SAY, THIS IS GETTING PRETTY EXCITING. I MEAN, WE'RE FINALLY GETTING A CHANCE TO REALLY FREAK OUT KANAKO.
I CAN HARDLY WAIT TO SEE THE LOOK ON THE EMOTIONLESS ONE'S FACE.
YOU MIGHT WANT TO DO A REALITY CHECK THERE.
SU, HOW'D THE REFERENCE HUNT GO?
PIECE OF CAKE!
THEN IT'S ALL YOU NOW, SHINOBU.
NARU, JUST LEAVE IT TO ME!
NICE TO SEE YOUR SMILE'S BACK TO NORMAL TOO.
HUH, YOU THINK?
YOU CALL THAT A SMILE? THAT'S A SMIRK.
......
THEY'RE ALWAYS HAVING SO MUCH FUN. MEOW.
BUT YOU'RE ALWAYS ALONE, KANAKO.
ALWAYS THE ONE LEFT OUT. MEOW.
I DON'T REALLY MIND.
AFTER ALL, THERE'S STILL ONE PERSON WHO'S KIND TO ME NO MATTER WHAT.

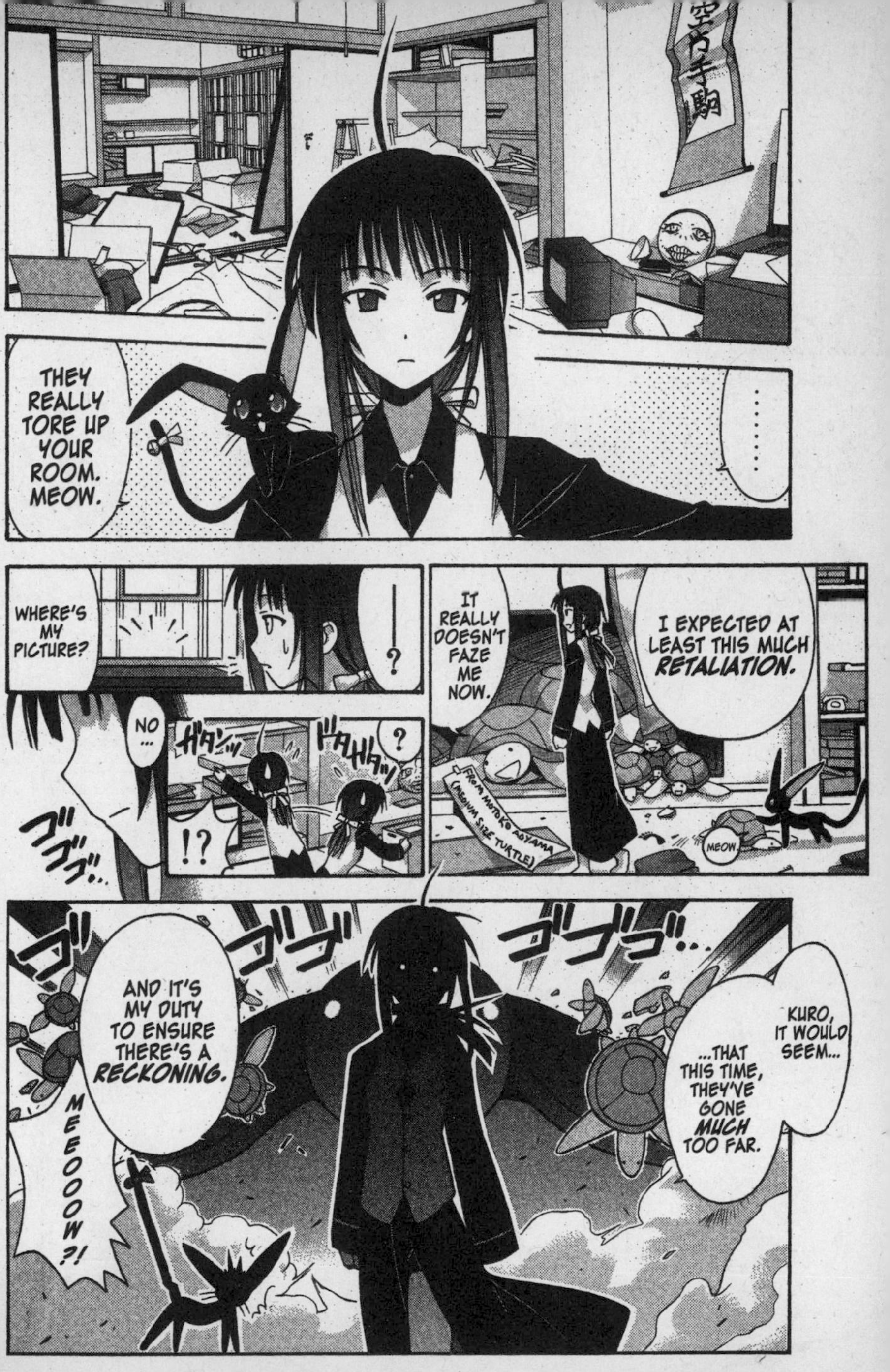
......
THEY REALLY TORE UP YOUR ROOM. MEOW.
I EXPECTED AT LEAST THIS MUCH RETALIATION.
IT REALLY DOESN'T FAZE ME NOW.
FROM MOTOKO AOYAMA (MEDIUM SIZE TURTLE)
MEOW
!?
WHERE'S MY PICTURE?
?
!?
NO...
ゴゴゴ...
KURO, IT WOULD SEEM...
...THAT THIS TIME, THEY'VE GONE MUCH TOO FAR.
AND IT'S MY DUTY TO ENSURE THERE'S A RECKONING.
ゴゴゴゴゴゴ...
MEEOOOOW?!

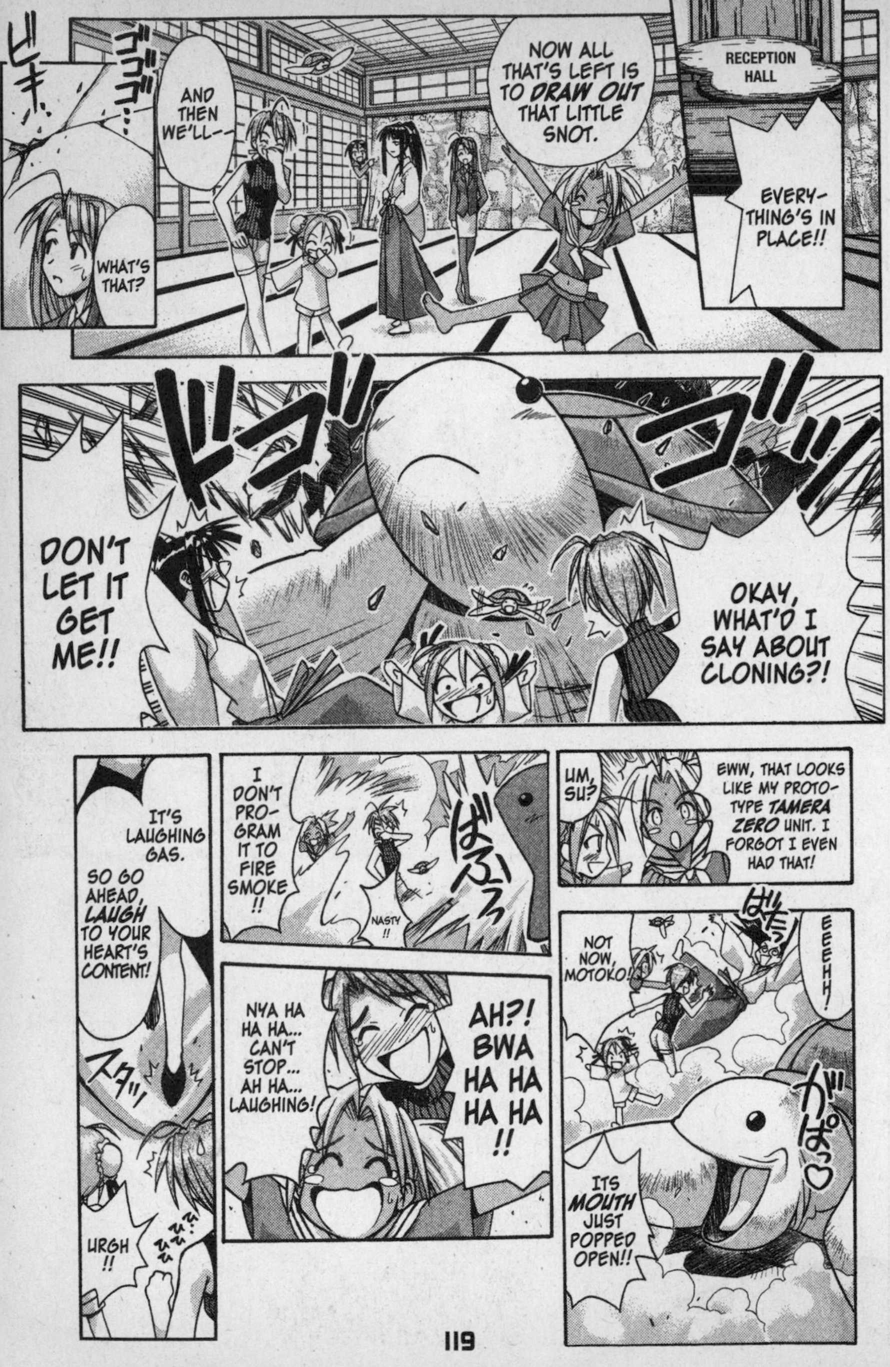
RECEPTION HALL
EVERY-THING'S IN PLACE!!
NOW ALL THAT'S LEFT IS TO DRAW OUT THAT LITTLE SNOT.
AND THEN WE'LL—
ゴゴゴ…
ビキ…
WHAT'S THAT?
ドゴゴッ
OKAY, WHAT'D I SAY ABOUT CLONING?!
DON'T LET IT GET ME!!
EWW, THAT LOOKS LIKE MY PROTO-TYPE TAMERA ZERO UNIT. I FORGOT I EVEN HAD THAT!
UM, SU?
I DON'T PROGRAM IT TO FIRE SMOKE!!
ばふっ
NASTY!!
EEEEHH!
NOT NOW, MOTOKO!
がぱっ♡
ITS MOUTH JUST POPPED OPEN!!
AH?! BWA HA HA HA HA HA!!
NYA HA HA HA... CAN'T STOP... AH HA... LAUGHING!
IT'S LAUGHING GAS.
SO GO AHEAD, LAUGH TO YOUR HEART'S CONTENT!
スタッ
URGH!!

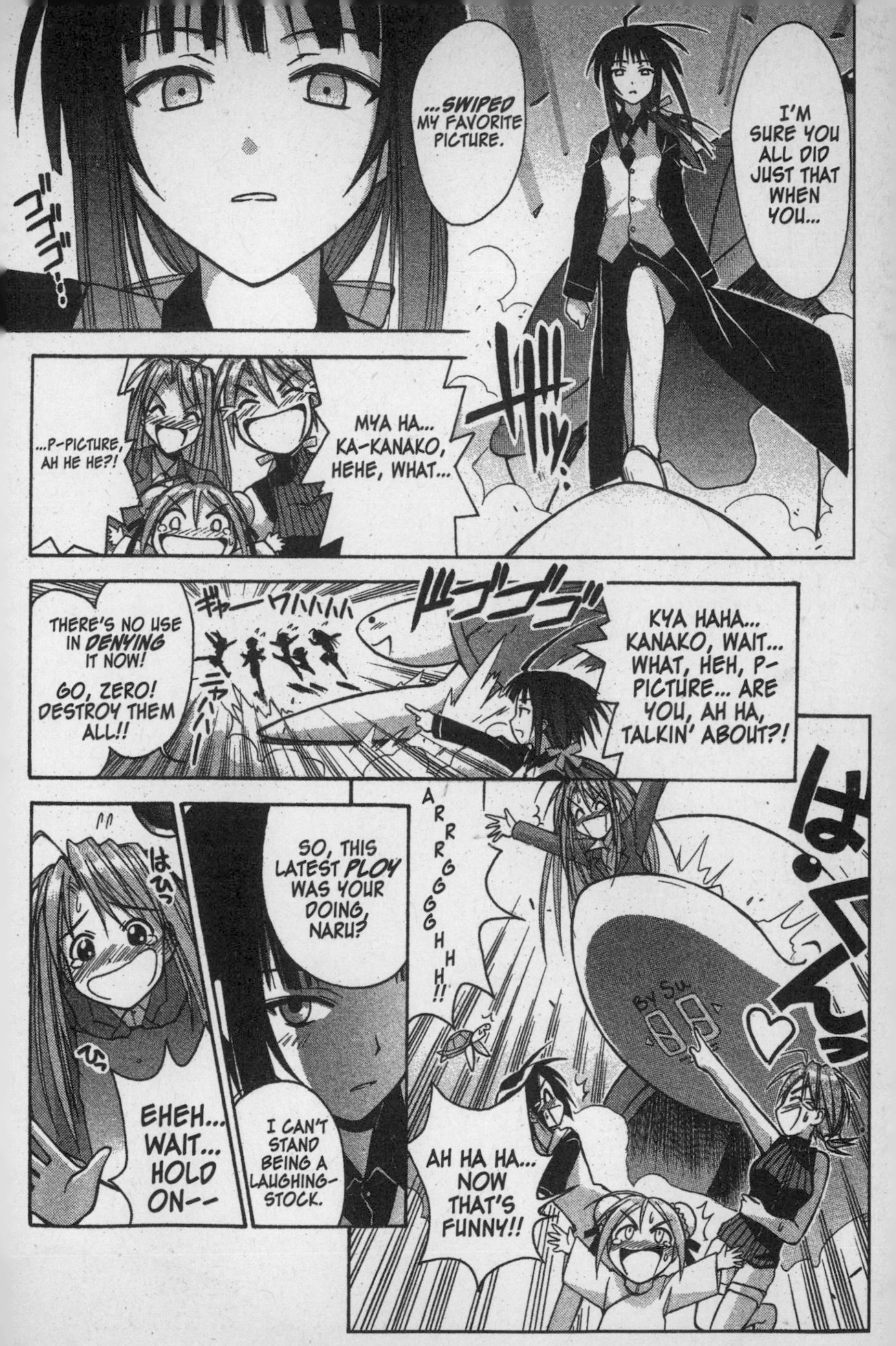

I'M SURE YOU ALL DID JUST THAT WHEN YOU...
...SWIPED MY FAVORITE PICTURE.
MYA HA... KA-KANAKO, HEHE, WHAT...
...P-PICTURE, AH HE HE?!
KYA HAHA... KANAKO, WAIT... WHAT, HEH, P-PICTURE... ARE YOU, AH HA, TALKIN' ABOUT?!
THERE'S NO USE IN DENYING IT NOW!
GO, ZERO! DESTROY THEM ALL!!
ARRRGGGGHHH!!
By Su
AH HA HA... NOW THAT'S FUNNY!!
SO, THIS LATEST PLOY WAS YOUR DOING, NARU?
I CAN'T STAND BEING A LAUGHING-STOCK.
EHEH... WAIT... HOLD ON--

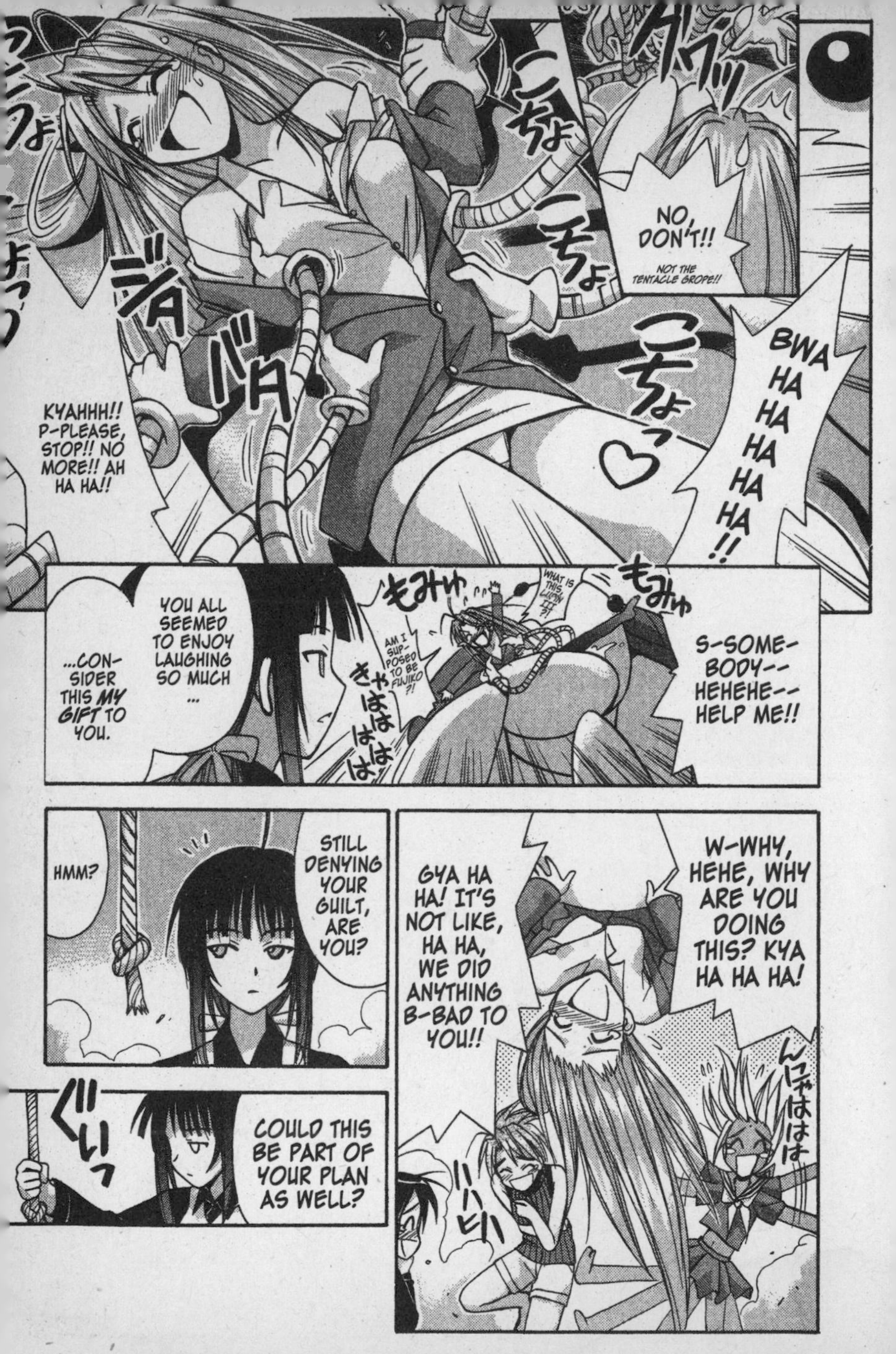

グワッ
こちょ
こちょ
NO, DON'T!!
NOT THE TENTACLE GROPE!!
BWA HA HA HA HA HA HA!!
こちょっ
ジタバタ
KYAHHH!! P-PLEASE, STOP!! NO MORE!! AH HA HA!!
S-SOMEBODY-- HEHEHE-- HELP ME!!
もみゅ
WHAT IS THIS LUPIN III?!
もみゅ
AM I SUPPOSED TO BE FUJIKO ?!
きゃははははは
YOU ALL SEEMED TO ENJOY LAUGHING SO MUCH ...
...CONSIDER THIS MY GIFT TO YOU.
STILL DENYING YOUR GUILT, ARE YOU?
HMM?
ぐいっ
COULD THIS BE PART OF YOUR PLAN AS WELL?
W-WHY, HEHE, WHY ARE YOU DOING THIS? KYA HA HA HA!
GYA HA HA! IT'S NOT LIKE, HA HA, WE DID ANYTHING B-BAD TO YOU!!
んにゃははは
ハハヒハ

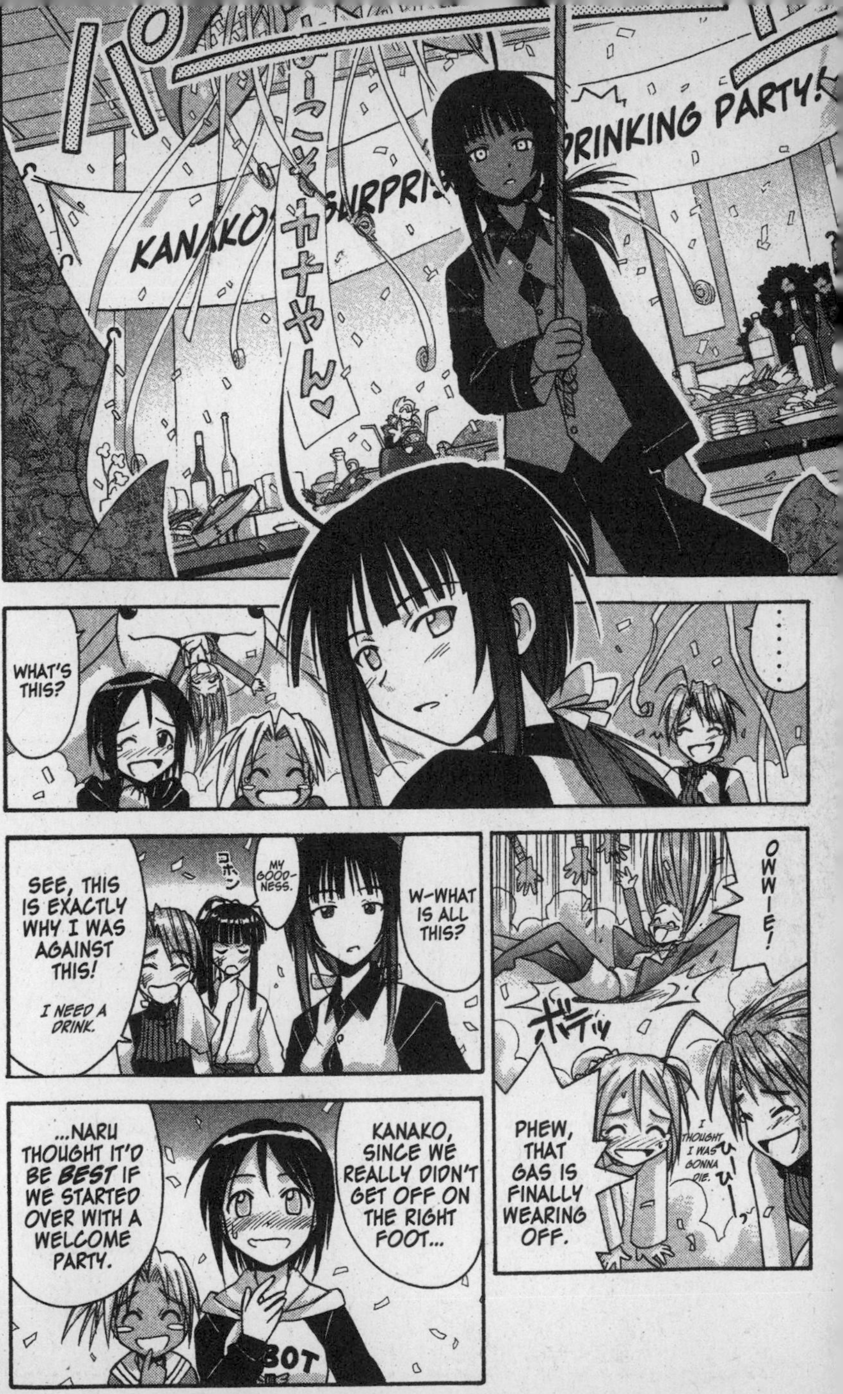

KANAKO SURPRIS
DRINKING PARTY!
カナやん♥
......
WHAT'S THIS?
OWWIE!
ボテッ
PHEW, THAT GAS IS FINALLY WEARING OFF.
I THOUGHT I WAS GONNA DIE.
W-WHAT IS ALL THIS?
MY GOODNESS.
コホン
SEE, THIS IS EXACTLY WHY I WAS AGAINST THIS!
I NEED A DRINK.
KANAKO, SINCE WE REALLY DIDN'T GET OFF ON THE RIGHT FOOT...
...NARU THOUGHT IT'D BE ***BEST*** IF WE STARTED OVER WITH A WELCOME PARTY.
BOT

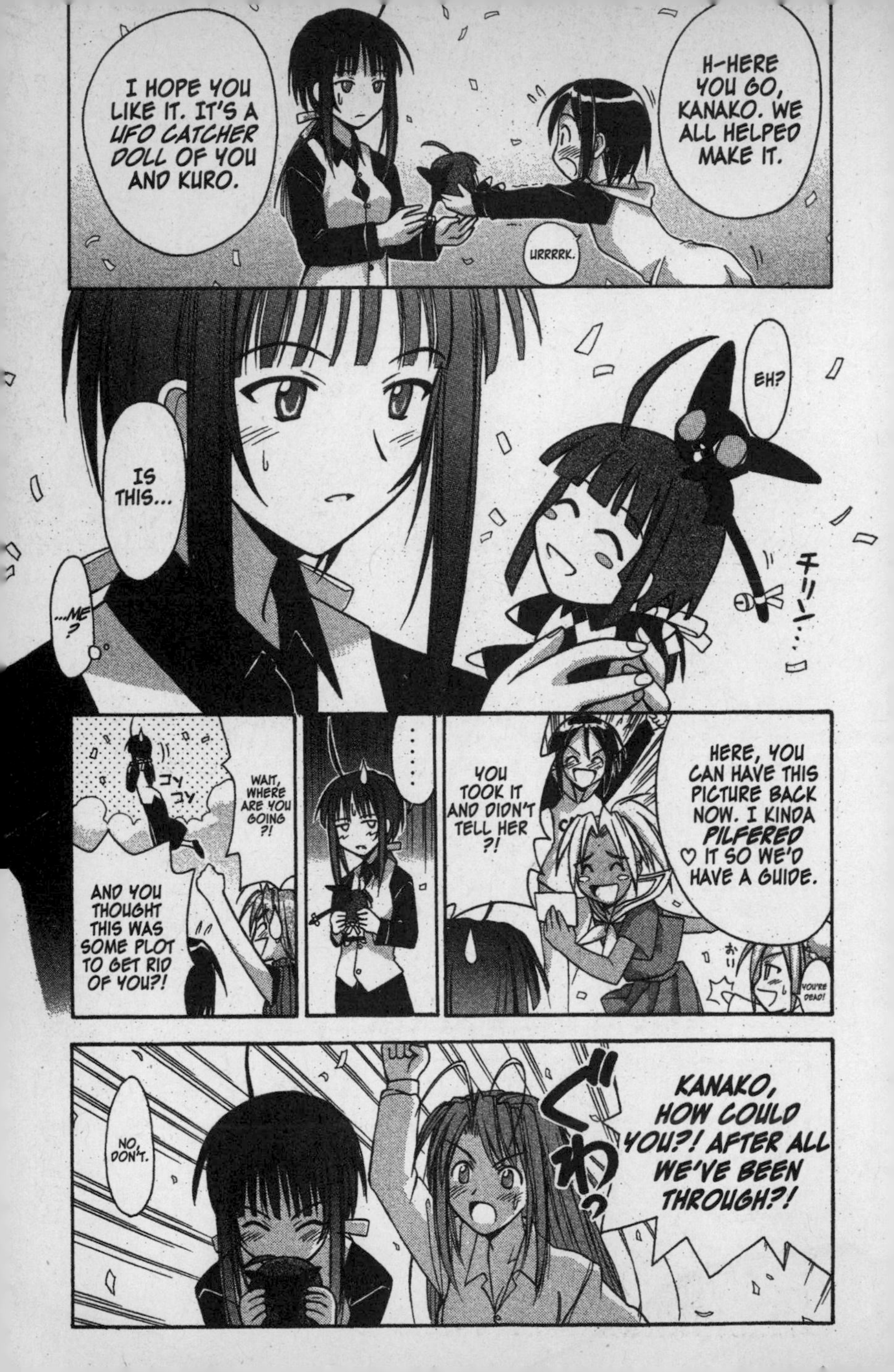
H-HERE YOU GO, KANAKO. WE ALL HELPED MAKE IT.
I HOPE YOU LIKE IT. IT'S A *UFO CATCHER DOLL* OF YOU AND KURO.
URRRRK.
EH?
チリン…
IS THIS...
...ME?
HERE, YOU CAN HAVE THIS PICTURE BACK NOW. I KINDA *PILFERED* ♡ IT SO WE'D HAVE A GUIDE.
おい
YOU'RE DEAD!
YOU TOOK IT AND DIDN'T TELL HER?!
......
WAIT, WHERE ARE YOU GOING?!
コソ コソ
AND YOU THOUGHT THIS WAS SOME PLOT TO GET RID OF YOU?!
KANAKO, HOW COULD YOU?! AFTER ALL WE'VE BEEN THROUGH?!
ぐわっ
NO, DON'T.

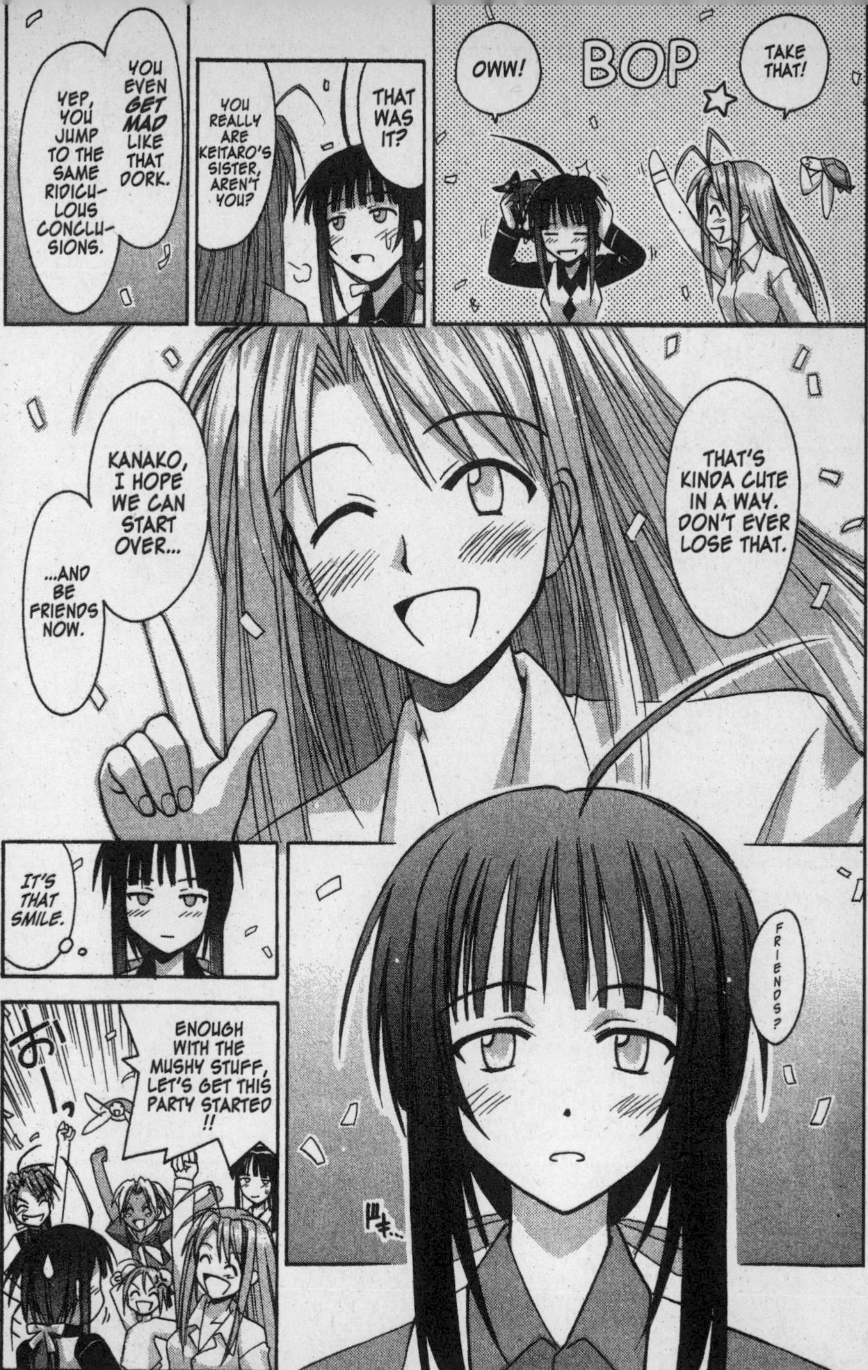
TAKE THAT!
BOP
OWW!
THAT WAS IT?
YOU REALLY ARE KEITARO'S SISTER, AREN'T YOU?
YOU EVEN GET MAD LIKE THAT DORK.
YEP, YOU JUMP TO THE SAME RIDICULOUS CONCLUSIONS.
THAT'S KINDA CUTE IN A WAY. DON'T EVER LOSE THAT.
KANAKO, I HOPE WE CAN START OVER...
...AND BE FRIENDS NOW.
FRIENDS?
IT'S THAT SMILE.
ENOUGH WITH THE MUSHY STUFF, LET'S GET THIS PARTY STARTED!!
おー、

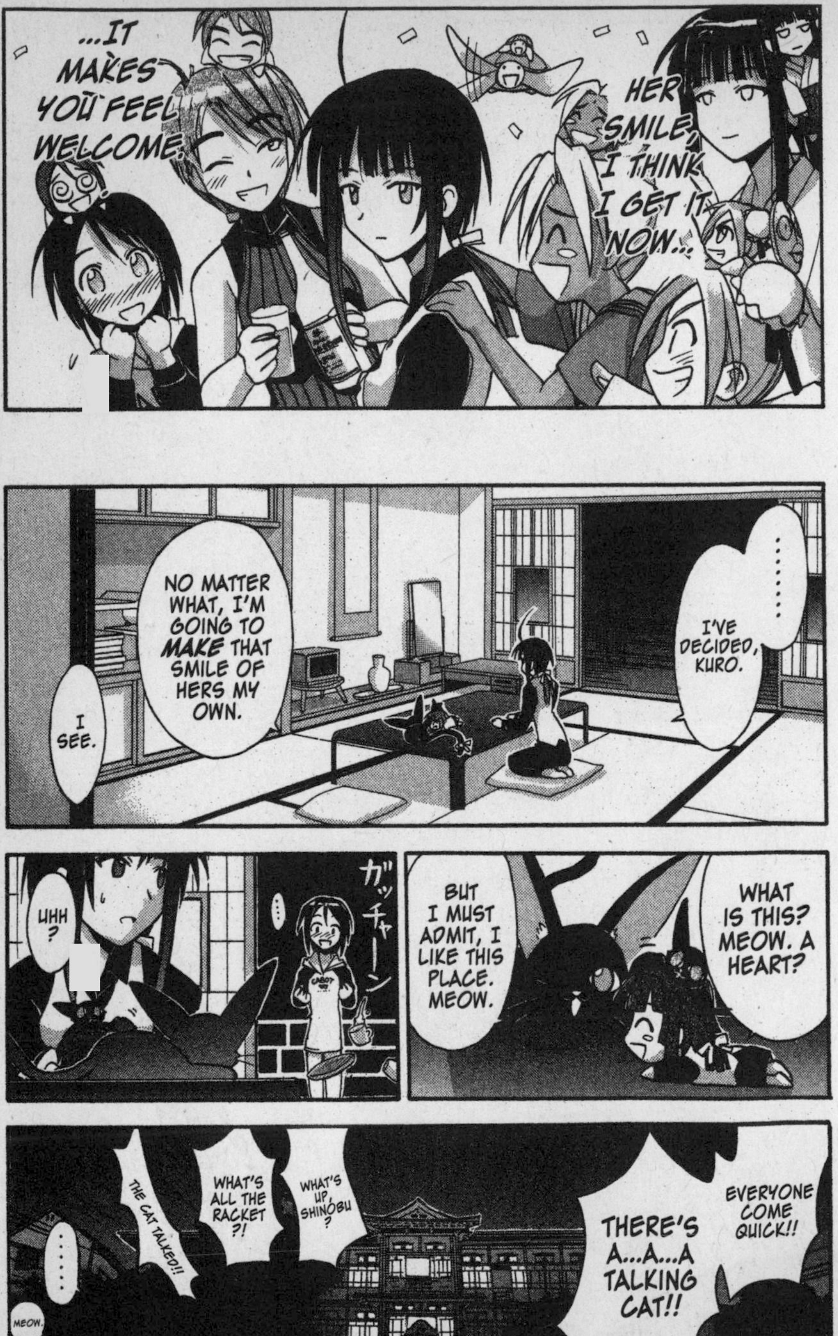
HER SMILE, I THINK I GET IT NOW...
...IT MAKES YOU FEEL WELCOME.
......
I'VE DECIDED, KURO.
NO MATTER WHAT, I'M GOING TO MAKE THAT SMILE OF HERS MY OWN.
I SEE.
WHAT IS THIS? MEOW. A HEART?
BUT I MUST ADMIT, I LIKE THIS PLACE. MEOW.
ガッチャーン
...
UHH?
EVERYONE COME QUICK!!
THERE'S A...A...A TALKING CAT!!
WHAT'S UP, SHINOBU?
WHAT'S ALL THE RACKET?!
THE CAT TALKED!!
......
MEOW.

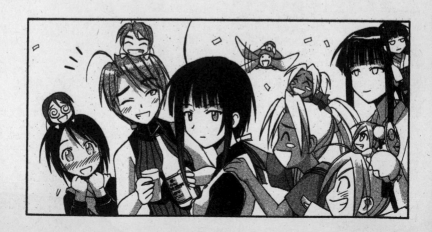

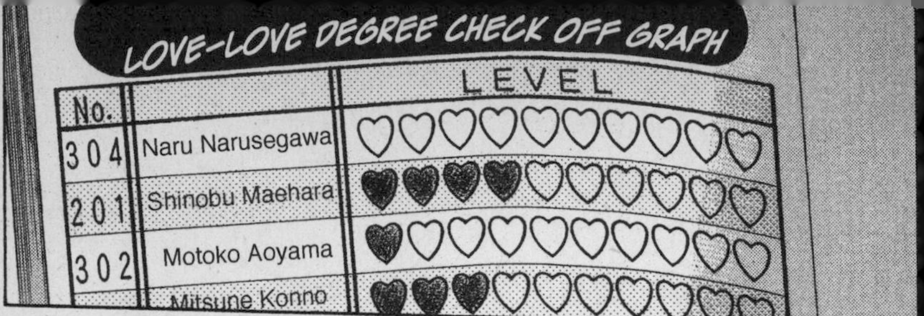
LOVE-LOVE DEGREE CHECK OFF GRAPH
LEVEL
No.
304 Naru Narusegawa
201 Shinobu Maehara
302 Motoko Aoyama
Mitsune Konno

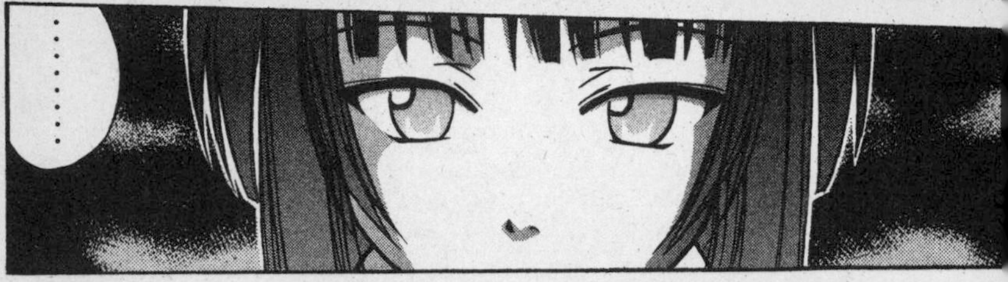
......

Love Hina

HINATA.94 A Love-Love Simulation

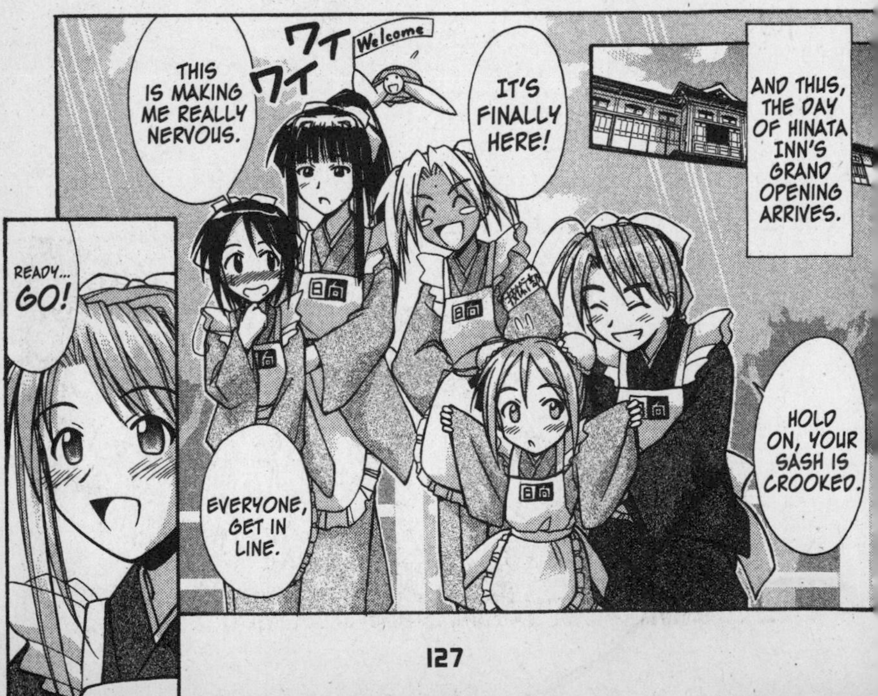
AND THUS, THE DAY OF HINATA INN'S GRAND OPENING ARRIVES.
IT'S FINALLY HERE!
ワイワイ
Welcome
THIS IS MAKING ME REALLY NERVOUS.
HOLD ON, YOUR SASH IS CROOKED.
EVERYONE, GET IN LINE.
READY... GO!

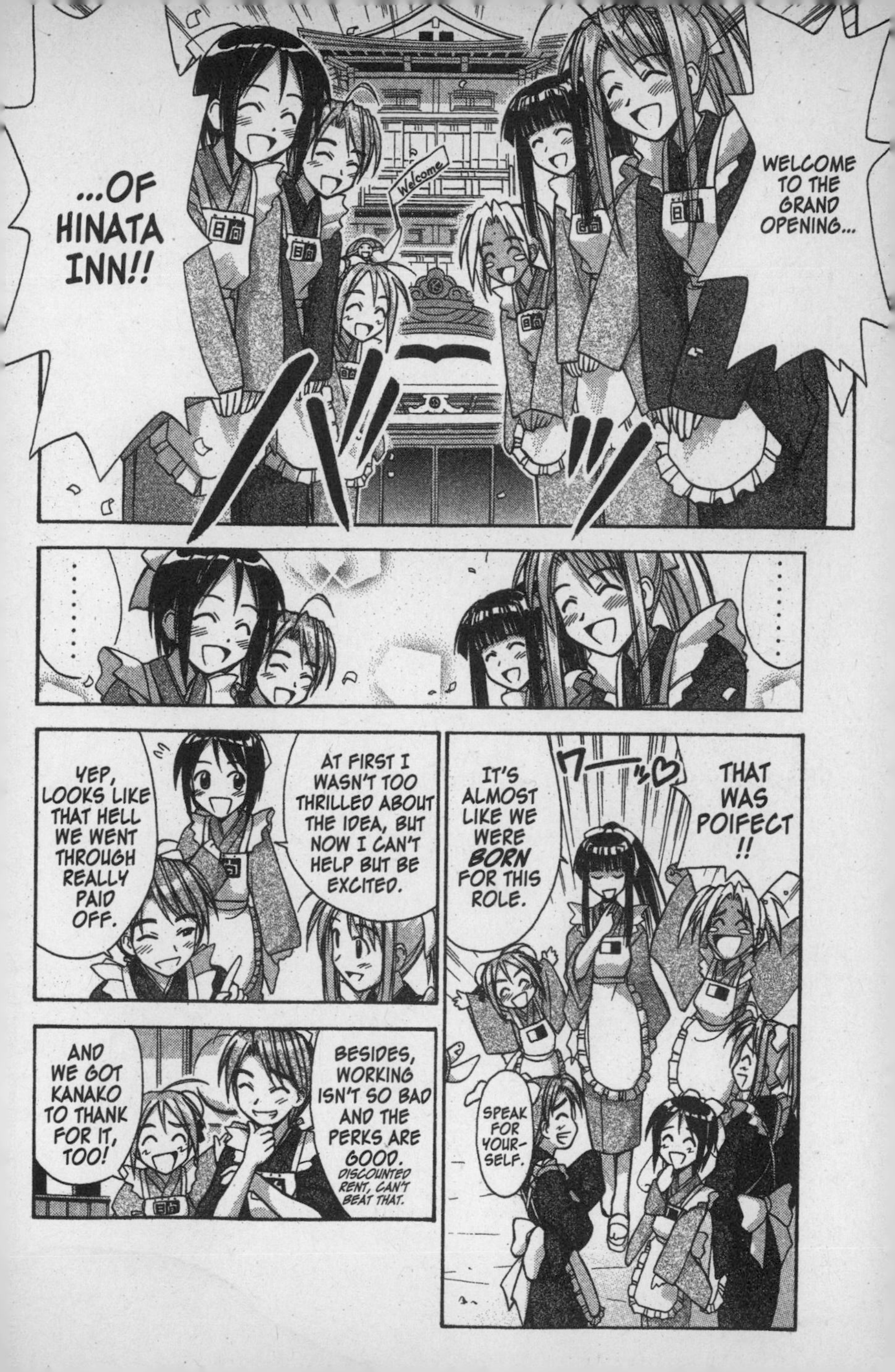
WELCOME TO THE GRAND OPENING...
...OF HINATA INN!!
......
......
THAT WAS POIFECT!!
ワーッ♡
IT'S ALMOST LIKE WE WERE BORN FOR THIS ROLE.
SPEAK FOR YOURSELF.
AT FIRST I WASN'T TOO THRILLED ABOUT THE IDEA, BUT NOW I CAN'T HELP BUT BE EXCITED.
YEP, LOOKS LIKE THAT HELL WE WENT THROUGH REALLY PAID OFF.
BESIDES, WORKING ISN'T SO BAD AND THE PERKS ARE GOOD.
DISCOUNTED RENT, CAN'T BEAT THAT.
AND WE GOT KANAKO TO THANK FOR IT, TOO!

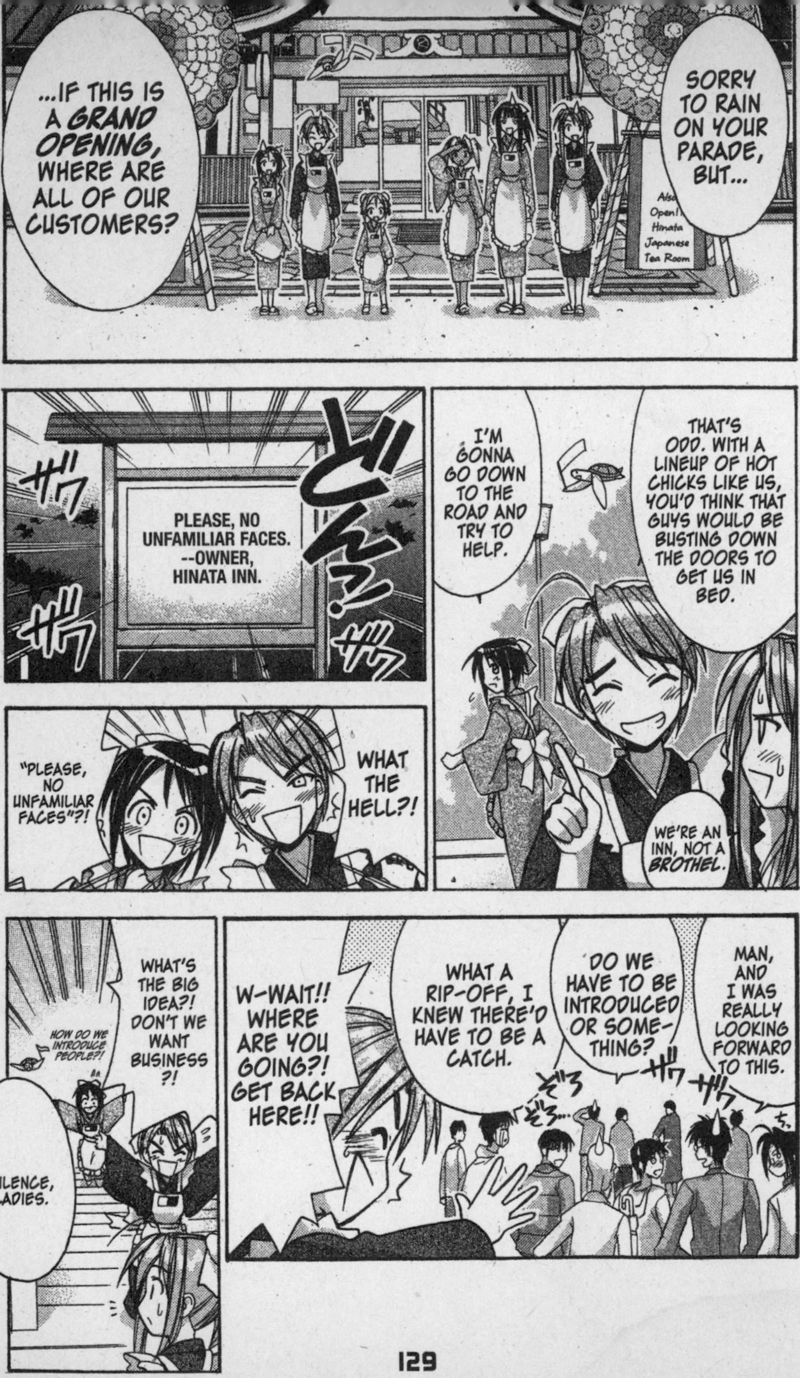
SORRY TO RAIN ON YOUR PARADE, BUT...
Also Open!! Hinata Japanese Tea Room
...IF THIS IS A GRAND OPENING, WHERE ARE ALL OF OUR CUSTOMERS?
THAT'S ODD. WITH A LINEUP OF HOT CHICKS LIKE US, YOU'D THINK THAT GUYS WOULD BE BUSTING DOWN THE DOORS TO GET US IN BED.
I'M GONNA GO DOWN TO THE ROAD AND TRY TO HELP.
WE'RE AN INN, NOT A BROTHEL.
PLEASE, NO UNFAMILIAR FACES. --OWNER, HINATA INN.
WHAT THE HELL?!
"PLEASE, NO UNFAMILIAR FACES"?!
MAN, AND I WAS REALLY LOOKING FORWARD TO THIS.
DO WE HAVE TO BE INTRODUCED OR SOME-THING?
WHAT A RIP-OFF, I KNEW THERE'D HAVE TO BE A CATCH.
W-WAIT!! WHERE ARE YOU GOING?! GET BACK HERE!!
WHAT'S THE BIG IDEA?! DON'T WE WANT BUSINESS?!
HOW DO WE INTRODUCE PEOPLE?!
SILENCE, LADIES.

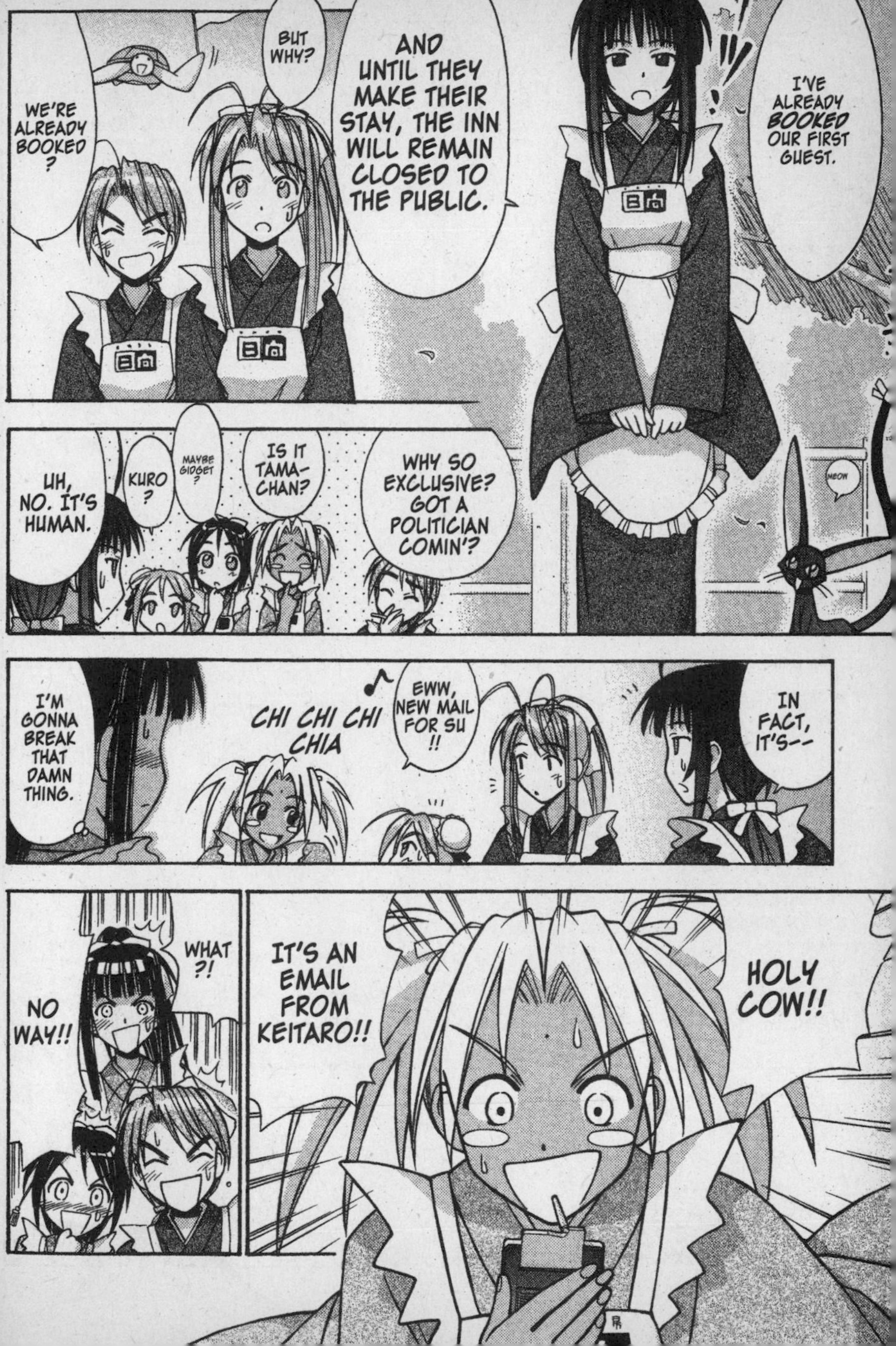
I'VE ALREADY BOOKED OUR FIRST GUEST.
MEOW
AND UNTIL THEY MAKE THEIR STAY, THE INN WILL REMAIN CLOSED TO THE PUBLIC.
BUT WHY?
WE'RE ALREADY BOOKED?
WHY SO EXCLUSIVE? GOT A POLITICIAN COMIN'?
IS IT TAMA-CHAN?
MAYBE GIDGET?
KURO?
UH, NO. IT'S HUMAN.
IN FACT, IT'S--
EWW, NEW MAIL FOR SU!!
CHI CHI CHI CHIA
I'M GONNA BREAK THAT DAMN THING.
HOLY COW!!
IT'S AN EMAIL FROM KEITARO!!
WHAT?!
NO WAY!!

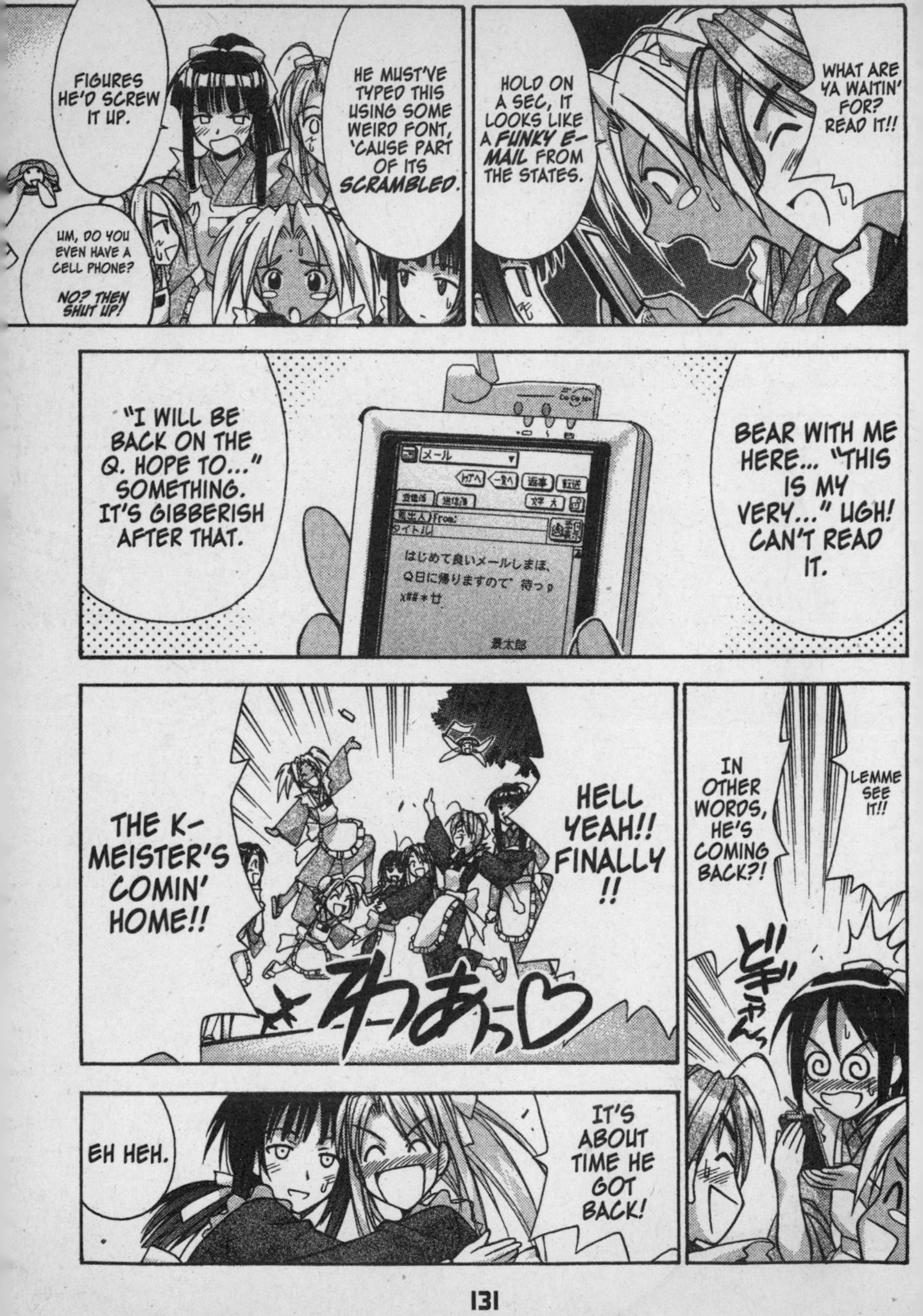
WHAT ARE YA WAITIN' FOR? READ IT!!
HOLD ON A SEC, IT LOOKS LIKE A FUNKY E-MAIL FROM THE STATES.
HE MUST'VE TYPED THIS USING SOME WEIRD FONT, 'CAUSE PART OF ITS SCRAMBLED.
FIGURES HE'D SCREW IT UP.
UM, DO YOU EVEN HAVE A CELL PHONE?
NO? THEN SHUT UP!
BEAR WITH ME HERE... "THIS IS MY VERY..." UGH! CAN'T READ IT.
メール
はじめて良いメールしまほ、
Q日に帰りますので 待っp
x##＊せ
景太郎
"I WILL BE BACK ON THE Q. HOPE TO..." SOMETHING. IT'S GIBBERISH AFTER THAT.
LEMME SEE IT!!
IN OTHER WORDS, HE'S COMING BACK?!
どぎゃん
HELL YEAH!! FINALLY !!
THE K-MEISTER'S COMIN' HOME!!
わあっ♡
IT'S ABOUT TIME HE GOT BACK!
EH HEH.

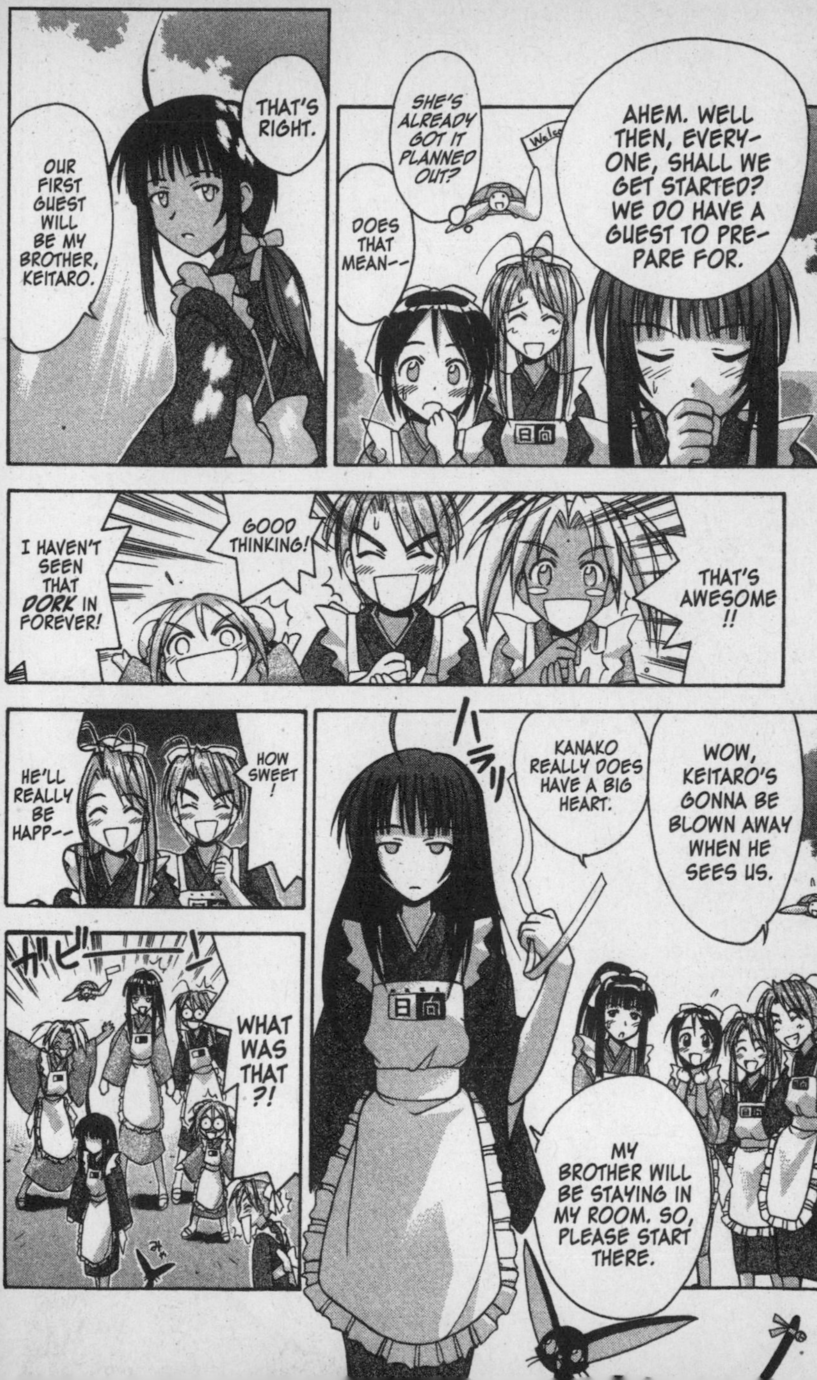
AHEM. WELL THEN, EVERY-ONE, SHALL WE GET STARTED? WE DO HAVE A GUEST TO PRE-PARE FOR.
SHE'S ALREADY GOT IT PLANNED OUT?
DOES THAT MEAN--
THAT'S RIGHT.
OUR FIRST GUEST WILL BE MY BROTHER, KEITARO.
THAT'S AWESOME!!
GOOD THINKING!
I HAVEN'T SEEN THAT DORK IN FOREVER!
WOW, KEITARO'S GONNA BE BLOWN AWAY WHEN HE SEES US.
KANAKO REALLY DOES HAVE A BIG HEART.
ハラリ
MY BROTHER WILL BE STAYING IN MY ROOM. SO, PLEASE START THERE.
HOW SWEET!
HE'LL REALLY BE HAPP--
WHAT WAS THAT?!

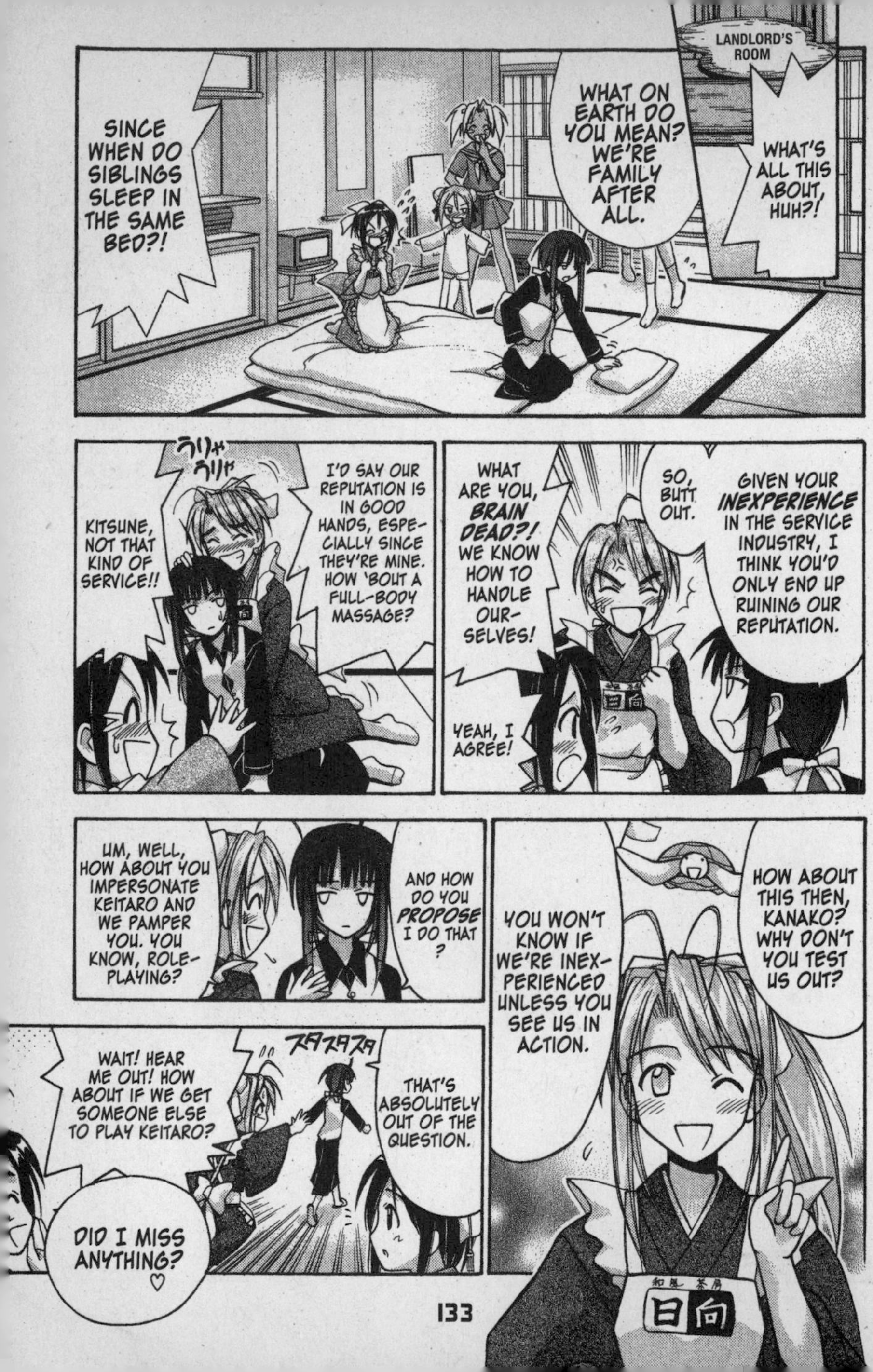
LANDLORD'S ROOM
WHAT'S ALL THIS ABOUT, HUH?!
WHAT ON EARTH DO YOU MEAN? WE'RE FAMILY AFTER ALL.
SINCE WHEN DO SIBLINGS SLEEP IN THE SAME BED?!
GIVEN YOUR INEXPERIENCE IN THE SERVICE INDUSTRY, I THINK YOU'D ONLY END UP RUINING OUR REPUTATION.
SO, BUTT OUT.
WHAT ARE YOU, BRAIN DEAD?! WE KNOW HOW TO HANDLE OURSELVES!
YEAH, I AGREE!
日向
I'D SAY OUR REPUTATION IS IN GOOD HANDS, ESPECIALLY SINCE THEY'RE MINE. HOW 'BOUT A FULL-BODY MASSAGE?
うりゃうりゃ
KITSUNE, NOT THAT KIND OF SERVICE!!
HOW ABOUT THIS THEN, KANAKO? WHY DON'T YOU TEST US OUT?
YOU WON'T KNOW IF WE'RE INEXPERIENCED UNLESS YOU SEE US IN ACTION.
和風 茶房
日向
AND HOW DO YOU PROPOSE I DO THAT?
UM, WELL, HOW ABOUT YOU IMPERSONATE KEITARO AND WE PAMPER YOU. YOU KNOW, ROLE-PLAYING?
THAT'S ABSOLUTELY OUT OF THE QUESTION.
スタスタスタ
WAIT! HEAR ME OUT! HOW ABOUT IF WE GET SOMEONE ELSE TO PLAY KEITARO?
DID I MISS ANYTHING? ♡

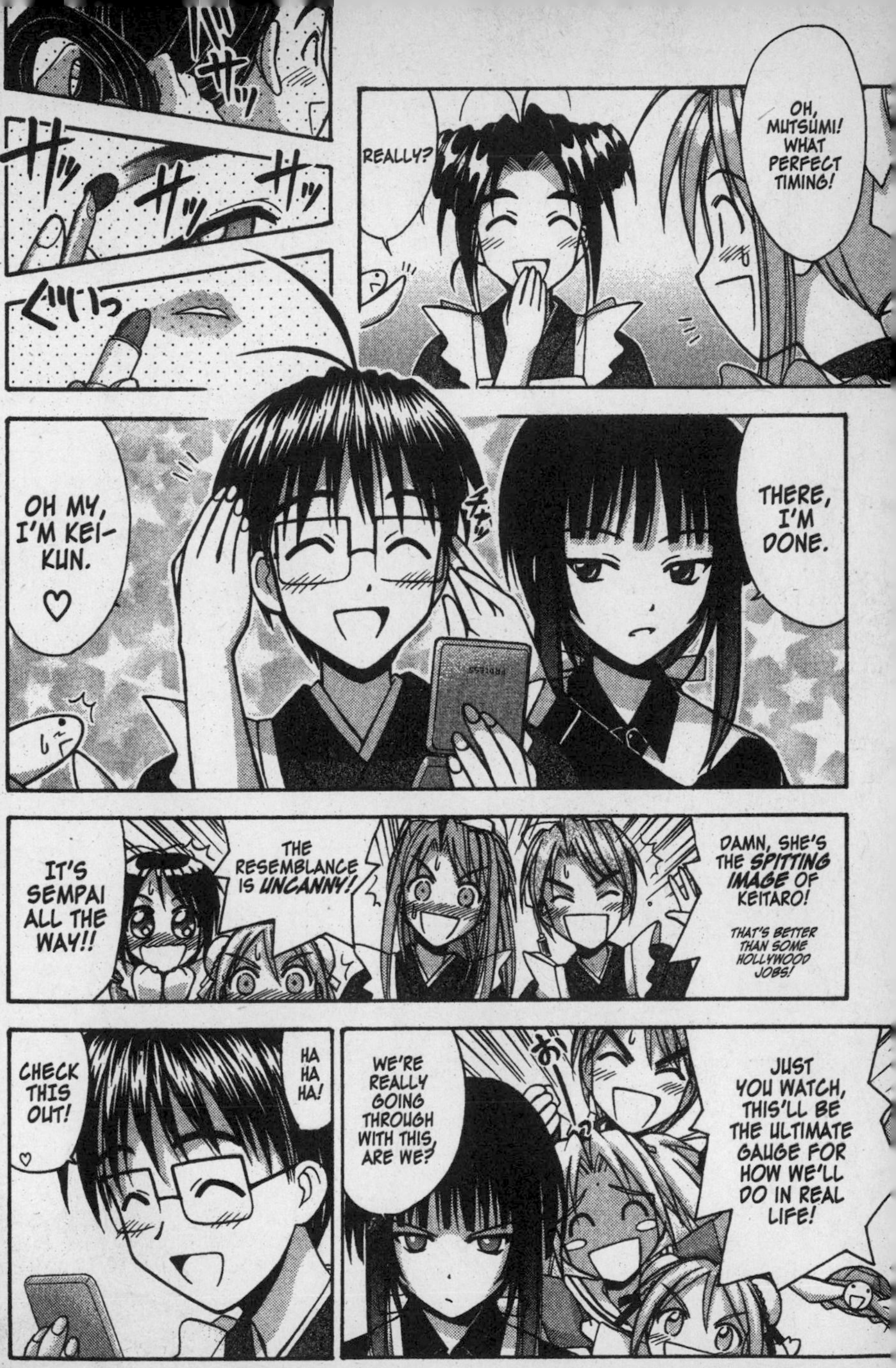
OH, MUTSUMI! WHAT PERFECT TIMING!
REALLY?
THERE, I'M DONE.
OH MY, I'M KEI-KUN. ♡
DAMN, SHE'S THE *SPITTING IMAGE* OF KEITARO!
THAT'S BETTER THAN SOME HOLLYWOOD JOBS!
THE RESEMBLANCE IS *UNCANNY*!
IT'S SEMPAI ALL THE WAY!!
JUST YOU WATCH, THIS'LL BE THE ULTIMATE GAUGE FOR HOW WE'LL DO IN REAL LIFE!
WE'RE REALLY GOING THROUGH WITH THIS, ARE WE?
HA HA HA!
CHECK THIS OUT! ♡

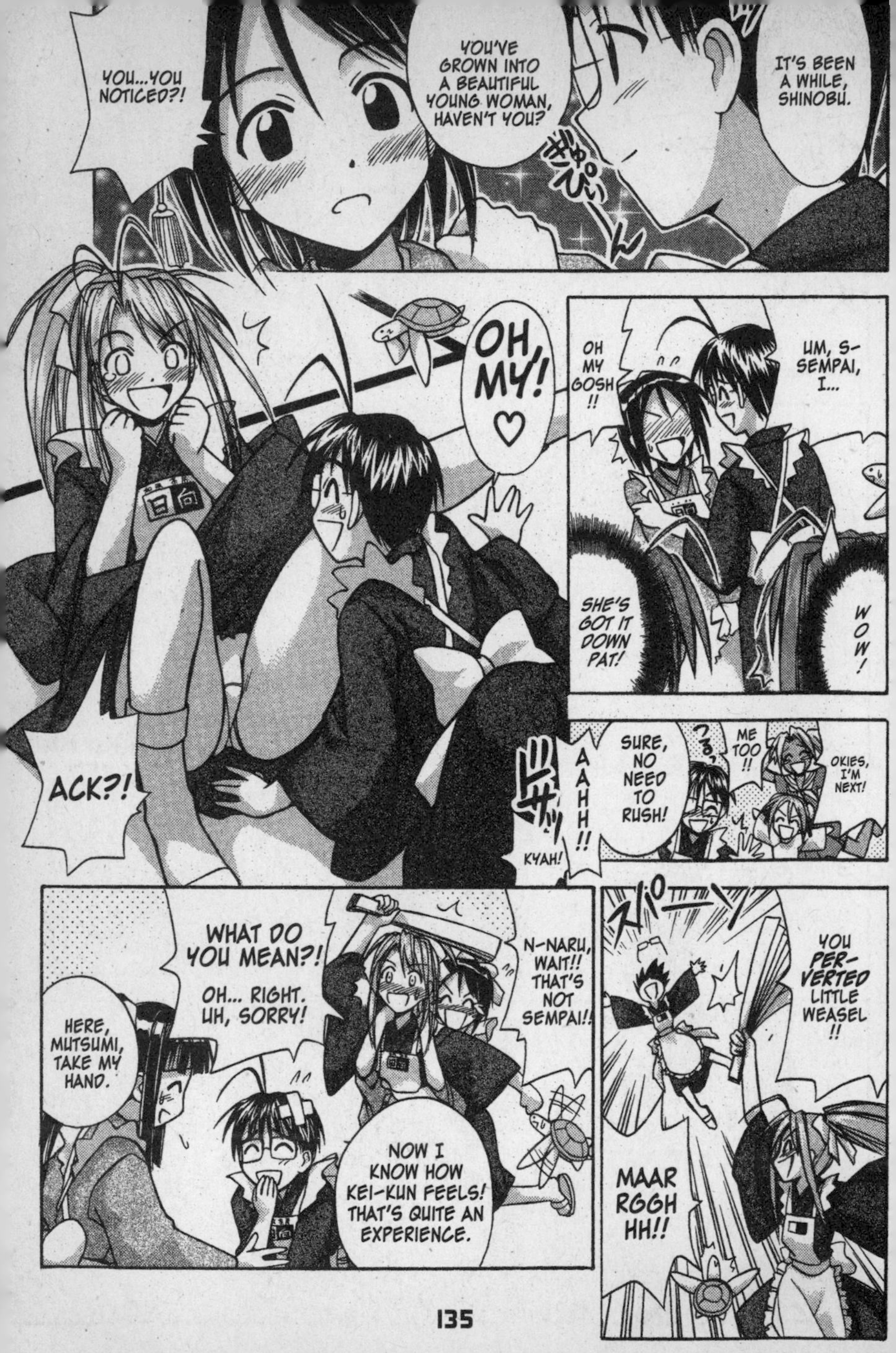
IT'S BEEN A WHILE, SHINOBU.
YOU'VE GROWN INTO A BEAUTIFUL YOUNG WOMAN, HAVEN'T YOU?
YOU...YOU NOTICED?!
UM, S-SEMPAI, I...
OH MY GOSH!!
WOW!
SHE'S GOT IT DOWN PAT!
OKIES, I'M NEXT!
ME TOO!!
SURE, NO NEED TO RUSH!
AAHH!!
KYAH!
OH, MY! ♡
ACK?!
YOU PERVERTED LITTLE WEASEL!!
MAARRGGHHH!!
N-NARU, WAIT!! THAT'S NOT SEMPAI!!
WHAT DO YOU MEAN?!
OH... RIGHT. UH, SORRY!
HERE, MUTSUMI, TAKE MY HAND.
NOW I KNOW HOW KEI-KUN FEELS! THAT'S QUITE AN EXPERIENCE.

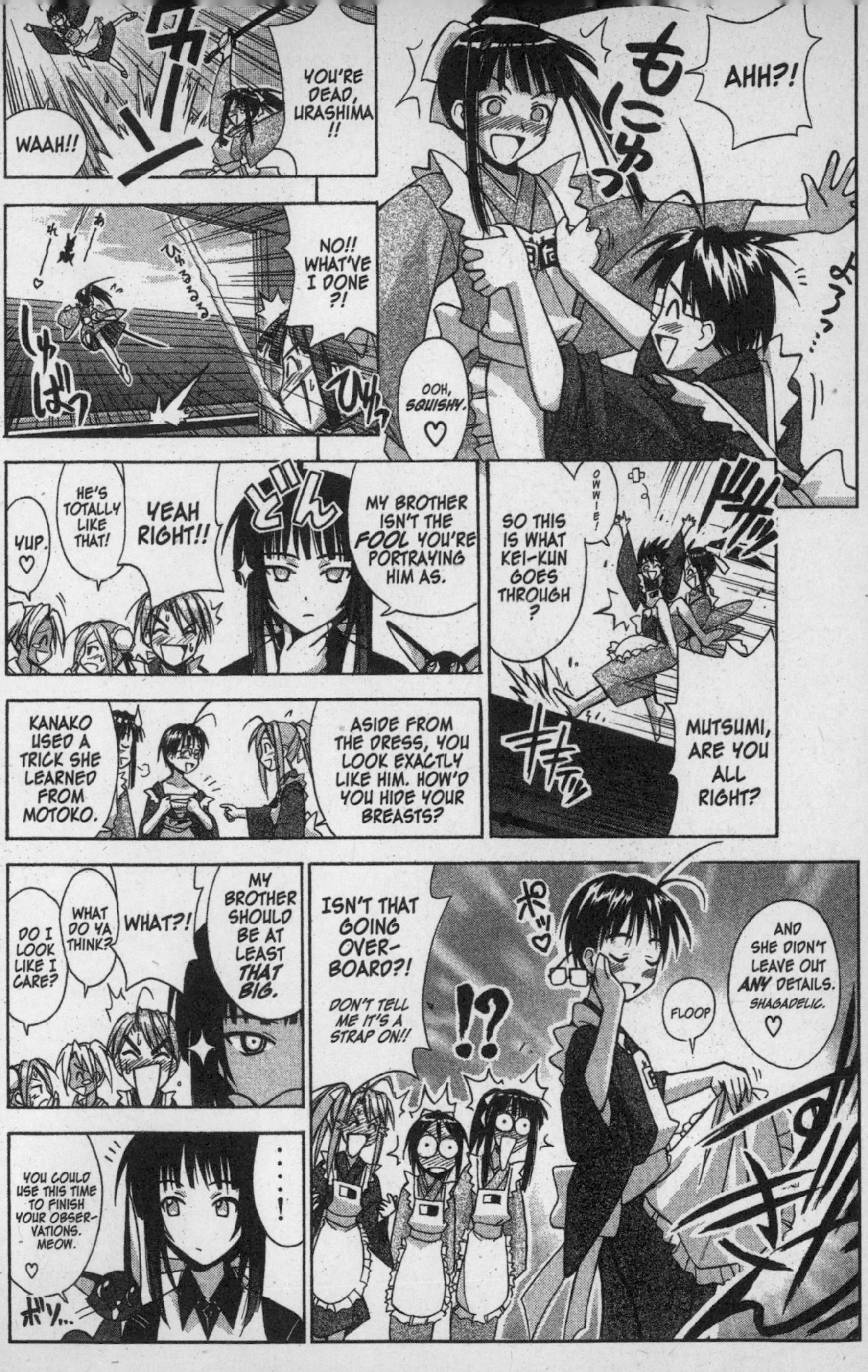
AHH?!
OOH, SQUISHY. ♥
YOU'RE DEAD, URASHIMA!!
WAAH!!
NO!! WHAT'VE I DONE?!
OWWIE!
SO THIS IS WHAT KEI-KUN GOES THROUGH?
MUTSUMI, ARE YOU ALL RIGHT?
MY BROTHER ISN'T THE FOOL YOU'RE PORTRAYING HIM AS.
YEAH RIGHT!!
HE'S TOTALLY LIKE THAT!
YUP. ♥
ASIDE FROM THE DRESS, YOU LOOK EXACTLY LIKE HIM. HOW'D YOU HIDE YOUR BREASTS?
KANAKO USED A TRICK SHE LEARNED FROM MOTOKO.
AND SHE DIDN'T LEAVE OUT ANY DETAILS. SHAGADELIC. ♥
FLOOP
!?
ISN'T THAT GOING OVER-BOARD?!
DON'T TELL ME IT'S A STRAP ON!!
MY BROTHER SHOULD BE AT LEAST THAT BIG.
WHAT?!
WHAT DO YA THINK?
DO I LOOK LIKE I CARE?
.....!
YOU COULD USE THIS TIME TO FINISH YOUR OBSER-VATIONS. MEOW. ♥

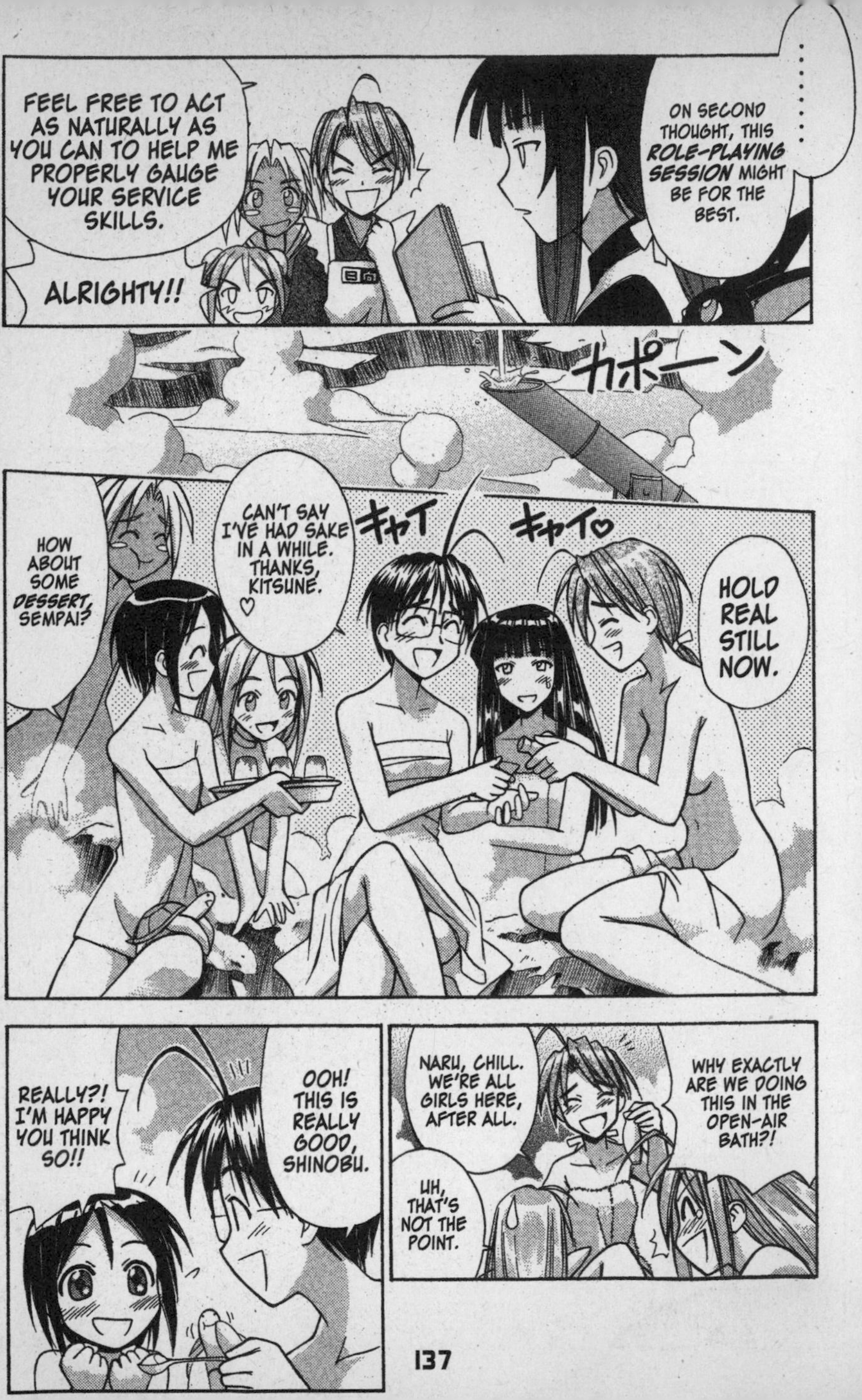
......
ON SECOND THOUGHT, THIS ROLE-PLAYING SESSION MIGHT BE FOR THE BEST.
FEEL FREE TO ACT AS NATURALLY AS YOU CAN TO HELP ME PROPERLY GAUGE YOUR SERVICE SKILLS.
ALRIGHTY!!
カポーン
HOLD REAL STILL NOW.
キャイ♡
キャイ
CAN'T SAY I'VE HAD SAKE IN A WHILE. THANKS, KITSUNE. ♡
HOW ABOUT SOME DESSERT, SEMPAI?
WHY EXACTLY ARE WE DOING THIS IN THE OPEN-AIR BATH?!
NARU, CHILL. WE'RE ALL GIRLS HERE, AFTER ALL.
UH, THAT'S NOT THE POINT.
OOH! THIS IS REALLY GOOD, SHINOBU.
REALLY?! I'M HAPPY YOU THINK SO!!

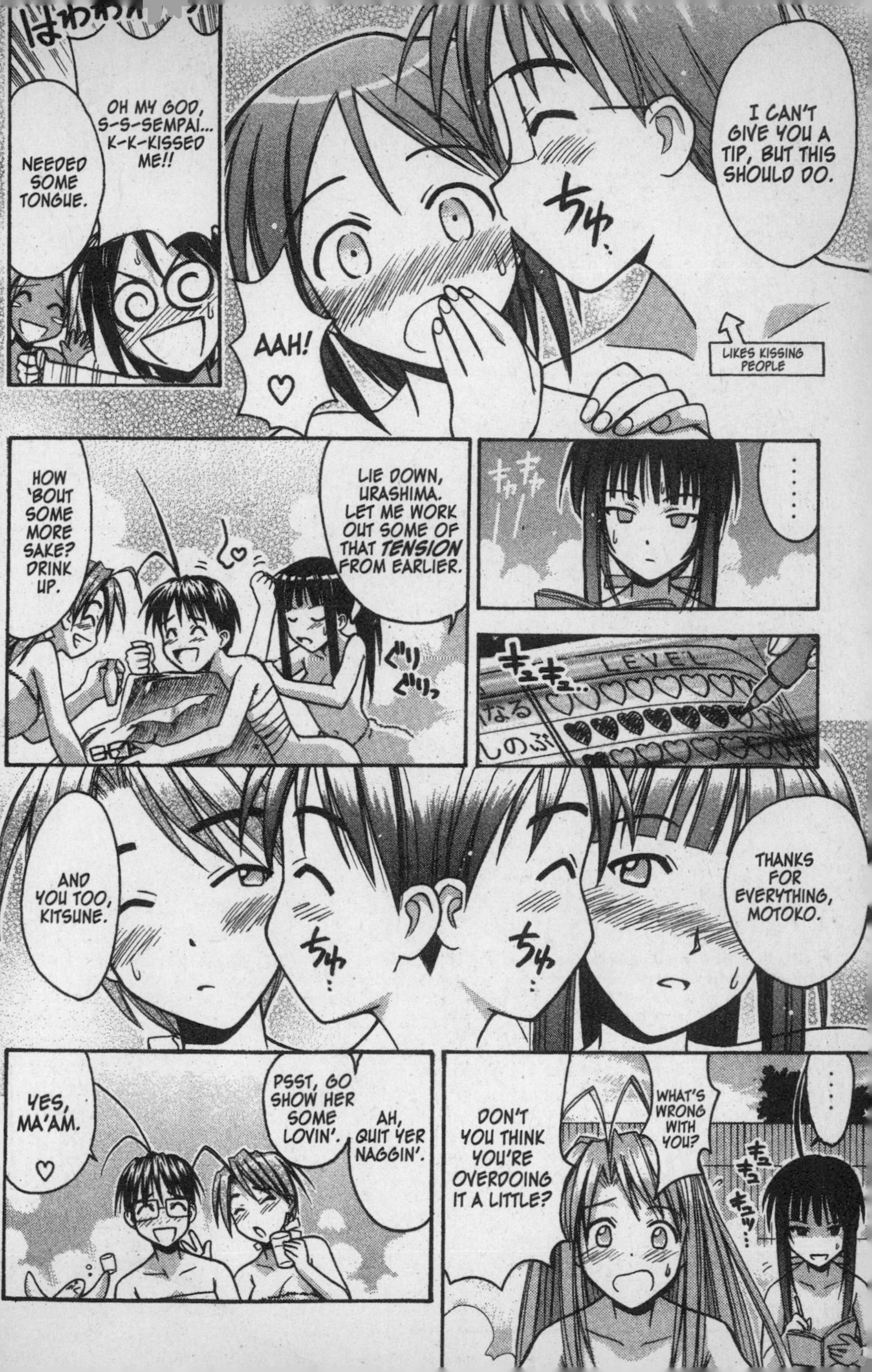
I CAN'T GIVE YOU A TIP, BUT THIS SHOULD DO.
ちゅ..
LIKES KISSING PEOPLE
AAH! ♡
ぱわわ
OH MY GOD, S-S-SEMPAI... K-K-KISSED ME!!
NEEDED SOME TONGUE.
......
キャキャ
キュキュ..
LEVEL
なる
しのぶ
LIE DOWN, URASHIMA. LET ME WORK OUT SOME OF THAT *TENSION* FROM EARLIER.
HOW 'BOUT SOME MORE SAKE? DRINK UP.
ぐりぐりっ
THANKS FOR EVERYTHING, MOTOKO.
ちゅ
ちゅ
AND YOU TOO, KITSUNE.
WHAT'S WRONG WITH YOU?
DON'T YOU THINK YOU'RE OVERDOING IT A LITTLE?
キュキュキュッ...
PSST, GO SHOW HER SOME LOVIN'.
AH, QUIT YER NAGGIN'.
YES, MA'AM. ♡

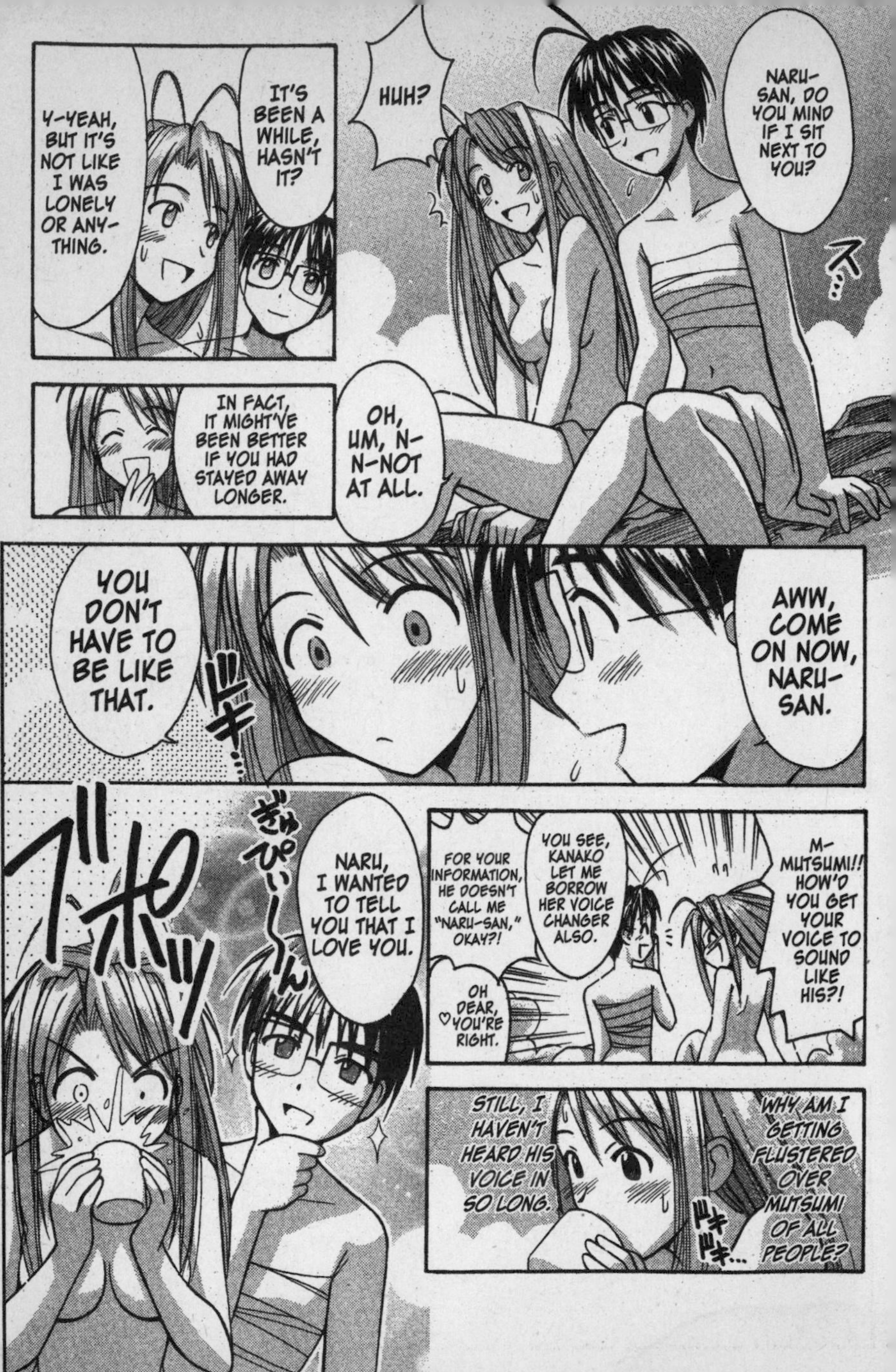
NARU-SAN, DO YOU MIND IF I SIT NEXT TO YOU?
HUH?
OH, UM, N-N-NOT AT ALL.
IT'S BEEN A WHILE, HASN'T IT?
Y-YEAH, BUT IT'S NOT LIKE I WAS LONELY OR ANY-THING.
IN FACT, IT MIGHT'VE BEEN BETTER IF YOU HAD STAYED AWAY LONGER.
AWW, COME ON NOW, NARU-SAN.
YOU DON'T HAVE TO BE LIKE THAT.
M-MUTSUMI!! HOW'D YOU GET YOUR VOICE TO SOUND LIKE HIS?!
YOU SEE, KANAKO LET ME BORROW HER VOICE CHANGER ALSO.
FOR YOUR INFORMATION, HE DOESN'T CALL ME "NARU-SAN," OKAY?!
OH DEAR, YOU'RE RIGHT.
WHY AM I GETTING FLUSTERED OVER MUTSUMI OF ALL PEOPLE?
STILL, I HAVEN'T HEARD HIS VOICE IN SO LONG.
NARU, I WANTED TO TELL YOU THAT I LOVE YOU.

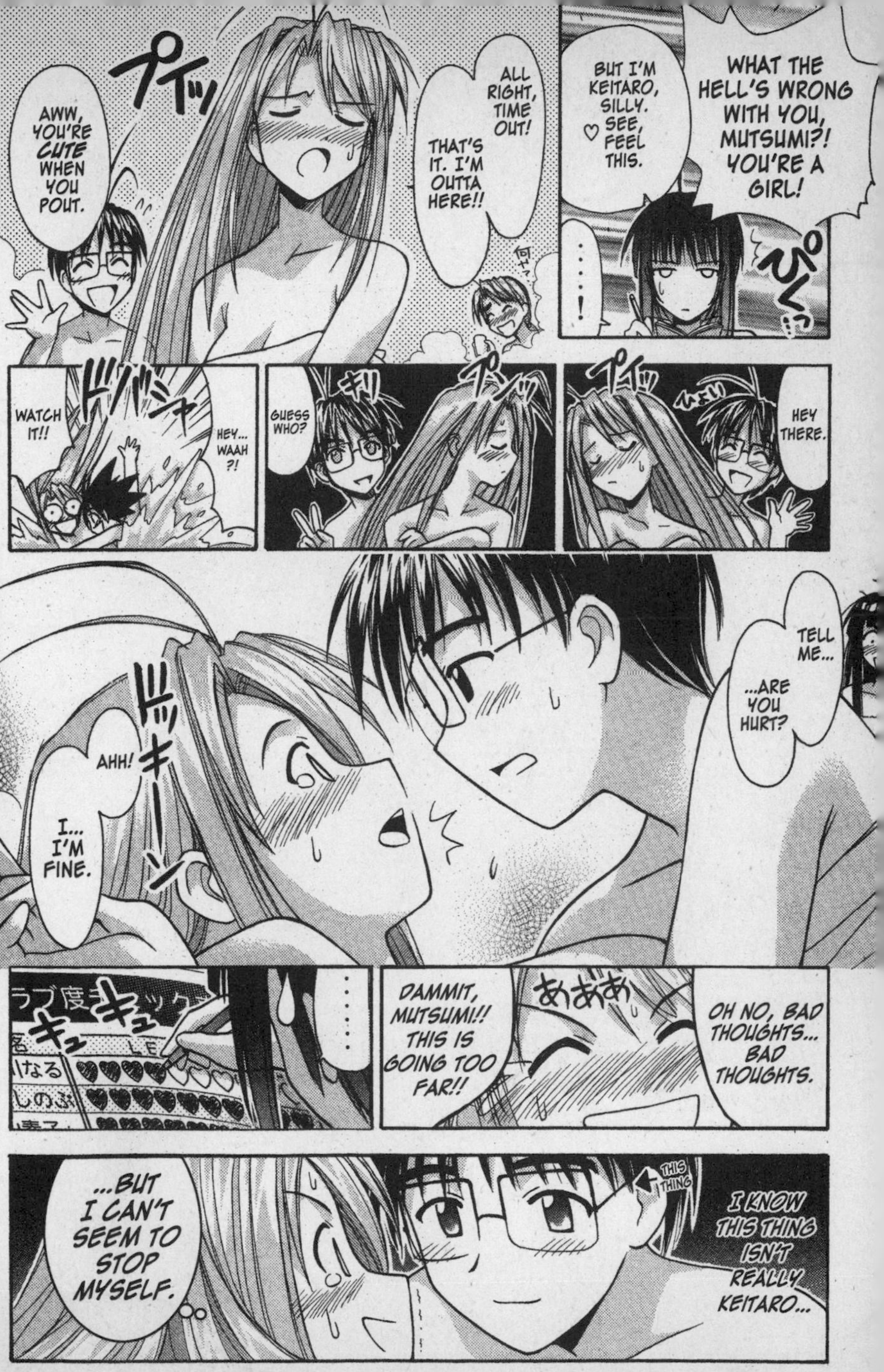
WHAT THE HELL'S WRONG WITH YOU, MUTSUMI?! YOU'RE A GIRL!
BUT I'M KEITARO, SILLY. ♡ SEE, FEEL THIS.
.....!
ALL RIGHT, TIME OUT!
THAT'S IT. I'M OUTTA HERE!!
AWW, YOU'RE CUTE WHEN YOU POUT.
HEY THERE.
GUESS WHO?
HEY... WAAH?!
WATCH IT!!
TELL ME...
...ARE YOU HURT?
AHH!
I... I'M FINE.
OH NO, BAD THOUGHTS... BAD THOUGHTS.
DAMMIT, MUTSUMI!! THIS IS GOING TOO FAR!!
......
I KNOW THIS THING ISN'T REALLY KEITARO...
THIS THING
...BUT I CAN'T SEEM TO STOP MYSELF.

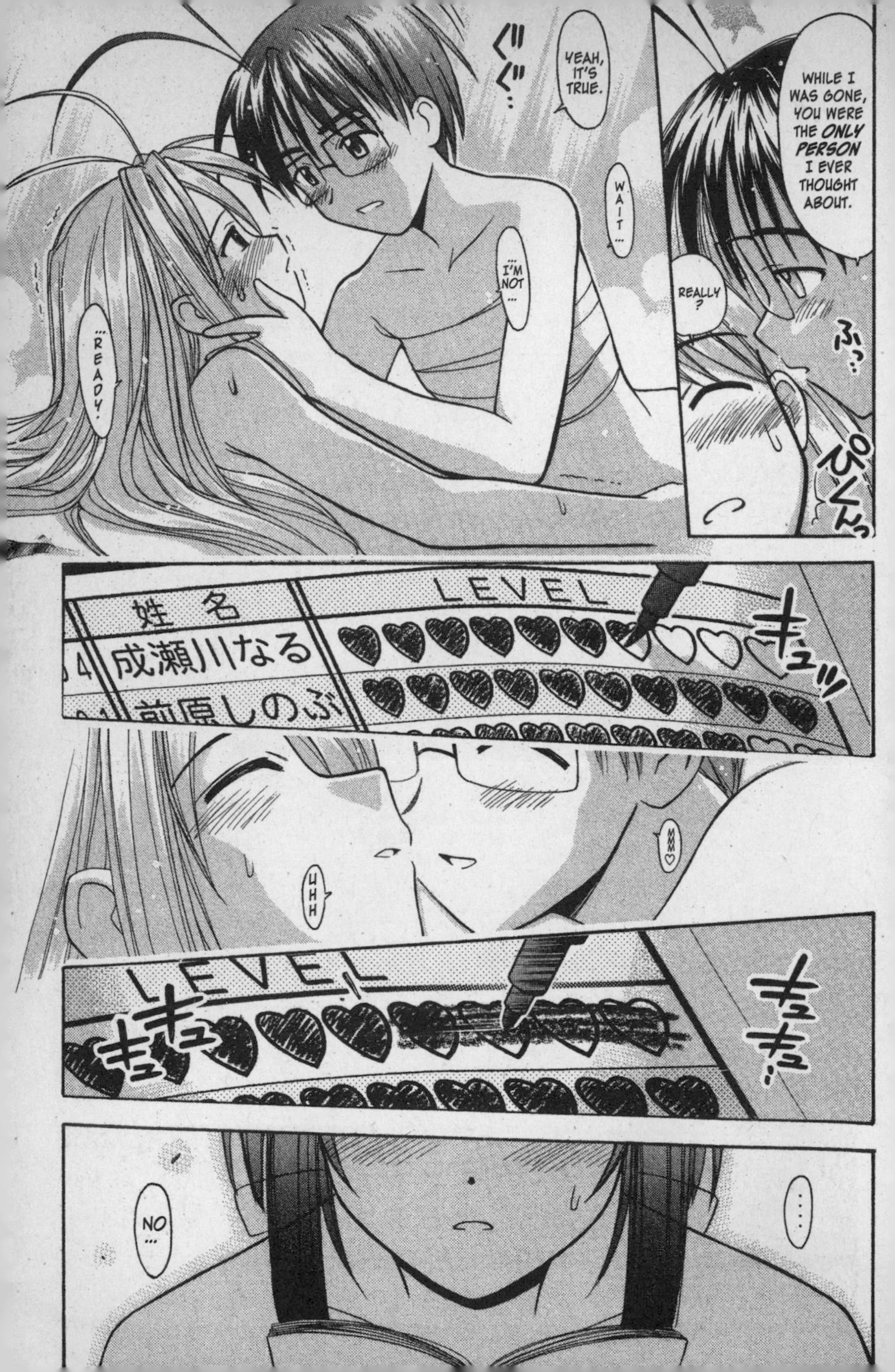
WHILE I WAS GONE, YOU WERE THE *ONLY PERSON* I EVER THOUGHT ABOUT.
REALLY?
ふっ…
ぴくんっ
YEAH, IT'S TRUE.
ぐぐ…
WAIT...
...I'M NOT...
...READY.
姓名
LEVEL
成瀬川なる
前原しのぶ
キュッ
MMM♡
UHH
LEVEL
キュキュ
キュキュ…
....
NO...

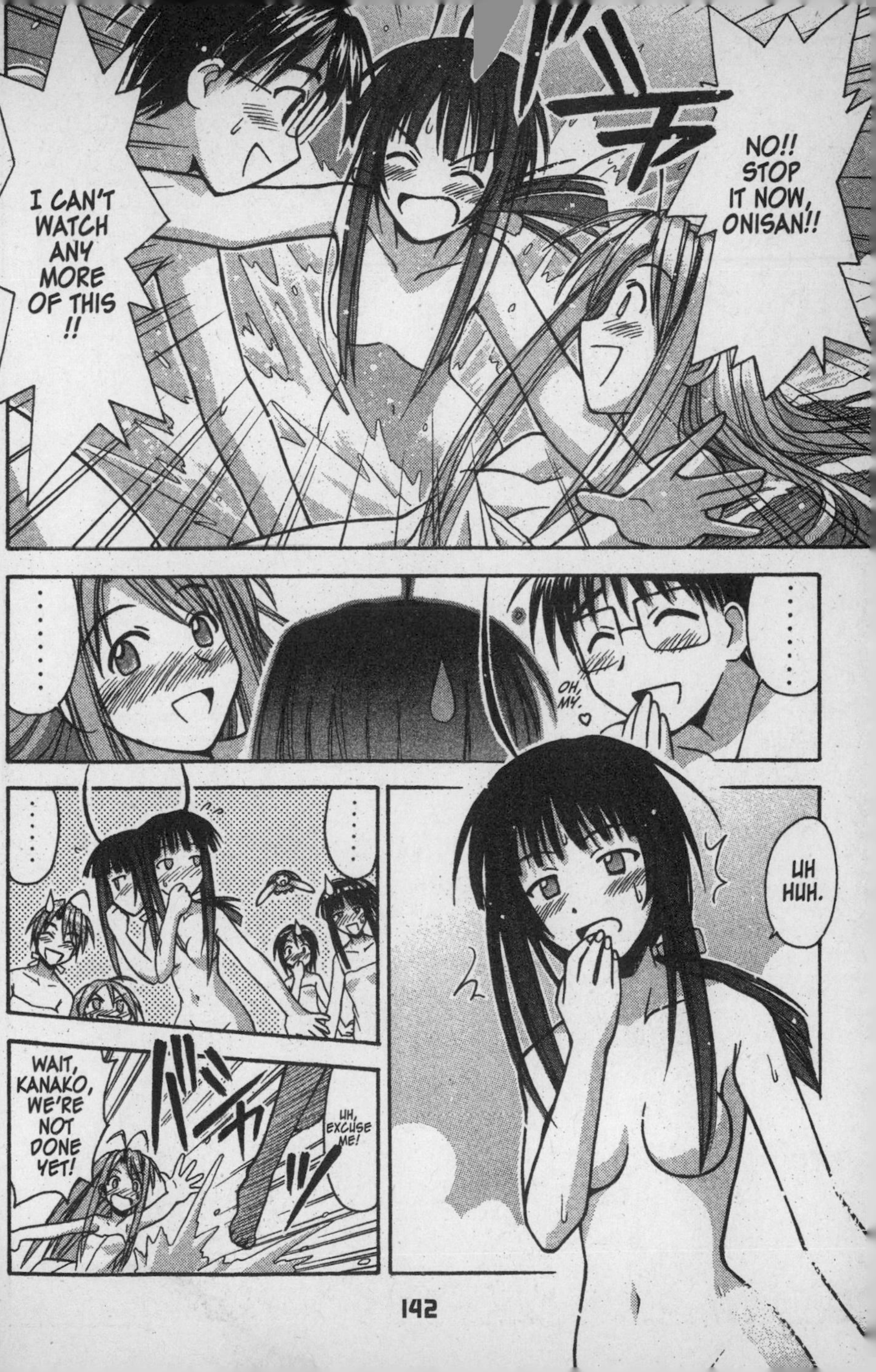
NO!! STOP IT NOW, ONISAN!!
I CAN'T WATCH ANY MORE OF THIS!!
......
OH, MY.
......
UH HUH.
......
UH, EXCUSE ME!
WAIT, KANAKO, WE'RE NOT DONE YET!

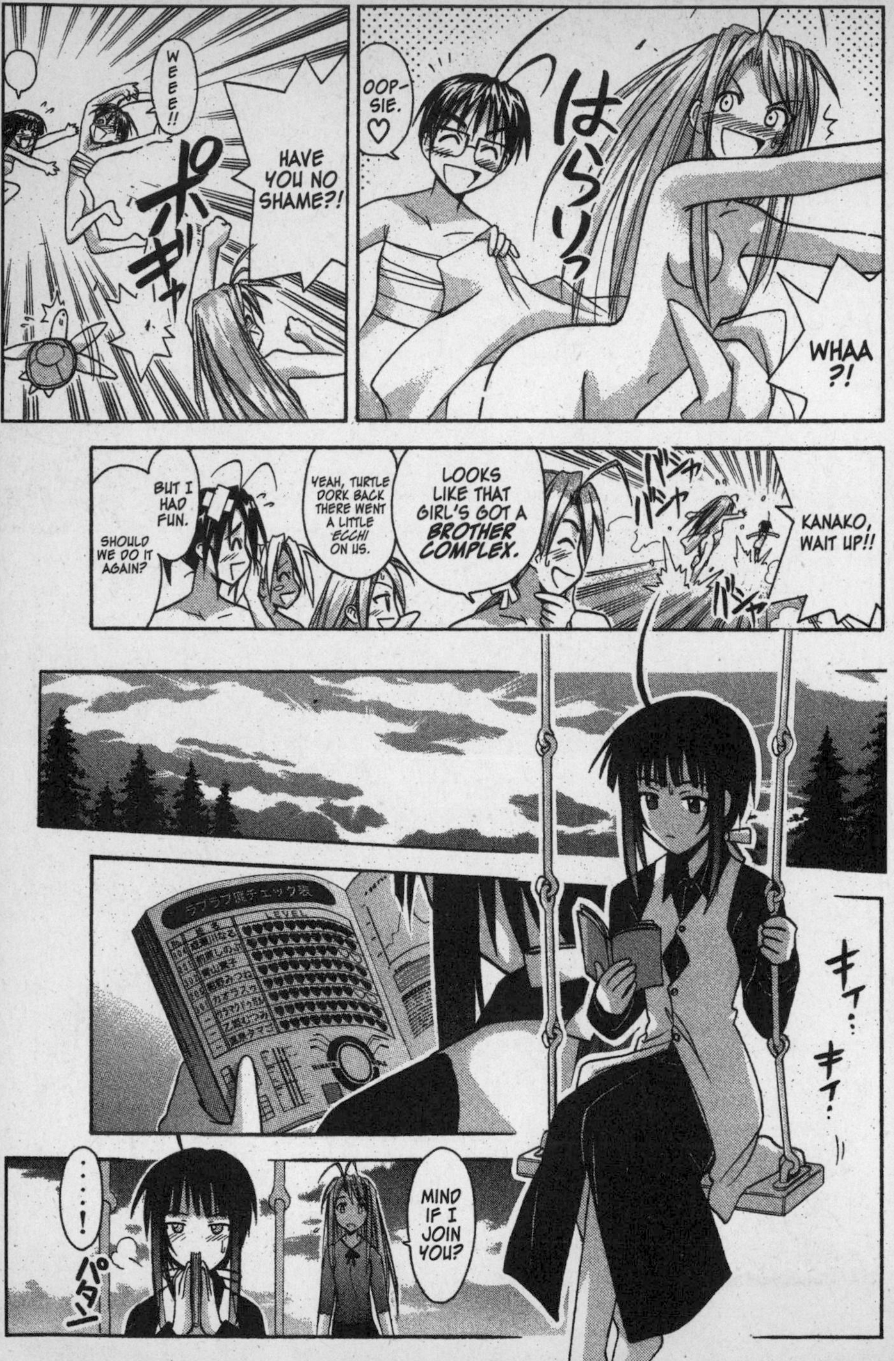

はらりっ
OOP-SIE. ♡
WHAA?!
WEEEE!!
HAVE YOU NO SHAME?!
ポギャ
KANAKO, WAIT UP!!
バシャ バシャ バシャ
LOOKS LIKE THAT GIRL'S GOT A BROTHER COMPLEX.
YEAH, TURTLE DORK BACK THERE WENT A LITTLE ECCHI ON US.
BUT I HAD FUN.
SHOULD WE DO IT AGAIN?
キィ… キィ…
LEVEL
MIND IF I JOIN YOU?
.....!
パタン

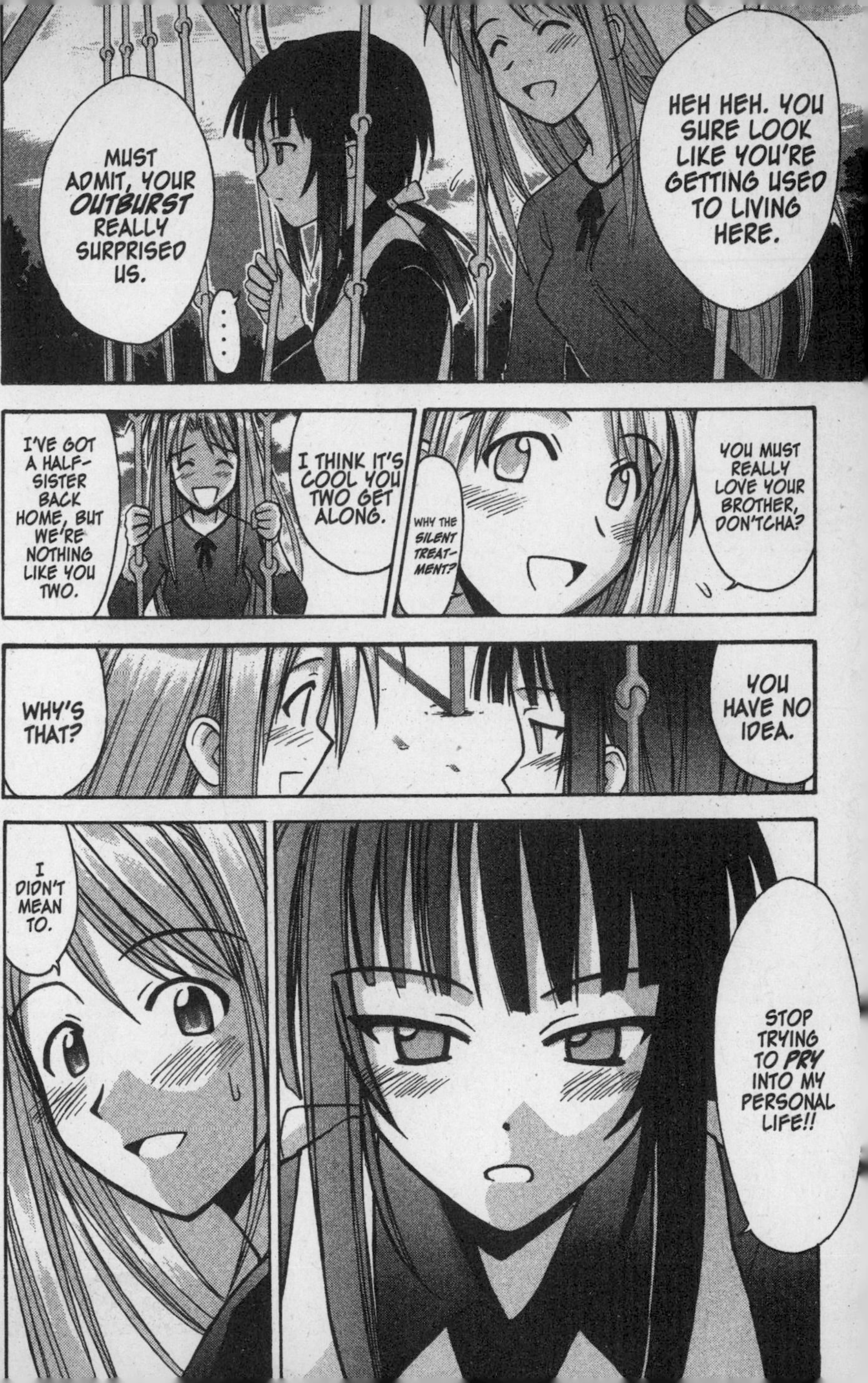
HEH HEH. YOU SURE LOOK LIKE YOU'RE GETTING USED TO LIVING HERE.
MUST ADMIT, YOUR *OUTBURST* REALLY SURPRISED US.
......
YOU MUST REALLY LOVE YOUR BROTHER, DON'TCHA?
WHY THE *SILENT TREATMENT?*
I THINK IT'S COOL YOU TWO GET ALONG.
I'VE GOT A HALF-SISTER BACK HOME, BUT WE'RE NOTHING LIKE YOU TWO.
YOU HAVE NO IDEA.
WHY'S THAT?
STOP TRYING TO *PRY* INTO MY PERSONAL LIFE!!
I DIDN'T MEAN TO.

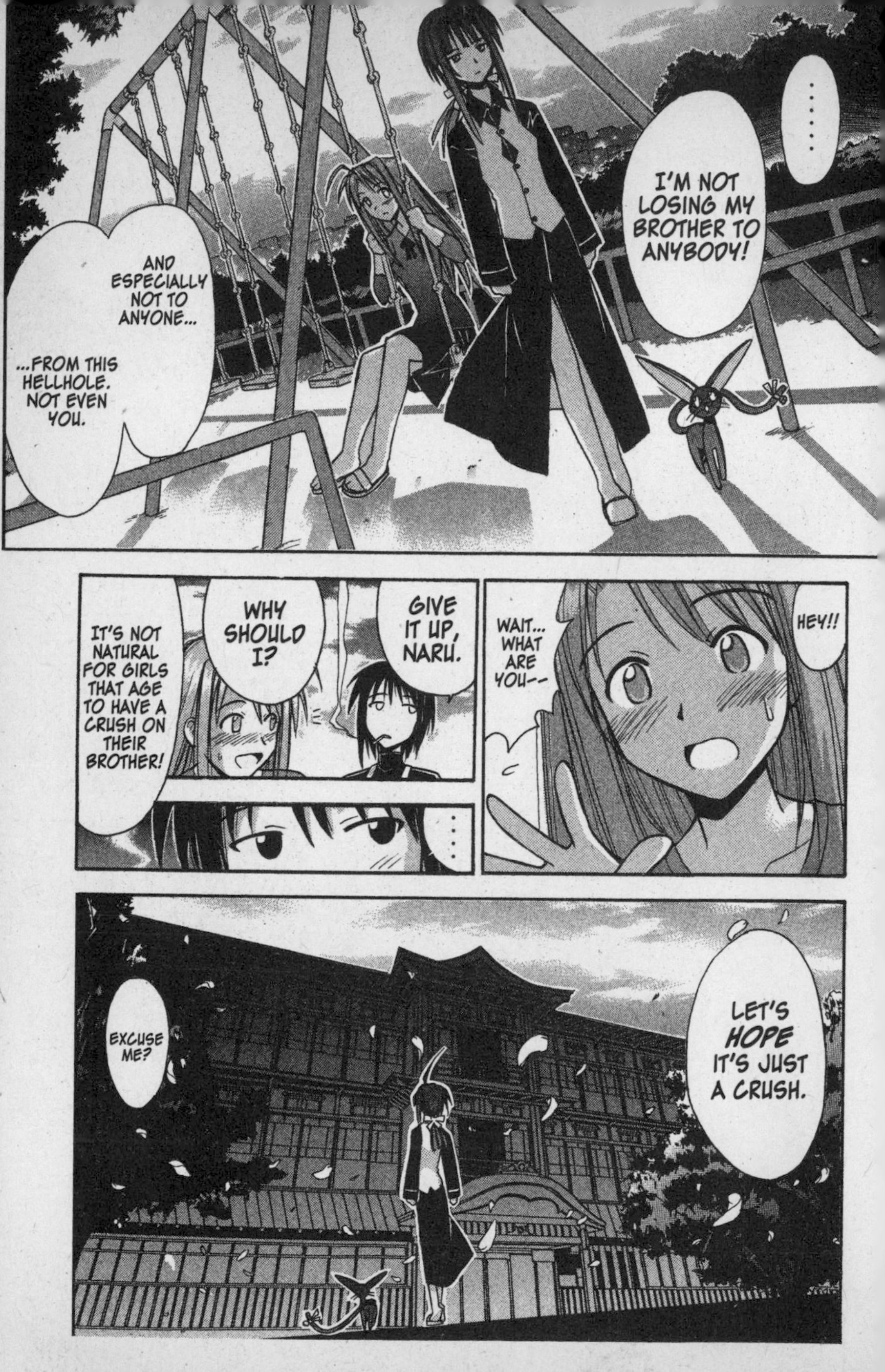
......
I'M NOT LOSING MY BROTHER TO ANYBODY!
AND ESPECIALLY NOT TO ANYONE...
...FROM THIS HELLHOLE. NOT EVEN YOU.
HEY!!
WAIT... WHAT ARE YOU--
GIVE IT UP, NARU.
WHY SHOULD I?
IT'S NOT NATURAL FOR GIRLS THAT AGE TO HAVE A CRUSH ON THEIR BROTHER!
....
LET'S *HOPE* IT'S JUST A CRUSH.
EXCUSE ME?

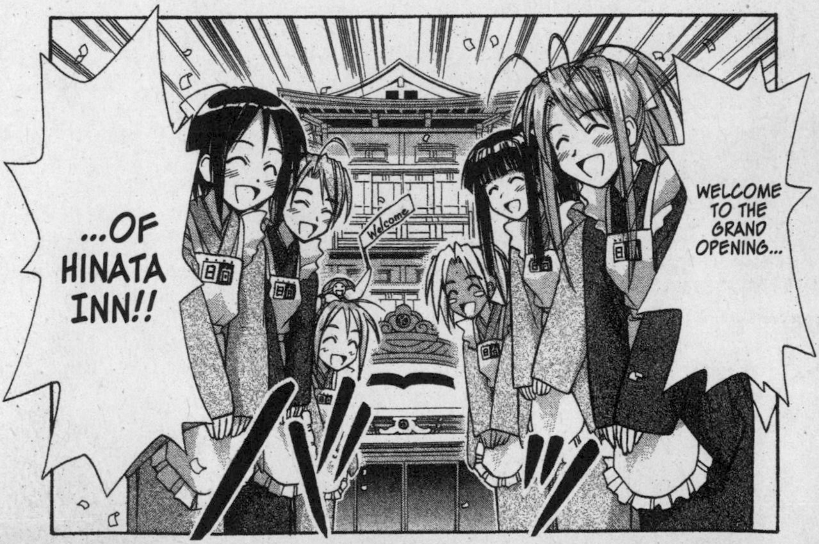
WELCOME TO THE GRAND OPENING...
...OF HINATA INN!!

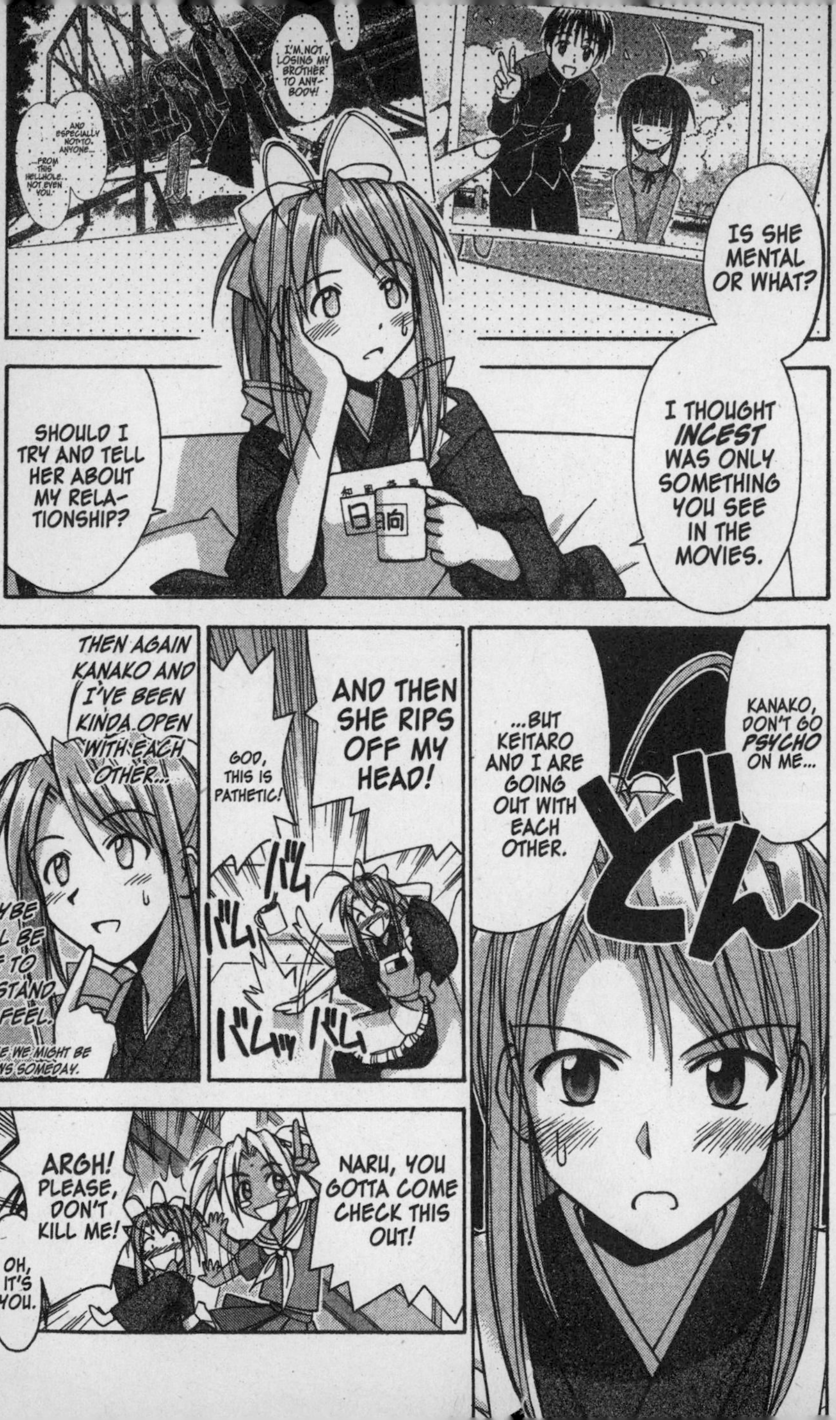
I'M NOT LOSING MY BROTHER TO ANYBODY!
AND ESPECIALLY NOT TO... ANYONE... ...FROM THIS HELLHOLE... NOT EVEN YOU.
IS SHE MENTAL OR WHAT?
I THOUGHT INCEST WAS ONLY SOMETHING YOU SEE IN THE MOVIES.
SHOULD I TRY AND TELL HER ABOUT MY RELATIONSHIP?
KANAKO, DON'T GO PSYCHO ON ME...
...BUT KEITARO AND I ARE GOING OUT WITH EACH OTHER.
どん
AND THEN SHE RIPS OFF MY HEAD!
GOD, THIS IS PATHETIC!
バム
バム
バムッ
バム
THEN AGAIN KANAKO AND I'VE BEEN KINDA OPEN WITH EACH OTHER...
...MAYBE SHE'LL BE ABLE TO NDERSTAND OW I FEEL.
BECAUSE WE MIGHT BE IN-LAWS SOMEDAY.
NARU, YOU GOTTA COME CHECK THIS OUT!
ARGH! PLEASE, DON'T KILL ME!
OH, IT'S YOU.

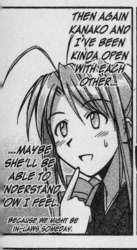

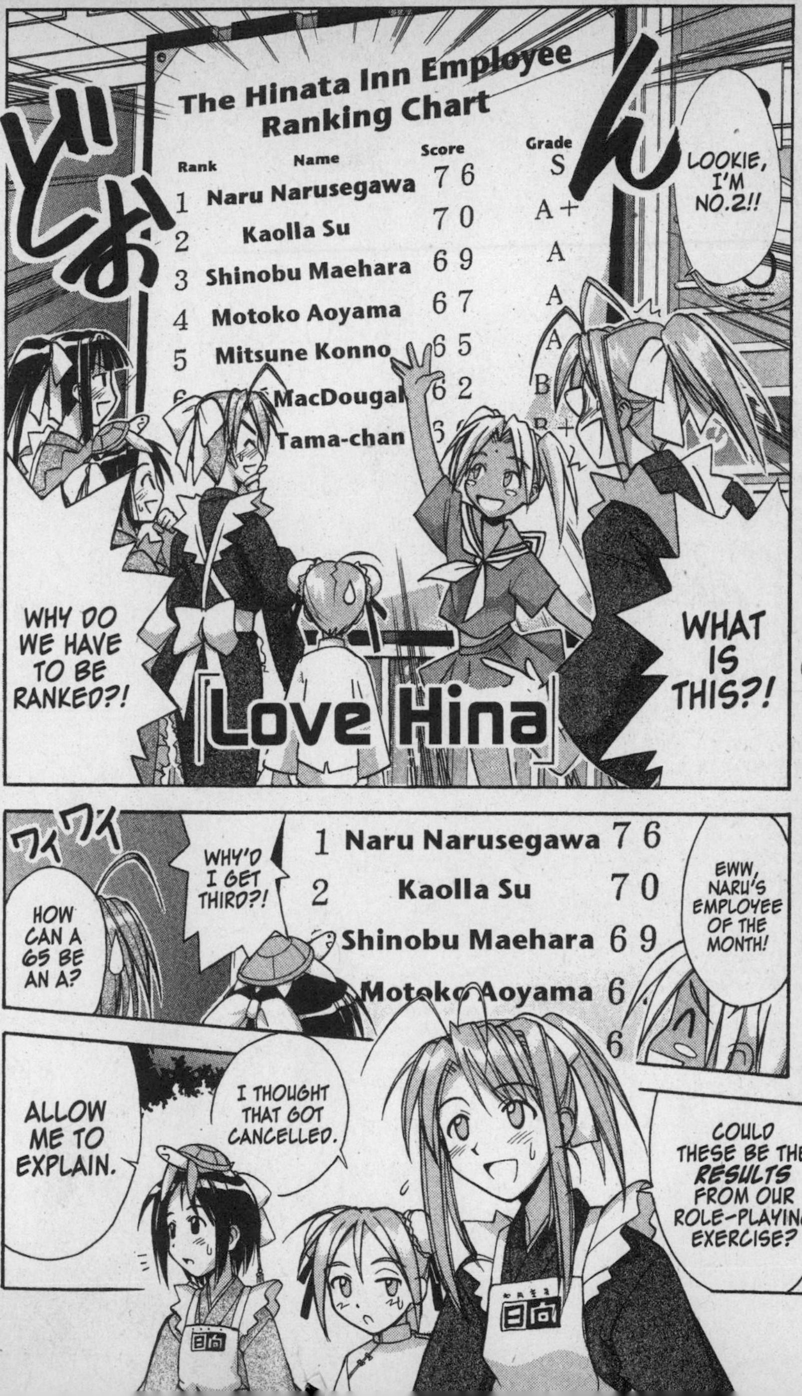
The Hinata Inn Employee Ranking Chart
Rank Name Score Grade
1 Naru Narusegawa 76 S
2 Kaolla Su 70 A+
3 Shinobu Maehara 69 A
4 Motoko Aoyama 67 A
5 Mitsune Konno 65 A
MacDougal 62 B
Tama-chan
LOOKIE, I'M NO.2!!
WHAT IS THIS?!
WHY DO WE HAVE TO BE RANKED?!
Love Hina
EWW, NARU'S EMPLOYEE OF THE MONTH!
1 Naru Narusegawa 76
2 Kaolla Su 70
Shinobu Maehara 69
Motoko Aoyama 6
6
WHY'D I GET THIRD?!
ワイワイ
HOW CAN A 65 BE AN A?
COULD THESE BE THE RESULTS FROM OUR ROLE-PLAYING EXERCISE?
I THOUGHT THAT GOT CANCELLED.
ALLOW ME TO EXPLAIN.
日向
日向

HINATA 95 Trouble on the Hinata Front?!

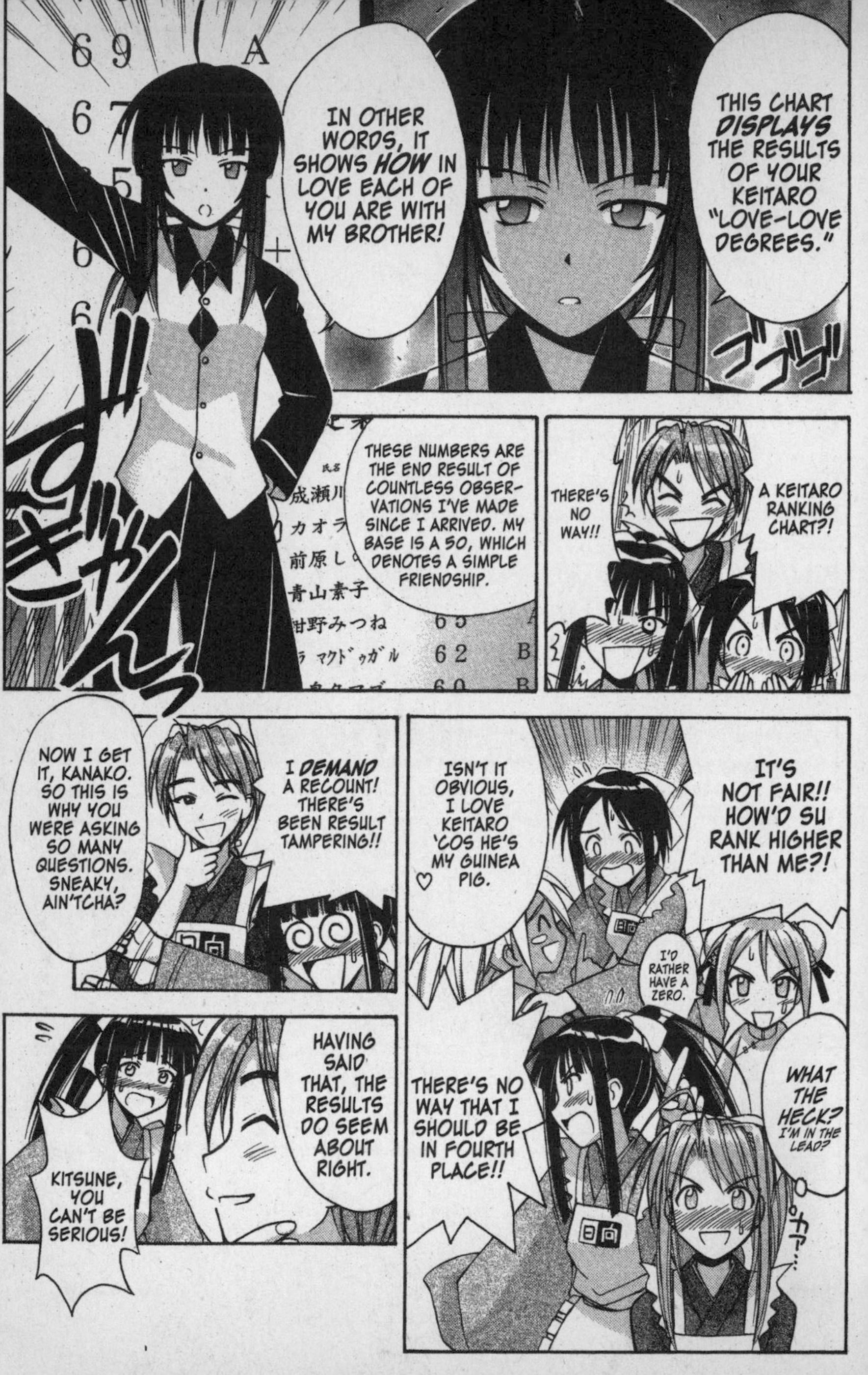
THIS CHART DISPLAYS THE RESULTS OF YOUR KEITARO "LOVE-LOVE DEGREES."
ゴゴゴ
IN OTHER WORDS, IT SHOWS HOW IN LOVE EACH OF YOU ARE WITH MY BROTHER!
THESE NUMBERS ARE THE END RESULT OF COUNTLESS OBSERVATIONS I'VE MADE SINCE I ARRIVED. MY BASE IS A 50, WHICH DENOTES A SIMPLE FRIENDSHIP.
ずぎゃーんっ
A KEITARO RANKING CHART?!
THERE'S NO WAY!!
IT'S NOT FAIR!! HOW'D SU RANK HIGHER THAN ME?!
ISN'T IT OBVIOUS, I LOVE KEITARO 'COS HE'S MY GUINEA PIG. ♡
I'D RATHER HAVE A ZERO.
WHAT THE HECK? I'M IN THE LEAD?
THERE'S NO WAY THAT I SHOULD BE IN FOURTH PLACE!!
カァ…
I DEMAND A RECOUNT! THERE'S BEEN RESULT TAMPERING!!
NOW I GET IT, KANAKO. SO THIS IS WHY YOU WERE ASKING SO MANY QUESTIONS. SNEAKY, AIN'TCHA?
HAVING SAID THAT, THE RESULTS DO SEEM ABOUT RIGHT.
KITSUNE, YOU CAN'T BE SERIOUS!

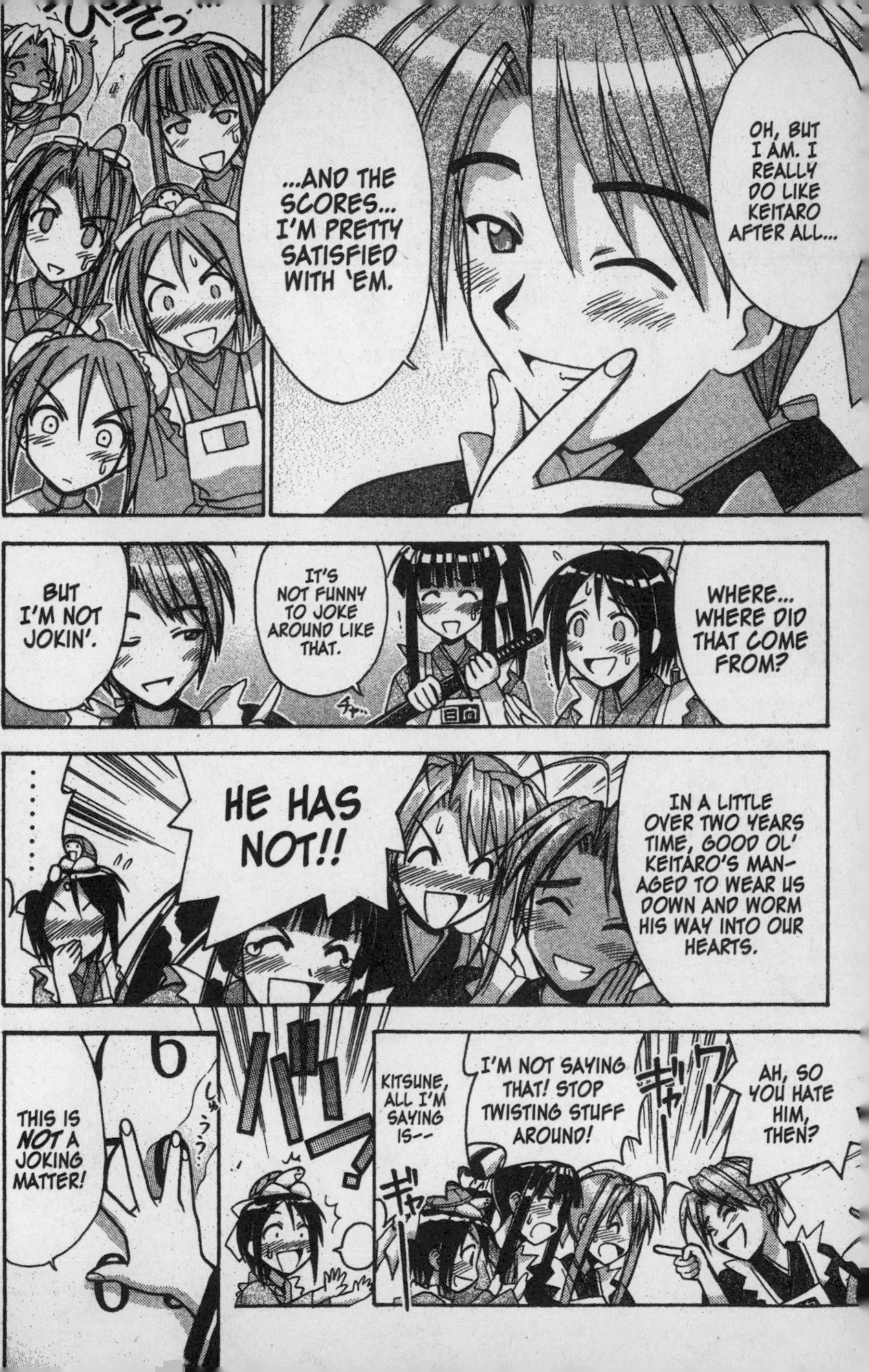
OH, BUT I AM. I REALLY DO LIKE KEITARO AFTER ALL...
...AND THE SCORES... I'M PRETTY SATISFIED WITH 'EM.
WHERE... WHERE DID THAT COME FROM?
IT'S NOT FUNNY TO JOKE AROUND LIKE THAT.
BUT I'M NOT JOKIN'.
IN A LITTLE OVER TWO YEARS TIME, GOOD OL' KEITARO'S MANAGED TO WEAR US DOWN AND WORM HIS WAY INTO OUR HEARTS.
HE HAS NOT!!
......
AH, SO YOU HATE HIM, THEN?
I'M NOT SAYING THAT! STOP TWISTING STUFF AROUND!
KITSUNE, ALL I'M SAYING IS--
THIS IS *NOT* A JOKING MATTER!

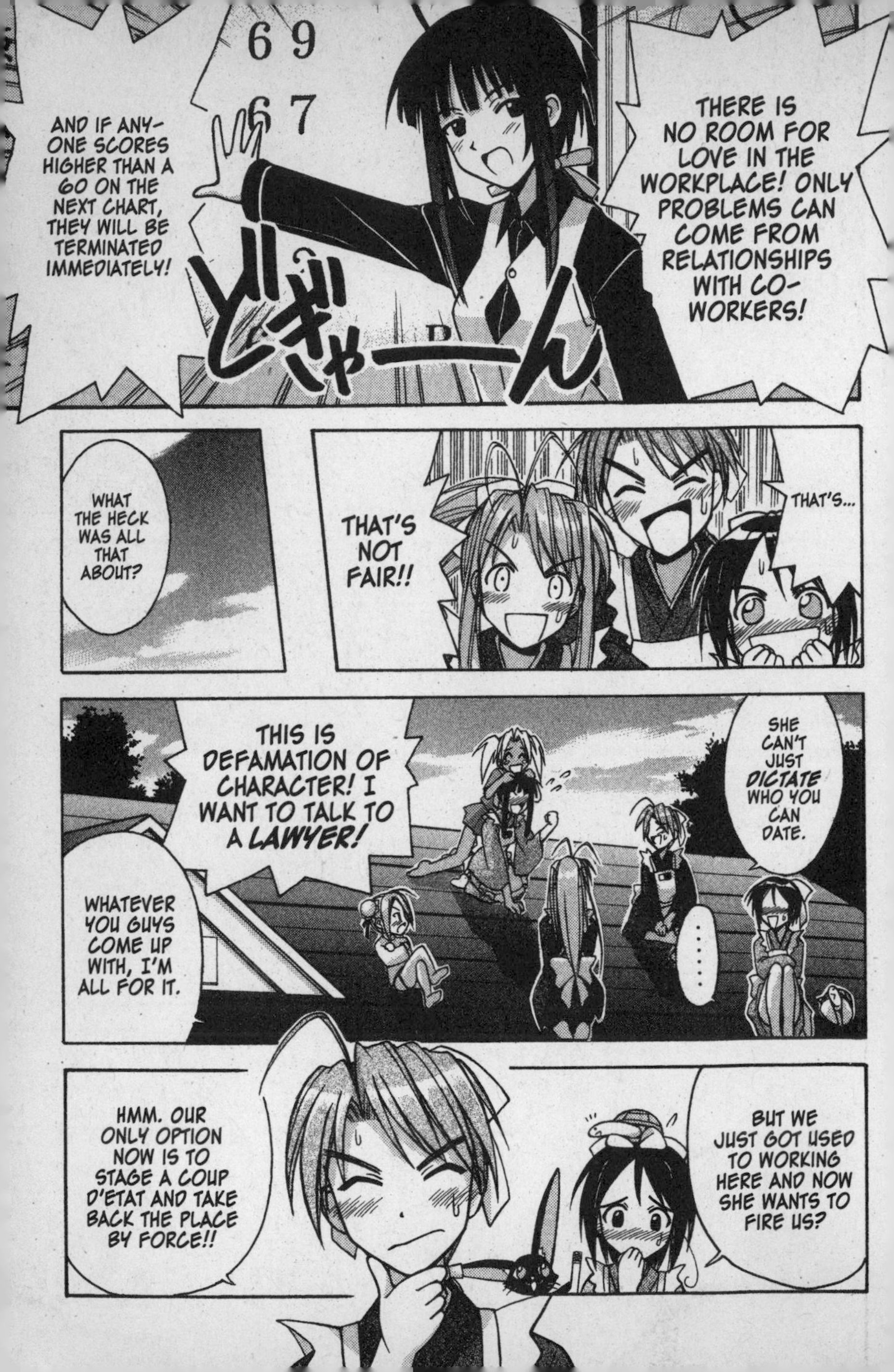

THERE IS NO ROOM FOR LOVE IN THE WORKPLACE! ONLY PROBLEMS CAN COME FROM RELATIONSHIPS WITH CO-WORKERS!
6 9
6 7
AND IF ANYONE SCORES HIGHER THAN A 60 ON THE NEXT CHART, THEY WILL BE TERMINATED IMMEDIATELY!
どぎゃーん
THAT'S...
THAT'S NOT FAIR!!
WHAT THE HECK WAS ALL THAT ABOUT?
SHE CAN'T JUST *DICTATE* WHO YOU CAN DATE.
......
THIS IS DEFAMATION OF CHARACTER! I WANT TO TALK TO A *LAWYER!*
WHATEVER YOU GUYS COME UP WITH, I'M ALL FOR IT.
BUT WE JUST GOT USED TO WORKING HERE AND NOW SHE WANTS TO FIRE US?
HMM. OUR ONLY OPTION NOW IS TO STAGE A COUP D'ETAT AND TAKE BACK THE PLACE BY FORCE!!

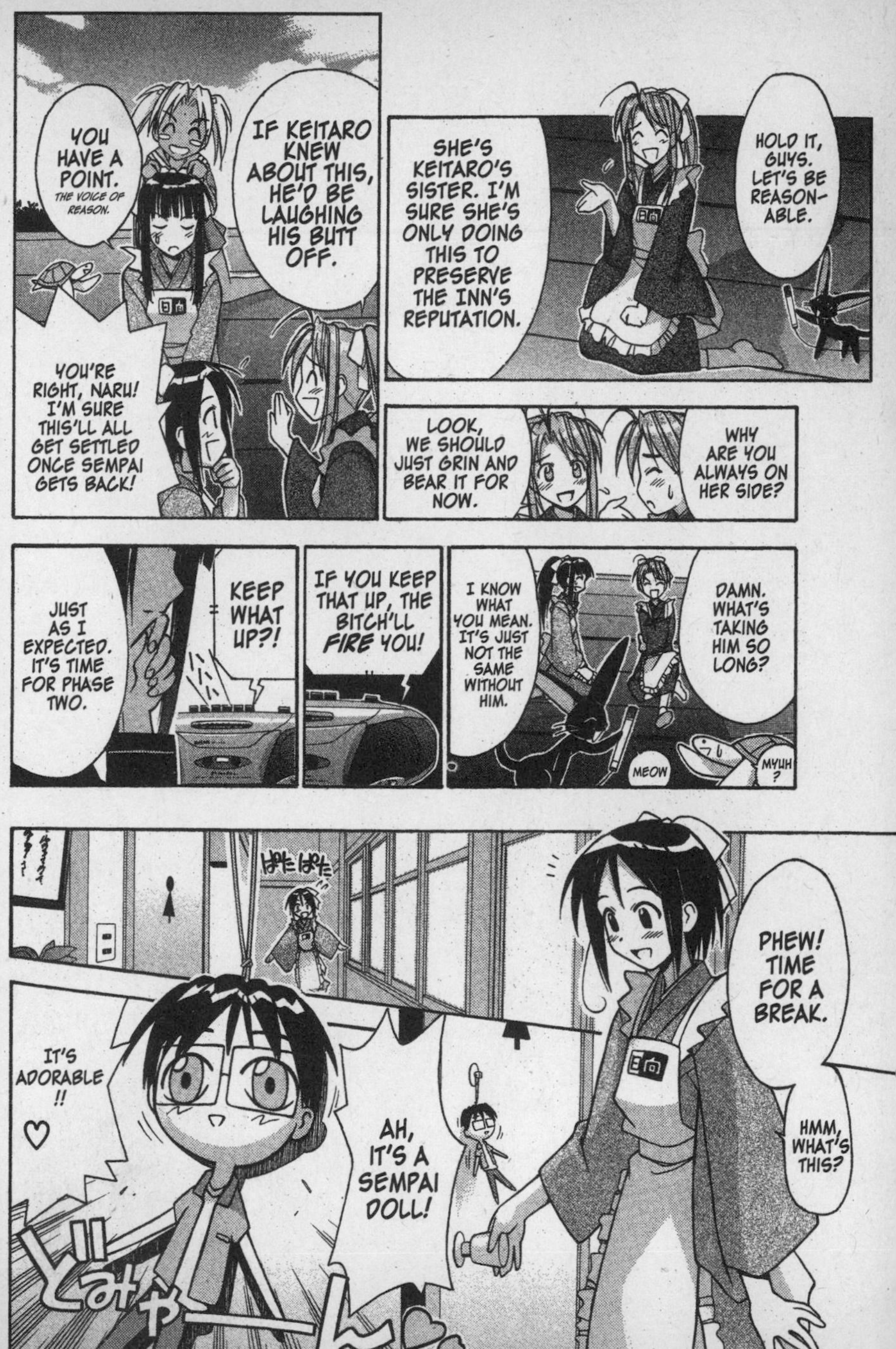
HOLD IT, GUYS. LET'S BE REASONABLE.
SHE'S KEITARO'S SISTER. I'M SURE SHE'S ONLY DOING THIS TO PRESERVE THE INN'S REPUTATION.
WHY ARE YOU ALWAYS ON HER SIDE?
LOOK, WE SHOULD JUST GRIN AND BEAR IT FOR NOW.
IF KEITARO KNEW ABOUT THIS, HE'D BE LAUGHING HIS BUTT OFF.
YOU HAVE A POINT.
THE VOICE OF REASON.
YOU'RE RIGHT, NARU! I'M SURE THIS'LL ALL GET SETTLED ONCE SEMPAI GETS BACK!
DAMN. WHAT'S TAKING HIM SO LONG?
I KNOW WHAT YOU MEAN. IT'S JUST NOT THE SAME WITHOUT HIM.
MYUH?
MEOW
IF YOU KEEP THAT UP, THE BITCH'LL FIRE YOU!
KEEP WHAT UP?!
JUST AS I EXPECTED. IT'S TIME FOR PHASE TWO.
PHEW! TIME FOR A BREAK.
ぱたぱた
HMM, WHAT'S THIS?
AH, IT'S A SEMPAI DOLL!
IT'S ADORABLE!!
どみゃーん

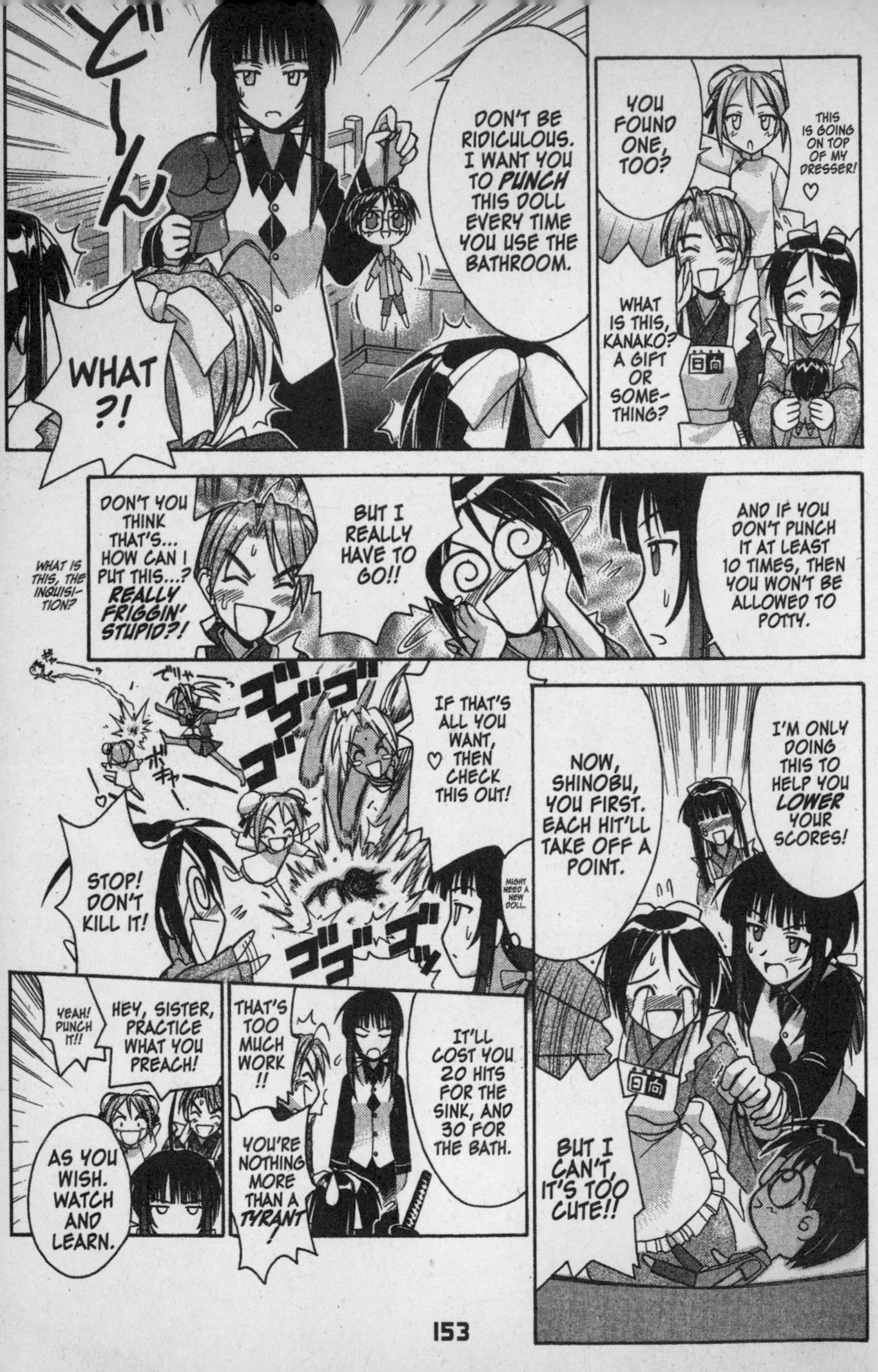
YOU FOUND ONE, TOO?
THIS IS GOING ON TOP OF MY DRESSER! ♡
WHAT IS THIS, KANAKO? A GIFT OR SOMETHING?
ど〜ん
DON'T BE RIDICULOUS. I WANT YOU TO PUNCH THIS DOLL EVERY TIME YOU USE THE BATHROOM.
WHAT ?!
AND IF YOU DON'T PUNCH IT AT LEAST 10 TIMES, THEN YOU WON'T BE ALLOWED TO POTTY.
BUT I REALLY HAVE TO GO!!
DON'T YOU THINK THAT'S... HOW CAN I PUT THIS...? REALLY FRIGGIN' STUPID?!
WHAT IS THIS, THE INQUISITION?
I'M ONLY DOING THIS TO HELP YOU LOWER YOUR SCORES!
NOW, SHINOBU, YOU FIRST. EACH HIT'LL TAKE OFF A POINT.
BUT I CAN'T, IT'S TOO CUTE!!
IF THAT'S ALL YOU WANT, THEN CHECK THIS OUT! ♡
MIGHT NEED A NEW DOLL.
STOP! DON'T KILL IT!
IT'LL COST YOU 20 HITS FOR THE SINK, AND 30 FOR THE BATH.
THAT'S TOO MUCH WORK !!
YOU'RE NOTHING MORE THAN A TYRANT !
HEY, SISTER, PRACTICE WHAT YOU PREACH!
YEAH! PUNCH IT!!
AS YOU WISH. WATCH AND LEARN.

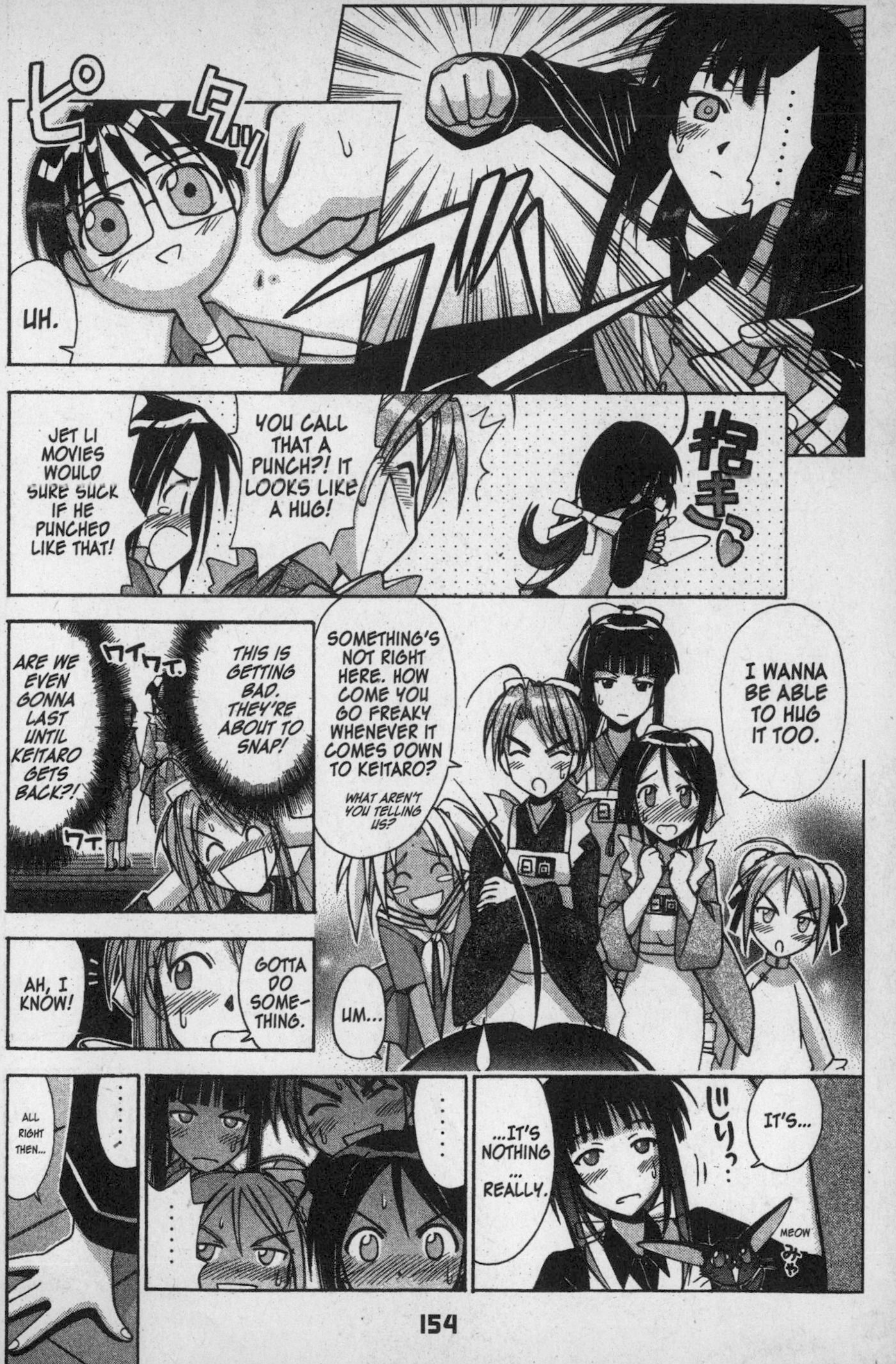
......
ピタッ
UH.
抱き♡
YOU CALL THAT A PUNCH?! IT LOOKS LIKE A HUG!
JET LI MOVIES WOULD SURE SUCK IF HE PUNCHED LIKE THAT!
I WANNA BE ABLE TO HUG IT TOO.
SOMETHING'S NOT RIGHT HERE. HOW COME YOU GO FREAKY WHENEVER IT COMES DOWN TO KEITARO?
WHAT AREN'T YOU TELLING US?
UM...
THIS IS GETTING BAD. THEY'RE ABOUT TO SNAP!
ワイワイ
ARE WE EVEN GONNA LAST UNTIL KEITARO GETS BACK?!
ワイ
GOTTA DO SOME-THING.
AH, I KNOW!
IT'S...
じりっ
...IT'S NOTHING ... REALLY.
MEOW
みゅ
......
......
......
ALL RIGHT THEN...

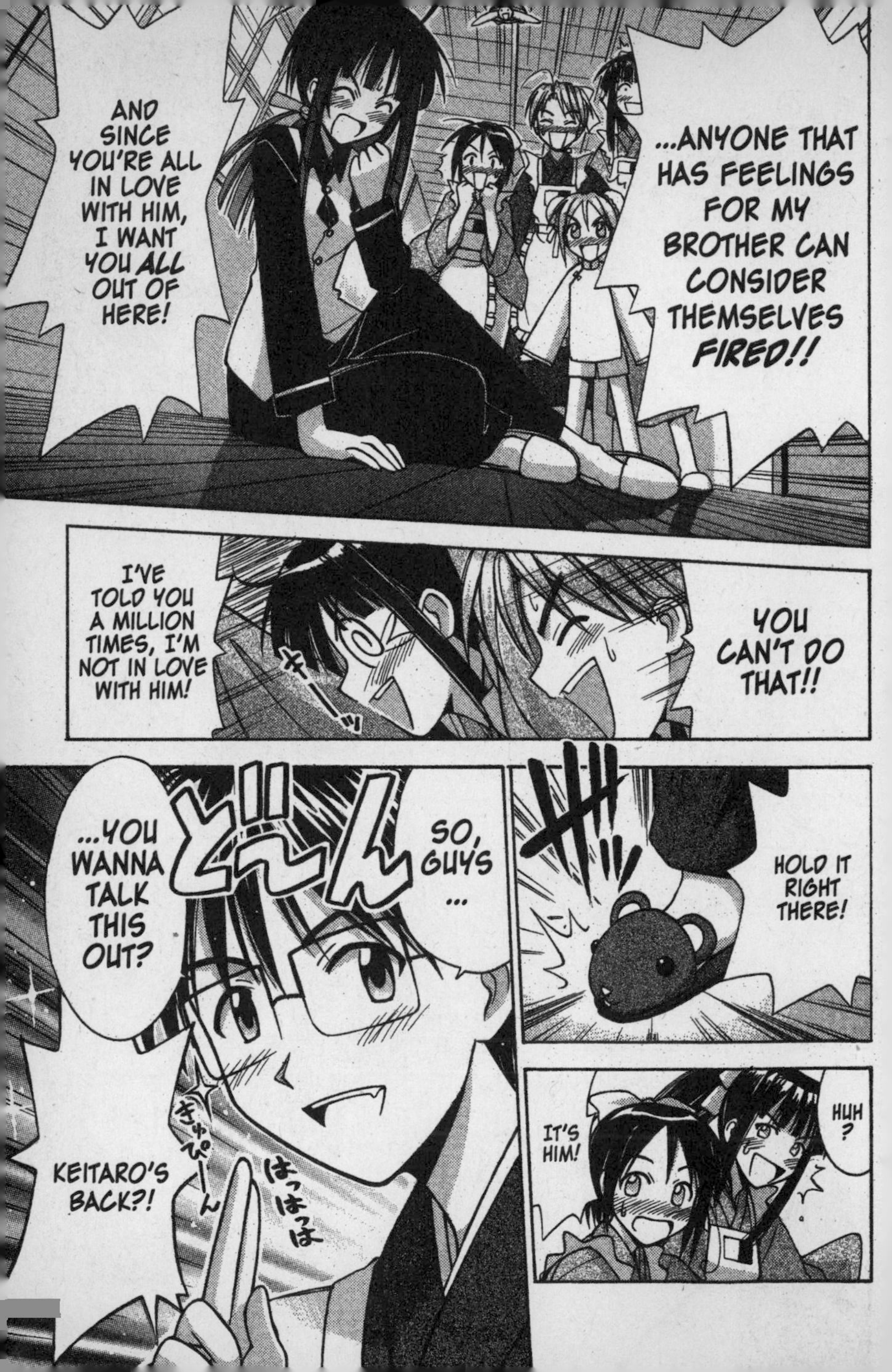
...ANYONE THAT HAS FEELINGS FOR MY BROTHER CAN CONSIDER THEMSELVES *FIRED!!*
AND SINCE YOU'RE ALL IN LOVE WITH HIM, I WANT YOU *ALL* OUT OF HERE!
YOU CAN'T DO THAT!!
I'VE TOLD YOU A MILLION TIMES, I'M NOT IN LOVE WITH HIM!
HOLD IT RIGHT THERE!
HUH?
IT'S HIM!
SO, GUYS...
どどん
...YOU WANNA TALK THIS OUT?
きゅぴーん
はっはっは
KEITARO'S BACK?!

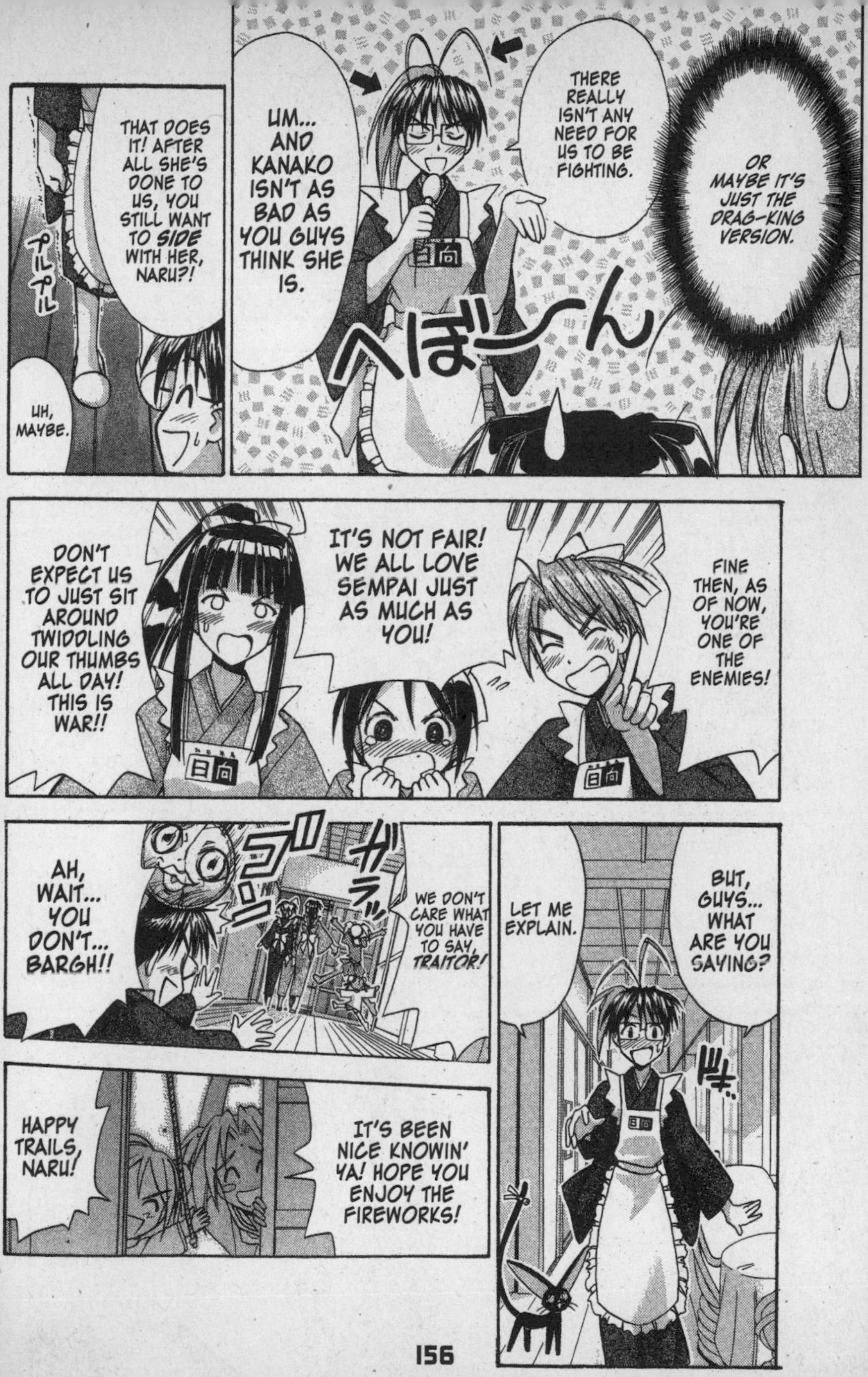
OR MAYBE IT'S JUST THE DRAG-KING VERSION.
THERE REALLY ISN'T ANY NEED FOR US TO BE FIGHTING.
UM... AND KANAKO ISN'T AS BAD AS YOU GUYS THINK SHE IS.
へぼ～ん
THAT DOES IT! AFTER ALL SHE'S DONE TO US, YOU STILL WANT TO SIDE WITH HER, NARU?!
プルプル
UH, MAYBE.
FINE THEN, AS OF NOW, YOU'RE ONE OF THE ENEMIES!
IT'S NOT FAIR! WE ALL LOVE SEMPAI JUST AS MUCH AS YOU!
DON'T EXPECT US TO JUST SIT AROUND TWIDDLING OUR THUMBS ALL DAY! THIS IS WAR!!
BUT, GUYS... WHAT ARE YOU SAYING?
LET ME EXPLAIN.
ドキ...
WE DON'T CARE WHAT YOU HAVE TO SAY, TRAITOR!
ガラッ
AH, WAIT... YOU DON'T... BARGH!!
IT'S BEEN NICE KNOWIN' YA! HOPE YOU ENJOY THE FIREWORKS!
HAPPY TRAILS, NARU!

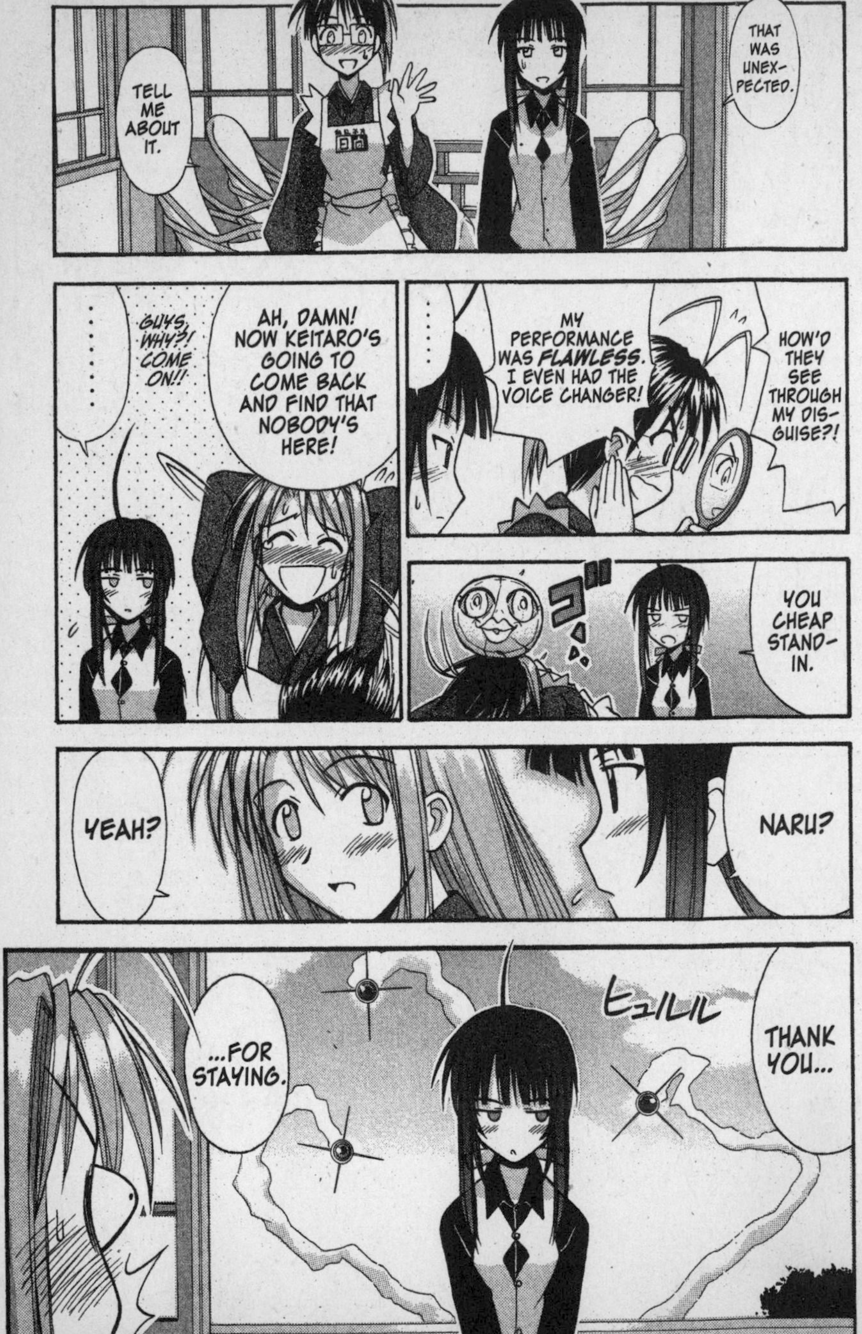
THAT WAS UNEXPECTED.
TELL ME ABOUT IT.
HOW'D THEY SEE THROUGH MY DISGUISE?!
MY PERFORMANCE WAS *FLAWLESS*. I EVEN HAD THE VOICE CHANGER!
......
YOU CHEAP STAND-IN.
AH, DAMN! NOW KEITARO'S GOING TO COME BACK AND FIND THAT NOBODY'S HERE!
GUYS, WHY?! COME ON!!
......
NARU?
YEAH?
THANK YOU...
ヒュルルル
...FOR STAYING.

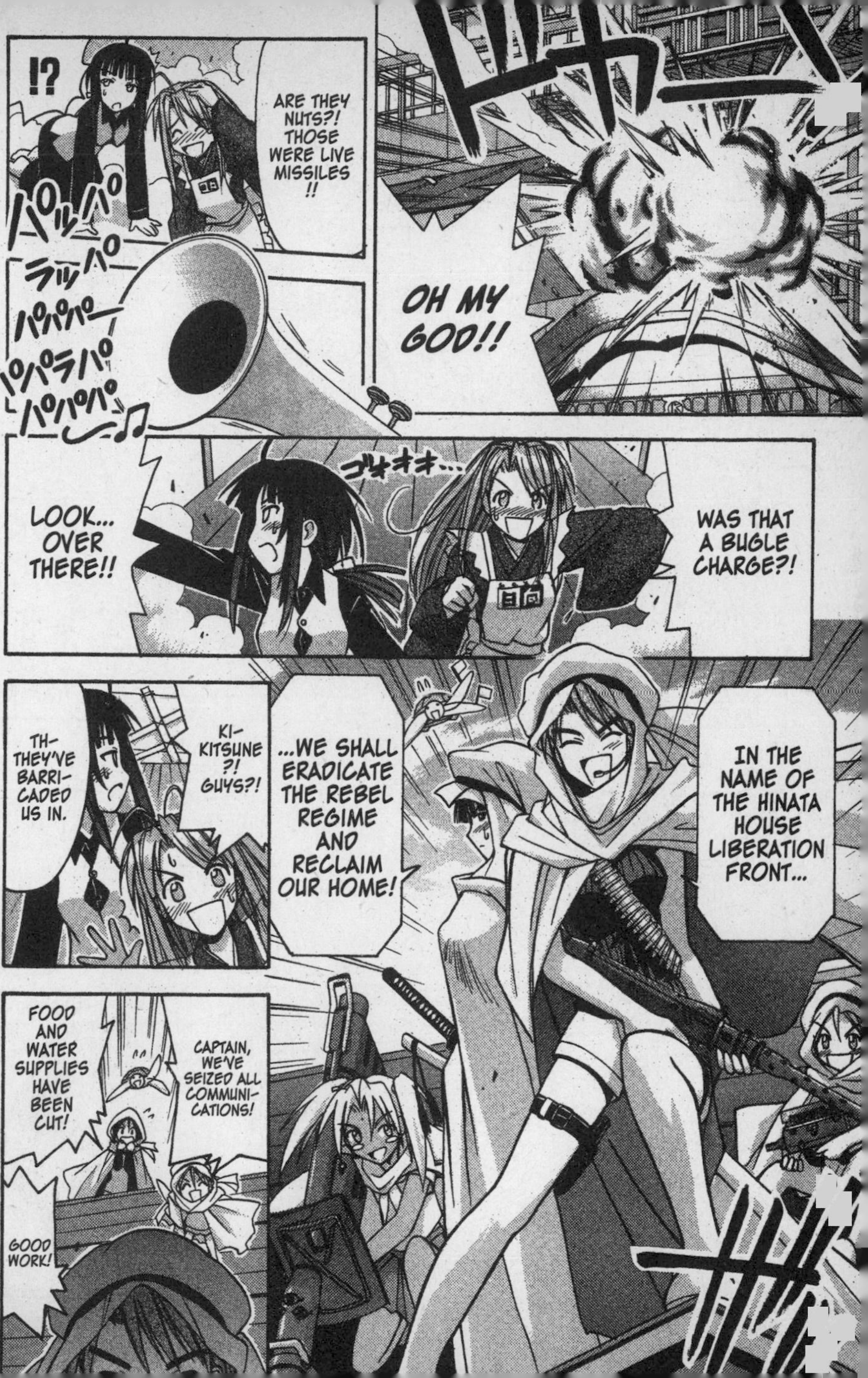
OH MY GOD!!
!?
ARE THEY NUTS?! THOSE WERE LIVE MISSILES!!
WAS THAT A BUGLE CHARGE?!
LOOK... OVER THERE!!
IN THE NAME OF THE HINATA HOUSE LIBERATION FRONT...
...WE SHALL ERADICATE THE REBEL REGIME AND RECLAIM OUR HOME!
KI-KITSUNE?! GUYS?!
TH-THEY'VE BARRICADED US IN.
CAPTAIN, WE'VE SEIZED ALL COMMUNICATIONS!
FOOD AND WATER SUPPLIES HAVE BEEN CUT!
GOOD WORK!

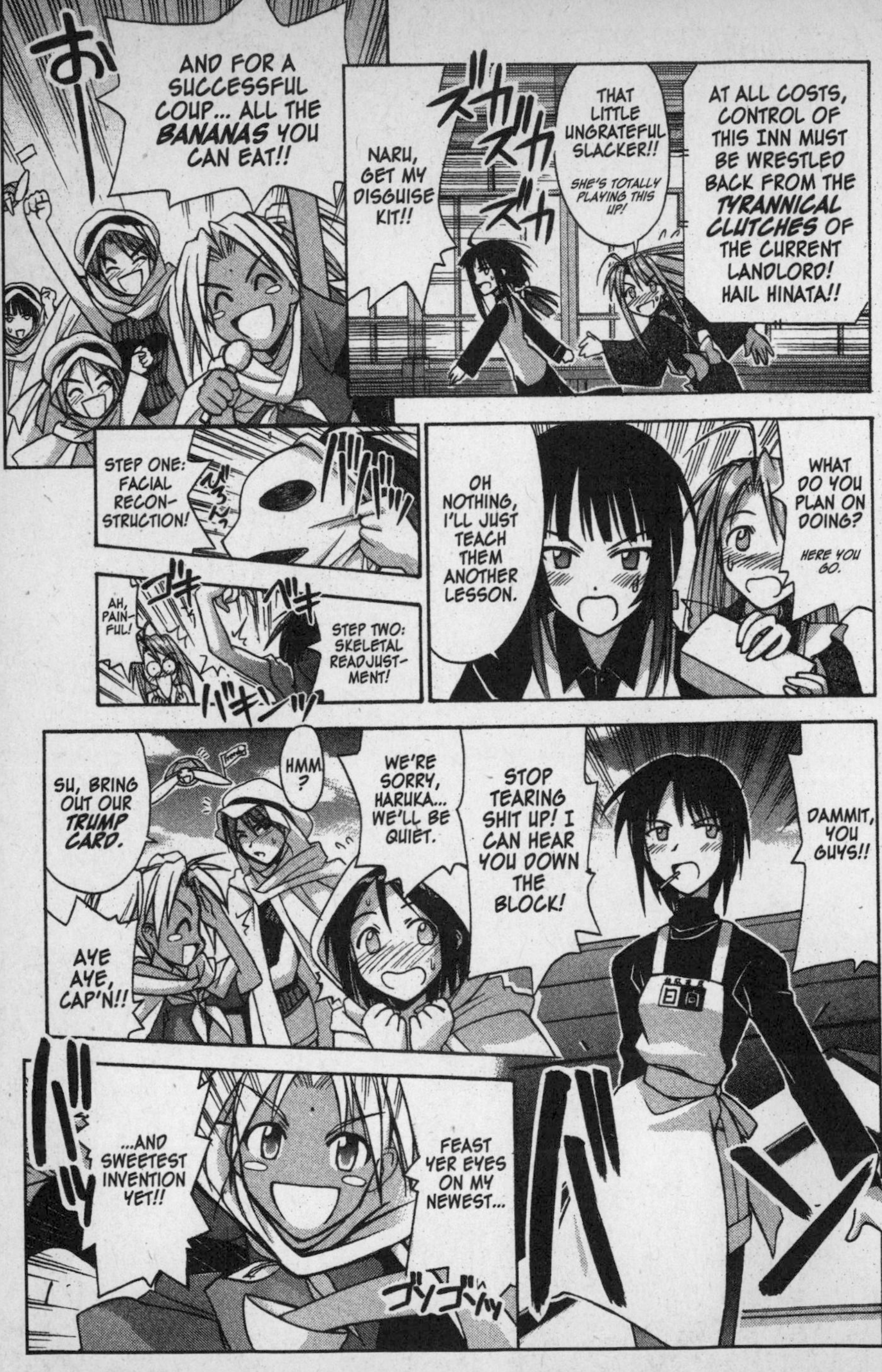
AT ALL COSTS, CONTROL OF THIS INN MUST BE WRESTLED BACK FROM THE TYRANNICAL CLUTCHES OF THE CURRENT LANDLORD! HAIL HINATA!!
THAT LITTLE UNGRATEFUL SLACKER!!
SHE'S TOTALLY PLAYING THIS UP!
NARU, GET MY DISGUISE KIT!!
AND FOR A SUCCESSFUL COUP... ALL THE BANANAS YOU CAN EAT!!
WHAT DO YOU PLAN ON DOING?
HERE YOU GO.
OH NOTHING, I'LL JUST TEACH THEM ANOTHER LESSON.
STEP ONE: FACIAL RECONSTRUCTION!
STEP TWO: SKELETAL READJUSTMENT!
AH, PAINFUL!
DAMMIT, YOU GUYS!!
STOP TEARING SHIT UP! I CAN HEAR YOU DOWN THE BLOCK!
WE'RE SORRY, HARUKA... WE'LL BE QUIET.
HMM?
SU, BRING OUT OUR TRUMP CARD.
AYE AYE, CAP'N!!
FEAST YER EYES ON MY NEWEST...
...AND SWEETEST INVENTION YET!!

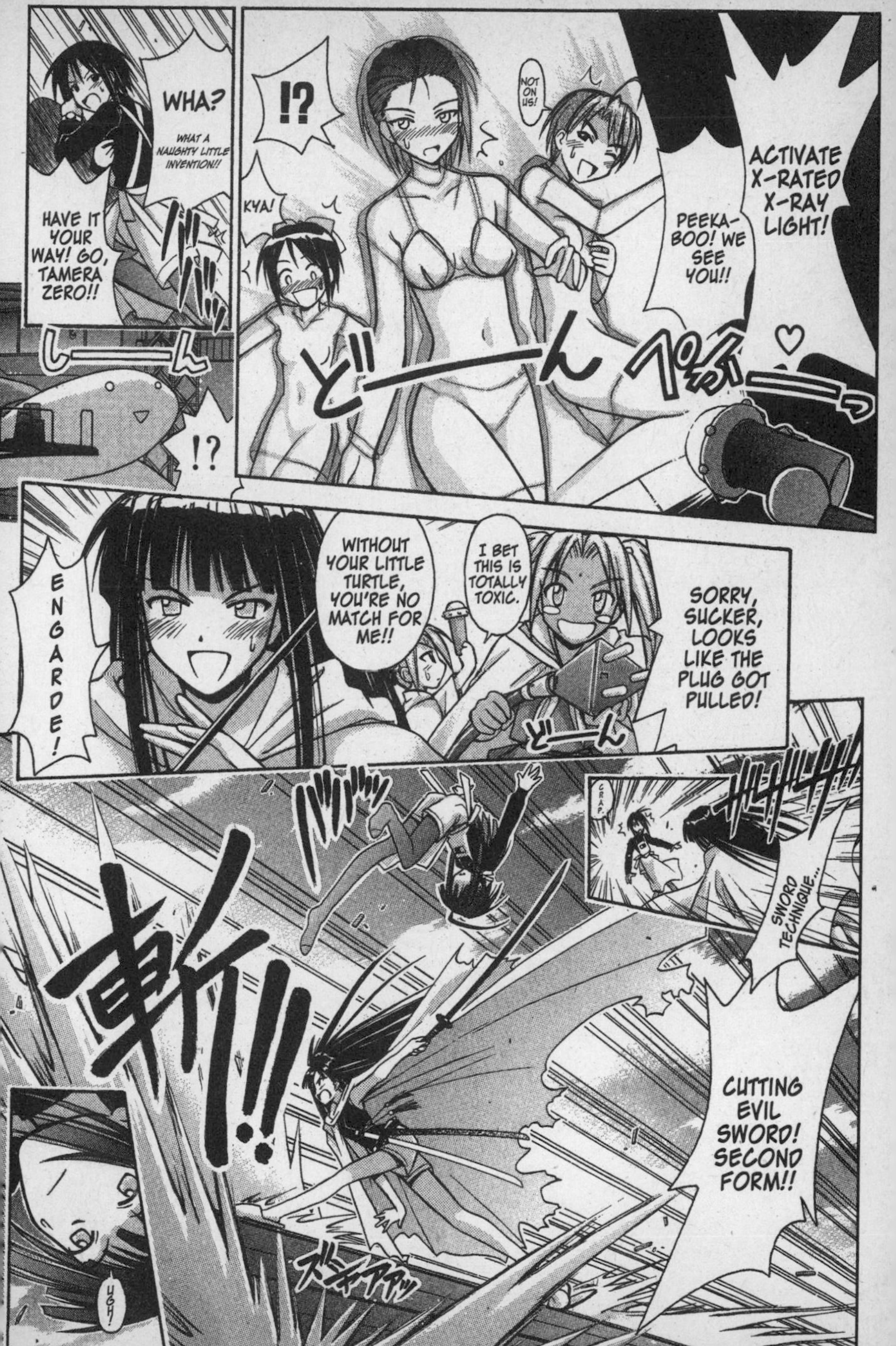
ACTIVATE X-RATED X-RAY LIGHT!
PEEKA-BOO! WE SEE YOU!!
NOT ON US!
!?
KYA!
どーーん
WHA?
WHAT A NAUGHTY LITTLE INVENTION!!
HAVE IT YOUR WAY! GO, TAMERA ZERO!!
!?
SORRY, SUCKER, LOOKS LIKE THE PLUG GOT PULLED!
I BET THIS IS TOTALLY TOXIC.
WITHOUT YOUR LITTLE TURTLE, YOU'RE NO MATCH FOR ME!!
ENGARDE!
どん
CRAP.
SWORD TECHNIQUE...
CUTTING EVIL SWORD! SECOND FORM!!
斬!!
UGH!

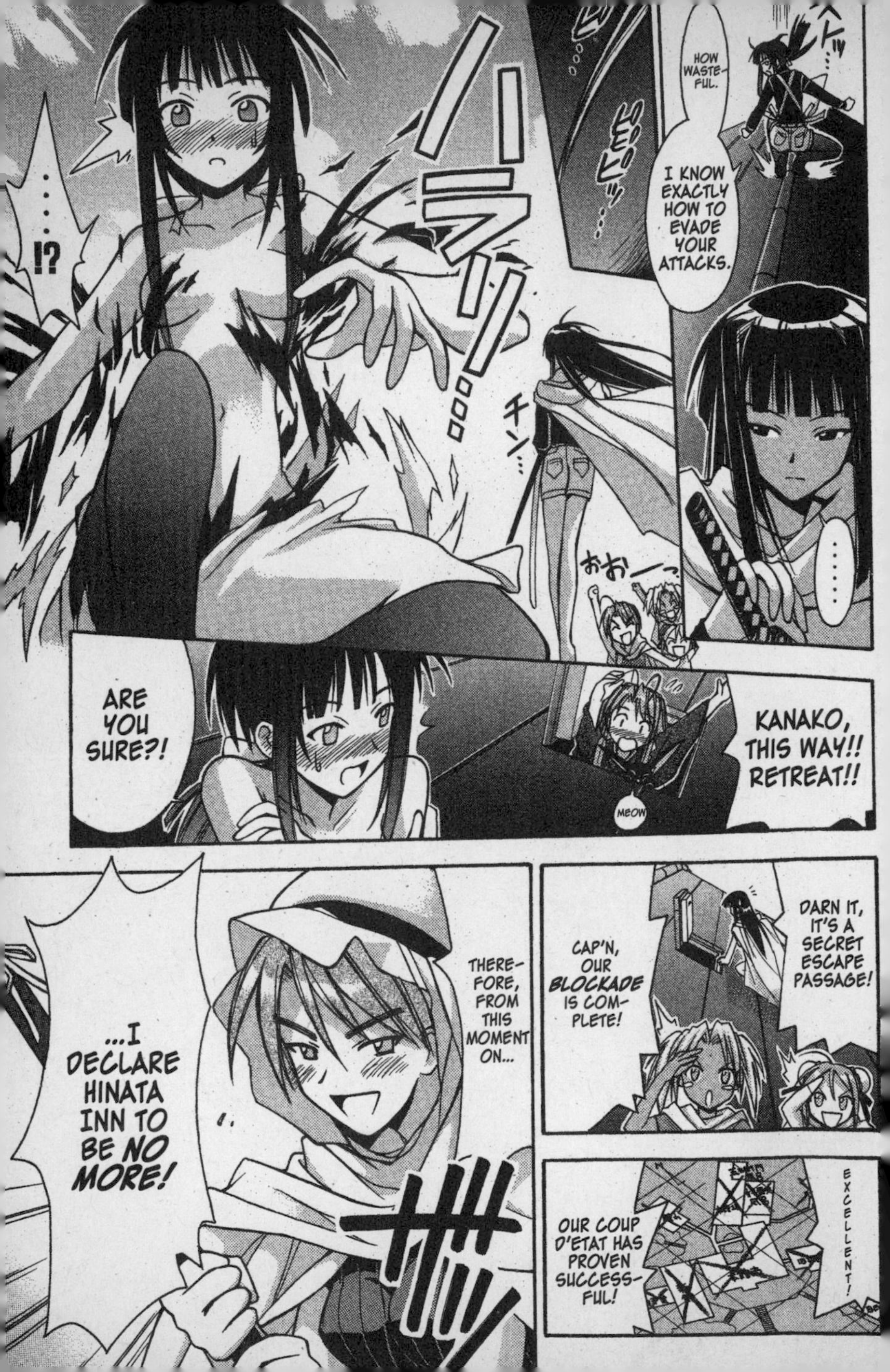

HOW WASTEFUL.
I KNOW EXACTLY HOW TO EVADE YOUR ATTACKS.
......
...!?
おおーっ
KANAKO, THIS WAY!! RETREAT!!
MEOW
ARE YOU SURE?!
DARN IT, IT'S A SECRET ESCAPE PASSAGE!
CAP'N, OUR BLOCKADE IS COMPLETE!
EXCELLENT!
OUR COUP D'ETAT HAS PROVEN SUCCESSFUL!
THEREFORE, FROM THIS MOMENT ON...
...I DECLARE HINATA INN TO BE NO MORE!

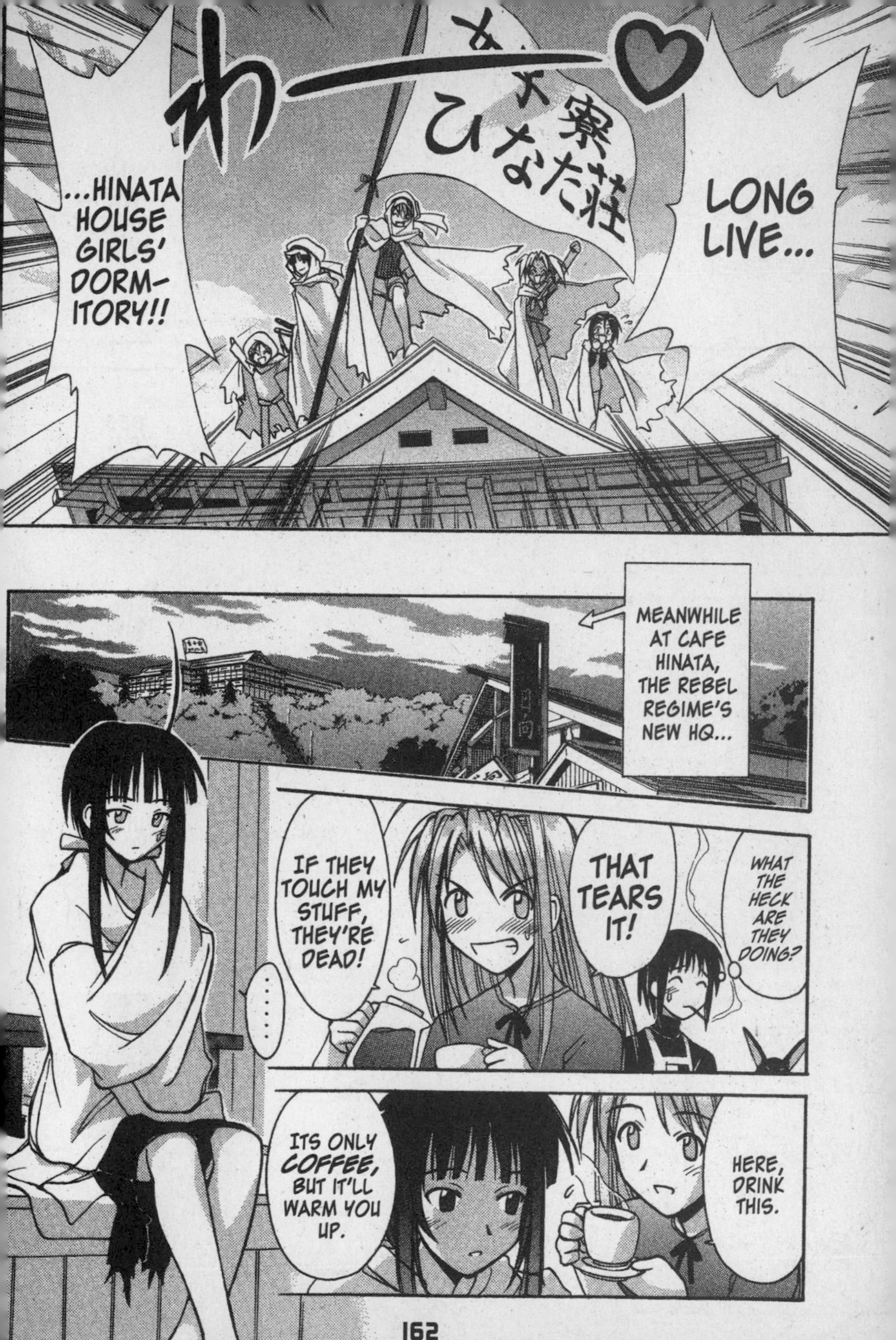
わーー♥
寮
ひなた荘
LONG LIVE...
...HINATA HOUSE GIRLS' DORM-ITORY!!
MEANWHILE AT CAFE HINATA, THE REBEL REGIME'S NEW HQ...
WHAT THE HECK ARE THEY DOING?
THAT TEARS IT!
IF THEY TOUCH MY STUFF, THEY'RE DEAD!
......
HERE, DRINK THIS.
ITS ONLY COFFEE, BUT IT'LL WARM YOU UP.

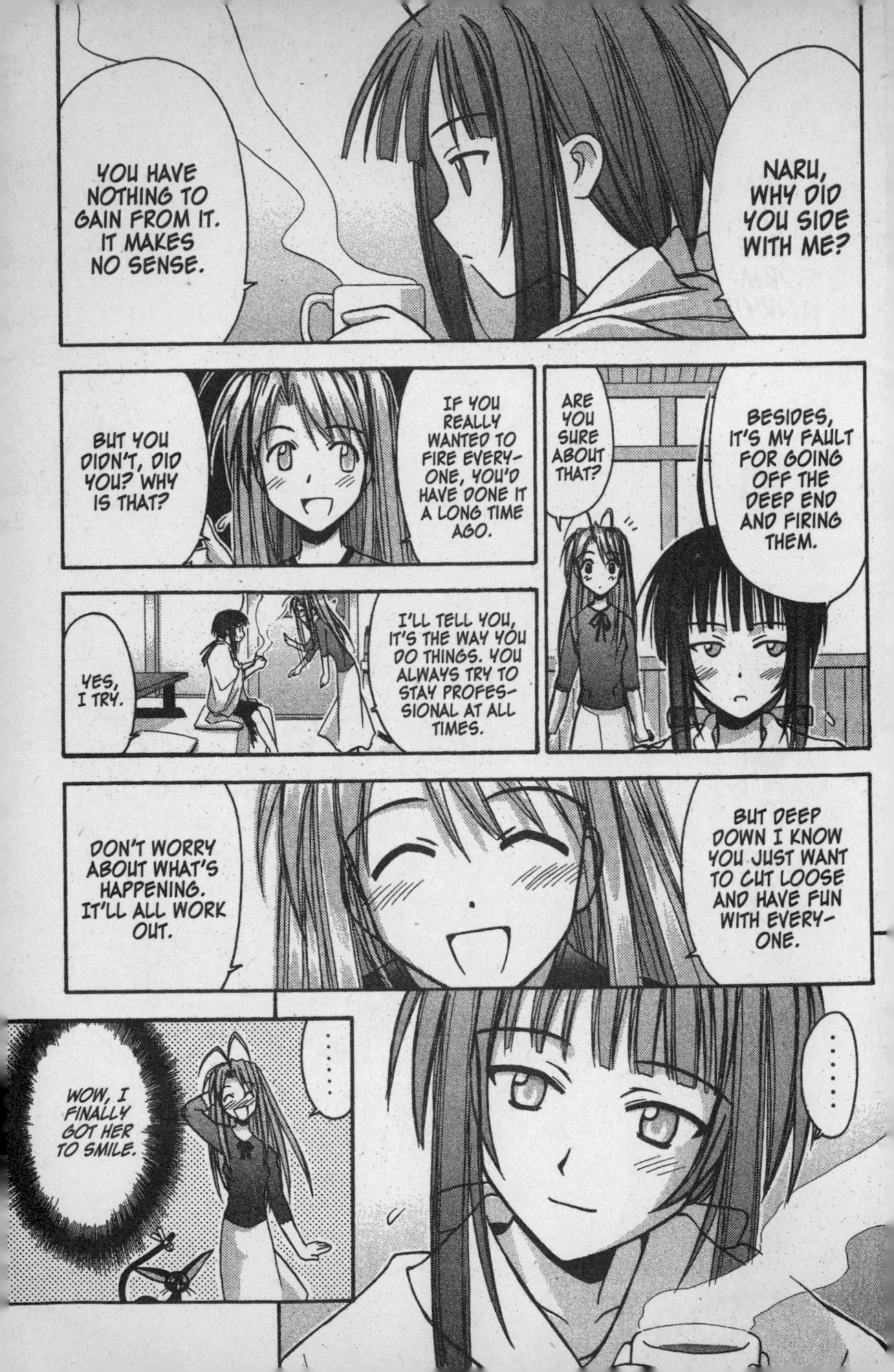
NARU, WHY DID YOU SIDE WITH ME?
YOU HAVE NOTHING TO GAIN FROM IT. IT MAKES NO SENSE.
BESIDES, IT'S MY FAULT FOR GOING OFF THE DEEP END AND FIRING THEM.
ARE YOU SURE ABOUT THAT?
IF YOU REALLY WANTED TO FIRE EVERY-ONE, YOU'D HAVE DONE IT A LONG TIME AGO.
BUT YOU DIDN'T, DID YOU? WHY IS THAT?
I'LL TELL YOU, IT'S THE WAY YOU DO THINGS. YOU ALWAYS TRY TO STAY PROFES-SIONAL AT ALL TIMES.
YES, I TRY.
BUT DEEP DOWN I KNOW YOU JUST WANT TO CUT LOOSE AND HAVE FUN WITH EVERY-ONE.
DON'T WORRY ABOUT WHAT'S HAPPENING. IT'LL ALL WORK OUT.
......
......
WOW, I FINALLY GOT HER TO SMILE.

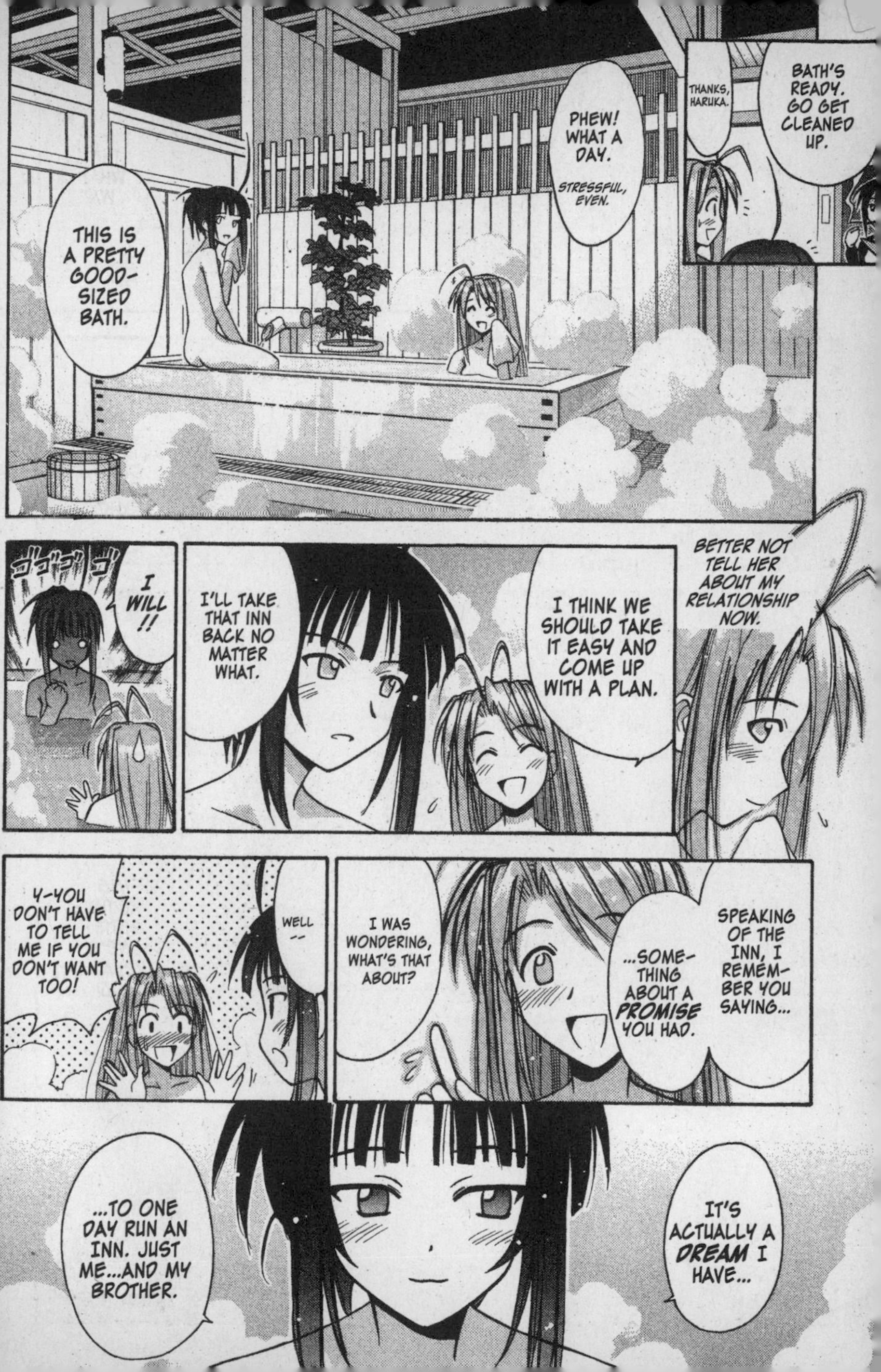
BATH'S READY. GO GET CLEANED UP.
THANKS, HARUKA.
PHEW! WHAT A DAY.
STRESSFUL, EVEN.
THIS IS A PRETTY GOOD-SIZED BATH.
BETTER NOT TELL HER ABOUT MY RELATIONSHIP NOW.
I THINK WE SHOULD TAKE IT EASY AND COME UP WITH A PLAN.
I'LL TAKE THAT INN BACK NO MATTER WHAT.
I WILL!!
SPEAKING OF THE INN, I REMEMBER YOU SAYING...
...SOMETHING ABOUT A PROMISE YOU HAD.
I WAS WONDERING, WHAT'S THAT ABOUT?
WELL--
Y-YOU DON'T HAVE TO TELL ME IF YOU DON'T WANT TOO!
IT'S ACTUALLY A DREAM I HAVE...
...TO ONE DAY RUN AN INN. JUST ME...AND MY BROTHER.

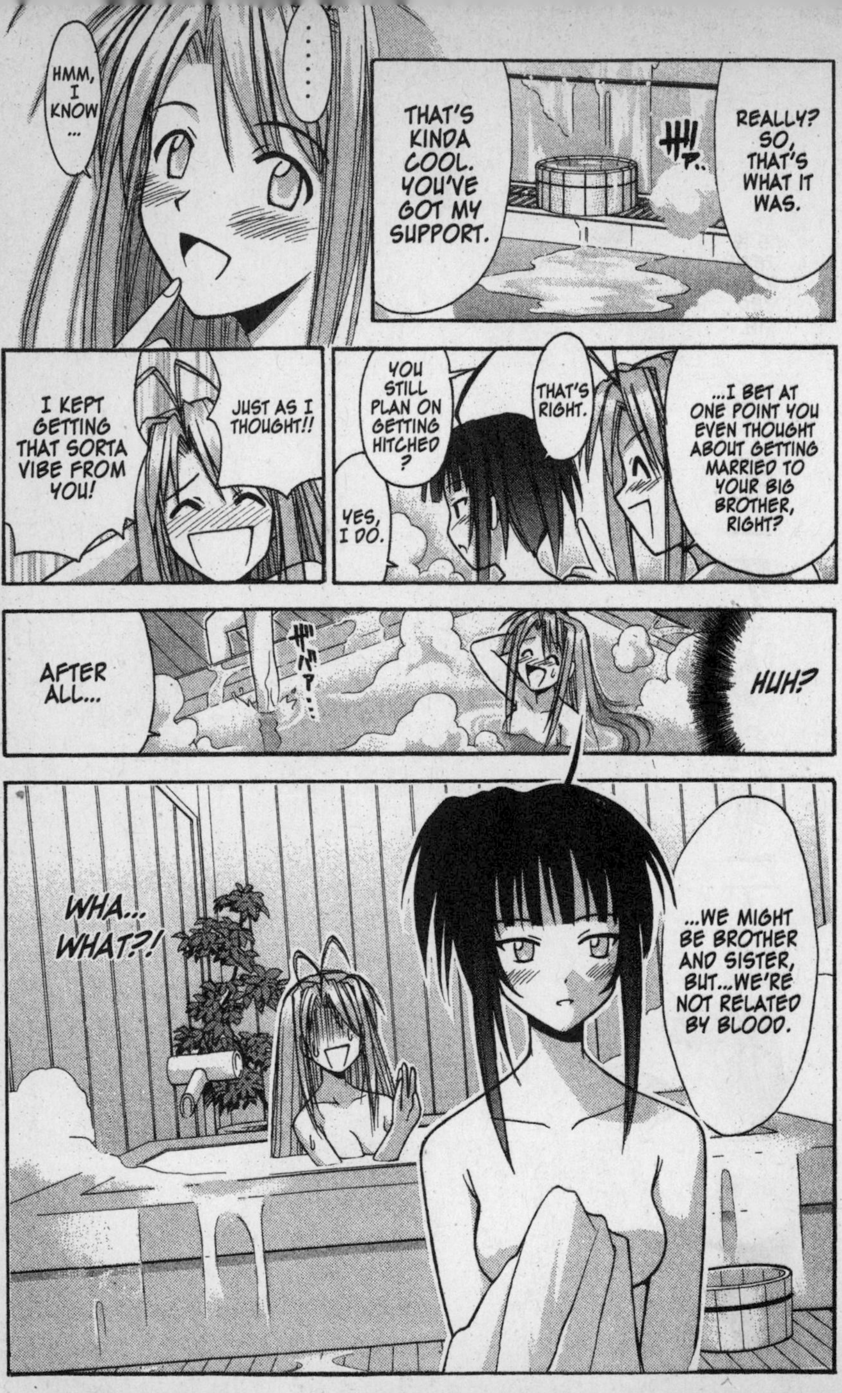
REALLY? SO, THAT'S WHAT IT WAS.
THAT'S KINDA COOL. YOU'VE GOT MY SUPPORT.
......
HMM, I KNOW...
...I BET AT ONE POINT YOU EVEN THOUGHT ABOUT GETTING MARRIED TO YOUR BIG BROTHER, RIGHT?
THAT'S RIGHT.
YOU STILL PLAN ON GETTING HITCHED?
YES, I DO.
JUST AS I THOUGHT!!
I KEPT GETTING THAT SORTA VIBE FROM YOU!
HUH?
AFTER ALL...
...WE MIGHT BE BROTHER AND SISTER, BUT...WE'RE NOT RELATED BY BLOOD.
WHA... WHAT?!

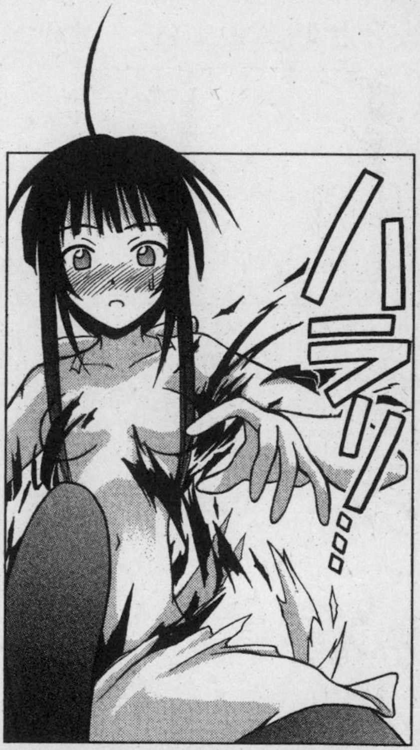
ハラッ…

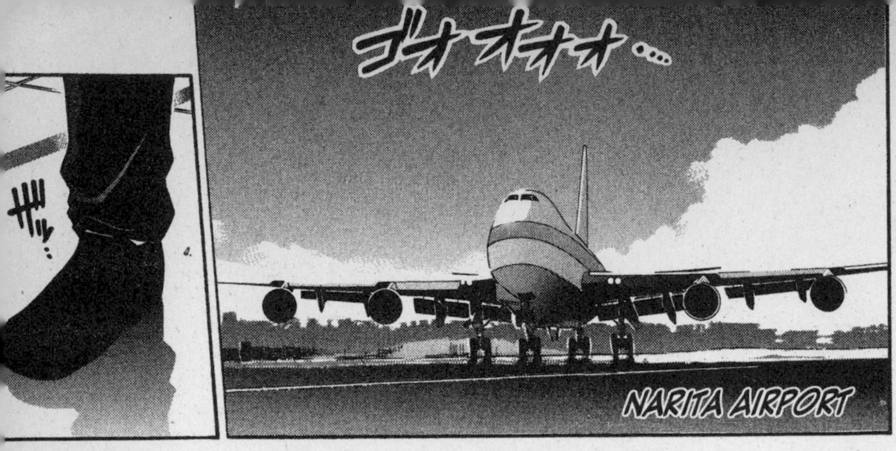
ゴォオオオ…
NARITA AIRPORT
ギッ…

Love Hina

HINATA.96 Assault on Fort Hinata

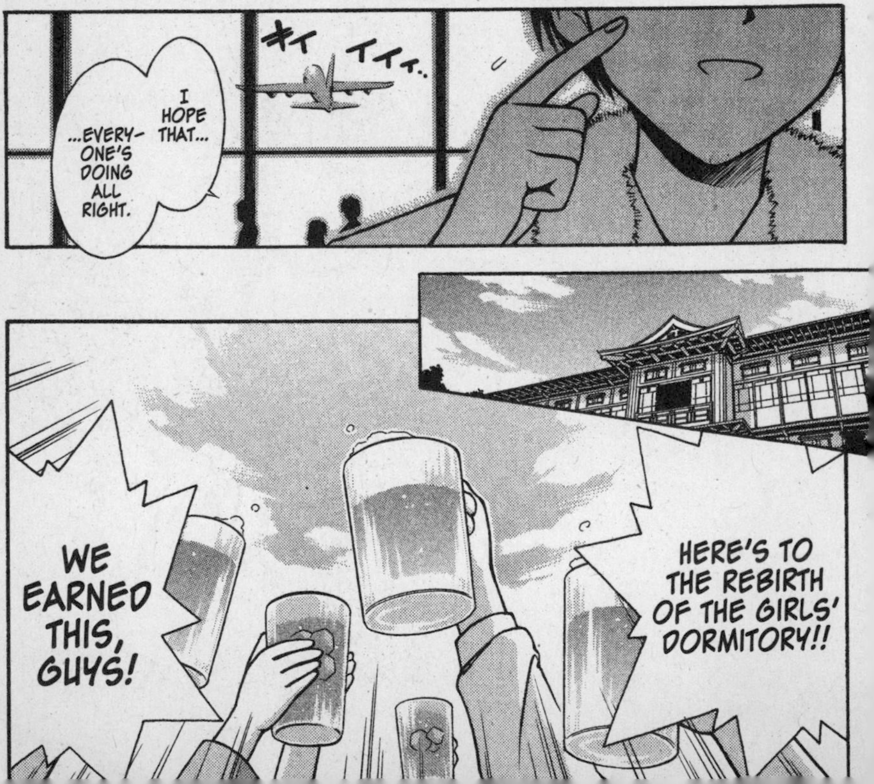
キイ イイィ..
I HOPE THAT...
...EVERYONE'S DOING ALL RIGHT.
HERE'S TO THE REBIRTH OF THE GIRLS' DORMITORY!!
WE EARNED THIS, GUYS!

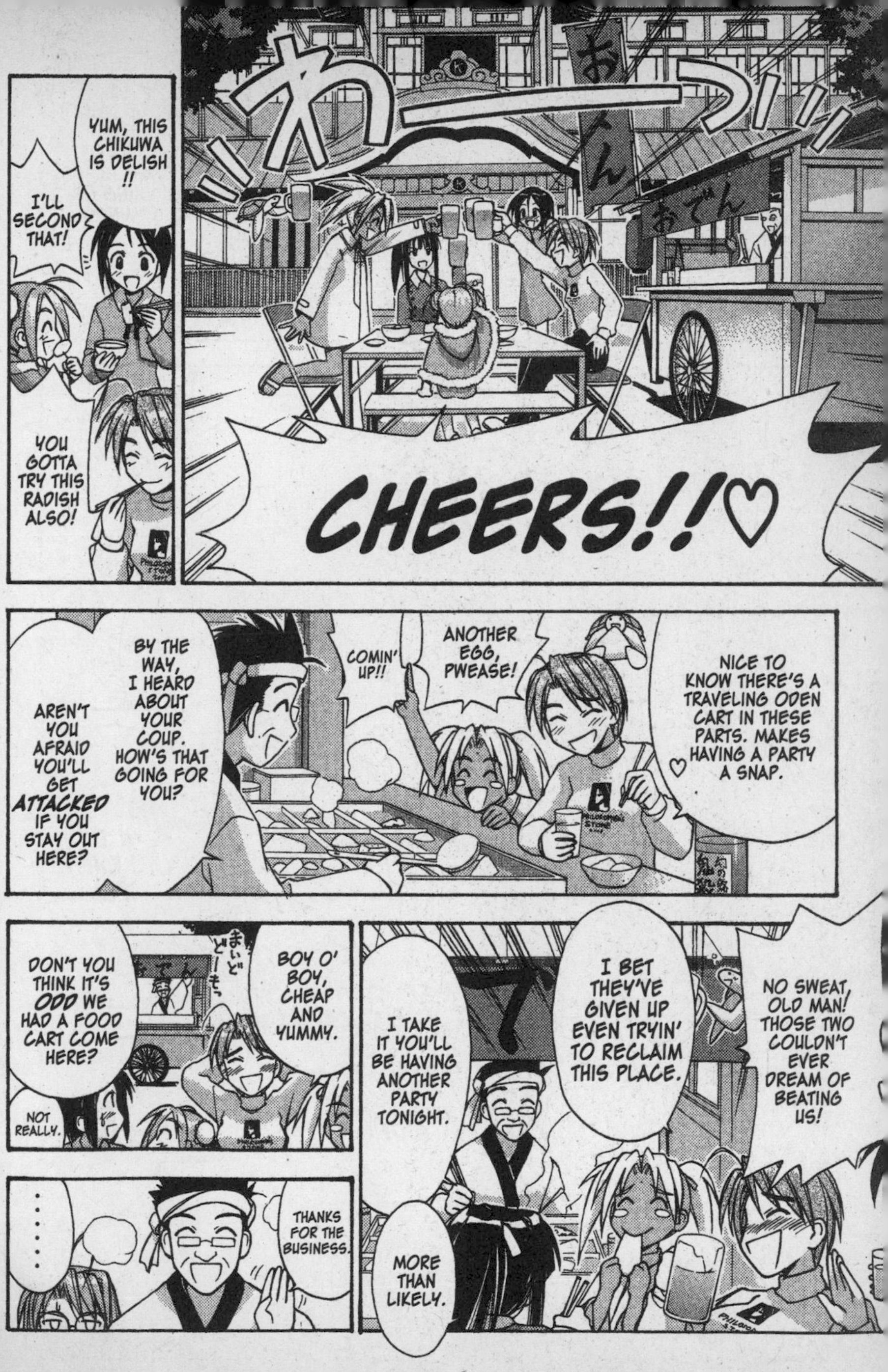

わーっ!!!
おでん
CHEERS!!♡
YUM, THIS CHIKUWA IS DELISH!!
I'LL SECOND THAT!
YOU GOTTA TRY THIS RADISH ALSO!
NICE TO KNOW THERE'S A TRAVELING ODEN CART IN THESE PARTS. MAKES HAVING A PARTY A SNAP. ♡
ANOTHER EGG, PWEASE!
COMIN' UP!!
BY THE WAY, I HEARD ABOUT YOUR COUP. HOW'S THAT GOING FOR YOU?
AREN'T YOU AFRAID YOU'LL GET ATTACKED IF YOU STAY OUT HERE?
NO SWEAT, OLD MAN! THOSE TWO COULDN'T EVER DREAM OF BEATING US!
I BET THEY'VE GIVEN UP EVEN TRYIN' TO RECLAIM THIS PLACE.
I TAKE IT YOU'LL BE HAVING ANOTHER PARTY TONIGHT.
MORE THAN LIKELY.
BOY O' BOY, CHEAP AND YUMMY.
まいど
DON'T YOU THINK IT'S ODD WE HAD A FOOD CART COME HERE?
NOT REALLY.
THANKS FOR THE BUSINESS.
......

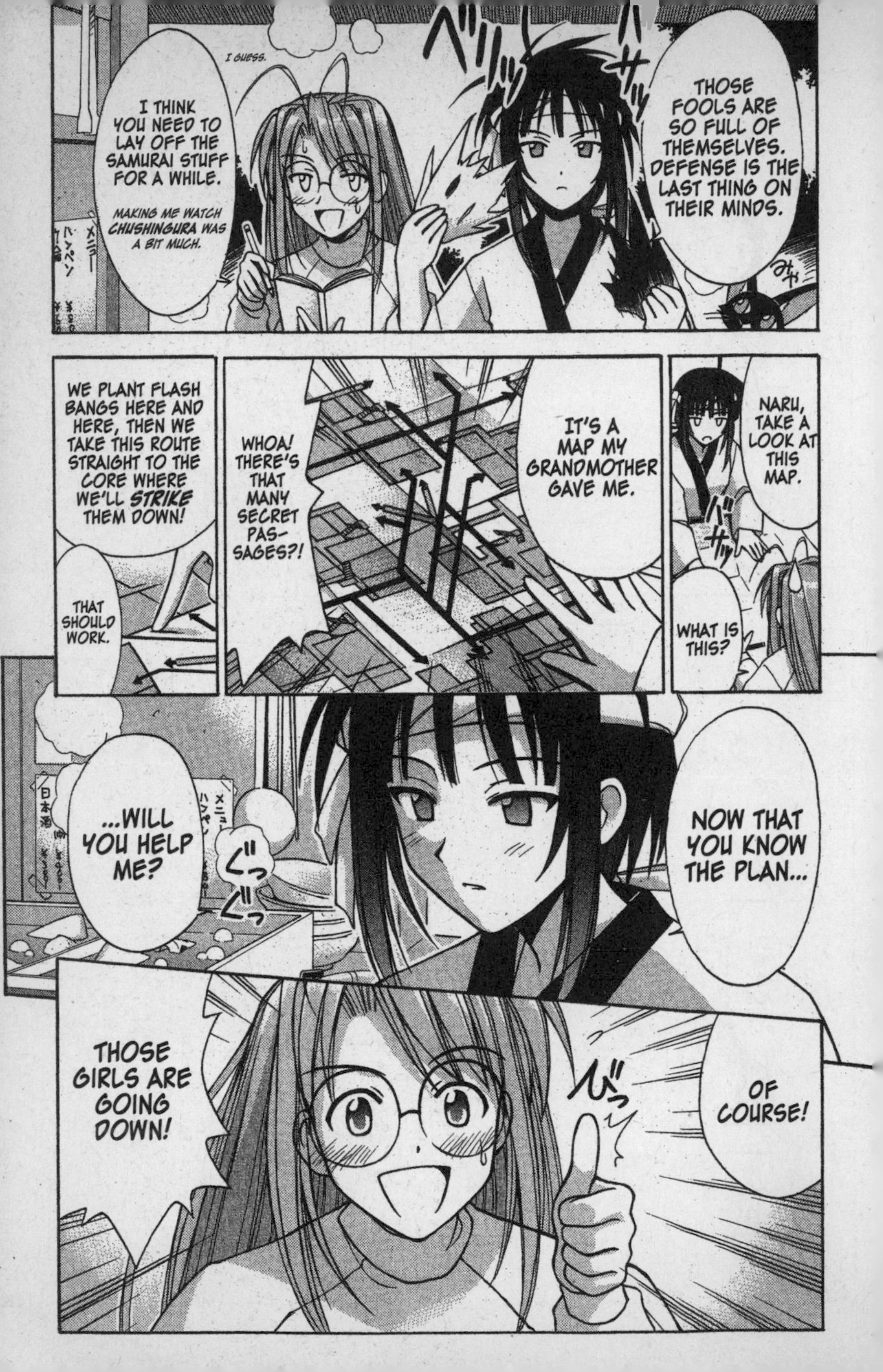
THOSE FOOLS ARE SO FULL OF THEMSELVES. DEFENSE IS THE LAST THING ON THEIR MINDS.
I GUESS.
I THINK YOU NEED TO LAY OFF THE SAMURAI STUFF FOR A WHILE.
MAKING ME WATCH *CHUSHINGURA* WAS A BIT MUCH.
NARU, TAKE A LOOK AT THIS MAP.
WHAT IS THIS?
IT'S A MAP MY GRANDMOTHER GAVE ME.
WHOA! THERE'S THAT MANY SECRET PAS-SAGES?!
WE PLANT FLASH BANGS HERE AND HERE, THEN WE TAKE THIS ROUTE STRAIGHT TO THE CORE WHERE WE'LL *STRIKE* THEM DOWN!
THAT SHOULD WORK.
NOW THAT YOU KNOW THE PLAN...
...WILL YOU HELP ME?
OF COURSE!
THOSE GIRLS ARE GOING DOWN!

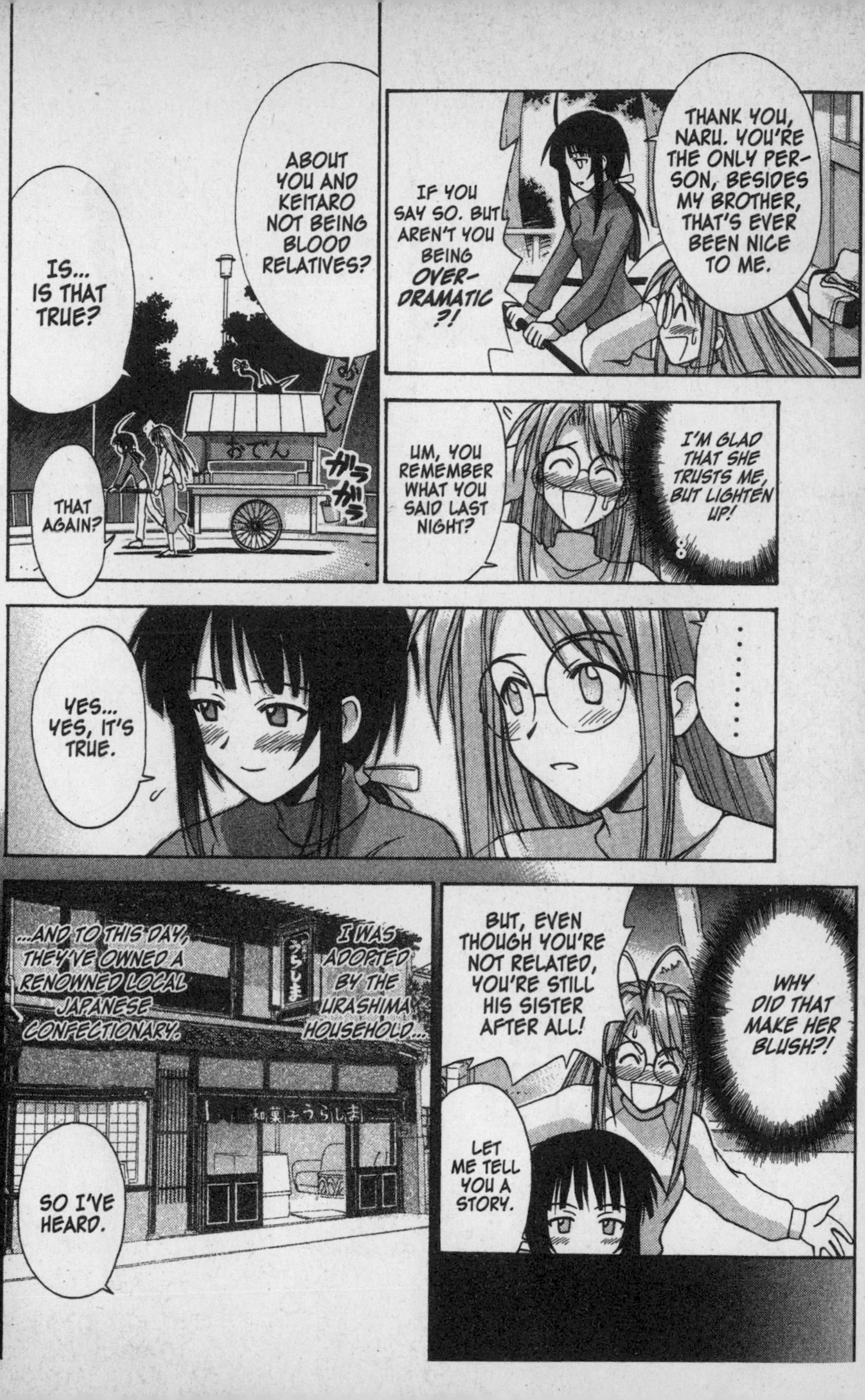
THANK YOU, NARU. YOU'RE THE ONLY PERSON, BESIDES MY BROTHER, THAT'S EVER BEEN NICE TO ME.
IF YOU SAY SO. BUT AREN'T YOU BEING OVER-DRAMATIC?!
I'M GLAD THAT SHE TRUSTS ME, BUT LIGHTEN UP!
UM, YOU REMEMBER WHAT YOU SAID LAST NIGHT?
ABOUT YOU AND KEITARO NOT BEING BLOOD RELATIVES?
おでん
ガラガラ
IS... IS THAT TRUE?
THAT AGAIN?
......
YES... YES, IT'S TRUE.
BUT, EVEN THOUGH YOU'RE NOT RELATED, YOU'RE STILL HIS SISTER AFTER ALL!
WHY DID THAT MAKE HER BLUSH?!
LET ME TELL YOU A STORY.
I WAS ADOPTED BY THE URASHIMA HOUSEHOLD...
...AND TO THIS DAY, THEY'VE OWNED A RENOWNED LOCAL JAPANESE CONFECTIONARY.
うらしま
和菓子うらしま
SO I'VE HEARD.

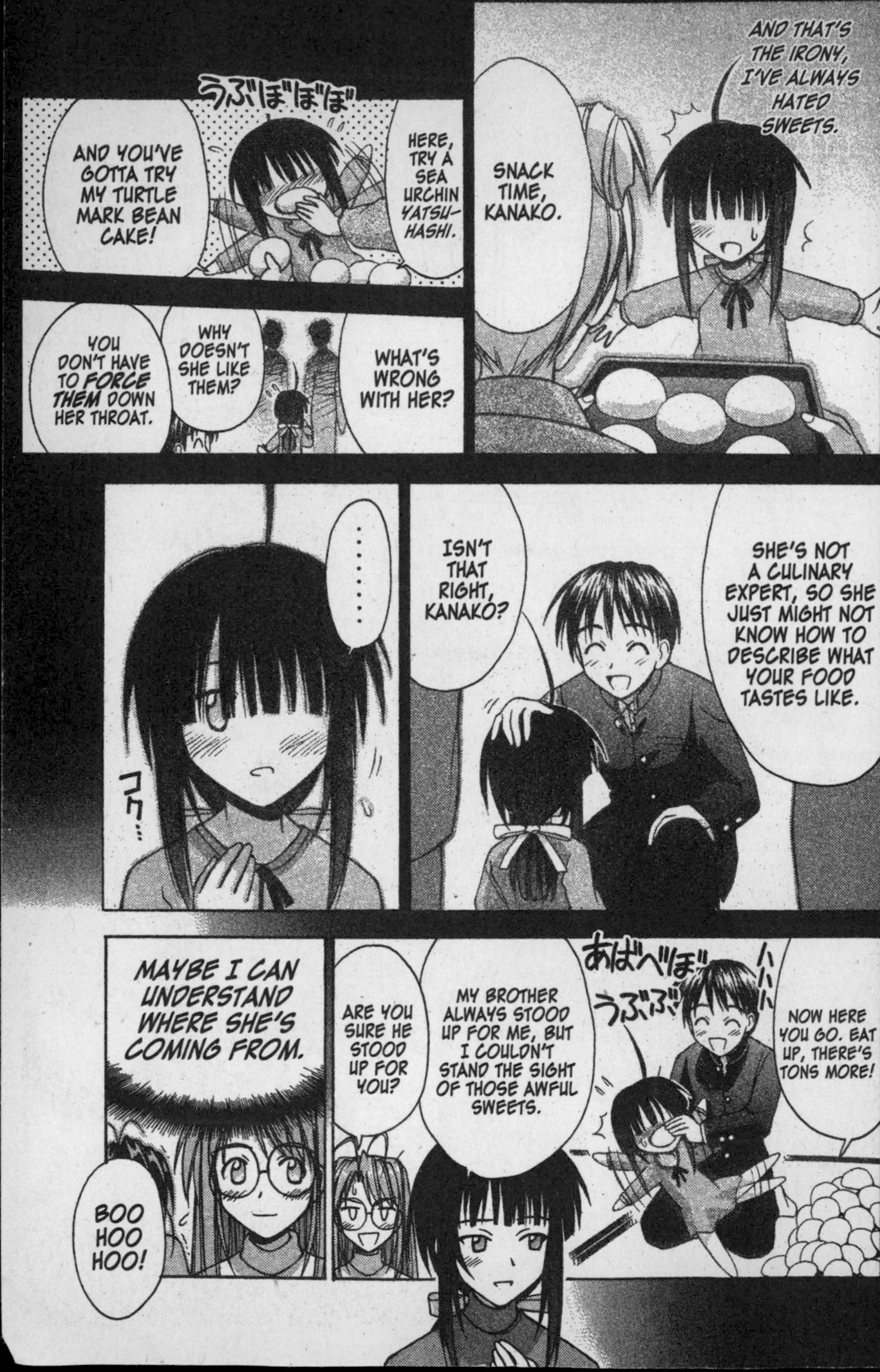
AND THAT'S THE IRONY, I'VE ALWAYS HATED SWEETS.
SNACK TIME, KANAKO.
うぶぼぼぼ
HERE, TRY A SEA URCHIN YATSU-HASHI.
AND YOU'VE GOTTA TRY MY TURTLE MARK BEAN CAKE!
WHAT'S WRONG WITH HER?
WHY DOESN'T SHE LIKE THEM?
YOU DON'T HAVE TO FORCE THEM DOWN HER THROAT.
SHE'S NOT A CULINARY EXPERT, SO SHE JUST MIGHT NOT KNOW HOW TO DESCRIBE WHAT YOUR FOOD TASTES LIKE.
ISN'T THAT RIGHT, KANAKO?
....
コク…
NOW HERE YOU GO. EAT UP, THERE'S TONS MORE!
ハハハ
あばべぼ
うぶぶ
MY BROTHER ALWAYS STOOD UP FOR ME, BUT I COULDN'T STAND THE SIGHT OF THOSE AWFUL SWEETS.
ARE YOU SURE HE STOOD UP FOR YOU?
MAYBE I CAN UNDERSTAND WHERE SHE'S COMING FROM.
BOO HOO HOO!

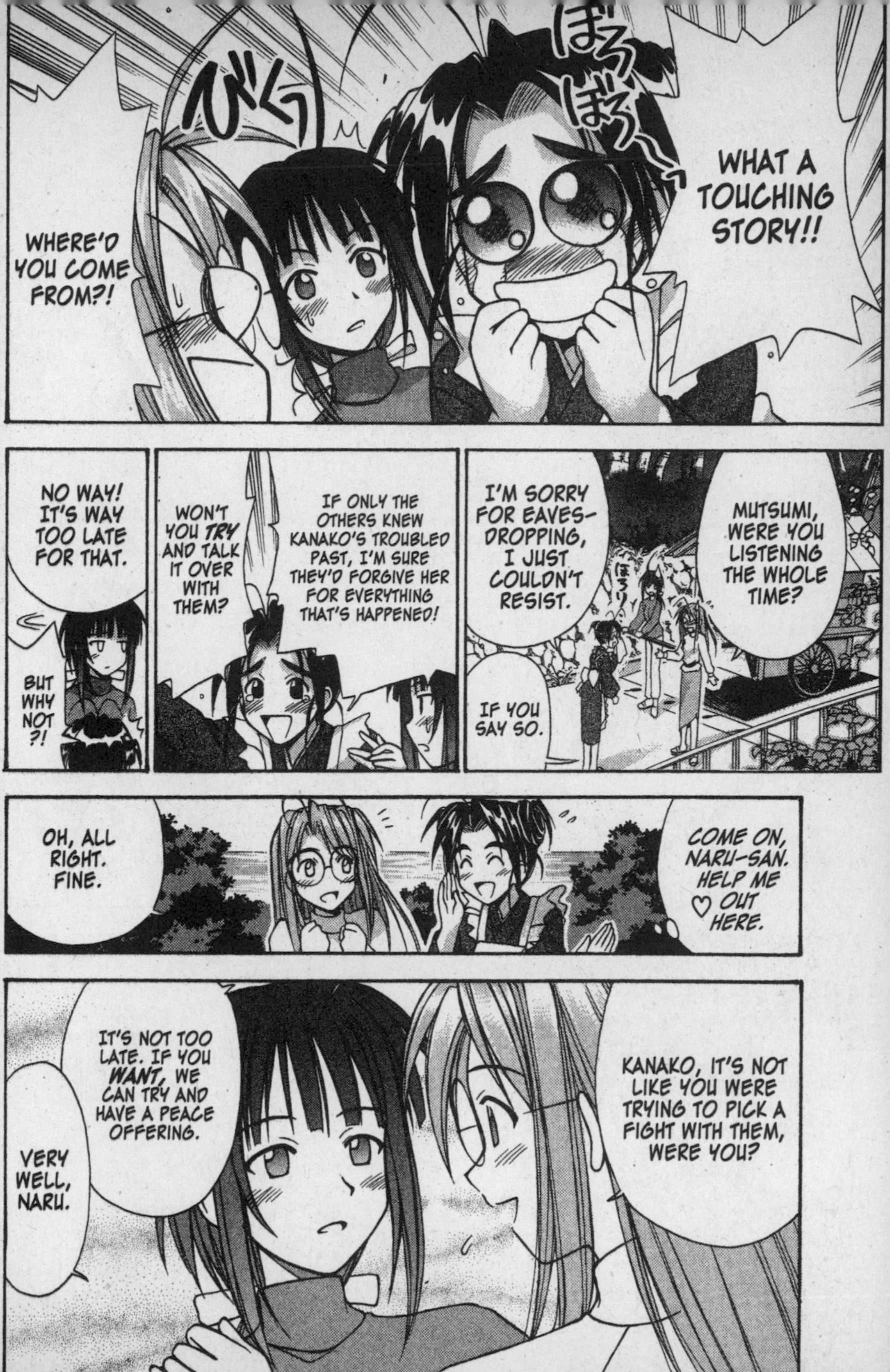

ぼろぼろ~~
WHAT A TOUCHING STORY!!
びくっ
WHERE'D YOU COME FROM?!
MUTSUMI, WERE YOU LISTENING THE WHOLE TIME?
I'M SORRY FOR EAVES-DROPPING, I JUST COULDN'T RESIST.
ぽろり
IF YOU SAY SO.
IF ONLY THE OTHERS KNEW KANAKO'S TROUBLED PAST, I'M SURE THEY'D FORGIVE HER FOR EVERYTHING THAT'S HAPPENED!
WON'T YOU *TRY* AND TALK IT OVER WITH THEM?
NO WAY! IT'S WAY TOO LATE FOR THAT.
BUT WHY NOT?!
COME ON, NARU-SAN. HELP ME ♡ OUT HERE.
OH, ALL RIGHT. FINE.
KANAKO, IT'S NOT LIKE YOU WERE TRYING TO PICK A FIGHT WITH THEM, WERE YOU?
IT'S NOT TOO LATE. IF YOU *WANT*, WE CAN TRY AND HAVE A PEACE OFFERING.
VERY WELL, NARU.

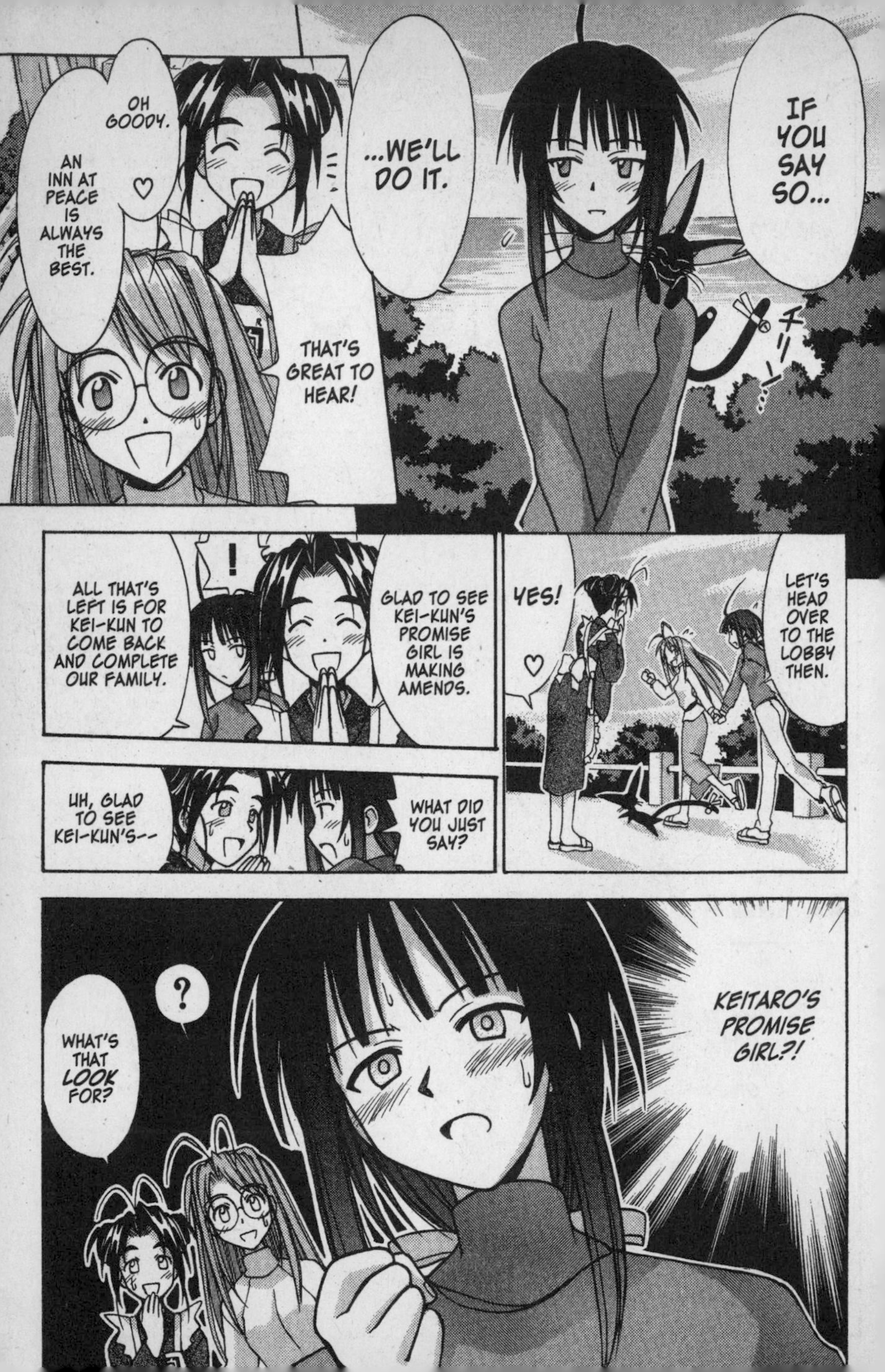
IF YOU SAY SO...
チリーン
...WE'LL DO IT.
OH GOODY.
AN INN AT PEACE IS ALWAYS THE BEST.
THAT'S GREAT TO HEAR!
LET'S HEAD OVER TO THE LOBBY THEN.
YES!
GLAD TO SEE KEI-KUN'S PROMISE GIRL IS MAKING AMENDS.
!
ALL THAT'S LEFT IS FOR KEI-KUN TO COME BACK AND COMPLETE OUR FAMILY.
WHAT DID YOU JUST SAY?
UH, GLAD TO SEE KEI-KUN'S--
KEITARO'S PROMISE GIRL?!
?
WHAT'S THAT *LOOK* FOR?

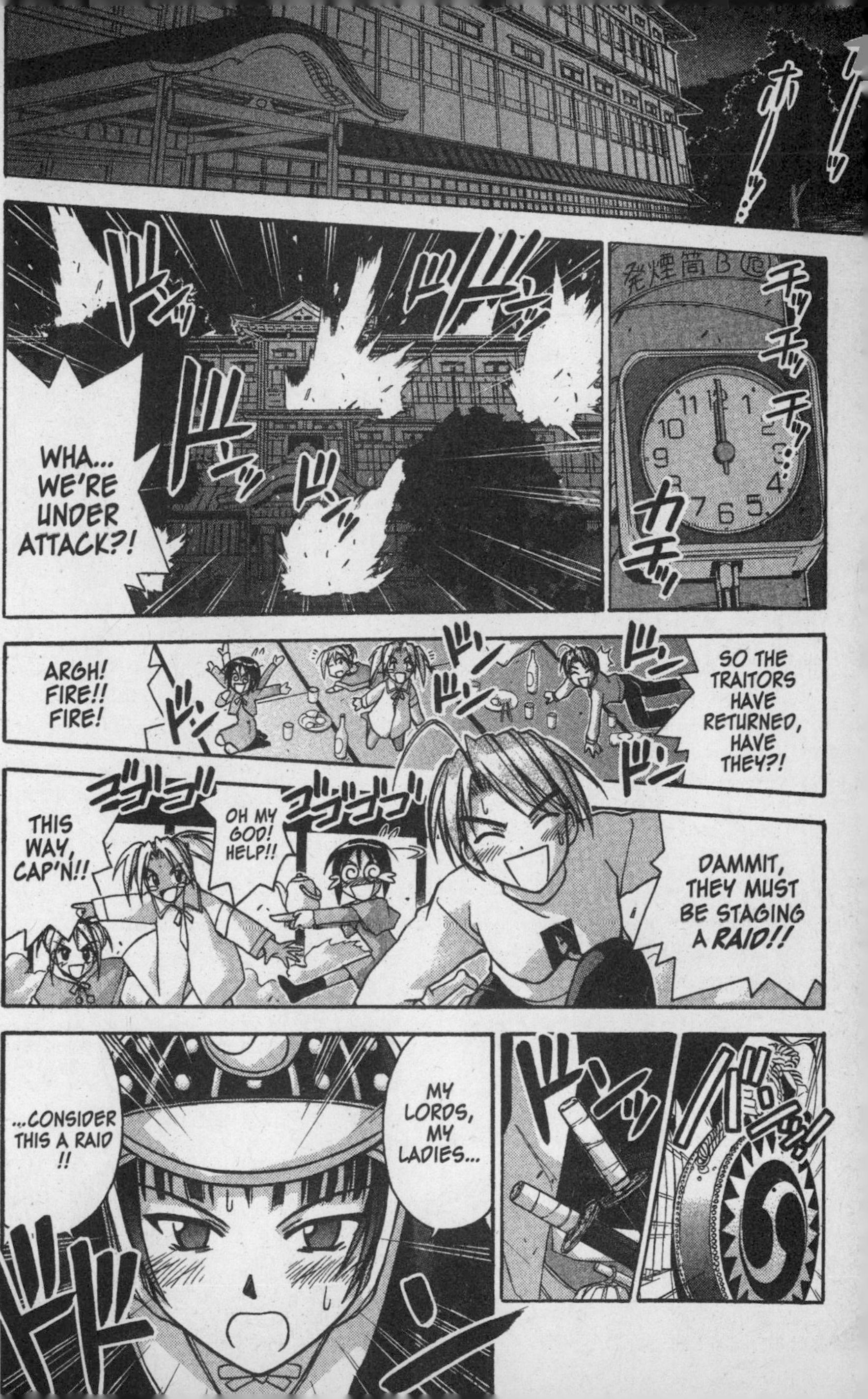

WHA... WE'RE UNDER ATTACK?!
SO THE TRAITORS HAVE RETURNED, HAVE THEY?!
ARGH! FIRE!! FIRE!
DAMMIT, THEY MUST BE STAGING A *RAID*!!
OH MY GOD! HELP!!
THIS WAY, CAP'N!!
MY LORDS, MY LADIES...
...CONSIDER THIS A RAID !!

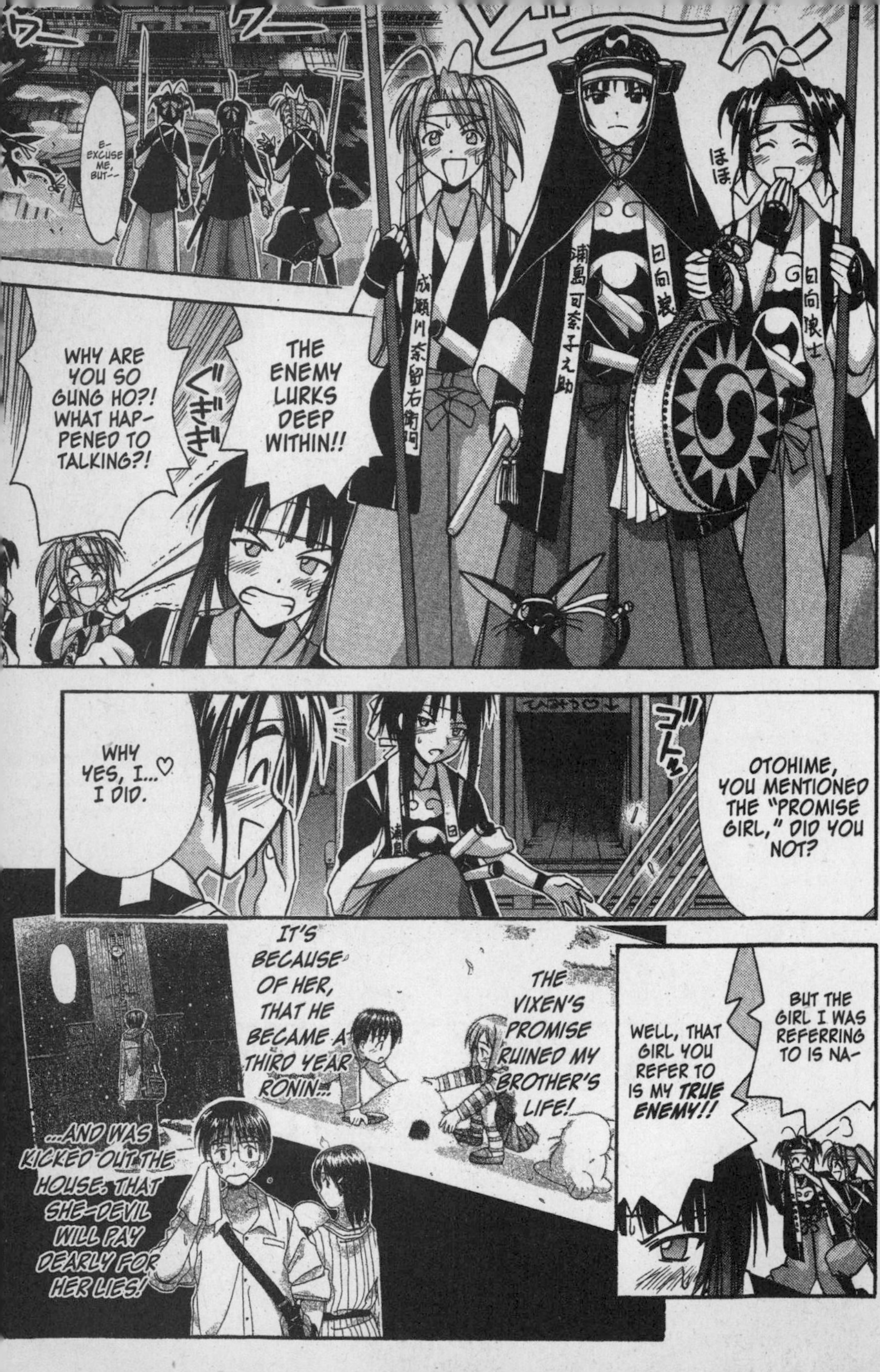
どーーん
ほほ
成瀬川奈留右衛門
浦島可奈子え助
日向狼士
E-EXCUSE ME, BUT--
THE ENEMY LURKS DEEP WITHIN!!
WHY ARE YOU SO GUNG HO?! WHAT HAP-PENED TO TALKING?!
ぐぎぎ
OTOHIME, YOU MENTIONED THE "PROMISE GIRL," DID YOU NOT?
ゴトッ
WHY YES, I...♡ I DID.
BUT THE GIRL I WAS REFERRING TO IS NA-
WELL, THAT GIRL YOU REFER TO IS MY *TRUE ENEMY!!*
THE VIXEN'S PROMISE RUINED MY BROTHER'S LIFE!
IT'S BECAUSE OF HER, THAT HE BECAME A THIRD YEAR RONIN...
...AND WAS KICKED OUT THE HOUSE. THAT SHE-DEVIL WILL PAY DEARLY FOR HER LIES!

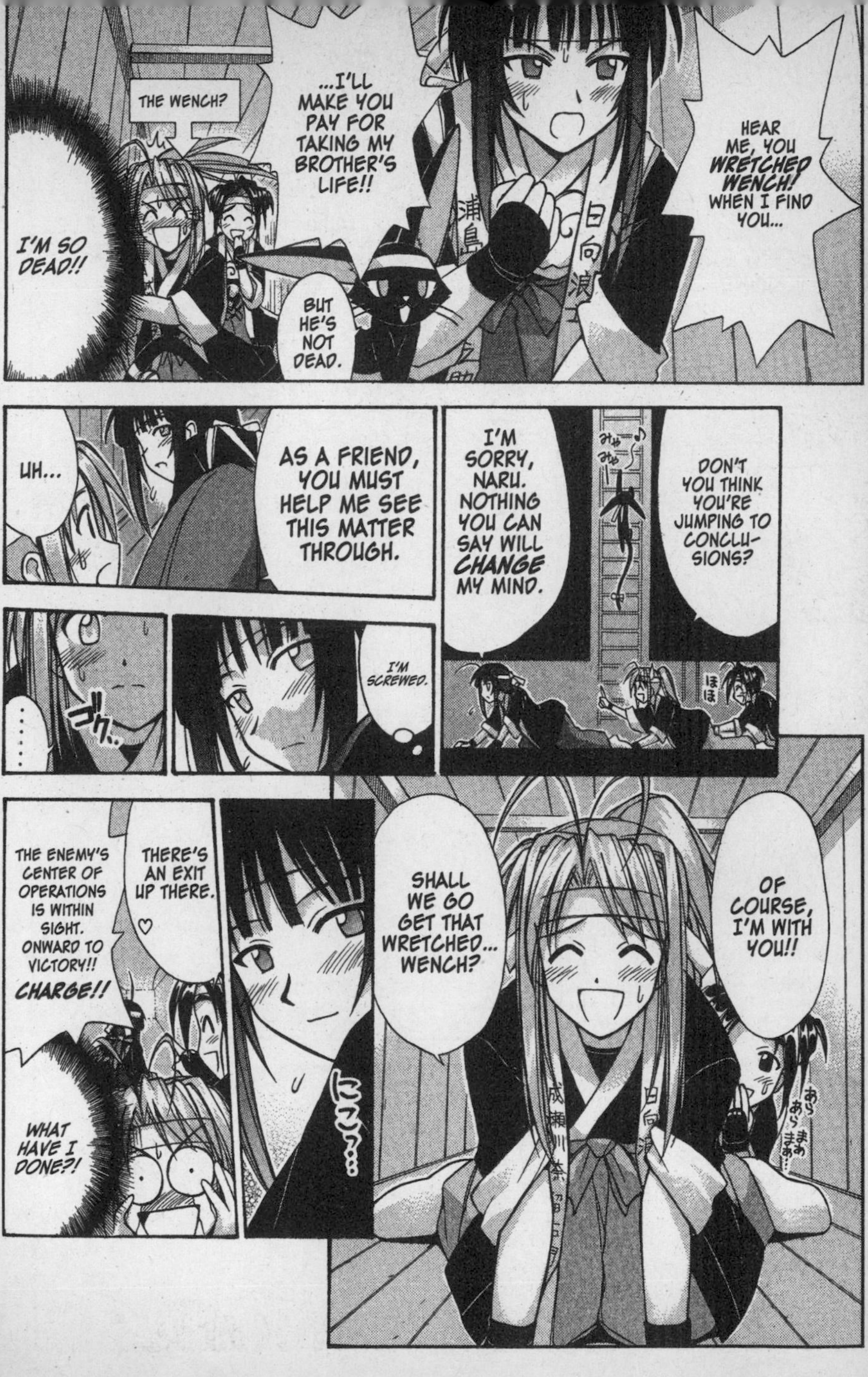
HEAR ME, YOU WRETCHED WENCH! WHEN I FIND YOU...
...I'LL MAKE YOU PAY FOR TAKING MY BROTHER'S LIFE!!
BUT HE'S NOT DEAD.
THE WENCH?
I'M SO DEAD!!
DON'T YOU THINK YOU'RE JUMPING TO CONCLUSIONS?
I'M SORRY, NARU. NOTHING YOU CAN SAY WILL CHANGE MY MIND.
AS A FRIEND, YOU MUST HELP ME SEE THIS MATTER THROUGH.
UH...
I'M SCREWED.
......
OF COURSE, I'M WITH YOU!!
SHALL WE GO GET THAT WRETCHED... WENCH?
THERE'S AN EXIT UP THERE.
THE ENEMY'S CENTER OF OPERATIONS IS WITHIN SIGHT. ONWARD TO VICTORY!! CHARGE!!
WHAT HAVE I DONE?!

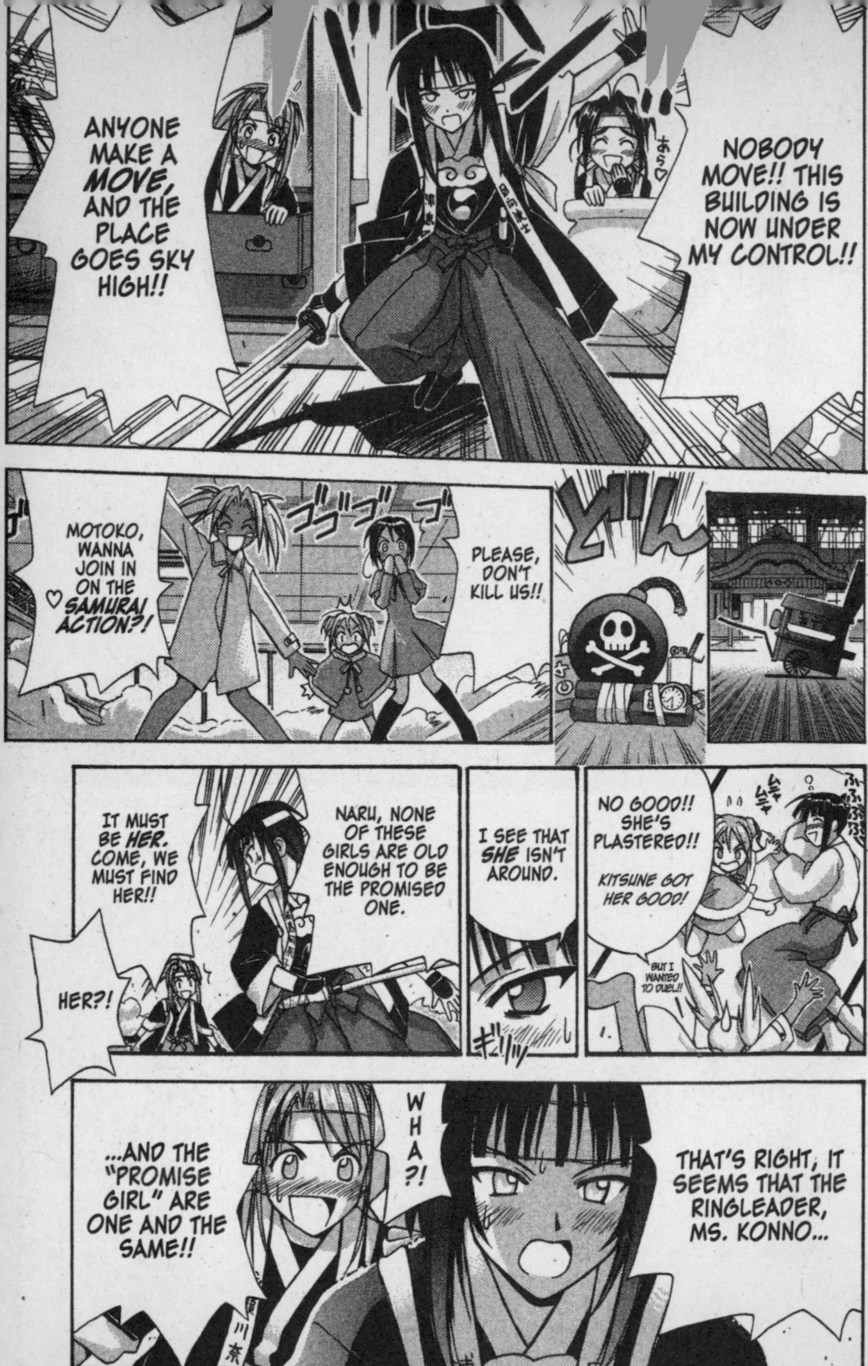

NOBODY MOVE!! THIS BUILDING IS NOW UNDER MY CONTROL!!
あら♡
ANYONE MAKE A MOVE, AND THE PLACE GOES SKY HIGH!!
どん
PLEASE, DON'T KILL US!!
MOTOKO, WANNA JOIN IN ON THE SAMURAI ACTION?! ♡
NO GOOD!! SHE'S PLASTERED!!
KITSUNE GOT HER GOOD!
BUT I WANTED TO DUEL!!
I SEE THAT SHE ISN'T AROUND.
NARU, NONE OF THESE GIRLS ARE OLD ENOUGH TO BE THE PROMISED ONE.
IT MUST BE HER. COME, WE MUST FIND HER!!
HER?!
THAT'S RIGHT, IT SEEMS THAT THE RINGLEADER, MS. KONNO...
WHA?!
...AND THE "PROMISE GIRL" ARE ONE AND THE SAME!!

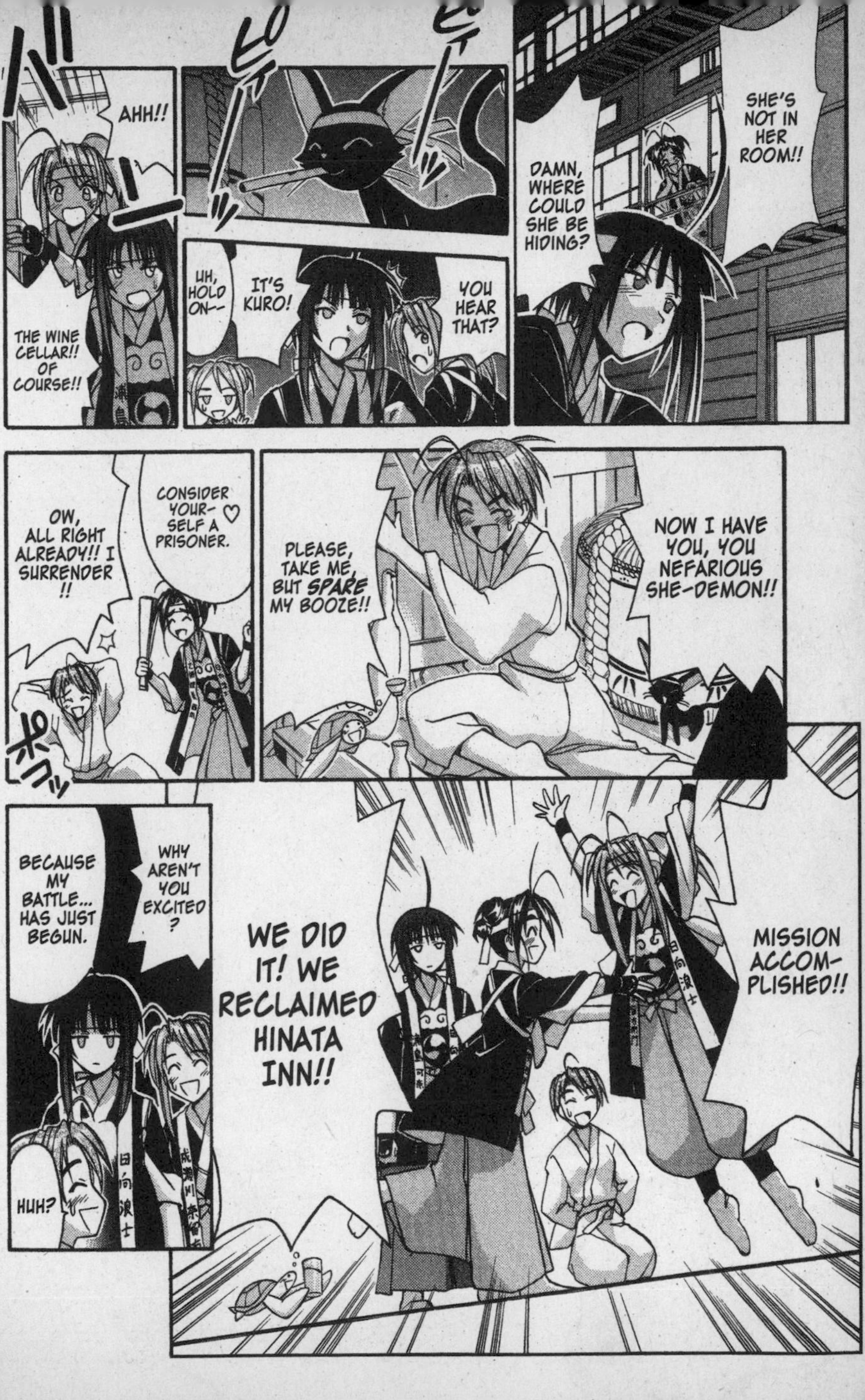
SHE'S NOT IN HER ROOM!!
DAMN, WHERE COULD SHE BE HIDING?
YOU HEAR THAT?
IT'S KURO!
UH, HOLD ON--
AHH!!
THE WINE CELLAR!! OF COURSE!!
NOW I HAVE YOU, YOU NEFARIOUS SHE-DEMON!!
PLEASE, TAKE ME, BUT SPARE MY BOOZE!!
CONSIDER YOURSELF A PRISONER. ♡
OW, ALL RIGHT ALREADY!! I SURRENDER!!
MISSION ACCOMPLISHED!!
WE DID IT! WE RECLAIMED HINATA INN!!
WHY AREN'T YOU EXCITED?
BECAUSE MY BATTLE... HAS JUST BEGUN.
HUH?

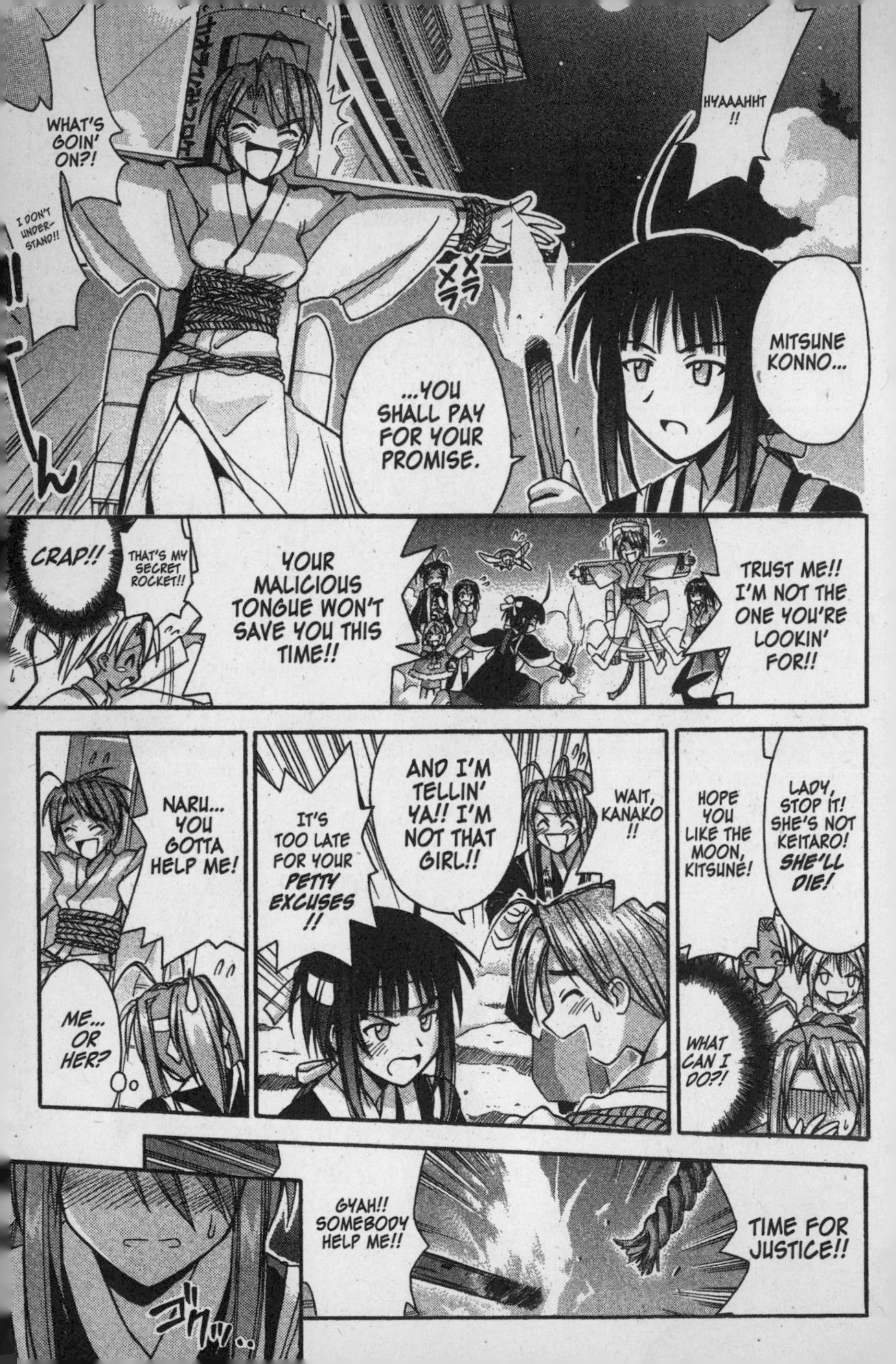
HYAAAHHT !!
MITSUNE KONNO...
...YOU SHALL PAY FOR YOUR PROMISE.
WHAT'S GOIN' ON?!
I DON'T UNDER-STAND!!
TRUST ME!! I'M NOT THE ONE YOU'RE LOOKIN' FOR!!
YOUR MALICIOUS TONGUE WON'T SAVE YOU THIS TIME!!
THAT'S MY SECRET ROCKET!!
CRAP!!
LADY, STOP IT! SHE'S NOT KEITARO! SHE'LL DIE!
HOPE YOU LIKE THE MOON, KITSUNE!
WHAT CAN I DO?!
WAIT, KANAKO!!
AND I'M TELLIN' YA!! I'M NOT THAT GIRL!!
IT'S TOO LATE FOR YOUR PETTY EXCUSES!!
NARU... YOU GOTTA HELP ME!
ME... OR HER?
TIME FOR JUSTICE!!
GYAH!! SOMEBODY HELP ME!!

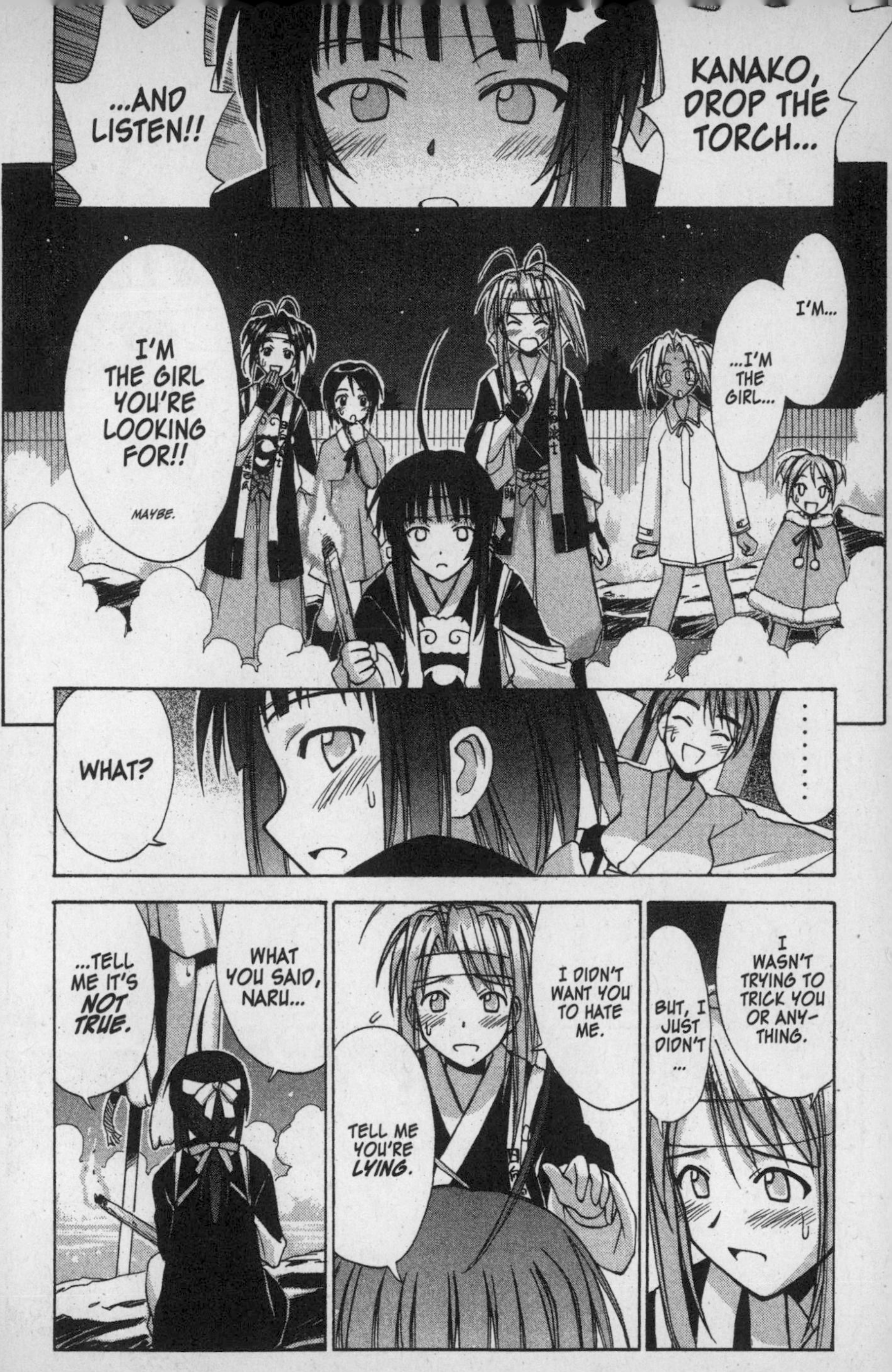
KANAKO, DROP THE TORCH...
...AND LISTEN!!
I'M...
...I'M THE GIRL...
I'M THE GIRL YOU'RE LOOKING FOR!!
MAYBE.
......
WHAT?
I WASN'T TRYING TO TRICK YOU OR ANY-THING.
BUT, I JUST DIDN'T ...
I DIDN'T WANT YOU TO HATE ME.
TELL ME YOU'RE LYING.
WHAT YOU SAID, NARU...
...TELL ME IT'S NOT TRUE.

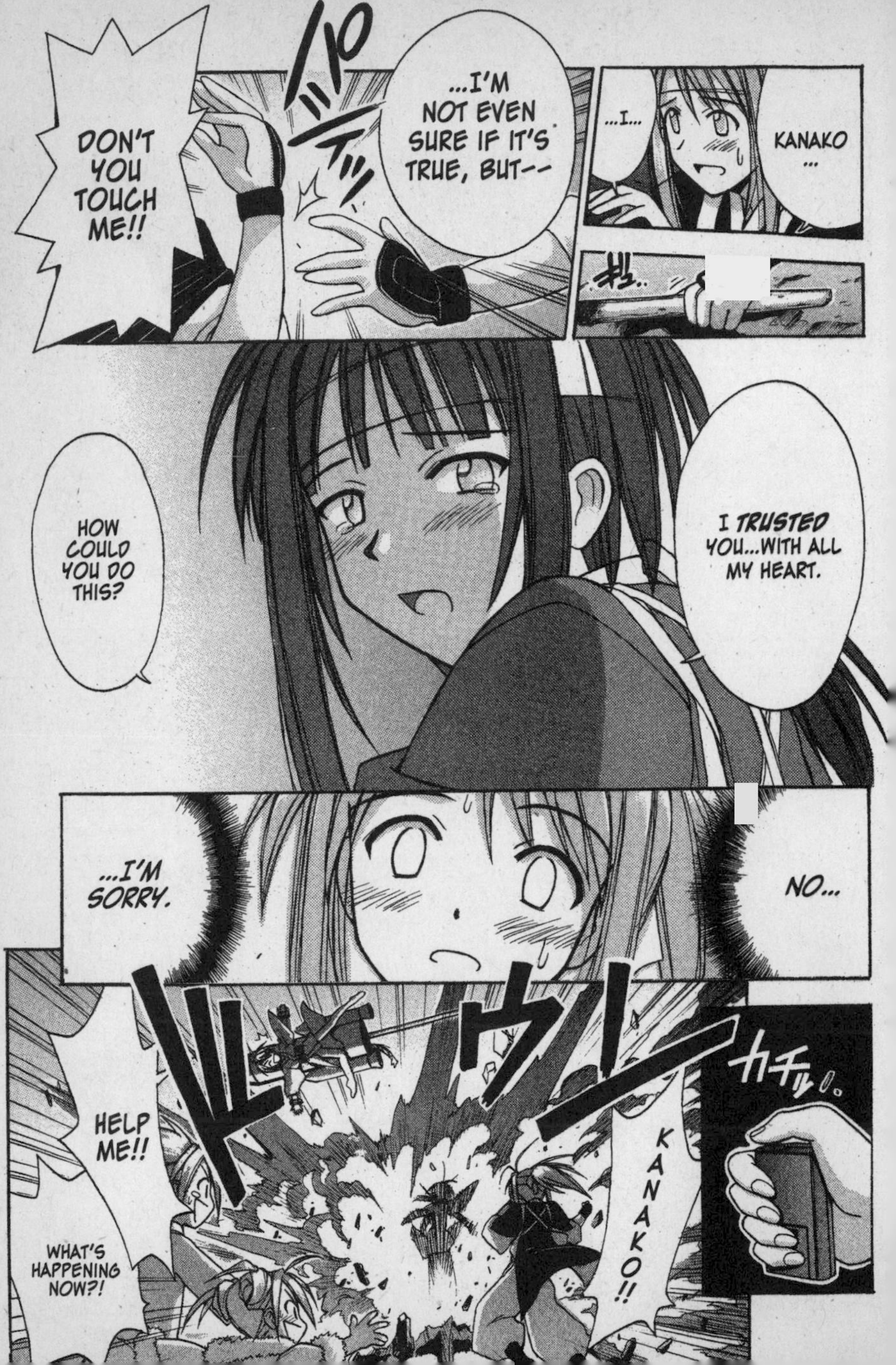
KANAKO ...
...I...
...I'M NOT EVEN SURE IF IT'S TRUE, BUT--
DON'T YOU TOUCH ME!!
I TRUSTED YOU...WITH ALL MY HEART.
HOW COULD YOU DO THIS?
NO...
...I'M SORRY.
KANAKO!!
HELP ME!!
WHAT'S HAPPENING NOW?!

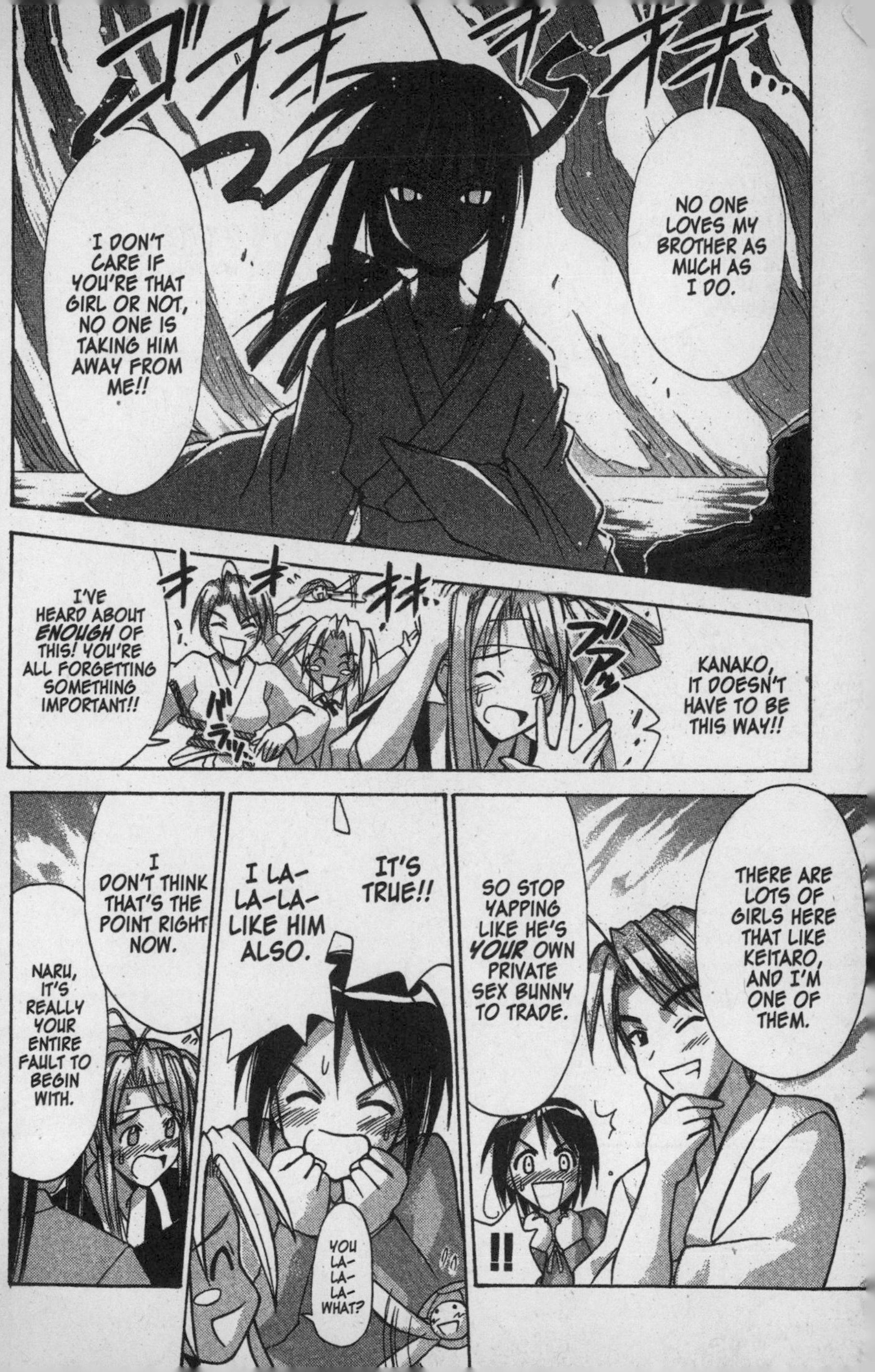
NO ONE LOVES MY BROTHER AS MUCH AS I DO.
I DON'T CARE IF YOU'RE THAT GIRL OR NOT, NO ONE IS TAKING HIM AWAY FROM ME!!
KANAKO, IT DOESN'T HAVE TO BE THIS WAY!!
I'VE HEARD ABOUT *ENOUGH* OF THIS! YOU'RE ALL FORGETTING SOMETHING IMPORTANT!!
THERE ARE LOTS OF GIRLS HERE THAT LIKE KEITARO, AND I'M ONE OF THEM.
SO STOP YAPPING LIKE HE'S *YOUR* OWN PRIVATE SEX BUNNY TO TRADE.
!!
IT'S TRUE!!
I LA-LA-LA-LIKE HIM ALSO.
YOU LA-LA-LA-LA-WHAT?
I DON'T THINK THAT'S THE POINT RIGHT NOW.
NARU, IT'S REALLY YOUR ENTIRE FAULT TO BEGIN WITH.

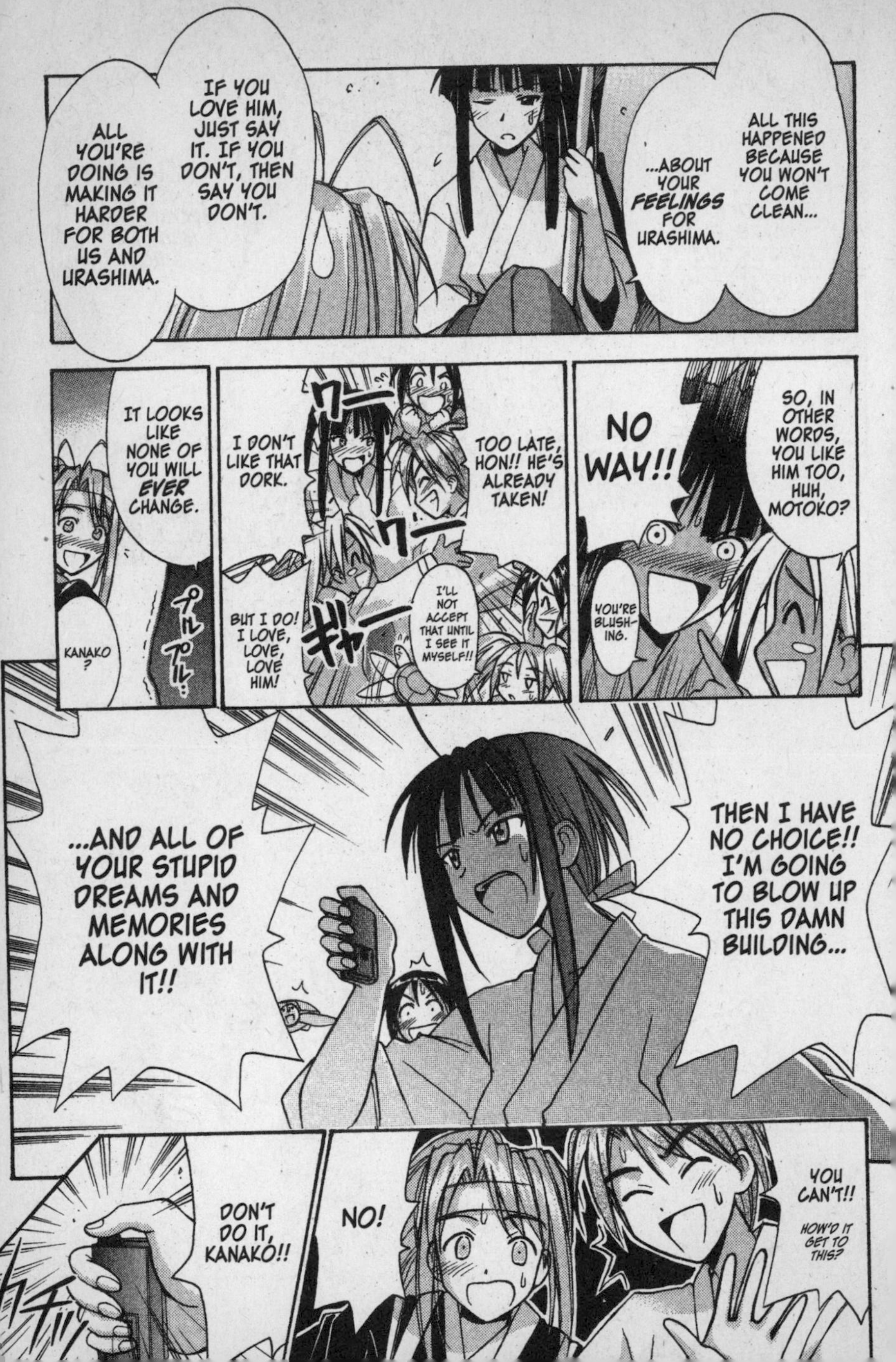
ALL THIS HAPPENED BECAUSE YOU WON'T COME CLEAN...
...ABOUT YOUR FEELINGS FOR URASHIMA.
IF YOU LOVE HIM, JUST SAY IT. IF YOU DON'T, THEN SAY YOU DON'T.
ALL YOU'RE DOING IS MAKING IT HARDER FOR BOTH US AND URASHIMA.
SO, IN OTHER WORDS, YOU LIKE HIM TOO, HUH, MOTOKO?
NO WAY!!
YOU'RE BLUSHING.
TOO LATE, HON!! HE'S ALREADY TAKEN!
ワー
I DON'T LIKE THAT DORK.
ワー
I'LL NOT ACCEPT THAT UNTIL I SEE IT MYSELF!!
ギャー
BUT I DO! I LOVE, LOVE, LOVE HIM!
IT LOOKS LIKE NONE OF YOU WILL EVER CHANGE.
プルプル
KANAKO?
THEN I HAVE NO CHOICE!! I'M GOING TO BLOW UP THIS DAMN BUILDING...
...AND ALL OF YOUR STUPID DREAMS AND MEMORIES ALONG WITH IT!!
YOU CAN'T!!
HOW'D IT GET TO THIS?
NO!
DON'T DO IT, KANAKO!!

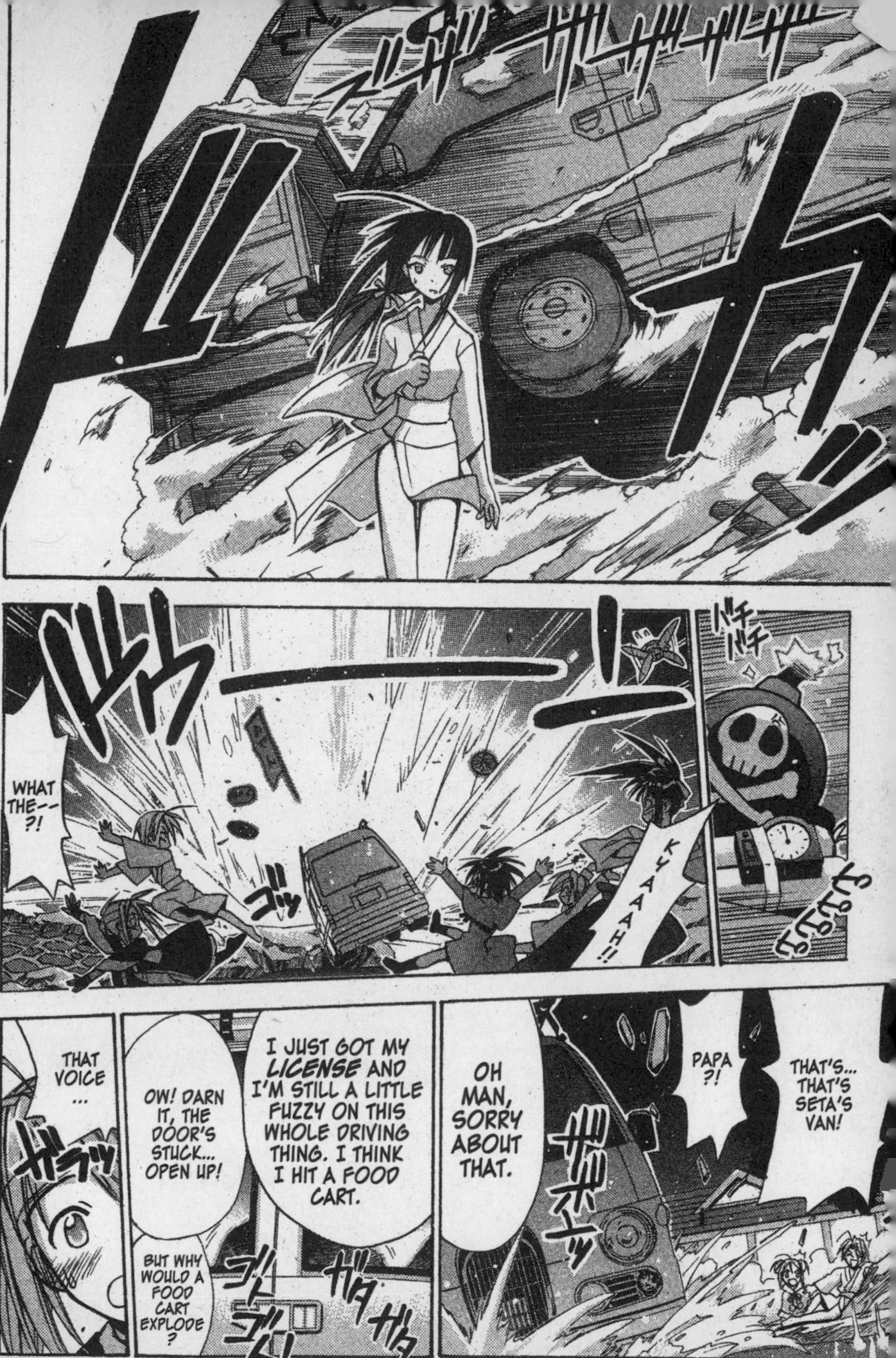

WHAT THE--?!
KYAAAAH!!
THAT'S... THAT'S SETA'S VAN!
PAPA?!
OH MAN, SORRY ABOUT THAT.
I JUST GOT MY LICENSE AND I'M STILL A LITTLE FUZZY ON THIS WHOLE DRIVING THING. I THINK I HIT A FOOD CART.
OW! DARN IT, THE DOOR'S STUCK... OPEN UP!
BUT WHY WOULD A FOOD CART EXPLODE?
THAT VOICE...

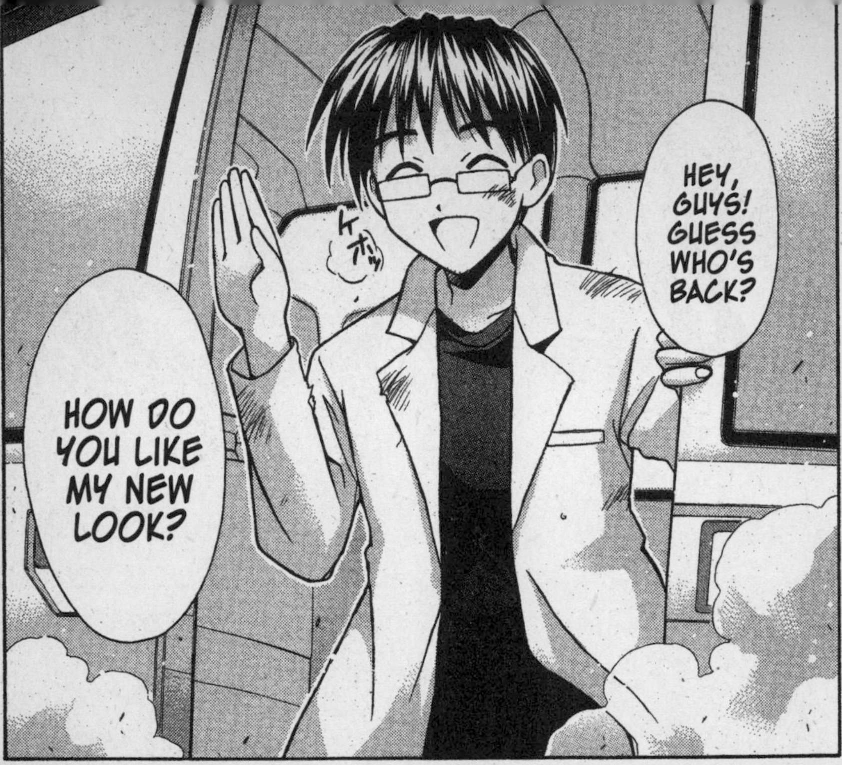
HEY, GUYS! GUESS WHO'S BACK?
ケホッ
HOW DO YOU LIKE MY NEW LOOK?

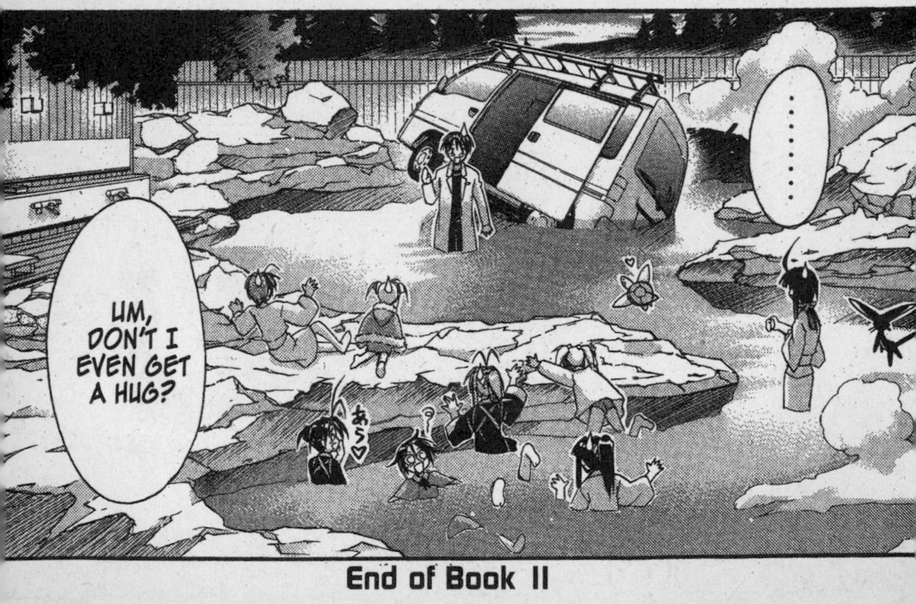
......
UM, DON'T I EVEN GET A HUG?
あら♡

End of Book II

STAFF

Ken Akamatsu
Takashi Takemoto
Kenichi Nakamura
Takaaki Miyahara
Tomohiko Saito
Masaki Ohyama
Ran Ayanaga

EDITOR

Noboru Ohno
Masakazu Yoshimoto
Yasushi Yamanaka

KC Editor

Mitsuei Ishii

In the next volume of

Love Hina

The North Land Emotional Journey

Keitaro's back, and he couldn't have picked a better time. Managing to force the warring girls into a temporary truce, he and the Hinata crew try to put differences aside and get on with their lives. Yet with all the changes that Keitaro's sister Kanako has made, that might be a feat in and of itself.

As Naru struggles with her true feelings for Keitaro, the rivalry between her and Kanako takes a bizarre turn when a magical spell is cast upon the two siblings. Now, whenever Naru tries to interfere with Kanako and Keitaro's relationship, she meets a hellish backlash that might just prove stronger than a childhood promise ever could.

With the strain of the situation mounting, and Naru's own indecisive nature tugging at her heart strings, she bolts from Hinata Inn on a non-stop journey to get as far away from Keitaro as she possibly can. But when Keitaro and the rest of the harem decide to track her down, Naru totally snaps. Will love ever prevail?

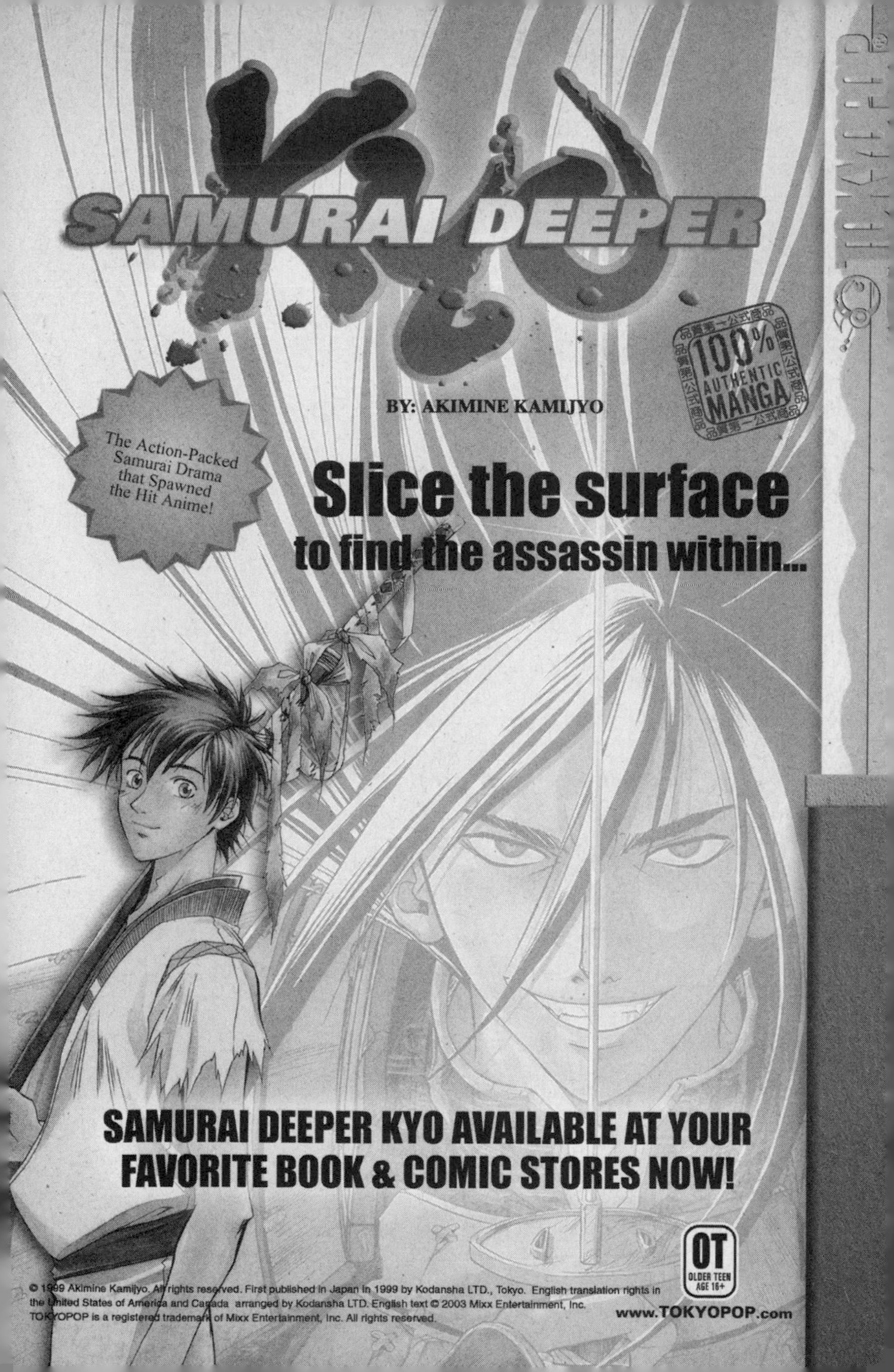
TOKYOPOP
SAMURAI DEEPER KYO
BY: AKIMINE KAMIJYO
100% AUTHENTIC MANGA
The Action-Packed Samurai Drama that Spawned the Hit Anime!
Slice the surface
to find the assassin within...
SAMURAI DEEPER KYO AVAILABLE AT YOUR FAVORITE BOOK & COMIC STORES NOW!
OT OLDER TEEN AGE 16+
© 1999 Akimine Kamijyo. All rights reserved. First published in Japan in 1999 by Kodansha LTD., Tokyo. English translation rights in the United States of America and Canada arranged by Kodansha LTD. English text © 2003 Mixx Entertainment, Inc. TOKYOPOP is a registered trademark of Mixx Entertainment, Inc. All rights reserved.
www.TOKYOPOP.com

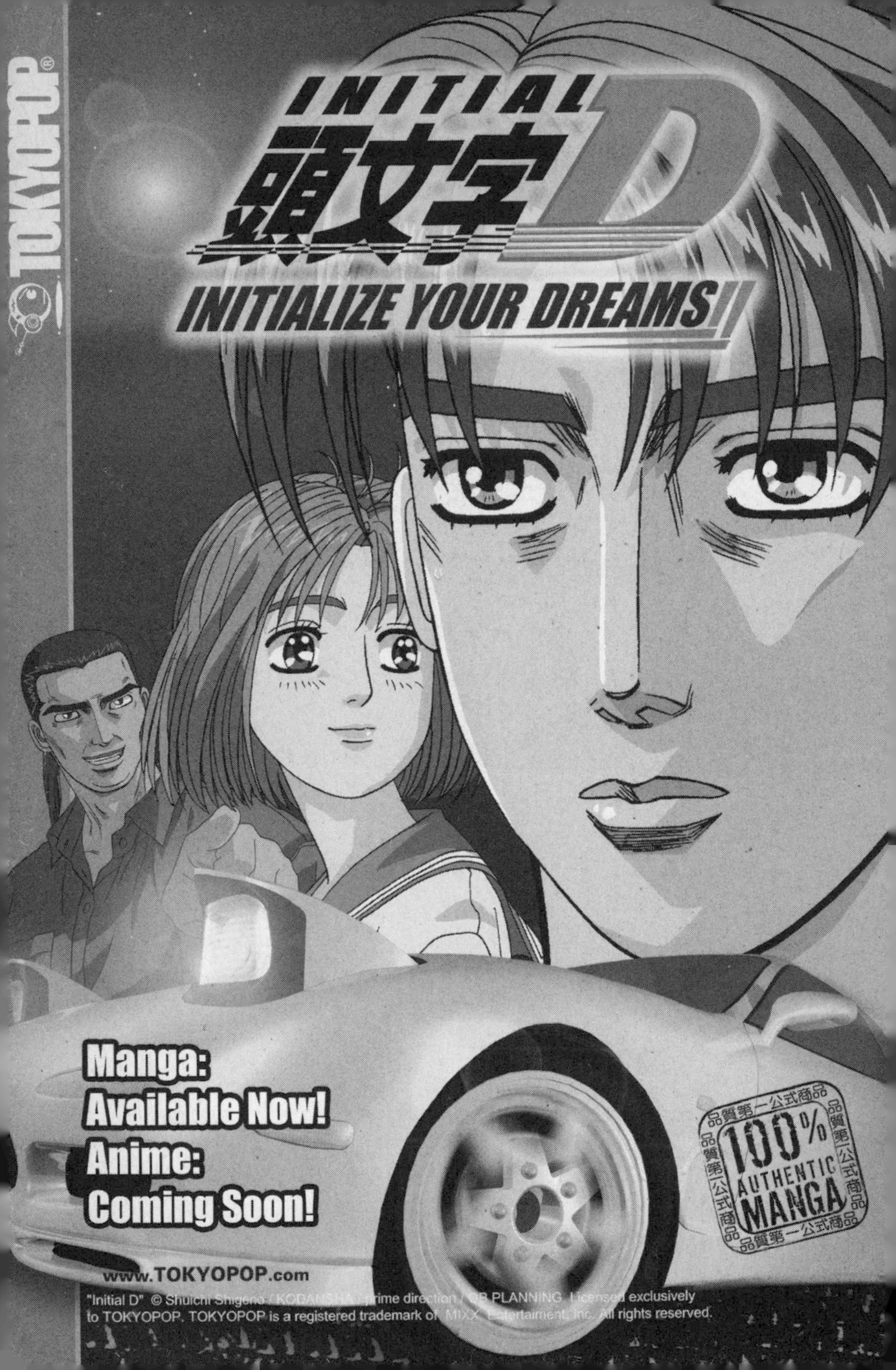
TOKYOPOP
INITIAL
頭文字D
INITIALIZE YOUR DREAMS!!
Manga:
Available Now!
Anime:
Coming Soon!
品質第一公式商品
100%
AUTHENTIC
MANGA
www.TOKYOPOP.com
"Initial D" © Shuichi Shigeno / KODANSHA / prime direction / OB PLANNING. Licensed exclusively
to TOKYOPOP. TOKYOPOP is a registered trademark of MIXX Entertainment, Inc. All rights reserved.

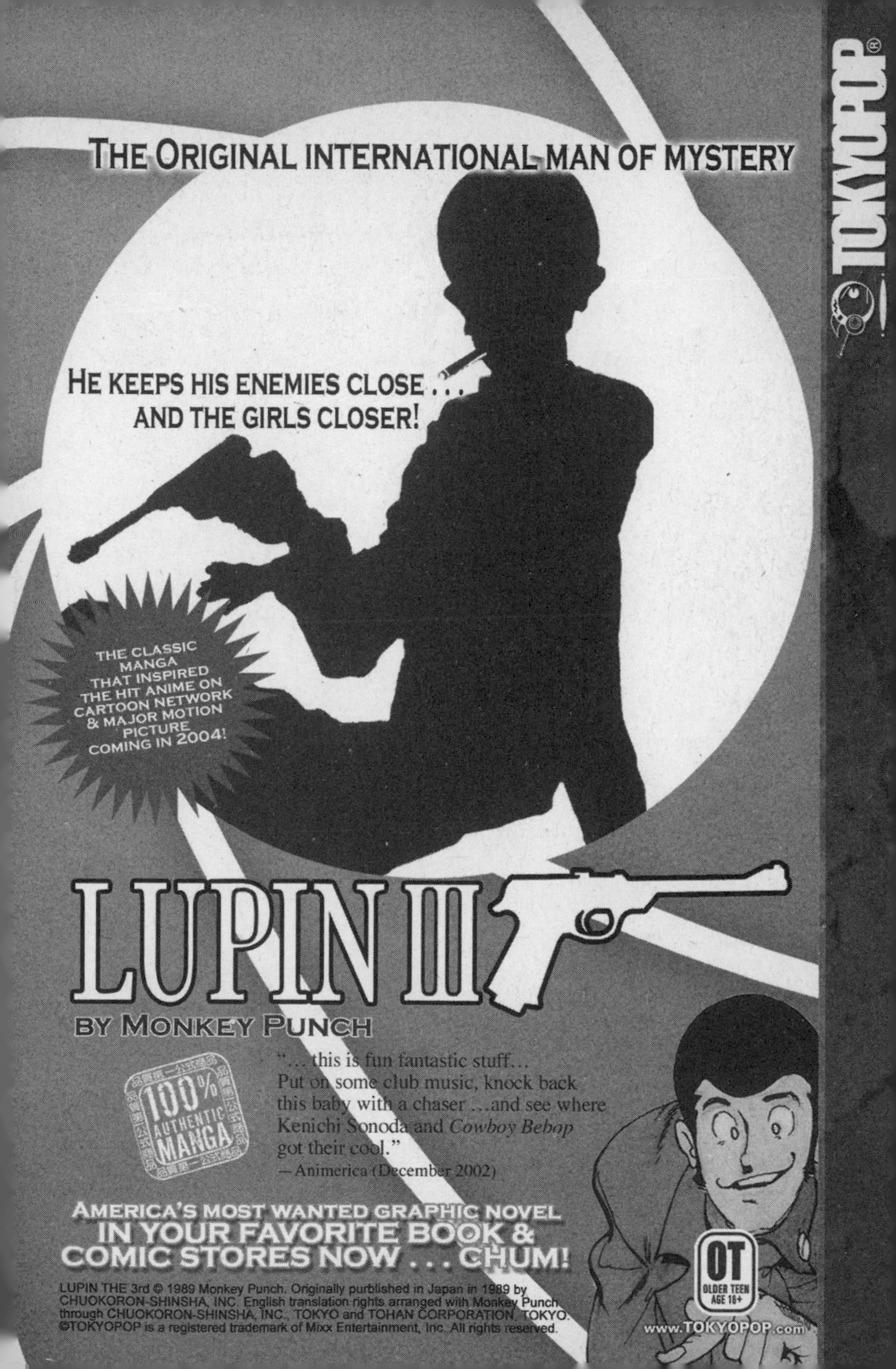

TOKYOPOP®
THE ORIGINAL INTERNATIONAL MAN OF MYSTERY
HE KEEPS HIS ENEMIES CLOSE . . .
. . . AND THE GIRLS CLOSER!
THE CLASSIC MANGA THAT INSPIRED THE HIT ANIME ON CARTOON NETWORK & MAJOR MOTION PICTURE COMING IN 2004!
LUPIN III
BY MONKEY PUNCH
100% AUTHENTIC MANGA
"... this is fun fantastic stuff... Put on some club music, knock back this baby with a chaser ...and see where Kenichi Sonoda and *Cowboy Bebop* got their cool."
—Animerica (December 2002)
AMERICA'S MOST WANTED GRAPHIC NOVEL
IN YOUR FAVORITE BOOK & COMIC STORES NOW . . . CHUM!
OT OLDER TEEN AGE 16+
LUPIN THE 3rd © 1989 Monkey Punch. Originally purblished in Japan in 1989 by CHUOKORON-SHINSHA, INC. English translation rights arranged with Monkey Punch through CHUOKORON-SHINSHA, INC., TOKYO and TOHAN CORPORATION, TOKYO. ©TOKYOPOP is a registered trademark of Mixx Entertainment, Inc. All rights reserved.
www.TOKYOPOP.com

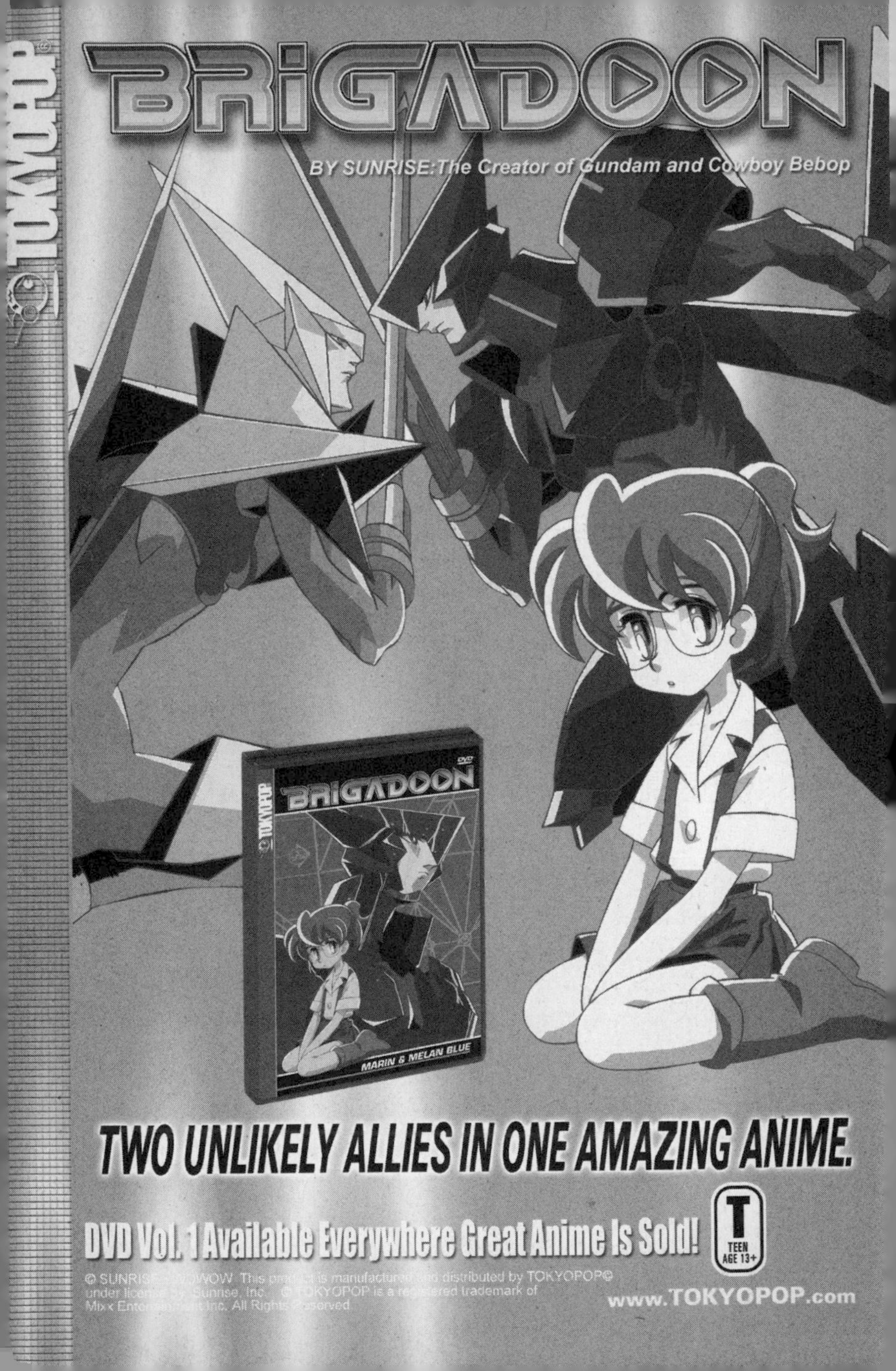
TOKYOPOP
BRIGADOON
BY SUNRISE: The Creator of Gundam and Cowboy Bebop
DVD
BRIGADOON
TOKYOPOP
MARIN & MELAN BLUE
TWO UNLIKELY ALLIES IN ONE AMAZING ANIME.
DVD Vol. 1 Available Everywhere Great Anime Is Sold!
T
TEEN
AGE 13+
© SUNRISE · WOWOW This product is manufactured and distributed by TOKYOPOP® under license by Sunrise, Inc. ® TOKYOPOP is a registered trademark of Mixx Entertainment Inc. All Rights Reserved.
www.TOKYOPOP.com

STOP!

This is the back of the book.
You wouldn't want to spoil a great ending!

This book is printed "manga-style," in the authentic Japanese right-to-left format. Since none of the artwork has been flipped or altered, readers get to experience the story just as the creator intended. You've been asking for it, so TOKYOPOP® delivered: authentic, hot-off-the-press, and far more fun!

DIRECTIONS

1
2
3
4
5
6
7
8
9
10

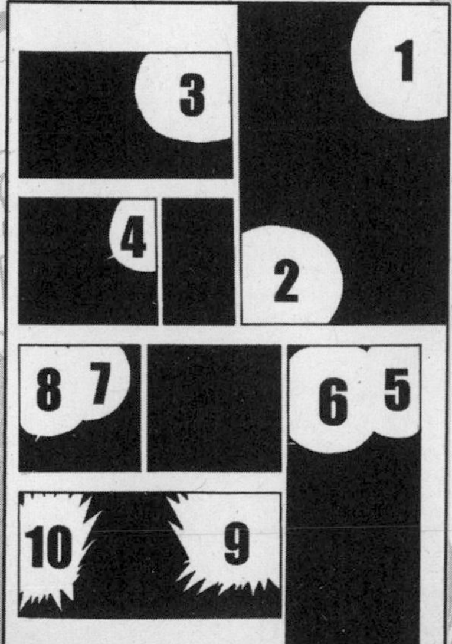

If this is your first time reading manga-style, here's a quick guide to help you understand how it works.

It's easy... just start in the top right panel and follow the numbers. Have fun, and look for more 100% authentic manga from TOKYOPOP®!

100% AUTHENTIC MANGA
品質第一公式商品

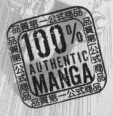